Land Policies for Equity and Growth

Thank you for choosing a SAGE product! If you have any comment, observation or feedback, I would like to personally hear from you. Please write to me at <u>contactceo@sagepub.in</u>

—Vivek Mehra, Managing Director and CEO,
SAGE Publications India Pvt Ltd, New Delhi

Bulk Sales

SAGE India offers special discounts for purchase of books in bulk. We also make available special imprints and excerpts from our books on demand.

For orders and enquiries, write to us at

Marketing Department
SAGE Publications India Pvt Ltd
B1/I-1, Mohan Cooperative Industrial Area
Mathura Road, Post Bag 7
New Delhi 110044, India
E-mail us at <u>marketing@sagepub.in</u>

Get to know more about SAGE, be invited to SAGE events, get on our mailing list. Write today to <u>marketing@sagepub.in</u>

This book is also available as an e-book.

————&℃℘————

Land Policies for Equity and Growth

Transforming the Agrarian Structure in

Uttar Pradesh

Edited by
Ajit Kumar Singh
Santosh Mehrotra

⑤SAGE www.sagepublications.com
Los Angeles • London • New Delhi • Singapore • Washington DC

First published in 2014 by

 SAGE Publications India Pvt Ltd
B1/I-1 Mohan Cooperative Industrial Area
Mathura Road, New Delhi 110 044, India
www.sagepub.in

SAGE Publications Inc
2455 Teller Road
Thousand Oaks, California 91320, USA

SAGE Publications Ltd
1 Oliver's Yard, 55 City Road
London EC1Y 1SP, United Kingdom

SAGE Publications Asia-Pacific Pte Ltd
3 Church Street
#10-04 Samsung Hub
Singapore 049483

Published by Vivek Mehra for SAGE Publications India Pvt Ltd, typeset in 10/12 pt Book Antiqua by Diligent Typesetter, Delhi and printed at Saurabh Printers Pvt Ltd, New Delhi.

Library of Congress Cataloging-in-Publication Data

Land policies for equity and growth : transforming the agrarian structure in Uttar Pradesh / edited by Ajit Kumar Singh and Santosh Mehrotra.

   pages cm

   Includes bibliographical references.

   1. Land reform—India—Uttar Pradesh. 2. Land use—Government Policy— India—Uttar Pradesh. 3. Agriculture and state—India—Uttar Pradesh. 4. Rural poor—India—Uttar Pradesh. I. Singh, Ajit Kumar, 1944– II. Mehrotra, Santosh K.

   HD1333.I42U84   333.3′1542—dc23   2014   2013050691

ISBN: 978-81-321-1360-7 (HB)

The SAGE Team: Shambhu Sahu, Vandana Gupta, Anju Saxena and
                 Dally Verghese

Contents

PART V
Emerging Issues

List of Illustrations

Tables

Figures

Preface

Land reforms have a prominent place in any strategy of rural transformation and poverty alleviation. Uttar Pradesh was among the pioneering states in the field of land reforms. The UP Zamindari Abolition Act was passed in 1950. It was a forward-looking measure that abolished the intermediary rights on land and banned sub-letting, thereby effectively achieving the goal of 'land to the tiller'. UP was also among the first states to carry out consolidation of land. The successful land reforms during the first phase created favourable conditions for Green Revolution in the state. The implementation of land ceiling legislation in UP was, however, lackadaisical as in the other states, though substantial numbers have been allotted land *pattas* on government-owned lands. As the intermediate castes, which were the main beneficiaries of the initial phase of land reforms, consolidated their economic position and acquired political clout, land reforms receded from the agenda of the state government.

Land relations and land situation have undergone substantial changes during the past five decades since the introduction of land reforms in the state. The demographic balance has further deteriorated, adversely affecting the land–man ratio. Today, arable land per capita has reduced to less than 10 cents. Nearly 90 per cent of the holdings are below 2 ha., with the result that they have become economically non-viable units. The preponderance of small holdings coupled with ban on leasing of land is adversely affecting agricultural progress, while restricting the access of land to the landless and the marginal farmers. This situation has brought the issue of agrarian reorganisation again into focus. Focusing on liberalisation and rapid economic development in the post-reform era accelerated the pace of transfer of agricultural land to non-agricultural uses causing deprivation and loss of livelihood to millions of small farmers. Land agitations cropped up in different parts of the country and coercive land acquisition became a politically explosive issue. These changes have again brought the land policy issues into the forefront of political agenda.

The present book examines the old and new issues related to land and land reforms, with particular reference to UP. It contains 17 chapters apart from the Introduction. Some of these chapters were presented in a national seminar organised by the Giri Institute of Development Studies, Lucknow, in August 2008 and were subsequently revised. Other chapters have been written specifically for the volume.

The chapters cover a large number of issues. The historical consequences of the Zamindari Abolition Act in UP (1950) and the land ceiling legislation (1960 and 1972) have been examined. Some chapters deal with the new emerging issues in land use and agrarian relations. The need for modernising and computerising land records has been examined. The chapters also look at the politically sensitive issue of land acquisition by government and the issue of purchase of farmland by private firms or by government on behalf of private firms, and its consequences for farmers. The proposed law on the rehabilitation and resettlement (R&R) has been discussed. Some chapters focus on the lower castes, the poor and the relatively marginalised, who form a majority of the landless. Some of the chapters are based on the analysis of secondary data sources that are well known as well as new ones, while some chapters are based on recent primary survey in the four agriclimatic zones of UP.

The editors would like to acknowledge with thanks the various debts incurred in bringing out this volume. Our foremost thanks is due to the authors of the chapters included in this volume who took the pain of revising their papers or contributing fresh papers. Thanks is also due to the Planning Commission and the Department of Land Resources, Ministry of Rural Development, Government of India, for providing funds for organising the seminar on land reforms in UP at the Giri Institute of Development Studies. Shri Vijay K. Saxena and Deepak Kumar of IAMR deserve special thanks for helping in putting together and editing the chapters.

We are thankful to the editors of *IASSI Quarterly* and *Journal of Rural Development* and Concept Publishers for granting permission to reprint the papers published earlier.

Finally, SAGE Publications and their editorial team deserve our praise for doing a prompt and excellent job in producing it.

6 June 2013   **Ajit Kumar Singh**
                                                     Santosh Mehrotra

1

Introduction: Agricultural Growth with Equity in Uttar Pradesh

Santosh Mehrotra

This is the first book of its kind on land issues, including land reforms, in one of India's largest and certainly its most populous states—Uttar Pradesh. The book discusses both old and new issues. It examines the historical consequences of the Zamindari Abolition Act in UP (1950) and the Land Ceiling Legislation (1960). It also examines new emerging issues in land and agrarian relations, e.g., land use policy (or rather its absence in UP). It discusses the need for modernising land records, computerising them and, most importantly, ensuring titling on the basis of ground-truthing actual landownership. Another new and extremely contentious issue examined is that of land acquisition by government, using its power of eminent domain and the issue of purchase of farm land by private firms (or by government on behalf of private firms) and its consequences for farmers. The new law on rehabilitation and resettlement (R&R), which is a component of the new Land Acquisition Bill, to finally put R&R on a firm legal footing is discussed, as opposed to leaving it to the realm of policy.

Importantly, the book is focused on the lower castes, the poor and the relatively marginalised, who in particular form a majority of the landless (i.e., without land of their own to cultivate) or those even without homestead land (i.e., land on which they can build their homes, and hence must live on either their landlord's or government-owned land). They are also the ones who constitute a significant share of the small or marginal farmers tilling less than 2 hectares (ha.) of land. Over time, with population increase combined with a very slow rate of absorption of agricultural workers in industry or services, there has occurred an incremental shrinking in the average size of farms, and small/marginal farmers account for 83 per cent of land cultivation in UP (and also in India). This shrinking farm size has had major consequences for agricultural productivity and output in UP.

In the first chapter in Part I of the book ('Overview'), Saha and Mehrotra (Chapter 2) examine the land ownership pattern currently prevailing by undertaking a detailed analysis of the All-India Debt and Investment Survey (of 2002–2003) and then the National Sample Survey (2009–2010). They first demonstrate how farm size has shrunk on average in India in general and UP in particular. They then examine the argument that the slow, in fact, stagnant growth in agriculture in UP (and India) has been majorly impacted by this shrinking farm size. Even though minimum support prices (MSP) for farm produce, especially wheat and rice, have been consistently rising in recent years, this price effect on output growth has been minimal, while non-price factors (i.e., falling average farm size and the inability of small/marginal farmers to access institutional credit) have led to rural impoverishment, with UP remaining one of the very few states in India (along with Bihar, Madhya Pradesh and Maharashtra) seeing a rise in the number of absolute poor.

In the second chapter in Part 1 of the book, Dhar (Chapter 3) discusses the politics of *zamindari* abolition in UP, especially in the context of the land-holding pattern before and after *zamindari* abolition. He then suggests that National Sample Survey data on landholding must be read along with the ground-reality of tenancy, and also the impact of the Land Ceiling Act of UP. He argues that the land reform of the 1960s abolished the absentee landlords but replaced it with rich peasants. The political class in UP was against the landlords, but not against landlordism. Their leader, G.B. Pant, the architect of the Zamindari Abolition Act (1950), was inflexibly moderate, and Charan Singh—the chief architect of the Land Ceiling Act (1960)—was a 'peasant patriarch'. On the basis of NSS data from the early 1950s to the early 1980s and Board of Revenue data, Dhar demonstrates that the land-owning community, mostly the backward caste (Yadavs mainly) and the upper caste (both Jats and Brahmins), in collusion with local government officials dominated by the upper castes, restricted the implementation of distribution of ceiling surplus land. Dhar shows that there was clear intent on the part of the political class to deceive: the time gap between the passing of the resolution for land reform and its actual initiation was long enough for the landlords to dispossess their tenants and hide that land as 'owned' in ingenious ways.

Part 2 of the book deals with the linkage between agrarian land ownership structure and agricultural output growth in UP, especially on the so-called inverse relationship between farm size and productivity. There are two chapters in this part of the book. Singh's (Chapter 4) objective is to examine the relationship between agrarian structure and agricultural growth in UP through a cross-section analysis of 42 districts of UP plains. He finds that average yields are positively and significantly correlated with average size of holdings as well as the proportion of area under holdings above 2 ha.

The second chapter in Part 2, by Richa Singh (Chapter 5), examines the farm-size productivity debate in the literature on agricultural economics. After presenting some descriptive statistics on the pattern of land holdings in UP she carries out a correlation analysis to examine whether there is any relationship between land holding size structure and key indicators of agricultural growth. She then tests the well-known hypothesis of the so-called inverse relationship between farm size and agricultural productivity. Richa Singh argues on the basis of correlation and multiple regressions that in UP a holding between 2 and 3 ha. is an optimum size holding. The area under this category of land shows a positive and a highly significant correlation with all the 10 indicators of agricultural development she uses in her analysis. It is thus a holding size that permits the most efficient use of available resources.

Part 3 of the book focuses on land access to the marginalised. It includes two chapters on how land reforms, such as they were in UP, affected the Dalit community (Chapter 6 by Siddharth Dube and Chapter 7 by Prashant Trivedi). In addition, it includes a chapter (Chapter 8) on a marginalised community that has rarely been discussed in the literature—the Bengali (or Bangladeshi) settlers on agricultural land in UP. Kripa Shankar (Chapter 9) examines how the caste and class position of a household influences the outcome of tenancy relations.

The chapter by Dube (Chapter 6) is a most unusual oral history, based on interviews conducted by Dube over several years of living in a village of Pratapgarh district (near Allahabad), with three generations of a Dalit household. This chapter is structured chronologically. It first sets the scene, the 'baseline', by analysing the agrarian situation in Baba ka Gaon at the outset of Indian Independence. Later sections then analyse the record of each decade since all the way through to 2007 paying particular attention to the epochal events in UP land reform, such as the abolition of *zamindari* and the several attempts at land ceilings and redistribution.

Trivedi (Chapter 7) discusses the abolition of *zamindari* and its impact and caste-wise ownership as it emerged after the abolition, and examines how effectively ceiling surplus land was distributed. He also examines the third major dimension of tenancy reform, and also the other important dimension of consolidation of fragmented land holdings. For each aspect, the caste dimension of the land ownership is analysed. He also reports the findings of a small field survey, focusing on 300 Dalit households, and concludes by spelling out the challenges for future land reform.

Saha (Chapter 8), based on his JNU doctoral thesis, provides a case study from Harevli, a village in Bijnor district of Western UP, about the impact of ownership of means of production on the nature of tenancy relations. Also, this chapter illustrates how the caste and class position of a household is intrinsically related to ownership of assets, and thereby influences the outcome of tenancy contracts. The chapter argues, on the basis of intensive fieldwork, that a skewed distribution of land and other productive assets resulted in a differential access of household to the tenancy markets. Thus, Saha finds that the asset-poor Dalit, Muslim and other backward caste (OBC) households obtained leased land under oppressive terms. On the contrary, asset-rich Tyagi households extracted substantial rent as lessors and extracted unpaid labour services through interlinked tenancy and wage labour contracts.

Kripa Shankar's chapter (Chapter 9) argues that at every stage of what has been called 'land reform' in UP has enlarged the bigger landowners, in terms of their both political and economic power. This is true for the *zamindari* abolition of 1956, the Land Ceiling Act that followed soon after or the spread of tenancy that resulted from the extreme inequality of landholding that was in turn created by the *zamindari* abolition and the ineffective implementation of land ceiling laws.

Chapters 10–12 in Part 4 of the book report the latest status of land relations, based on field surveys carried out by the faculty of the Giri Institute of Development Studies (Lucknow): Singh (Chapter 10) examines the various dimensions of land reform in UP and presents farmers' views on them; Fahimuddin (Chapter 11) focuses on tenancy (which is banned legally but yet is practised widely); and Singh and Garia (Chapter 12) discuss the impact of distribution of ceiling surplus land to the poor.

Singh's chapter (Chapter 10) describes the sample of the primary survey on which the chapter is based, presents farmers' views on land consolidation and its impact, presents their views on land ceiling and its effects, and then their views on land leasing and tenancy. He finds the following:

1. Consolidation of holdings is one of the most successful land reform measures. It has reduced time and drudgery of farmers on moving from one field to another and enabled them to make investment on development of land. It has a clear favourable impact on agricultural productivity. There is an overwhelming support among the farmers for consolidation measures. However, there are some procedural problems and malpractices associated with the process that need to be removed.

2. Land ceilings did not affect the majority of the sample farmers directly. However, by and large they favour land-ceiling measures as it has a positive impact on the economic and social status of the land allottees. In fact, a good proportion of farmers feel that the land ceiling size may be further reduced to below 10 acres of irrigated land. The majority of respondents are small and marginal farmers, who think that a reduction in ceiling can make more land available for them as well as for the landless labourers.

3. Though sub-letting of land is prohibited under the Zamindari Abolition Act of UP except for certain categories of handicapped persons, the practice of oral lease is quite common. Land leasing is being practised mostly among the small and marginal farmers and is a mechanism to make adjustment in their investment and income requirements. The most common term of leasing out is the 50–50 per cent sharing of paid-out costs and output. However, the practice of advance cash payment is emerging in some parts. The survey also indicates that the landowners are not in a dominant position in the land lease market, which is largely determined by market forces of demand and supply of land. Over two-thirds of the farmers who reported leasing out land favoured the view that leasing should be legalised as they felt that it will make

the process easier, will allow retention of land ownership and will allow fair sharing of costs and outputs. Overall, the study lends support to the view that land leasing should be allowed as it will increase access of marginal farmers and the landless labourers to land and improve their economic condition.

Fahimuddin (Chapter 11) has interesting findings to report, based on the primary survey of tenancy relations in UP:

1. Despite the legislative regulations and restrictions on the tenancy, it is being widely practised in UP as well as in India. The NSS figures show that the percentage of tenant holdings was 20.5 per cent in UP during 1980–1981, which declined to 11.7 per cent in 2002–2003. The percentage of leased-in area in total area has remained around 10 per cent in UP during 1980–1981 to 2002–2003.
2. The socio-economic conditions of the sample tenants have revealed that majority of them belonged to backward castes followed by scheduled castes, while very few tenants were from upper castes. Agriculture was the main occupation of about 60 per cent of tenants, while about 20 per cent of them were rural labourers.
3. The majority of landlords who rented out their land also belonged to OBCs and around half of them were engaged in agriculture and the rest were in service and trade professions.
4. Average land leased-in per household was 1.61 acres, which was higher than the land owned per household (1.19 acres).
5. Better income was the main reason for leasing-in of land. The leased-in land did provide an average annual income of ₹5,163 per household, which accounted for 22.34 per cent of average annual income per household.
6. All lease agreements are oral. The length of lease was generally of short duration. In most of the cases, duration of lease was of 1–2 years. The terms of lease were generally decided according to the prevalent lease practices in the area. The dominant form of leasing was based on the sharing of produce and cost on a 50:50 basis. Generally, the cost of fertilisers and irrigation was shared on a 50–50 per cent basis between tenants and landlords. The practice of leasing-in on

the basis of cash payment was also found to be emerging in some districts.

7. Insecurity of lease contract was the most serious problem perceived by tenants. About one-third of tenants have reported taking loan from the land owners for production or consumption purposes. One-fourth of the tenants have reported that their landowners sought undue favour in lieu of leasing-in of land to them in the form of payment of lower wages for labour.

8. The majority of tenants who were interviewed expressed the view that tenancy should be legislated.

The prohibition of tenancy has not really ended the practice. This, in turn, also depresses employment opportunities for the landless agricultural labourers. The ban on tenancy, which was meant to protect tenants, has only ended up hurting the economic interests of the tenants as they are not even recognised as tenants. As a result, they are denied the benefits of laws that provide security of tenure and regulate rent.

Chapter 12 (Singh and Garia) examines the impact of land distribution of rural UP based on a sample survey conducted by the Giri Institute of Development Studies. The chapter presents the details of the ceiling surplus and *Gram Sabha* lands distributed, and goes on to examine the social, demographic and income characteristics of the allottees. It also presents the problems faced by allottee households in obtaining ownership title and physical possession of the land allotted to them. It also examines the problems the allottee households faced in actually cultivating the land allotted to them, and the impact such land had on net income, employment and yield. The chapter makes a number of suggestions on the basis of its primary survey. First, if degraded land is acquired for distribution the government should make the land cultivable by measures like levelling, treatment of sodic soil and so on. Second, land allotted to the person should be in the form of a single plot rather than scattered ones. Third, resale of land by the allottee should be prohibited. And finally, government should provide adequate support in terms of credit to enable the land allotted to properly cultivate the land.

Part 4 of the book turns to new and emerging issues: the land use pattern in UP (Chapter 13); forest land and the injustices deriving from its diversion and the insensitivity of the UP Forest Department (Chapter 14); the acquisition of land from farmers for non-agricultural uses (e.g., by private firms for industrial use, or government acquisition for infrastructure, housing complexes to be built by private developers, or industry [in the form of special export processing zones]) (Chapter 15); and finally, land record management and titling (Chapter 16), which has been relatively neglected in government policy by most Indian states, including UP, though not by significant major states (e.g., Karnataka, Goa).

Chapter 13 (Ambekar and Singh) examines the land use pattern in UP, both before and after the bifurcation of the state into Uttarakhand and UP. There are a number of dimensions of land use that show little or no change since 2000 (when Uttarakhand became a separate state). The base reporting area has not changed in the period between 2000 and 2010. The area under forest has not changed (though as the next chapter on forest land in UP argues, forest land has been a source of major social conflict).

The big change has occurred in the quantum of land called 'barren and uncultivable' and also 'land put to non-agriculture use' since 2000. Barren land was 6.17 lakh ha. in 2000 and fell to 5.07 lakh ha. by 2007–2008, due to setting up of industrial estates and habitations in these areas. Similarly, land being put to non-agricultural uses has been increasing at a faster pace since 2000. It was 24 lakh ha. in 2000 and increased to 27.6 lakh ha. by 2007–2008 – or an increase to 40,000 ha. per year compared to only 14,000 ha. per year in the1990s. Hence, Ambekar and Singh argue in the chapter that the state is in urgent need of land-use policy.

Another issue of concern arising from Chapter 12 on land use is the high and rising land lying fallow. Thus, current fallow land rose from 10.5 lakh ha. in 2000–2001 to 14.1 lakh ha. in 2007–2008. The authors suggest absentee landlords as one possible reason and non-availability of irrigation/droughts as another. There is need for action by policy-makers, since the phenomenon of absentee landlords could be either small farmers where males have migrated in search of work to cities, and with tenancy being illegal are not willing to risk leasing out their cultivable land to resident farmers in the village. This is a matter of concern since, as the chapter shows, net sown area has not increased since 2000.

Chapter 14 (Choudhary and Roma) examines the issue of the rights of forest-dependent people. The forest-dependent *adivasi* people (who constitute a very tiny proportion of UP's population) have been victims of first a rapacious colonial state, and since Independence have been meted out a similar treatment by the state's Forest Department, which took control over all forests after *zamindari* abolition (*zamindars* had controlled forests on behalf of the coloniser and continued in that role until *zamindari* abolition in 1950 in UP). The chapter examines the disputes between the revenue department and the forest department of the state, and those between the forest department and the people, and suggests a series of policy measures that are needed to ensure that the Forest Rights of Act 2006 becomes an enabler to correct historical injustices.

An exceedingly important emerging issue is the one of land acquisition by government or land purchase for non-agricultural uses by private firms, which displaces farming families, and often whole farming communities (Chapter 15). Singh discusses the legal framework for land acquisition (i.e., the Land Acquisition Act, 1894) and problems inherent therein; the structural issues in land markets in India contributing to market failure; and the public policy responses to the challenges in land acquisition, rehabilitation and re-settlement (R&R). Provisions for R&R have been systematically neglected by governments in the past in India, with the result that some two-thirds of the nearly 60 million persons who have been displaced by 'development'-related land acquisition by the state or private purchases of agricultural land have never been rehabilitated or properly compensated. This is sought to be now corrected by the Act on Land Acquisition and R&R passed by the Parliament (2013), which replaces the Act of 1894. UP government's policies in this regard and the new bill Act are critically examined by the author.

Singh's next chapter (Chapter 16) deals with an important yet equally neglected issue historically, that of the management of the land record and tilting system in India, especially for agricultural land. Revenue collection was the primary purpose of land management by the British in India, for whom this was the biggest source of revenue. After Independence, the Constitution put the matters related to land in the State List, and state governments were supposed to carry out survey and settlement operations periodically and to update the records and maps. Because land records in colonial times were merely an aid to revenue collection, there was less emphasis on maintaining accurate and up-to-date textual and spatial records of individual ownership. After Independence, land revenue as a source of revenue for state governments fell sharply, and most state governments did not carry out survey and settlement operations. As a result, land records today are in a terrible state, in most states in India (except in a small minority like Karnataka and Goa), including UP.

This is a situation beset with problems, since it is the cause of serious market failures. Without proper land records and clear, written, up-to-date record of titles, land owners are fearful of selling, potential buyers fear buying and potential tenants do not want to lease land (and yet an informal, unrecorded tenancy market flourishes), thereby causing all kinds of distortions.

Alagh in his chapter (Chapter 17) addresses a number of emerging issues in land reforms and policy: first, the question of tenancy in India and the controversies of legalising it; second, the present context of leveraging small farmer advantages in the emerging institutional models; third, the issues raised by the spread of urban land use and spaces to rural areas; and finally, the problems related to forest or mining land, which have long-term sustainability or rehabilitation concerns.

Alagh re-visits the debate about legalising tenancy. He points out that *benami* tenancies and increasingly reverse tenancy exist as recent NSS and other studies show. He argues that the use of operational farm distribution data to test the hypothesis of reverse tenancy is somewhat suspicious. According to him the marginalisation of small-holder farming remains a problem in the fast-changing agriculture in India and other Asian economies. In this context, he refers to the institutional reform and agricultural growth in Vietnam since the 1990s of the last century. Globalisation induced price volatility in these agrarian economies, particularly downward pressure on prices and a proliferation of intermediaries in supply and marketing chains, which has disadvantaged more vulnerable farmers. Vulnerability is more in less-fertile or less-populated areas, the forest, the 'remote and mountainous areas' and the 'ethnic minorities'.

Alagh stresses that recognition of land rights is central to re-form in rural India because land can then become collateral for investment. This is evident in states like Gujarat, Karnataka and Andhra Pradesh where progress has been made; this is also very important for forest areas. He asserts that we cannot go on with a government-owned forest model.

Alagh points out that land scarcity is going to be perhaps the single greatest constraint to Indian development. This problem is particularly severe in tribal areas. He argues that we need to build models of cooperation rather than confrontation. His stand on the land question is that the powers of the Land Acquisition Act are gone, and with the reestablishment of land rights the market would take over. In his view, there is little logic in denying the farmer his share in the gain from land prices. Instead of making the farmer a sullen outsider, we should make him a stakeholder.

Alagh supports producer companies of farmers. Groups of stakeholders, including the smallest peasants, can cooperate for well-defined and limited purposes for land development and water projects. He points out that farmer-level irrigation management systems, watershed development projects and groundwater cooperatives are all thriving, and many more and very promising possibilities are there.

Tenancy records have to be straightened so that tenants who farm around two-fifth of the land can leverage their assets in bargains with the corporates. The question of the organisation of small farmers and their links with higher-level organisations like input supplying or selling companies, or irrigation systems, is a complex one. Possibility of small farmers to form their own companies, without loss of control on their land, now exists under the law and needs to be strengthened. Later on, they may be allowed to have joint ventures with big companies, if they so decide. A problem visualised in contract farming is the organisation of farmer groups to interact with large companies. One solution is to encourage farmer groups in this context.

Alagh underlines the need for a civil society initiative in policy making and implementation as the state gets weaker and corporatised. He ends by supporting the laws for judicious use of land.

The book concludes (Chapter 18) with a series of clear policy imperatives for the UP government. As this book's authors have shown, and this chapter has emphasised, UP's rural citizenry are in a state of chronic crisis. Agricultural growth/income in the state has grown very slowly, and the number of rural poor in UP would have grown even after 2005, as they did between 1999–2000 and 2004–2005. As many as 3.5 million persons employed in agriculture in UP in 2004–2005 left to work as construction workers or in services by 2009–2010. Farm size has been shrinking on average. The antecedents of the shrinking average farm size lie in policy neglect of both basic health and education services, which led to UP's women having a total fertility rate of 3.6 in 2009, one of the highest for any state in India. The antecedents also lie in the complete neglect of redistributive land reforms (especially the land ceiling legislation).

This book's agenda for action is suggested below, based on the research presented in this book.

1. Legalise tenancy to enable use of fallow land, reassure landlords/tenants and counter farm size shrinkage.
2. Intensify land consolidation to counter adverse effects of farm size shrinkage and reduce inefficiency.
3. Implement land ceiling, at least to ensure homestead rights to homeless.
4. Develop a public land bank to enable tenancy.
5. Encourage group farming to enable small and marginal farmers to get access to inputs and enter the contract farming market.
6. Develop a land-use policy for the state to restrict inefficient conversion of agricultural land to non-agricultural use.
7. Adopt the new Land Acquisition Act, especially the R&R measures for old and future displaced.
8. Implement the central government's land records modernisation programme speedily.
9. Stop the diversion of forestland for non-forest use to protect tribal people.
10. Ensure women's rights in land through legal changes.

With growing agrarian distress, slow agricultural growth, growing marginalisation of holdings and sluggish pace of economic transformation, the issues of agrarian reform have again assumed importance for economic growth and political stability. The situation is more serious in populous and agriculture-dominated states like UP. As the chapters in this volume argue, fresh approaches to the land question are required at the present juncture of our economic development. The costs of ignoring these questions would be enormous.

PART I

Overview

2

Land Issues Then and Now in India: New Challenges and Policy Dilemmas

Partha Saha and Santosh Mehrotra

Introduction

Agriculture and rural citizens in India (including in Uttar Pradesh — UP) are in a chronic state of distress, and agrarian structure is only part of the problem. Rarely, since Independence in 1947, has agricultural output grown faster than 3 per cent per annum. The Eleventh Plan (Planning Commission, 2008) notes that in the pre–Green Revolution period (1951–1992 to 1967–1998) agriculture and allied sectors grew at 2.54 per cent per annum, and slightly slower during the Green Revolution period (1968–1969 to 1980–1981) at 2.44 per cent per annum. It was only during the period of wider Green Revolution technology dissemination (1981–1982 to 1990–1991) that agriculture's growth rate picked up to 3.52 per cent per annum. That growth was sustained only for a limited period (1991–1992 to 1996–1997) at 3.66 per cent per annum after India's economic reforms began in 1991 (although agriculture was pretty much left untouched by the economic reforms). However, agriculture returned to its pre–Green Revolution levels of 2.5 per cent per annum over 1997–1998 to 2006–2007. Agriculture has grown at an average rate of 3.3 per cent in the Eleventh Plan (2007–2012), but with a drought in 2012–2013, output dipped again. The higher agricultural output growth during the Eleventh Plan period compared to the previous decade, however, is not much ground for rejoicing. The faster growth was due to higher agricultural prices, partly driven by higher premium support prices given by the central government to procure grains for supply to the public distribution system of ration shops at highly subsidised prices. In other words, higher agricultural growth has not been driven by higher production.

In fact, the index of crop production has risen by just 1.2 per cent per annum during 1996–2012 (leading to lower national per capita availability of cereals) (Ministry of Finance, 2013).

Between 1984–1985 and 1995–1996 the growth rate of agricultural NSDP (net state domestic product) of UP averaged less than the national average (2.82 per cent per annum as against 3.62 per cent). Similarly, between 1995–1996 and 2004–2005 UP's agricultural growth rate was the same as that of India (1.87 per cent as against 1.85 per cent).

UP's agricultural growth rate should have been much better, given its natural resource endowment. The proportion of cultivable land that is rain-dependent is one of the lowest in UP. In other words, despite being less vulnerable to the vagaries of monsoon, since most of its land is irrigated,[1] UP has barely managed an agricultural growth rate either below or the same as India as a whole from the mid-1980s to the mid-2000s. The same holds for the period since the mid-2000s.

Why is the agricultural growth rate important, especially in a state where the share of employment in agriculture is higher (58 per cent) than the national average (53 per cent) in 2009–2010. The instrumental value of agriculture was recognised by David Ricardo when he noted that the growth of agricultural output sets an upper limit to the growth of the non-agricultural sector. Why this might be the case has been summarised in more recent literature as the four ways in which greater agricultural output contributes to an economy's development: (1) supplying food stuff and raw materials to other expanding sectors in the economy; (2) providing an investible surplus of savings and taxes to support investment in another expanding sector; (3) selling for cash a marketable surplus that will generate demand from the rural population for products of other expanding sectors; and (4) relaxing the foreign exchange constraint by earning foreign exchange through exports or by saving foreign exchange through import substitution (Meier, 1976).

---

[1] Planning Commission (2008), based on the Central Statistical Organisation, states that 32 per cent of UP's agriculture is rain-fed (as against 60 per cent for India). On the other hand, the All-India Debt and Investment Survey 2002–2003 finds that gross irrigated area as a per cent of gross cropped area in UP is 80 per cent (48 per cent India).

However, the purpose of agricultural development cannot be, to use Meier's phrase, "simply to underwrite the expansion of non-agricultural sectors—even at the expense of an 'agricultural squeeze'" (p. 566).[2] In fact, Sukhamoy Chakravarty (1987, p. 21) had noted that in the early Five Year Plans of India, agriculture had been treated with neglect as a 'bargain sector'—which did not happen in East and South-east Asian economies. The historical evidence of the now industrialised countries as well as that of the miracle-economies of Asia shows they experienced an agricultural revolution prior to their industrial revolution.[3]

The longer term objective in Indian planning has always remained a structural transformation—the absorption of a larger fraction of the rural workforce in new income-earning opportunities in industry and services, but clearly the planners have not managed to solve the complex problem of the timing of the transformation and the inter-temporal sequence of policies to accomplish it. This chapter examines the structural factors underlying how the agrarian situation came to this pass at the commencement of the second decade of the new millennium.

The objective of this chapter is to locate the issues of the ownership distribution of land (i.e., essentially the shrinking over time of average farm size with four-fifths of farmers being marginal/small) as one of many factors holding back agricultural growth in India. The section titled 'Land Tenure System Prior to and Since Independence' briefly traces the development of various land tenure systems prior to Independence with special reference to UP. The next section (Land Reform Policies Post Independence) traces various policy discussions related to land reforms at the national level, and for UP. The section titled 'Land Distribution in UP in the 2000s' analyses the land distribution data across different regions of UP in different time periods. Based on the historical pattern of development of the land tenure system and the present agrarian structure, the last section locates the worsening distribution of land ownership and the resulting shrinkage in average farm size as a factor in the slow agricultural growth in UP as well as in India.

---

[2] Lipton (1968) had argued that the lessons of recent history showed that an 'urban bias' can discriminate against agriculture.

[3] Saith (1995) argued that East Asia experienced agricultural growth rates twice those found in India between 1950 and 1980.

Land Tenure System Prior to and Since Independence

In ancient times as well as during most of the medieval period in India, the first person to clear the land had the right to that land, and there was no intermediary between the state and the cultivator. This situation could continue as long as there was no shortage of land and population was small, and the land–man ratio was not adverse. Even though the king could gift land from his own proprietorship or wasteland to the scholars or notable personalities for their services, the king was by no means the owner of all land within his jurisdiction. The king's share varied between one-sixth and one-third (in different time periods), and the king took a share in exchange of protection that the king provided to his subjects (Powell, 1974). Land revenue was collected from the cultivators directly by the officials.

It was only after Akbar's death that all over the Mughal Empire land revenue was collected by the intermediaries (ruling chiefs, *jagirdars*, village headman, etc.). All these heterogeneous sets of intermediaries over time came to be known as *zamindars* (Powell, 1974). The share of the produce, arrangement with the state and the number of layers of intermediaries varied over time and space.

The origin of colonial rule in India was the purchase of *zamindari* rights over 38 villages of Calcutta by the East India Company from the Nawab of Bengal, and the company agreed to pay a stipulated sum to the Nawab annually. Subsequently, during the period of colonisation, the colonial rulers practised different methods of land revenue collection in different parts of the country. The permanent settlement in Bengal province was characterised by *zamindars* being declared as proprietors of soil with property rights, and the *zamindar's* share was fixed at one-tenth of the total land revenue. Along with the creation of different layers of intermediaries, another devastating change that took place in this system was the conversion of millions of *raiyats* to the status of tenants-at-will. With the passage of time, the *zamindars*, in order to free themselves from the burden of collecting land revenue, created subordinate tenures, thereby encouraging subinfeudation (Powell, 1974).

In addition to the *zamindari* system, there was also another system of land revenue known as the *raiyatwari* system, which was prevalent in Madras and Bombay presidencies (but not in UP). This system was based on the assessment of land revenue directly from cultivators by the state, and there was no middleman between the cultivator and the colonial ruler. The *raiyatwari* system involved assessment of land revenue on the field itself and then deciding what that field ought to pay, which included both rent and land tax (Appu, 1996).

The British land revenue system consistently ignored the rights of the peasantry, be it in the *zamindari* area or in the *raiyatwari* area. The clear policy of the colonial rulers was to protect and safeguard the rights of the landlords (whom they considered their natural ally), and the land laws and land records totally ignored share croppers and oral tenants (Appu, 1996). The condition of the actual tillers of land was miserable and the unambiguous policy of the colonial rulers was "to do no more for the wretched of the land than what was absolutely necessary to stave off open revolt" (Appu, 1996). Added to this was the increasing dependence of the Indian peasantry on stagnant agriculture as a result of complete destruction of Indian cottage industries (Dutt, 1976).

During the colonial period, there were three types of land revenue systems in UP: *taluqdari, zamindari* and *bhaichara*. The *taluqdari* system was the land revenue system in the Awadh region (presently central UP). In rest of UP, both *zamindari* and *bhaichara* coexisted together, although the extent of land under different systems varied across regions. *Bhaichara* was the dominant system in the western region (Upper Doab region), whereas *zamindari* was more prevalent in the eastern region of the state (Singh, 1992).

*Taluqdar*s were non-cultivating large landowners having permanent heritable proprietary rights in their estates, and were essentially the large *zamindar*s. They were responsible for the payment of fixed land revenue to the government, which was realised as rent from their tenants. To realise the rents, the *taluqdar*s could seize and sell the crops of the tenants and in extreme cases could also evict tenants from their estates (Whitcombe, 1971). When the colonial rulers annexed Awadh in 1856, *taluqdar*s were considered to be the natural ally of the colonisers and several enactments were passed, which "buttressed the already privileged position of the taluqdars" (Jassal, 1980). Between the *taluqdar* and tenants, there existed different layers of subproprietors, which only added to the total appropriation from the peasantry.

The *bhaichara* system was a system of owner cultivation by the members of the community (mostly Jats and Tyagis in the western region), which settled in an area after occupying and colonising it and dividing the land among themselves (Neale, 1962). The peasant proprietors had individual and hereditary rights on the land. The peasants were not free to alienate their land and they paid their rents to the state through the village headman. Land was mostly cultivated by the family members of the peasant proprietors who were assisted by the *riaya* (non-peasant castes like Chamars) and over whom the peasant proprietors exercised direct social and economic control (Singh, 1992). The necessity for the *bhaichara* system was primarily to protect the peasant proprietors who were exposed to waves of invasions by different groups or clans and "it was necessary for bhaichara system to continue for the purpose of resisting the encroachments from predatory hordes".[4] However, none of the attacking clans could wholly uproot the existing groups from the soil. Hence, in those districts which were subject to repeated invasions (the western district of UP), the society was intermingled but vertically stratified with the most recent group of conquerors at the top. The NorthWestern Province came under the British rule during 1801–1803 and scarcity of large landholders in the western region meant that the British had no option but to deal directly with the *bhaichara* community and the village-level *zamindars* (Whitcombe, 1971).

Benaras division came under British rule in 1775 and the permanent land revenue settlement on the Bengal pattern was put in place. The permanent *zamindari* settlement in the eastern region of the state was characterised by high and inflexible revenue demand, stratified rural society comprising several layers of tenants and subtenants and almost complete alienation of the cultivators from the land (Whitcombe, 1971).

Thus the historical process of development of agrarian societies across different regions of UP varied on account of differences in revenue settlement systems practised by the colonial rulers. The *zamindari* land revenue system of eastern UP was fundamentally different from the *bhaichara* system of western UP, which provided some kind of tenurial security for cultivators and witnessed the rise of a class of rich occupancy tenants. This class of independent tenants had an incentive to invest in land and improve productivity. In contrast, in eastern UP, tenurial insecurity, exorbitant rent and

---

[4] This was the observation of M.H. Elliot, the first settlement officer of Meerut during the colonial period and was cited in Singh (1992).

the lion's share of the produce being taken away by the layers of intermediaries discouraged any kind of productive investment by the tenants.

From the foregoing discussion, it is clear that the problem of different layers of intermediaries was not confined to UP alone but persisted across different regions of the country. In fact, the problem was so severe in certain cases that in Bengal there were instances where as many as 50 layers of intermediaries were created between the *zamindar* and the actual cultivator.[5] In addition to the economic exploitation (where the landlord's profit ranged between 5 and 7 times the land revenue), there were non-economic forms of exploitation as well, in the form of forced labour, and compulsory contribution to the *zamindars* during the time of festivals (Driver, 1949).

Based on a detailed study, it was estimated that in India at the time of Independence, 55–60 per cent of land came under the *zamindari* system (Kotosky, 1964). Abolition of intermediary land rights was therefore one of the most important policy interventions required at the dawn of Independence. Improving the condition of the peasantry in general and actual tillers in particular was reflected in various documents and in declarations of the Congress and Kissan Sabha since the mid-1930s onwards. Abolition of intermediary rights was the first step towards progressive land reform. But even in this, the enormity of the task and the complexities involved soon became evident, and it was realised post Independence by the Economic Programme Committee under the Chairmanship of Jawaharlal Nehru that "there being great divergence in the condition and background of the landlord system from State to State, the States should be free to deal with the question of abolition of the system in accordance with their particular circumstances".

Land Reform Policies Post Independence

UP, which had experienced substantial peasant mobilisation during the Independence struggle, was in the forefront of legal enactments of land reform. As a result, land reforms were carried out by the

---

[5] Report of the Land Revenue Commission of Bengal, Vol. 1 (cited in Appu, 1996).

elected government of the United Provinces in the 1920s and the 1930s. The first Congress government of 1935–1937 started a land reform process that culminated in the post-Independence *zamindari* abolition. Security of tenure improved after the first Congress government's efforts. By 1937, *zamindars* only had control over the orchards, i.e., non-cultivated land. They had lost control over cultivated lands, and even before Independence tenancy in UP could be transferred as a result of the tenancy reforms of the Congress government. The Uttar Pradesh Zamindari Abolition and Land Reforms Act, 1951, abolished all intermediary rights in land, and brought the actual tiller of the soil in direct contact with the state (in the sense that land revenue would now go to the state government and no longer to the *zamindar*).Therefore, certain types of land rights were recognised. It created four categories of rights on land (*Bhumidars, Sirdars, Asamis* and *Adivasis*).[6] An important feature of this Act was that it prohibited sub-leasing out while allowing for crop-sharing arrangement. This arrangement encouraged the upper classes (not willing to cultivate land themselves) to lease out land under the garb of crop-sharing arrangement. Therefore, this Act did not provide any protection to the tenants-at-will and share croppers. The implementation was fraught with lack of political will, clash of interest among various stakeholders, absence of reliable land records and a complicated legal system. In some cases, the entire Act or some parts of it were challenged in the courts, which further delayed the process (Appu, 1996).

Apart from abolition of intermediary rights, tenancy reform is another important measure of land reform. At the national level, since Independence, tenancy reform has been a subject of discussion in various Five Year Plans. The policy suggestions on tenancy reforms have primarily centred on the resumption of land

---

[6] All ex-intermediaries were granted Bhumidari Right (absolute right over land including the right to sell) on their self-cultivated land. All occupancy tenants and hereditary tenants were granted Sirdari Right (permanent and heritable right over land without the right to sell or mortgage). The Sirdar could acquire Bhumidari Right by paying hefty lump sum money. *Asamis* and *Adivasis* were non-occupancy tenants who were sub-tenants on *sir* and *khudkast* lands of *zamindars*. They were basically tenants-at-will and could remain tenant for a stipulated time period. They were therefore the most insecure of the lot. *Adivasis* could acquire Bhumidari or Sirdari Rights on certain terms and conditions, which were much beyond their ability. For a detailed discussion of various land rights, refer to Appu (1996).

for personal cultivation, and rent to be paid to the landowner by the tenant.[7] The tenancy reform measures suggested in the policy documents gave ample opportunity to the landowners to evict tenants under the pretext of resuming land for self-cultivation, which indirectly made imposition of fair rents totally ineffective. The fear of being evicted in case of non-compliance with the demand of the landowners loomed large among the tenants, and landowners could extract rent that was much higher than the stipulated norms. It should be noted that compared to other states, the degree of eviction of tenants was least in UP because of superior land records that existed in UP, combined with the pre-Independence tenancy reforms, which considerably reduced the control of *zamindar*s over cultivated land. Unfortunately, the land record system deteriorated from the 1960s onwards. A systematic compilation of comprehensive land records is not only essential from the perspective of land reforms, but also important for carrying out production activities, as access to formal credit is dependent on land titles. The Eleventh Five Year Plan observed that unless land records are accurate and updated, the process of computerisation will have very limited benefits.

Under UP law, share-cropping is legally permitted, but subletting is not. From the point of view of increasing production and productivity, it should be noted that share-cropping does not encourage investment on the land by the share-cropper. The current situation in UP is that after the Green Revolution, share-cropping declined, as the earlier landlords simply decided to take back the land, since they would make the necessary investments to make the land provide the higher yields that the Green Revolution technology made possible. Meanwhile, sub-tenancy remained illegal, and the sub-tenants' name cannot be entered into government records as the law does not provide for it. Knowledgeable observers noted to the authors that writing the name of the sub-tenant down in the administrative records would lead to an increase in corruption in a state where governance remains of poor quality. They also note that, in any case, feudal-type tenancy (which was usually of a long-term nature) has been replaced by capitalist

---

[7] Tenants' cultivating land that exceeded the ceiling limit of the landowner were to be given permanent and heritable rights over land. However, landowners could choose the plots for their personal cultivation.

tenancy (which is seasonal), and hence less in need of a recording of the tenancy.[8]

The third aspect of land reform, namely ceiling on agricultural holding, was never given any priority by the policy-makers in India. It was feared that implementation of ceiling would lead to preponderance of uneconomic holding, thereby endangering the food security of the nation. However, the Planning Commission (First Five Year Plan) stressed on imposition of ceiling on future acquisitions of agricultural land. The concern over food security was reiterated in successive plan documents and was used as a pretext of not implementing ceiling law. In fact there were a number of variations across states on the level of ceiling, and this — in conjunction with numerous loopholes and slow process of implementation — made the ceiling laws absolutely ineffective (Appu, 1996). In fact, the Eleventh Five Year Plan noted that "the amount of land declared surplus was far short of amount of land that was estimated to be surplus". Besides, possession of ceiling surplus land is itself a very big challenge given the rural hierarchy.

As in the rest of India, the ceiling laws enacted in UP were largely ineffective. Uttar Pradesh Imposition of Ceilings of Land Holding Act, 1960, was a failure because it provided a fairly liberal ceiling and allowed for a large number of exemptions. As a result of this, the landlords took full advantage of the various loopholes in the Act and various studies indicated that a large number of bogus transfers took place, defeating the main purpose of the Act.

Uttar Pradesh Consolidation of Holdings Act, 1953, was successful to some extent despite all its malpractices, and made investment on land more viable and profitable, which contributed to increased agricultural production (Singh, 1992). This programme was initially undertaken in the agriculturally more progressive western districts of the state and subsequently extended to the eastern districts. It is argued that this consolidation of land holdings was one among a host of factors (especially increases in irrigation after Independence) that contributed to agricultural dynamism in eastern UP (Singh, 1992).

To put things in a nutshell, despite early enactment of various land reform legislations, the agrarian structure of UP remained

---

[8] We are grateful to Naresh Saxena, an ex-bureaucrat belonging to the IAS, and a scholar, for this insight.

unequal, with a high degree of concentration of land (although it might have been less unequal compared to other states).

Land Distribution in UP in the 2000s

In this section, we analyse data pertaining to landholding from various rounds of National Sample Surveys. The latest round of employment and unemployment survey (NSS 66th round, 2009–2010) and the last round of All India Debt and Investment Survey (NSS 59th round, 2002–2003) have been used in this analysis. The employment and unemployment survey has information on land ownership and it has been used to analyse ownership distribution of land across various social groups in different regions of UP. In addition to information on land ownership, All-India Debt and Investment Survey (AIDIS) collects information on operational holding, and hence it makes possible analysis of access to land in case of different social groups. Further, AIDIS has different categories of land (homestead land, agricultural land, orchard, etc.), and therefore it allows for a detailed analysis of distribution of land among different social groups. Since the objectives of the two rounds of NSS surveys are different, they are not strictly comparable over time. However, the broad trends and patterns are more or less similar. In what follows, we first present the analysis of AIDIS, followed by the analysis of the 2009–2010 round of employment and unemployment survey. It may be noted here that in UP, scheduled tribe (ST) households constituted less than 1 per cent of households in the state. Therefore, ST households have not been considered in this analysis.

Analysis of All India Debt and Investment Survey, NSS, 2002–2003

In AIDIS, 2002–2003, information on household land ownership was collected for different categories of land. The different categories of land considered in the survey were crop land (irrigated and unirrigated), orchards and plantations, water bodies, land used exclusively for non-farm business, land put to other non-agricultural uses, homestead land and other areas. In the present analysis, all categories of land except crop land and homestead land have been clubbed together as other land. In rural India, the average values for each of these different categories of land were the least in the case of scheduled caste (SC) households and highest in the case of other households (Table 2.1).

From Table 2.1 it may be pointed out that in rural India, close to 60 per cent of SC households did not own any agricultural land in 2002–2003. Land being the most important means of production in rural India, not owning it is clearly a huge disadvantage, and it gets further reflected in the socio-economic backwardness of the specified groups. However, a vast majority of SC households owned some homestead land. Any claim of landlessness declining should be verified as per the type of land, because inclusion of homestead land drastically reduces the incidence of landlessness. In terms of land value, the average value of land owned by OBCs and Others is 2.5 times the average value of land owned by SC households. Therefore, it can be concluded that SC households owned small plots of land and/or poor quality of unirrigated tracts of land.

In UP, the average value of crop land owned by 'other households' was 4.4 times the average value for SC households (Table 2.2). Further, 28 per cent of all rural households and 38 per cent of SC households in rural UP did not own any crop land. This disparity in the average value of different categories of land across social groups was observed in all the four regions of the state.[9]

All across the state, SC households were characterised by the small size of landownership, and this phenomenon was particularly severe in the eastern region of the state, where more than half of SC households owned less than half of a hectare of agricultural land. Land scarcity was not much of an issue in the southern region, but then land is of very poor quality and unsuitable for crop cultivation (Table 2.3).

Inequality in ownership holding is sought to be corrected by access to land through tenancy contracts (even though informal) for the land-poor households (so the inequality of operational holdings is lower than that for ownership of holdings). On the contrary, there

[9] For a detailed analysis, refer to Saha (2009).

Table 2.1

Average Value of Land (₹ 000) and Proportion of Households (%) Owning, by Social Groups, Rural India, 2002–2003

Land type	Scheduled caste		OBC		Others		All households	
	Average value	*% of households owning*	*Average value*	*% of households owning*	*Average value*	*% of households owning*	*Average value*	*% of households owning*
Crop land	48	40.7	127	57.8	227.4	61.5	130.3	55.9
Homestead land	18.3	94	28.2	92.5	40.5	92.5	27.6	92.6
Other land	1.8	4.1	9.1	7	16.8	10.3	9.2	7.2
All categories of land	68.5	94.6	165.3	93.4	286	93.7	167.9	93.5

Source: Calculated from NSS Database, 59th round, AIDIS, 2002–2003.

Table 2.2
Average Value of Land (₹ 000) and Proportion of Households (%) Owning, by Social Groups, Rural UP, 2002–2003

Land type	Scheduled caste		OBC		Others		All households	
	Average value	% of households owning	Average value	% of households owning	Average value	% of households owning	Average value	% of households owning
Crop land	80.3	62.3	205.4	75.4	355.3	77.7	199.6	72.1
Homestead land	18.3	98.6	25.6	98.4	35	97.9	25.3	98.3
Other land	1.5	4.5	6.9	7	12.4	11.2	6.4	7.1
All categories of land	101.1	99	240.3	98.7	404.3	98.3	233.3	98.7

Source: Calculated from NSS Database, 59th round, AIDIS, 2002–2003.

Table 2.3

Proportion of Households in Terms of Ownership of Agricultural Land, by Social Groups, by Region, Uttar Pradesh, 2002–2003 (%)

	Owning less than 0.5 ha.			Owning more than 4.0 ha.		
Region	SC	OBC	Others	SC	OBC	Others
Western	35.5	32.2	22.9	0	1	2.3
Central	47.4	35.8	18.7	0	0.5	4.7
Eastern	54	50.5	31.8	0	0.7	3.4
Southern	18.7	14.1	12.4	3.1	11.8	9

Source: Calculated from NSS Database, 59th round, AIDIS, 2002–2003.

Table 2.4

Proportion of Land Operated by Households

	Operated by top 5% of households		Operated by bottom 70% of households	
Country/state/region	1991–1992	2002–2003	1991–1992	2002–2003
All India	39.0	41.0	14.2	11.7
Uttar Pradesh	30.0	31.6	22.3	20.8
Western Uttar Pradesh	28.9	31.4	19.9	18.6
Central Uttar Pradesh	25.3	29.1	28.0	24.2
Eastern Uttar Pradesh	28.6	30.8	25.1	22.6
Southern Uttar Pradesh	28.3	28.7	21.5	24.7

Source: Calculated from NSS Database, 48th and 59th rounds, AIDIS, 2002–2003.

has been a concentration of operational holding by the land-rich households (Table 2.4). The proportion of land operated by the top 5 per cent of households increased in 2002–2003 as compared to that in 1991–1992. However, what is noticeable from Table 2.4 is that the share of holdings operated by top 5 per cent of holdings in UP was lower in 1992–1993 than for India as a whole, and that situation did not change a decade later. In fact, the share of land operated by the bottom 70 per cent of the households is correspondingly much greater in UP than in the rest of India.

Whatever be the reason for concentration of operational holding, the net result of land concentration is increasing incidence of landlessness (Table 2.5), and their magnitude being more severe among SC households (Table 2.6).

Table 2.5
Landlessness in Terms of Operational Holding, Rural Households

Country/State/Region	Proportion of landless households	
	1991–1992	*2002–2003*
All India	33.9	39.7
Uttar Pradesh	23.6	24.3
Western Uttar Pradesh	31.3	33.9
Central Uttar Pradesh	21.6	23.6
Eastern Uttar Pradesh	17.7	19.3
Southern Uttar Pradesh	28.7	21.3

Source: Calculated from NSS Database, 48th and 59th rounds, AIDIS, 2002–2003.

At the all-India level, the incidence of landlessness in terms of operational holding increased by about 6 percentage points in 2002–2003 as compared to 1991–1992; in UP much less so the only exception to the increase in landlessness was the southern region of the state, which registered a considerable decline in the incidence of landlessness in terms of operational holding (Table 2.5).

Across social groups, the incidence of landlessness in UP was the highest in the case of SC households. The higher incidence of landlessness among SC households prevailed across all the regions of the state, except the central region (Table 2.6). It may be further noted that across all social groups, the incidence of landlessness was extremely high in the western region of the state.

Table 2.6
Landlessness in Terms of Operational Holding, by Social Groups, 2002–2003

Country/State/Region	Proportion of landless households		
	SC	*OBC*	*Others*
Uttar Pradesh	29.9	21.1	24.6
Western Uttar Pradesh	43.8	27.5	32.3
Central Uttar Pradesh	19.2	18.6	36.8
Eastern Uttar Pradesh	25.2	17.3	14.0
Southern Uttar Pradesh	34.5	14.8	11.8

Source: Calculated from NSS Database, 59th round, AIDIS, 2002–2003.

From the above analysis it is clear that there is a higher incidence of landlessness among SC households in terms of agricultural land and such households are primarily characterised by the ownership of extremely small plots of low-value land. Furthermore, the process of concentration of operational holding has grown over the years; here again, SC households are the ones with limited access to land for cultivation. This process was captured by the two rounds of AIDIS survey (the latest round being almost a decade old). The latest round of NSS employment and unemployment survey indicates continuation of broad overall trends in terms of distribution of land, and this has been captured in the next sub-section.

Land Distribution Based on Employment and Unemployment Survey Round, 2009–2010, National Sample Survey

As mentioned in the introduction to this chapter, data on landownership collected in the employment and unemployment survey of the NSS pertain to all categories of land together, and do not classify them as per their usage. However, consistent with the analysis presented in Section titled 'Analysis of All India Debt and Investment Survey, NSS, 2002–2003', SC households were characterised by a lack of ownership of land across all the regions of the state.[10] The proportion of land owned by SC households was much less than their numerical strength (Table 2.7). On the other hand, OBCs and Others have a clear advantage in terms of land ownership in rural areas.

The lack of ownership of land among SC households gets highlighted in the form of lower size of landownership across all the regions of the state (Table 2.8). By and large, average size of land owned by SC households is less than one-third that of Other households. This is not only true for UP, but also holds true at the all-India level.

As per size class distribution of land preponderance of small landholding was observed among all social groups. The average size

---

[10] It may be pointed out here that in the 66th round (2009–2010), the western region of UP has been divided into two regions viz., North Upper Ganga Plains and South Upper Ganga Plains.

Table 2.7

Proportion of Households and Proportion of Land Owned in Rural Area, by Social Groups, 2009–2010

Region/State/ Country	Scheduled caste		Other backward classes		Others	
	% of households	% of land owned	% of households	% of land owned	% of households	% of land owned
North Upper Ganga Plains	23.1	12.7	54.1	54.7	22.2	32.6
South Upper Ganga Plains	26.2	11.1	49.9	53.6	23.7	35.4
Central region	36.8	18.7	42.9	43.5	20.0	37.8
Eastern region	27.2	11.1	56.7	57.9	15.3	30.9
Southern region	33.3	11.4	45.3	41.4	21.1	47.2
Uttar Pradesh	28.4	12.6	51.8	52.0	19.2	35.5
All India	22.2	10.9	42.2	50.4	24.7	38.7

Source: Calculated from NSS Database, 66th round, Employment & Unemployment Survey, 2009–2010.

Table 2.8

Average Size of Land Owned in Rural Area (in Hectares), by Social Groups, 2009–2010

Region/State/Country	Scheduled caste	Other backward classes	Others	All social groups
North Upper Ganga Plains	0.27	0.50	0.72	0.49
Central region	0.29	0.57	1.07	0.57
Eastern region	0.18	0.44	0.88	0.44
Southern region	0.44	1.19	2.90	1.30
South Upper Ganga Plains	0.30	0.76	1.06	0.71
Uttar Pradesh	0.24	0.52	1.06	0.53
All India	0.29	0.71	0.93	0.68

Source: Calculated from NSS Database, 66th round, Employment & Unemployment Survey, 2009–2010.

of land ownership has been steadily declining over time and this has been primarily due to sub-division of land and fragmentation. However, the smallness of size of holding was more acute among SC households, 95 per cent of whom owned less than 1 ha. of land

Table 2.9

Size Class Distribution of Land Owned in Rural Uttar Pradesh, by Social Groups, 2009–2010 (% of Households)

Size class	Scheduled caste	Other backward classes	Others	All social groups
Landless	4.6	3.2	1.8	3.4
Less than 1 ha.	90.4	81.4	64.4	81.0
1–2 ha.	3.5	10.8	15.9	9.6
2–4 ha.	1.5	3.7	13.9	4.9
Above 4 ha.	0.0	0.9	3.9	1.2
All size classes	100.0	100.0	100.0	100.0

Source: Calculated from NSS Database, 66th round, Employment & Unemployment Survey, 2009–2010.

in rural UP, and none of the SC households owned above 4 ha. of land (Table 2.9).

Clearly, the major trends that emerged from the analysis of AIDIS data on landholding were reflected in the employment and unemployment survey results as well. Smallness of size of landholding and land scarcity among the marginalised sections of the society are the two overwhelming conclusions that can be drawn from the analysis of the NSS rounds. Given the historical experience of failed attempts at land reform measures, and the present reality of smallness of size of landholding in general on the one hand and land scarcity among the marginalised sections of the society on the other, the larger question that we need to address is what should be the focus of any future land policy.

Agrarian Structure and Its Role as a Constraint on Agricultural Growth

In this section, we turn to an explanation for the sustained slow growth in Indian agriculture, and the role of the agrarian structure in that slow growth. In this context, it is useful to examine the long-standing analytical controversy around the relationship between farm size and productivity.

The literature finds that imperfections in a single market would not be sufficient to introduce a systematic relationship between farm size and productivity per unit of land. For instance, if credit is rationed according to farm size, but all other markets are perfect (a rather unlikely condition in India), land and labour market transactions will produce a market structure that equalises yields across farms of different operational size. However, if there are imperfections in two markets (land rental and insurance, or credit and labour, as exists in these markets in India), a systematic relationship can arise between farm size and productivity.

After examining a large number of studies across Latin America, Africa and Asia (including India), Binswanger et al. (1995) note that the studies are consistent with the following generalisations:

1. The productivity differential in favour of small farms over large ones increases with the differences in size. This implies it is the largest where inequalities in land holdings are the largest, in the relatively land-abundant countries of Latin America and Africa, and the smallest in land-scarce Asian countries where farm size distributions are less unequal. In other words, in India the relationship would hold, but would be much weaker compared to other regions.
2. The highest output per unit area is often achieved not by the smallest sub-family but by the second highest farm size class. This suggests that the smallest farms may be the most severely credit constrained; the latter is exactly the situation that we find in India.
3. When land is adjusted for differences for quality, the negative productivity relationship with farm size weakens but does not disappear, especially where land quality difference is very large.
4. Introduction of the Green Revolution technology in India led to a weakening but not the disappearance of the productivity differentials between farm sizes.

In the section titled 'Land Tenure System Prior to and Since Independence', we saw that 84 per cent (81 per cent in UP) of all operational holdings in India are less than 1 ha. in size (i.e., less than 2.5 acres). In fact, over time there has been a persistent shrinkage in the size of the average firm as population has increased. For long the effective argument was made that land distribution of ceiling surplus land is necessary because there is an inverse relationship between farm size and productivity (Bhardwaj, 1962). Over time, there has been consistent decline in the share of holdings of larger size.

Sen and Bhatia (2004) note that as the farm size falls, family members are compelled to migrate to other forms of work to add to their means of livelihood, leading to a worsening of production management, thereby resulting in slower agricultural output growth. They note that at least half the Indian states have average holdings below the minimum size required to maintain a family of five above the poverty line. States with a rate of growth of agriculture higher than the average had holdings on average greater in size than the minimum required.

It may be noted that high total fertility rates continue to be a problem in some of the backward states like UP and Bihar (3.6 per woman) where agriculture is the principal source of livelihood for a majority of the population, and fragmentation and shrinking of farm size is a serious problem. Among the major states (leaving out Delhi, which is largely urban), Bihar has the highest population density in the country, while UP has the fourth highest population density (Table 2.10). The high population density and fragmentation of landholding implies that a large chunk of the population in these two states have to depend on non-agricultural sources of incomes for their livelihood. Unfortunately, in the past decade, except construction, no other sector has generated employment opportunities (Mehrotra, 2014). This in turn implies large-scale out-migration from these two states. UP alone accounts for 41 per cent (i.e., 16 million) of the 40 million of all inter-state migrations in India between 1991 and 2001 (Census, 2001). This 16 million

Table 2.10
Population Density by State, 2001 and 2011

India/States/UT	2001	2011
India	324	382
Delhi (UT)	9,294	9340
Chandigarh (UT)	7,903	9252
Pondicherry (UT)	2,029	2598

(Table 2.10 Continued)

(Table 2.10 Continued)

India/States/UT	2001	2011
Lakshadweep (UT)	1,894	2013
Bihar	880	1102
West Bengal	904	1030
Kerala	819	859
Uttar Pradesh	689	828
Haryana	477	573
Tamil nadu	478	555
Punjab	482	550
Dadra & Nagar Haveli (UT)	449	491
Jharkhand	338	414
Assam	340	397
Goa	363	394
Maharashtra	314	365
Tripura	304	350
Karnataka	275	319
Gujarat	258	308
Andhra Pradesh	275	308
Orissa	236	269
Madhya Pradesh	196	236
Rajasthan	165	201
Uttaranchal	159	189
Chhattisgarh	154	189
Meghalaya	103	132
Himachal Pradesh	109	123
Manipur	107	122
Nagaland	120	119
Daman & Diu (UT)	1,411	112
Sikkim	76	86
Jammu and Kashmir	99	56
Mizoram	42	52
Andaman & Nicobar Islands (UT)	43	46
Arunachal Pradesh	13	17

Source: Registrar General of India Census, 2001 and 2011.

includes both in-migrants and out-migrants. If we consider the net effect of both out-migration and in-migration, then the number of net out-migrants from UP was 2.6 million, which was the highest in the country, followed by Bihar (1.7 million).

Balakrishnan (2010) draws two very important conclusions from the shrinking farm size. First, the majority of India's farmers would be unable to access new technology as their access to credit falls. Of course, one could argue that this is an administrative issue, not a structural one; however, the fact remains that for banks there is a greater transaction cost when lending to hundreds of thousands of small and marginal farmers. New technology is capital-intensive and their asset base is too small for them to access the institutional lenders for credit. In fact, there is evidence that small and marginal farmers are today unable to access institutional lenders and tend to rely on informal moneylenders, who charge higher rates and have transfer terms than public sector banks. In fact, the shrinking farm size has made it difficult for these farmers to grow enough to meet their own consumption needs, and hence borrowing from money-lenders to meet their consumption needs has grown. Balakrishnan (2010) notes that their inability to invest in land improvements is a probable reason for the slower growth of yield in the period since 1991, compared to the Green Revolution period (1967–1968 to 1990). Second, an improvement in farm relative prices (such as through an increase in minimum support prices) may have little impact "when structural factors governing production, such as farm size, turn adverse irreversibly" (p. 197). It is not surprising that NSS finds that 40 per cent of farmers report that farming is not profitable. Even less surprising is that the number of those employed in agriculture fell in UP between 2004–2005 and 2009–2010 by over 3.5 million. In fact, there was a decline in the numbers employed in agriculture in India by 14 million over the same period. Of this decline, half of the fall was accounted for by only two states, UP and Bihar.

Rural distress is one reason for males leaving agriculture in UP but this situation is compounded by the fact that women too have been withdrawing from agricultural work (other than public works, especially when created by MGNREGA). In addition, with growing rural open market wages (thanks to MGNREGA) and male migration leading to shortage of labour, there has been a growth in mechanisation in agriculture, in UP and elsewhere. Thus, very few families will till their farms, including small and marginal farmers, using a bullock or male bull, which was normal in the past. There has been an explosion of the tractor population in UP. Threshing at harvesting time is also done by tractor-driven threshers, thus again reducing the demand for labour. Demand for women's labour is thus declining, even as agriculture is increasingly dependent upon them (Mehrotra, 2014). Hence, women too need help to move into non-agricultural work, while remaining in the village.

This implies that roughly 7.5 million people gave up agriculture in these two states alone. The question therefore is, where are these people going? Part of the answer is given by the Census data (2011). Between 2001 and 2011, these two states accounted for 4.3 million net out-migrants—UP with 2.6 million net out-migrants (highest in the country), followed by Bihar (1.7 million). Unless and until non-agricultural employment opportunities are created in these two states, out-migration from these two states will continue, given that these two states have very high population density (828 persons per sq. km in UP and 1,102 persons per sq. km in Bihar).

The policy approach to agriculture since the 1990s has been to secure increased production through subsidies on inputs such as power, water and fertiliser, and by increasing the MSP rather than through building new capital assets in irrigation, power and rural infrastructure in less-endowed regions. This has shifted the production base from low-cost regions to high-cost ones, causing an increase in the cost of production, regional imbalance and the burden of storage and transport of food grains (Balakrishnan, 2010).

The equity, efficiency and sustainability of the current approach are questionable. Subsidies do not improve income distribution or the demand for labour. The boost in output from subsidy-stimulated use of fertiliser, pesticides and water has the potential to damage aquifers and soils—an environmentally unsustainable approach that may partly explain the rising costs and slowing growth and productivity in agriculture, notably in Punjab and Haryana. Although private investment in agriculture has grown, this has often involved macroeconomic inefficiencies (such as private investment in diesel-generating sets instead of public investment in electricity supply). Public investment in agriculture has fallen dramatically since the 1980s and so has the share of agriculture in the total gross capital formation (Balakrishnan, 2010). Instead of promoting low-cost options that have a lower capital–output ratio, present policies have resulted in excessive use of capital on the farms, such as too many tube wells in water-scarce regions.

Concluding Remarks

The state of rural distress in UP is evident from the fact that 3.5 million workers left agriculture for non-agricultural activities within a matter of 5 years (2004–2005 and 2009–2010). UP accounts for the largest number of those who migrated in search of non-agricultural work, especially construction work, more than in any other state. Mechanisation of agricultural work has also reduced the demand for labour. The highest total fertility rates found in any state has, over time, resulted in a dramatic shrinking of average farm size causing rural distress. This rural distress is occurring notwithstanding the much greater advantage UP's agriculture enjoys relative to other states of the country (e.g., 72 per cent of agricultural land is irrigated in UP, as against 48 per cent in the rest of the country). Yield gaps with other states remain high. Although rising minimum support prices for the wheat and rice grown by UP farmers should have served as an offsetting factor, the non-price factors underlying slow agricultural growth seem to have been overwhelming.

It is for these reasons that a number of radical policy decisions will urgently need to be taken to revive agricultural incomes in UP, while at the same time encouraging an orderly transition out of agriculture for workers into both rural and urban non-farm economic activities. First, tenancy, which remains illegal in UP (one of the few states of India where it is illegal), must be legalised to enable use of fallow land and also counter the shrinking of farm size. Second, land consolidation efforts would also need to be intensified in order to reduce inefficiency. Third, ceiling surplus land should be used to at least ensure homestead rights to those who are homeless in rural areas. Fourth, the state should develop a public land bank to enable tenancy, and thus allow land to be used. At the same time this would reassure small and marginal farmers, who want to lease out their lands to bigger farmers and migrate in search of non-agricultural work, are encouraged to do so. However, no one should underestimate the challenges of attempting this task in a state where governance levels are perhaps among the worst in the country. Fifth, the UP government will have to encourage group farming, especially among small and marginal farmers, so that they can get access to input and credit, and also enter the contract farming market.

Finally, the UP government should ensure changes to the Hindu Succession Act to enable women to own land, since there is large-scale male migration ocurring along with feminisation of agriculture. Moreover, the UP Government will have to facilitate the formulation of self-help groups among women farmers, and support them with credit and other inputs.

References

Appu, P.S. (1996), *Land Reforms in India*, Vikas Publishing House, New Delhi.

Balakrishnan, P. (2010), *Economic Growth in India. History and Prospects*, Oxford University Press, Delhi.

Bhardwaj, K. (1962), *Production Conditions in Indian Agriculture*, Cambridge University Press, Cambridge.

Binswanger, H., P.K. Deininger and G. Feder (1995), 'Power Distortions, Revolt and Reforms in Agricultural Land Relations', in J. Behrman and T.N. Srinivasan (eds.), *Handbook of Development Economics*, pp. 2659–2672, Elsevier, Amsterdam.

Birdsall, N. and J.L. Londono (1997), 'Asset Inequality Does Matter: Lessons from Latin America', *OCE Working Paper*, Inter American Development Bank.

Chakravarty, S. (1987), *Development Planning: The Indian Experience*, Oxford University Press, Delhi (Paperback edition).

Driver, P.N. (1949), *Problems of Zamindari and Land Revenue Reconstruction in India*, New Book Company, Bombay.

Dutt, R.C. (1976), *Economic History of India*, Government of India, New Delhi.

Jassal, S. (1980), 'Agrarian Contradictions and Resistance in Faizabad District of Oudh (India), 18581970', *Journal of Peasant Studies*, 7 (3), 312–337.

Kotosky, G. (1964), *Agrarian Reforms in India*, People's Publishing House, New Delhi.

Mehrotra, S. (2014), *Seizing the Demographic Dividend. Policies to Achieve Inclusive Growth in India*, Cambridge University Press.

Meier, G.M. (1976), *Leading Issues in Economic Development*, Oxford University Press, New York.

Ministry of Finance (2013), Economic Survey 2012–2013, Government of India, New Delhi.

Neale, W.C. (1962), *Economic Change in Rural India: Land Tenure and Land Reform, 1800–1955*, Yale University Press, New Haven, CT.

Powell, B. (1974), *The Land System of British India*, Oriental Publishers, New Delhi.

Saha, P. (2009), 'Land Relations and Asset Holdings: A Study Based on Village-Level Evidence from Uttar Pradesh', Unpublished Ph.D. Thesis, Submitted to Jawaharlal Nehru University, New Delhi.

Sen, A. and M.S. Bhatia (2004), *The State of the Indian Farmers: A Millennium Study*, Academic Foundation & Ministry of Agriculture, New Delhi.

Singh, J. (1992), *Capitalism and Dependence: Agrarian Politics of Western Uttar Pradesh, 1951-1991*, Manohar Publishers, New Delhi.

Whitcombe, E. (1971), *Agrarian Conditions in North India: Vol. 1; The United Province Under British Rule 18601900*, University of California Press, Berkeley, CA.

3

Landlordism without Landlord: The UP Land Reform

Hiranmay Dhar

Introduction

"She is a messiah. People like me have been getting disenchanted with her as nothing was coming to us despite having a Dalit Chief Minister. But then I got this piece of land. Now we realise that the administration listens to us." This was Raju, a Dalit landless labour, quoted in *Hindustan Times* (HT), Lucknow (21 July 2008) on Mayawati, the UP Chief Minister, after getting an acre of land as part of the redistribution of 191 acres of land, which became *gaon-sabha* land after *chakbandi* (consolidation). This land was redistributed among 212 erstwhile landless labourers of Kalpi (Jalaun district), which included 145 scheduled castes and 64 other backward castes.

Rigizin Samphel, the District Magistrate of Jalaun district, was quoted by the HT correspondent as saying, "It was one of the toughest tasks that we have accomplished. We did not stop at only allotment. Within a week of allotment, we deployed the Provincial Armed Constabulatory, the police and over two dozen *tehsil* officials to give possession of the plots to the beneficiaries." For the poor beneficiaries, police help was necessary as this *gaon-sabha* land was under the control of the upper-caste people who are unwilling to leave.

The sub-divisional magistrate added, "We are going further: not all the plots of land are good — some are uneven or barren. We have decided to suggest means to use a particular piece of land. We will also give options to plant cash crops and provide saplings free of costs."

According to Mayawati's announcement in 2007–2008 the *pattas* (or ownership title document) of 10,078 ha. of agricultural land have been allotted to 51,319 poorest of the poor among the scheduled castes and scheduled tribes, compared to 19,500 *pattas* given in the last year. This year the target has been doubled (*Hindustan Times*, Lucknow, 27 July 2008).

In UP, most of the *gaon-sabha* land (i.e., government-owned land) is under the illegal occupation of the dominant landowning communities — mostly upper castes and backward castes. People like Raju need police help for the occupation of the land that they have been given. Further, they need institutional help for the supply of inputs, credit and marketing facilities for the productive use of the land.

Land reform is not a once-for-all solution of the agrarian transformation of any economy. It is necessary, but not the sufficient condition for rural transformation. There are, in fact, three basic conditions for genuine land reform. Land reform is the dispossession of a class of landlords without, or little, compensation and the distribution of the land to the peasantry and the agricultural workers who were dispossessed by the landlords. The second point is that land reform is a non-market intervention usually initiated from below by mass organisation, which also has to have state support for its success and sustenance. A land reform, in order to be successful, has to be implemented within a short period of historical time. It also needs inclusive agricultural policy with active state support — the institutional arrangements for credit and marketing facilities, etc.[1]

The chapter is organised in four parts. First part discusses the politics of *zamindari* abolition in UP. Second part discusses the land-holding pattern before and after *zamindari* abolition. It also examines how National Sample Survey data on landholding must be read along with the ground-reality of tenancy. The impact of the Land Ceiling Act of UP is discussed in third part. The final part of the chapter gives the main conclusions.

---

[1] Major land reforms have occurred either as a part of social revolution, e.g., in Mexico, Bolivia, Nicaragua, Cuba, Russia in 1917, China in 1949, or as an outcome of war, e.g., in Japan, Taiwan, South Korea, eastern and central Europe or as part of a process of systemic change, e.g., in Ethiopia, Vietnam, China after 1979, in former Soviet Union in 1991; more limited land reform occurred in other countries whose impact has not been transformative; see Agrarian Studies in this connection (Ramachandran and Swaminathan, 2002).

Land Reform in UP: The Politics of Zamindari Abolition

Land reform entered the mainstream of UP politics in the 1945–1946 election. On the election-eve campaign, Jawaharlal Nehru, Congress's most radical face at the time, emphasised repeatedly that the nawabs and rajas would find no place in the new order. In the election, the Congress won overwhelmingly in the general seats, but was rejected badly by the Muslims in the Muslin seats. The ministry that was formed was distinctly moderate in its approach to the reform. The then Chief Minister G.B. Pant was, to quote Peter Revees, 'inflexibly moderate'. True to their election manifesto, the government announced the formation of the UP Zamindari Abolition Committee (UPZAC henceforth) in October 1946. Except Ajit Prasad Jain—who talked about the neglect of the landless field labourers in the report—and Vishambar Prasad Tripathy—who talked about cooperative farming replacing entirely individual farming and also village community taking control of land—all other members were protagonists of the 'peasant proprietorship' and distinctly moderate in their approach to the *zamindari* abolition. One member—Begam Aizaz Rasool—was the landlord's representative. The socialists and the communists were completely out of the reckoning in this process after they resigned from the Congress.

The Congress Chief Minister, G.B. Pant, 'inflexibly moderate' in his approach, was not hostile to the *zamindars* as a class. He entrusted Charan Singh with the task of drafting the UP Zamindari Abolition Committee Report (UPZAC report henceforth). In his *Abolition of Zamindari* in 1947, Charan Singh talked about private property and 'peasant proprietor' as he who 'seek the elimination of the 'Zamindar' who is not a landlord but ... is a mere holder of land or tiller of the soil in his ownership. 'Abolition of Zamindari' simply means, and ought to mean, abolition of the landlord-tenant system and no more" (Singh, 1946, p. 131).

Scholars have described Charan Singh variously. To Baxter (1975), he was "spokesman for the middle farmer and individual ownership". Duncan (1979) found in him "the most prominent spokesman and champion (in UP) ... of the more prosperous section of the peasantry". Brass (1965), more specific according to T. Byres, identified Charan Singh as the 'the leading spokesman for the interests of the middle-level and rich peasant proprietors' (Brass, 1980). For us, however, Byre's comment on Charan Singh is at the same time more specific and contextual: 'Charan Singh's significance', Byres said, 'lies in the contribution he made to the emergence and consolidation of rich peasants as a class in North-west India. In so doing, he cleared some of the way for an agrarian capitalism from below in western UP. ... Charan Singh argued a neo- populist case against capitalism. That is not inconsistent with his reducing some of the barriers to agrarian capitalism ....' (Byres, 1991).

The UPZAC report was explicit in its assertion that they would not like to confiscate land for redistribution, as the hardship and discontent that it might cause will not be commensurate with its achievement, and further, the land that will be so available for redistribution will not be enough to make the innumerable small units economically viable. Only the land, the report emphasised, not under cultivating possession of the landlords will be taken over on payment of appropriate compensation (UPZAC report, 1948, p. 389). 'Cultivator' or 'tiller of the soil' in this connection was defined as the person who 'performs the manual task of cultivation', 'provides the finance', 'manages and supervises the holding' and 'takes the risks involved'. The employment of casual labour was allowed so long as the owner performs the last three tasks (UPZAC report, 1948, p. 389).

This definition of 'cultivation' gives 'the zamindari abolition in UP a particular shape'. Reeves (1991) described the process succinctly thus:

> Abolition on this basis became fairly straightforward: identify the 'cultivator' and confirm the cultivator in that position with secure rights by eliminating the right of any other person which interposed between the cultivator and the State. Thus zamindar would retain their sir and khudkast, and their grove land (since in all these types of land they were in cultivating possession); and tenant-in- chief would then retain the land which they now held from any zamindar or other intermediary, all right of the zamindar having been extinguished. (p. 286)

At the time of the abolition 10,235,000 acres, let and un-let, has been recorded as *sir* and *khudhkast* land, which is 18 per cent of the recorded land. The *zamindar* succeeded in restoring 79.5 per cent of them through eviction and other means (Hasan, 1998, 1989a, 1989b, p. 75). The delay in the passage of the act further helped the *zamindars* in their depredations. Six years had elapsed since the passing of a formal resolution announcing the abolition of *zamindri* in UP in August 1946 to the time of sending direction to the rural record keeper in 1952 for updating the land records, giving the *zamindars* ample[2] time to restore their land.[3]

Bewildering varieties of tenure in the pre-*zamindari* period was replaced by the two main forms of tenure in the Act: *bhumidar* and *sirdars*. Under the new arrangement, the vast majority of the peasants were to become *bhumidars*. Ex-intermediaries were to be treated as *bhumidars* in respect of their *sir* and *khudkast* land and so also will be the tenants who pay 10 times of their rent. *Bhumidars* paid low rent and were entitled to transfer their rights and use their land for non-agricultural purposes. Under the new scheme, the *sirdars* could acquire *bhumidari* right and, with it, 50 per cent reduction in land revenue by depositing 10 times of their annual rent for their land with the Zamindari Abolition Fund (ZAF). In addition, a minor tenure in the form of *asami* was created, who were mostly the former non-occupancy tenants having no stable rights.[4]

The ZAF was created at the initiative of Charan Singh, supported by G.B. Pant, to organise funds to compensate the ex-intermediaries—some 390 of them. Provisions like no confiscation and no redistribution of land, on the other hand, were meant to satisfy the relatively better-off peasants (owning more than 10 acres of land) and thus create a political support base of the Congress. Sir Jagdish Prasad, the landlord leader opposed to the *zamindari* abolition, was not beside the point when he was quoted in the Pioneer (22 January 1950) saying that the *bhumidari* system was a way of ensuring political support for the Congress in the ensuing election. Writing in the *National Herald* in the pen-name 'Sekhar', Prof. V.B. Singh was more explicit and to the point:

> Politically it (the abolition scheme) is a device to extend and stabilise the social base of the present government for getting votes in the

[2] See Uttar Pradesh Zamindari Abolition and Land Reforms Act, pp. 2–3.
[3] For a lucid description of the process, see Whitcombe (1975).
[4] UPZALR, p. 2.

next election. Economically it will create a new class of rural bour-
geoisie who will exploit the peasant and other sections of the rural
population in a much more intense form.[5]

Landholding Pattern Before and After *Zamindari* Abolition

After about three decades of land reform the land ownership in UP
had become more concentrated. In 1976–1977, a mere 15 per cent
of the households controlled more than 64 per cent of the land as
compared to about 19 per cent controlling more than 60 per cent
of the total holding in the pre-land reform period. In the mean
time, however, the average size of the holding fell from 3.5 acres
to 2.88 acres in response to subdivision of holding as well as sale
and purchase of land (Table 3.1).

The analysis of the NSS gives a clearer picture of the land distribution pattern of the UP in the post-land-reform period.[6] In the
initial five decades after the land reform, there was some decline
in the large holding and area owned by them for a number of
reasons. In 1950, there was some increase due to large-scale and
indiscriminating eviction of tenants by the landlords in the pretext
of self-cultivation under *sir* and *khudkast*. The 1960s, however, saw
some fall in their area owned owing to large-scale disposing of
their land to their former tenants and *benami* transfer of land to
avoid ceiling laws that came into force during the period, which
as followed by big landowners holding on to their land due to
ineffective implementation of the ceiling laws (see Sharma, 1994).

So far as the landholders at the bottom of the landownership
hierarchy is concerned, i.e., those with 0.01–0.99 size holding, their
numerical strength increased rapidly, but the size of their holding
did not increase very significantly.

The greatest benefit of the land reform has accrued to the marginal (1.00–2.49 acres), small (2.50–4.90 acres) and medium holdings

---

[5] *National Herald*, 8 June 1948.

[6] There are many studies of this aspect of the land question in the Independence
period. We have, however, mainly depended on the works of Dantwala and Shah
(1973), Singh and Mishra (1984), Khusro (1958), Bandyopadhyay (1986) and Sharma
(1994).

Table 3.1
Pattern of Land Ownership Prior to and After Zamindari Abolition (in Percentage)

Size of ownership holding (in acres)	Prior to abolition of zamindari		Period of National Sample Survey							
			1953–1954		1961–1962		1971–1972		1976–1977	
	Households	Area owned	Household	Area owned	Household	Area owned	Household	Area owned	Household	Area owned
Below 1.0 acre	37.80	6.00	38.69	2.37	44.21	1.59	50.20	4.09	50.98	5.33
Below 5.0 acres	81.20	39.10	78.43	31.83	75.22	19.99	86.22	42.37	84.15	35.55
5.0–10.0 acres	12.70	26.10	14.25	29.08	12.86	20.54	9.45	27.82	9.60	24.47
Above 10.0 acres	6.10	34.80	7.32	39.09	11.92	59.47	4.33	29.81	6.25	39.98
Average size of holding (in acres)	3.50		3.40		4.39		2.35		2.88	

Source: Cited in Reeves (1991).

(5.00–14.99 acres) in comparison to the other categories of holdings. In UP the number of medium landholders fell significantly during the period, while their land ownership fell only marginally, thus making this class of landholder better off compared to the others (see Sharma, 1994, p. A-122).

The NSS data on the ownership pattern, however, gives the *de jure* position. It ignores the effect of the institution of tenancy, which is almost universal in UP rural areas (though the conditions of tenancy had undergone radical transformation). On this issue of the operational holding, the following points can be noted.

First, in spite of the definitional change in the concepts of the household between the 8th round and the 17th round, it can be pointed out that the number of households owning no land increased especially after 1961–1962. Analysis by scholars has also shown that the numerical preponderance of the sub-marginal (0.01–0.99 acre) holdings at the bottom of the farm size ladder has increased continuously, especially after 1961. The proportion of their farm size area, on the other hand, remained lower in UP, creating an adverse land–man ratio. This forced this section of the peasantry to supplement their income from their uneconomic holding and seek non-agricultural occupation and sometimes migrate, which has assumed enormous proportion in recent times. *Palayan* is the name of this menace in the UP countryside today. This also has important implications for the radical land reforms itself. Historical experience has shown that in order to be successful the state should intervene to create institutions that would provide adequate access to these classes of framers—who usually constitute the largest segment of the rural population—cheap and easy access to inputs, water, etc., as well as proper marketing facilities. But in this era of liberalisation, with the state increasingly withdrawing from its economic responsibility, such a possibility seems to be becoming remote.

Second, both the number of large households and area operated by them declined in UP since 1953–1954. In fact, since 1953–1954 increasingly very few of these households owned disproportionately large amount of area. In the early 1980s, 1.70 per cent household owned 15.12 per cent of the area in UP (Table 3.2).

Third, the real gain of change in operational holding went to the marginal, small and medium households. These categories of farmers gained considerably. The medium households gained most among them. In this category, the decrease in the proportions of

Table 3.2
Trends in the Distribution of Ownership and Operational Holdings in UP (in Percentage)

Size of ownership holding (in acres)	Trends of distribution	Period			
		1953–1954	*1961–1962*	*1971–1972*	*1982*
I. Trends in ownership holding					
1. Households owning no land		9.36	2.77	4.55	4.85
2. Sub-marginal holdings	H	30.32	33.90	30.83	38.71
(0.01–0.99 acres)	A	4.29	4.11	6.83	4.42
3. Marginal holdings	H	20.34	20.78	22.20	24.40
(1.00–2.49 acres)	A	10.13	9.88	13.57	15.73
4. Small holdings	H	18.40	21.39	18.60	17.38
(2.50–5.00 acres)	A	19.39	22.21	24.66	24.38
5. Medium holdings	H	18.12	17.82	13.79	12.92
(5.00–14.99 acres)	A	42.97	41.87	41.08	40.92
6. Large holdings (15.00	H	3.46	3.34	2.03	1.74
and above acres)	A	25.13	23.59	16.78	15.35
7. All households	H	100.00	100.00	100.00	100.00
	A	100.00	100.00	100.00	100.00
II. Trends in operational holding					
1. Households operating no land		5.14	20.76	24.26	20.00
2. Sub-marginal holdings	H	30.41	14.64	15.22	25.77
(0.01–0.99 acres)	A	2.17	2.51	2.85	4.06
3. Marginal holdings	H				
(1.00–2.49 acres)	A				
4. Small holdings	H	20.40	21.59	20.48	17.69
(2.50–5.00 acres)	A	20.46	25.42	25.43	24.53
5. Medium holdings	H	19.49	19.21	15.75	13.42
(5.00–14.99 acres)	A	43.41	34.98	42.76	42.36
6. Large holdings (15.00	H	3.53	3.32	2.12	1.70
and above acres)	A	24.03	25.98	16.14	15.12
7. All households	H	100.00	100.00	100.00	100.00
	A	100.00	100.00	100.00	100.00

Source: Adapted from Sharma (1994).
Note: H — household ownership; A — area in operation.

households is considerable in comparison to that in area. In UP the decline in the proportions of household was from 19.49 to 13.42 per cent between 1953–1954 and 1982, while the decline in the proportion in their operated area was from 43.41 to 42.36 per cent, thus making the middle farmers comparatively better off in terms of land: household ratio. The trend continued in 1992 and 2003 also.[7]

Impact of Land Ceiling

Similar to land reform in UP, which abolished absentee landlordism (on compensation) to establish peasant proprietorship, the ceiling on land holding generated much debate. Lot of arguments were heard around such words as 'social question', 'equality', 'private property', 'individual incentive', 'socialism', 'confiscation', 'higher food production', etc. (Thorner, 1956, pp. 52–68). Nehru, of course, came out with the most far-reaching and radical proposal for ceiling of *income* itself at 40 times the national minimum, which would gradually be reduced to 20 times the minimum necessary. The Report of the UPZAC, however, rejected all such talks about ceiling in favour of the right of cultivators to cultivate land under their possession. In the draft of First Plan, however, the equity consideration returned possibly due to all round agrarian distress and the defeat of the Congress in the state election (Thorner, 1956).

With this objective in view, the UP Imposition of Ceiling on Land Holding Act was enacted for ensuring increased agricultural production, providing land to the landless agricultural labourers and for public purposes. The original act imposed a ceiling of 40 acres of fair-quality land (80 acres of inferior land) for a family of five. The ceiling did not apply to *Khalian* and residential area. This original act was not effective and did not succeed in releasing much land. So, it was drastically amended in 1973, which reduced the effective ceiling limit to 7.30 ha. (or 18.25 acres) or its equivalent of un-irrigated land for a family of five.

The status of the UP Land Ceiling Act up to March 2008 is given in Table 3.3. Land of 3,68,351 acres was identified as surplus. About

---

[7] See NSS report nos. 491 and 492 (Thorner, 1976, 1980).

Table 3.3
Status of UP Land Ceiling Act: March 2008

Status of UP land			Area (in acres)
1. Land declared surplus			3,68,351 (100.00)
2. Land taken possession of by the state government			3,38,349 (91.86)
3. Reasons for failure in taking possession			
a. Land under stay order in different courts	28,377 (94.58)		
b. Land under consolidation process	377 (1.25)		
c. Land under consideration	1,248 (4.17)		30,002 (8.14) (100.0)
4. Reason for not settling surplus land			
a. Land under stay order in different courts	15,111 (70.31)		
b. Joint enquiry	2,693 (12.52)		
c. Land proposed to be given to gaon-sabha	1,142 (5.30)		
d. Land proposed to be given to other departments	844 (3.93)		
e. Land under consolidation	112 (0.52)		
f. Land under illegal possession	466 (2.17)		
g. Land included in consolidation by mistake	986 (4.59)		
h. Land not distributed for other reasons	139 (0.66)		
i. Total			21,493 (100.00)
5. Land available for settlement			3,16,856 (100.00)
6. Settlement of land under possession	Number of beneficiaries	Area in acres	Acres per head
a. Land distribute to SC	2,07,430 (68.24)	1,84,642 (58.27)	0.89
b. Land distributed to ST	487 (00.16)	974 (0.31)	2.00
c. Land distributed to others	96,067 (31.60)	77,337 (17.01)	0.80
d. Land under gaon-sabha and other departments	53,903 (17.01)		
7. Total land settled			3,16,856 (100.00)

Source: Board of Revenue, UP.
Note: Figures in the parentheses indicate percentage.

92 per cent of that declared surplus, i.e., 3,38,349 acres, was taken possession of by the state government. About 8 per cent of those declared surplus could not be taken possession of due to issuance of stay order by various courts — almost 95 per cent of these 8 per cent — and the rest could not be taken possession of as they were under consolidation process and also due to various other government procedural reasons. Out of those 3,38,349 acres of land was taken possession of by the government, another 6.78 per cent, i.e., 21,493 acres of land, could not be settled: more than 82 per cent of these lands could not be settled due to various types of legal wrangling (Table 3.3) and for other procedural delays.

Legal wrangling and procedural reasons were the two most important reasons that undermined the effectiveness of the Ceiling Act in UP like many of its predecessors. One civil servant, posted in the Board of Revenue, said in an interview that due to slackness on the part of the Revenue Administration, it took almost 3 years to collect details and file return to the landowners in the initial stage of the Act. He further said that the average time taken by the prescribed authority in all the cases is about 1–3 years from the date of institution of the ceiling cases. At the stage of Appellate Authority, the average time taken for the disposal of cases is about 1.5–2 years. Reasons for these are normal procedural requirements: courts allowing landowners to give their opinion about surplus land, at the end of enquiry landowners pleading falsely that the land is to be used for government schemes, spot inspection being demanded by the party, filling of irrelevant sale deeds, etc. The delay in disposal of ceiling cases is the highest at the High Court stage. About two-thirds of the pending cases in each district remain pending for more than 3 years at a minimum and in certain cases it takes up to 16–17 years.

Two types of land are usually available in UP for redistribution: common *gaon-sabha* land and land declared surplus under the ceiling laws. In UP, however, most of the *gaon-sabha* land are under the illegal occupation of the powerful landowners. The redistribution of surplus land poses still greater problems. In an intensive study of four districts of Kheri, Jalaun, Gorakhpur and Saharanpur, it was found that 20 per cent of the surplus land is under the illegal possession of the government. Similar stories can be heard from the districts of Lucknow, Nainital, Shajahanpur and Bariely.[8]

---

[8] See Bandyopadhyay (1986, *Land Reform in India*, pp. 4–6).

In another study of 26 districts out of 62 districts of UP by IAS probationers, carried out between 1988 and 1992, it was found that the average area owned by surplus ceiling owners was 63.27 acres, average finally declared surplus is 31.63 acres and the average area finally taken possession of by the government is 16.57 acres (Implementation of the Land Ceiling Programme in Uttar Pradesh, 1992). In further elaboration of this information collected from this survey, another study reported that these probationers studied 37 villages and identified 208 surplus ceiling owners; 22.3 per cent of these owners own more than 50 acres and 37.3 per cent of them had their land outside their village of residence (i.e., absentee landlord). It pointed out that out of the total of 8,172.5 acres initially declared surplus in these sampled villages, 80.1 per cent of the area has been finally declared surplus, but 17.8 per cent of the land was released to the landlord on various pretexts (Iyer, 1992). Land ceiling cases against 394 *khatedar* owning 7890 ha. were instituted in Lucknow district in 1989, out of which only 3,128 cases were finally declared surplus and out of this only 44 per cent could be distributed. The situation is much worse in Lakhimpur Khiri, where at least four persons were found to own more than 1,000 acres. The majority of the owners in Lakhimpur Khiri are upper caste, some are backward caste and a few Muslim (Implementation of Land Ceiling Programme in Uttar Pradesh, quoted in Hasan, 1998).

In another study of nine villages, in five districts of Etawah, Jhansi, Sonebhadra, Bahraich and Shahjahanpur, it was found that initially 1,939.64 acres of land was declared surplus, out of which only 733.28 acres of land, i.e., 37.81 per cent, was finally declared surplus (Bobade, 1992).

A study of 26 districts of UP in the last decade identified eight distinct methods used by the landholders of different classes — but mostly the bigger ones — to circumvent various provisions of the Ceiling Act:

1. Lands were sold off to near relations;
2. False construction of residential houses;
3. Filing false partition deeds;
4. Formal decrees of divorce;
5. Manipulation of birth certificate;
6. Creation of religious deeds;

7. Prolongation of litigation (especially by big landlords); and

8. Through wrong classification of land.

Even after the land was declared surplus the landlords used a number of ruses to get back the land: (1) Part of the land was shown under orchards. (2) Number of family members was inflated. (3) Partition suits under section 176 of ZALR were initiated, indicating that the land has been divided long back. (4) Landlord had not initially, intentionally, indicated plots to be declared surplus and subsequently filed objection against the decision of the prescribed authority. (5) Good-quality land was shown as waste and/or barren land. (6) Minor declared as major fraudulent. (7) Land shown as falling under flood-prone area. (8) The plea taken that sons have already inherited father's land and the original case to be filed again separately, which delays the proceedings. (9) Other frequently taken plea is that the details of land prepared by the tehsil staff ignored certain facts that are basic to the case.[9]

Out of 3,16,856 acres of land distributed by the UP government, the scheduled castes got 2,07,430 acres, which works out to be 0.89 acre per head. A total of 487 scheduled tribes got 974 acres, which makes it 2.00 acres per scheduled tribe beneficiaries. Another 96,067 other caste beneficiaries got 77,337 acres, i.e., 0.8 acres per head (Table 3.3, rows 6a, 6b and 6c).

This macro-level statistical information does not reveal the effort made by locally dominated land-owning communities in collusion with local government officials to thwart redistribution of land and to recapture land from the beneficiaries of land given to them.

Table 3.4 gives a snapshot of such machination of the landowners in nine districts of UP, e.g., Ambedkar Nagar, Vadauna (Banda), Bahraich, Balia, Chitrakut, Jaunpur, Shahjahnpur, Saharanpur and Sonebhadra.

Victims are mostly Dalits and tribals and the perpetrators are mostly landlords, government officials and the police. The linkages of the landowners and the local government officials are caste and class. The mass of these poor farmers and the agricultural labourers need protection as did Raju, the delighted Dalit labourer of Jalgaon

---

[9] See Iyer (1992), and also see *Implementation of Land Ceiling Programme in Uttar Pradesh* (1992). The study was carried out by IAS probationers in 26 out of 62 districts, covering 40 per cent of the district between 1988 and 1992.

Table 3.4
Status of Land Distributed to the Dalits

Sl. no.	Item	No. of dalits affected
A.	Got *patta*, not the possession	279
B.	Asami *patta* cancelled	39
C.	Possession without *patta*	7
D.	Got *patta*, possession of which later taken away	14
E.	Invalid *patta*	5
F.	Land reoccupied by declaring owner dead	3
G.	Double entry (in forest and revenue dept)	31
H.	False will	10

Source: From *Dalits of UP to the Citizen of India*; A Report of the Public Hearing held in Lucknow on 5 and 6 October 2001.

Note: 'Double entry': entry in the record book of both revenue and forest departments. This type is usually found in Sonebhadra district of UP. Often the tribals there have been uprooted by the Forest Department who claim that land in question belongs to them. To the tribal of Sonebhadra the forest officials are the most dreaded landlords.

district who got help from his district magistrate. Like Raju, these labourers also need help in developing skill in modern agriculture with emphasis on diversification, in supply of cheap seeds, proper marketing facilities and other necessary institutional help.[10]

Conclusion

The radical nature of the land reform in UP lies in the abolition of the absentee landlord and its replacement by rich peasants. From landlords to peasant proprietorship was the basis of this transformation. The political class that was in the saddle at the time of Independence was against the landlords, not against landlordism. Their leaders like G.B. Pant, 'inflexibly moderate',

[10] See Bhalla (2006), for a comprehensive review of the evolution of Indian Agricultural Policy from its accent on structural changes with land reform as a basic condition for investment in agricultural development to its almost exclusive emphasis on technological innovation for agricultural growth.

and Charan Singh, 'peasant patriarch', the chief architect of the Act and the 'radical peasant leader' protected their class interest. The Act in its final form rejected the confiscation of land and its redistribution (for fear of discontent that it might cause and the decline in food production that it might lead to).

Private property was the basis of this reform. Land under self-cultivation (with the hired labour) — called *sir* and *khudkast* — was allowed to be retained and the land above that was taken after liberal compensation. The time gap between the passing of the resolution for land reform and its actual initiation was long enough for the landlords to dispossess their tenants and 'hide' their land as owned in diverse ingenious ways.

Despite the initial reservation of the framers of land reform to redistribute land, the talk of redistribution of land declared surplus above ceiling returned to the discourse of the land laws precisely for the same reason for which it was rejected earlier: to contain social discontent. In this connection, terms like 'social question', 'equality', etc., came into circulation. The Ceiling Law came into force in 1962, which was amended in 1973. But this enactment imposed from above on a rural social structure, which was dominated by the landowning community — mostly backward caste and upper caste — who, in collusion with local government officials dominated by the former upper castes, restricted its implementation.

Some surplus land has been distributed. But the landowners are making it difficult for the beneficiaries to occupy it and maintain it.

It is clearly evident that the land reform in UP is radical in the sense that it ended the era of absentee landlords and instituted the dominant peasant proprietorship in the rural areas of UP. The enactment, however, does not satisfy the basic conditions of genuine reform: it did not confiscate the landlords' land, paid them compensation and was implemented after an immense time gap, which gave the landlords time to protect their interest.

References

Bandyopadhyay, D. (1986), 'Land Reform in India: An Analysis', *Economic and Political Weekly*, Vols. 25 and 26.

Baxter, C. (1975), 'The Rise and Fall of the BKD in Uttar Pradesh', in Weiner and Field (eds.) (1968), *State Politics in India*, Princeton University Press, Princeton, NJ.

Bhalla, G.S. (2006), *Indian Agriculture since Independence,* National Book Trust, New Delhi.

Bobade, S.M. (1992), 'Land Ceiling Situation in UP', paper presented at the GIDS seminar, Lucknow.

Brass, P.R. (1965), *Factional Politics in an Indian State: the Congress Party in Uttar Pradesh,* University of California Press, Berkley, CA.

Brass, P.R. (1980), 'The Politicization of the Peasantry in a North Indian State: Part II', *Journal of Peasant Studies,* 8 (1 [October]), pp. 3–36.

Byres, T.J. (1991), 'Charan Singh (1902–1987): An Assessment', *The Journal of Peasant Studies,* 15 (2), pp. 139–189.

Dantwala, M.L. and C.H. Shah (1973), 'Pre-reform and Post-Reform Agrarian Structure', *Indian Journal of Agricultural Economics,* XXVI (3), pp. 183–200.

Duncan, I. (1979), 'The Politics of Foodgrains Procurement: A Study of Northern India', paper presented to the Peasant Seminar of the Center for International and Area Studies, University of London, 29 June, pp. 78–79.

Hasan, Z. (1989a), *Dominance and Mobilization: Rural Politics in Western Uttar Pradesh, 1930-80,* SAGE Publications, New Delhi.

Hasan, Z. (1989b), 'Power and Mobilization: Pattern of Resilience and Change in Uttar Pradesh Politics', in Frankel, F. and Rao, M.S.A. (1989), *Dominance and State Power in Modern India,* Kali for Women Press, Delhi.

Hasan, Z. (1998), *Quest for Power Oppositional Movements Post-Congress Politics in Uttar Pradesh,* Oxford University Press, New Delhi.

Iyer, K.G. (1992), 'Land Ceiling in Uttar Pradesh', paper presented at the seminar on land reform at the GIDS, Lucknow.

Khusro, A.M. (1958), *Economic and Social Effects of Jagirdari Abolition and Land Reform in Hyderabad,* Osmania University Press, Osmania.

Lal Bahadur Shastri National Academy of Administration (Land Reform Unit), Mussoorie (1992), 'Implementation of Land Ceiling Programme in Uttar Pradesh', paper presented at the Worksop in Land Reforms, Giri Institute of Development Studies, Lucknow.

Ramachandran, V.K. and M. Swaminathan (2002), *Agrarian Studies, Essays in Agrarian Relations in Less Developed Countries,* Tulika, New Delhi.

Reeves, P. (1991), *Landlords and Governments in Uttar Pradesh: A Study of their Relation until Zamindari Abolition,* Oxford University Press, Bombay.

Sharma, H.R. (1994), *Economic and Political Weekly,* 24.

Singh, B. and S. Mishra (1984), *A Study of Land Reform in Uttar Pradesh,* Oxford Book Co., Calcutta.

Singh, C. (1946), *Abolition of Zamindari: Two Alternatives,* Kitabsthan, Allahabad.

Thorner, D. (1956), *The Agrarian Prospects in India,* pp. 52–68, Delhi School of Economics, University Press, Delhi.

Thorner, D. (1976), *The Agrarian Prospect in India,* Allied Publishers, Mumbai.

Thorner, D. (1980), *The Shaping of Modern India,* Allied Publishers, Mumbai.

United Provinces Zamindari Abolition Committee Report, vol. 1 (1948), UP Government Press, Allahabad.

Whitcombe, E. (1975), 'Whatever Happened to the Zamindars', in E.J. Hobsbawm, W. Kula, A. Mitra, K.N. Raj and I. Sachs (eds.), *Peasant in History Essays in Honour of Thorner Daniel,* pp. 177–179, Oxford University Press, Calcutta.

PART II

Agrarian Structure and Agricultural Growth

4

Land Reforms and Agricultural Development in UP: Retrospect[*]

Ajit Kumar Singh

Introduction

Right from the inception of planned economic development land reforms were assigned a high priority with a view to removing obstacles in the transformation of agriculture imposed by the exploitative land tenure system in the country and to create a more egalitarian rural society. However, land reforms in the country have remained confined to the objective of creating individual proprietary rights and granting security of tenure to the actual tiller of land, and did not attempt any basic transformation of agrarian relations. Even in the limited objectives which the political leadership set itself the success attained has fallen much short of expectations. Over the years the political commitment to land reforms has weakened considerably.

The success of land reform measures and their impact on the rural economy have also varied from state to state. In the present chapter, we have attempted an overview of land reforms in Uttar Pradesh. We first examine the three phases of the land reform process in Uttar Pradesh from 1950 to the 1980s. We then go on to assess their impact on agrarian structure and agricultural growth in the state, using regression analysis. Finally, we have also tried to examine the implications of changes in the agrarian structure on future agricultural growth.

[*] This chapter was previously published in *IASSI Quarterly*, 1992. This text has been edited for typographical errors, stylistic consistency and sequential organisation in order to make it suitable for inclusion in this book.

Land Reforms in Uttar Pradesh

Uttar Pradesh, which had seen the political mobilisation of the peasantry during the Independence struggle on a large scale, was among the more progressive states of the country during the first phase of land reforms initiated after Independence. In this phase, land reforms in the state aimed at the abolition of all forms of intermediary land rights with a view to giving land to the tiller. In the second phase, attention was focused on the consolidation of the fragmented holdings. The next phase aimed at a more equitable distribution of land through two rounds of land ceiling legislation.

Reorganisation of agriculture on cooperative lines was never given a serious thought. Cooperative farming societies were more often than not an attempt by the large landowners to circumvent the land ceiling legislation and to get various concessions from the government. This is clearly reflected in the jump in the number of cooperative farming societies from 387 in 1960–1961 to 1359 in 1965–1966, when the first round of ceiling legislation was implemented. Growth of cooperative farming societies stagnated thereafter, and is reported to be 1502 in 1988–1989 with a membership of 33,063 and area of 139,348 ha.

Tenurial Reforms

The Uttar Pradesh Zamindari Abolition and Land Reforms Act, 1951, which was one of the most progressive measures of land reforms introduced in the country, abolished all intermediary rights in land and brought the actual tiller of the soil in direct contact with the state. The Act substituted the bewildering variety of land rights prevalent in the state by a new and simplified tenure system, which recognised two major types of land rights, namely, *bhumidari* and *sirdari*. While both the land rights were permanent and heritable, the latter right was constrained by restrictions on transfer and use of land, while carrying higher revenue charges payable to government. A *sirdar* could, however, acquire *bhumidari* rights on payment of 10 times the rent. In 1977 complete uniformity of land tenures was created in the state when all *sirdars* were conferred *bhumidari* rights by the government.

The Uttar Pradesh Zamindari Abolition and Land Reforms Act 1951 reduced the bewildering variety of land rights from 40 to 4 categories, removed a large parasitic class of intermediaries and, by conferring permanent and heritable rights on the tiller of the land, removed the motivational hurdle for raising agricultural productivity (Singh and Mishra 1964a).

Though the impact of *zamindari* abolition on agricultural production in the state is difficult to assess, it can be safely said that the land tenure system based on peasant proprietorship that was created by the Act removed the disincentive for investment in agriculture and provided the necessary precondition for agricultural growth in the state. Thus, area irrigated by tube wells in the state nearly doubled within a decade rising from 2.76 lakh ha. in 1950–1951 to 5.43 lakh ha. in 1960–1961. The positive impact of the land reforms on agricultural growth in Uttar Pradesh is also reflected by the fact that the average yield of the major crops which had maintained a downward trend in the decades preceding 1951 showed a clear jump in the decade 1951–1961 as can be seen from Table 4.1. Foodgrains output in the decade in UP registered a growth of 23.0 per cent and foodgrain yield of 14.7 per cent (Table 4.2).

The peaceful and swift abolition of the vested interests of over two million zamindars was no mean achievement by any standard. However, a serious lacuna that remained in the tenurial structure of the state was the continuation of the practice of sub-letting (which was legally barred except in certain specific circumstances) in the garb of share cropping (Singh and Misra, 1964b). The share croppers

Table 4.1

Per Acre Yield of Major Crops in Uttar Pradesh from 1931 to 1961 (in Quintals)

Year	Major crops		
	Rice	Wheat	Sugarcane
1931	7.07	9.55	26.82
1941	6.27	8.66	30.00
1951	4.76	8.56	30.22
1961	8.05	9.95	39.23

Source: R.S. Mathur, *Dynamics of Labour Force*, Yash Printers, Lucknow, 1991, p. 74.

Table 4.2

Indicators of Agricultural Development in Uttar Pradesh from 1950–1951 to 1988–1989

	Indicators of agricultural development			
Year	Foodgrains output (in lakh tonnes)	Foodgrains yield (in quintals/ hectare)	Net irrigated area (in '000 hectare)	Fertiliser consumption (in lakh tonnes)
1950–1951	117.8	6.9	4,840	N.A.
1955–1956	120.6 (2.4)	6.7 (–2.9)	4,952 (2.3)	0.20
1960–1961	144.9 (20.1)	7.9 (+17.9)	5,024 (1.5)	0.30 (50.0)
1965–1966	152.5 (5.2)*	8.4 (+6.3)*	5,875 (16.9)	0.93 (210.0)
1970–1971	194.7 (27.7)	10.0 (+19.0)	7,218 (22.9)	4.11 (341.9)
1975–1976	194.6 (–0.1)	10.3 (3.0)	7,933 (9.9)	4.87 (18.5)
1980–1981	249.5 (28.2)	12.2 (18.4)	9,453 (19.2)	11.51 (136.3)
1985–1986	314.3 (26.0)	15.2 (24.6)	10,132 (7.2)	19.72 (71.3)
1988–1989	354.9 (12.9)	17.4 (14.5)	10,043 (–0.9)	21.36 (8.3)

Source: Compiled from *Bulletin of Agricultural Statistics, UP* (annual).
Notes: 1. *Referred for the year 1964–1965.
       2. Figures in parenthesis show per cent change over the previous period.

usually bear the entire cost of cultivation and pay as much as half of the produce as rent, while they are not allowed to remain on the same land for any length of time (Planning Commission, 1965).

The NSS rounds reveal a moderate level of leasing in the state, though there are considerable inter-region variations in the extent of leasing (Singh, 1987a). Thus, in 1971–1972 the proportion of household-leasing in land varied from 13.67 per cent in the Western Region to as much as 57.13 per cent in the Himalayan Region, and the proportion of area leased in varied from 10.15 per cent in the Eastern Region to 19.71 per cent in the Himalyan Region (Table 4.3). The variation in leasing operation among regions seems related to the extent of agricultural development as well as demographic pressure.

Looking at changes in leasing over the years, we observe that the pattern of leasing across different size classes remained more or less unchanged over the period 1953–1954 and 1971–1972. However, between 1971–1972 and 1982, we find a sharp decline in the proportion of leased in land in case of sub-marginal and marginal holdings accompanied by a sharp rise in the area leased in case of large holdings (Table 4.4). To some extent decline in the

Table 4.3
Region-wise Extent of Leasing in Uttar Pradesh, 1971–1972

	Per cent leasing land	
Region	Per cent of households leasing in land	Per cent of operated area leased in
Himalayan region	57.13	19.71
Western region	13.67	12.71
Central region	28.96	15.18
Eastern region	27.08	10.15
Southern region	19.61	16.38
Uttar Pradesh	25.01	13.90

Source: NSSO, 26th round, 1971–1972.

proportion of leased area in case of sub-marginal (below 1 acre) and marginal holdings (1.0–2.5 acres) and the corresponding increase in the proportion of owned area reflects the impact of the land redistribution programme undertaken in the seventies under which 2.36 lakh acres were distributed in September 1982 (Singh, 1987b). At the same time, it reflects the practice of reverse tenancy which has been strengthened in the wake of Green Revolution. In fact, one observes a distinct decline in the proportion of sub-marginal holding in total households leasing in as well as in area leased in between 1971–1972 and 1982. Sub-marginal holdings account for nearly one-fourth of the holdings reporting leasing out of land.

Table 4.4
Per cent of Area Leased in to Operated Area by Size Categories in Uttar Pradesh

		Per cent of area leased		
Size	Category	1953–1954	1971–1972	1982
1	Sub-marginal holdings (Up to 1.0 acre)	22.3	21.2	11.2
2	Marginal holdings (1.0–2.5 acres)	18.2	18.3	12.7
3	Small holdings (2.5–5.0 acres)	16.3	14.9	13.0
4	Medium holdings (5.0–15.0 acres)	9.8	11.7	10.5
5	Large holdings (Above 15.0 acres)	7.2	8.1	13.5
	All categories	11.3	13.0	12.0

Source: NSSO, 8th, 26th and 37th rounds, 1953–1954, 1971–1972 and 1982.

Consolidation of Holdings

Another reform of major importance for agricultural development undertaken in Uttar Pradesh was the consolidation of fragmented holdings, which existed in an acute form in the state (Agarwal, 1971). Though the history of land consolidation in Uttar Pradesh goes back to 1918–1919 when consolidation was introduced on a cooperative basis, work on consolidation picked up only after passing of the *Uttar Pradesh Consolidation of Holdings Act*, 1953, which provided for compulsory consolidation. Plan-wise progress of consolidation in Uttar Pradesh has been shown in Table 4.5. By the end of Third Five Year Plan nearly 67.43 lakh ha. had been consolidated. By the end of the Fifth Five Year Plan the target of 146 lakh ha., which were expected to be covered by the consolidation measure, had been nearly achieved. Since the Sixth Five Year Plan, a second round of consolidation was taken up in selected tehsils.

Though not devoid of malpractices, consolidation of holdings has been one of the most successful programmes of land reform, which has made investment on land more viable and profitable and has contributed to increased agricultural production. This has been brought out by a number of studies (Agarwal 1971; PEO 1969). Initially the programme was undertaken in western

Table 4.5
Progress of Consolidation of Holdings in Uttar Pradesh by Five Year Plan-wise

Period	Area consolidated (in lakh hectares)	Cumulative achievement (in lakh hectares)
First Five Year Plan (1951–1956)	0.76	0.76
Second Five Year Plan (1956–1961)	21.06	21.82
Third Five Year Plan (1961–1966)	45.61	67.43
Annual Plans (1966–1969)	21.53	88.96
Fourth Five Year Plan (1969–1974)	26.38	115.34
Fifth Five Year Plan (1974–1979)	22.74	138.08
Sixth Five Year Plan (1980–1985)	21.80	159.88
Seventh Five Year Plan (1985–1990 till 1988–1989)	13.07	172.95

Source: Complied from Five Year Plan Documents, UP Government.

districts of the state, which have been agriculturally more progressive. The coverage to eastern districts was extended in subsequent years. Consolidation of holdings is among the important factors which have contributed to the dynamism of agriculture in eastern Uttar Pradesh, visible since the early seventies. Thus, the growth rate of agricultural output in this region jumped from 2.02 per cent per annum in the period 1950–1953 to 1963–1966 to 2.58 per cent per annum in the period 1963–1966 to 1976–1979 and further to 3.48 per cent per annum in the period 1968–1971 to 1983–1986.

Land Redistribution Programme

While one can look at with some degree of satisfaction at the first phase of land reforms which aimed at the abolition of the parasitic intermediary land interests, the performance of Uttar Pradesh, state in the second round of land reforms, which aimed at a more equitable distribution of land, has been by and large depressing as in other parts of the country. As we have argued elsewhere,

> The success of the first phase in a way was responsible for the failure of the second stage of land reforms. The old zamindars, who were allowed to retain large tracts under *sir* and *khudkast* for self cultivation, emerged as rich farmers and retained their political and economic clout not only dominating the rural society and cornering the benefits of the developmental programmes, but also occupying seats in the state legislatures and the Parliament in sizeable numbers. Their vested interest in land had become stronger with growing commercialization of agriculture, which had become a profitable economic activity. (Singh, 1989)

As a result, while land ceiling laws were passed for their populist appeal, enough loopholes were left in them both at the legislation and implementation stage to make them self-defeating. The fate of the two rounds of land ceiling legislations in Uttar Pradesh is an ample testimony to this (Singh, 1975).

The Uttar Pradesh Imposition of Ceiling of Land Holding Act, 1960, provided for a ceiling of 40 acres of 'fair quality land' for a family. For a family of more than five members eight acres of land were allowed for every additional member subject to a ceiling of 64 acres. Not only the Act provided a fairly liberal ceiling, it allowed for a large number of exemptions. Full advantage was taken by the landlords of the various loopholes in the Act and the large number of fictitious transfers took place defeating the main purpose of the Act. No wonder that till 1973 only, 2,32,000 acres of land could be declared surplus against about four lakh acres of expected surplus.

The Uttar Pradesh Land Ceiling (Amendment) Act, 1972, reduced the ceiling to 7.30 ha. of irrigated land taking the family of a tenure holder excluding major sons as unit. In addition two hectares for each additional member of a family with more than five members were allowed subject to a maximum of 6 ha. The amended Act ended some of the exemptions granted earlier such as for grove land held by farms. The impact of the Act was further diluted by the fact that while the decision to lower the ceiling was announced on 24 February 1970, the revised Act recognised transfers of land made prior to 24 January 1971 as valid.

Defective as the revised ceiling legislation was, its tardy implementation in the face of stiff opposition by the landlords rendered it a practically ineffective measure of agrarian change. The affected landlords fought pitched and prolonged legal battles right from the court of the prescribed authority to the Supreme Court. Nearly 90 per cent of persons to whom notices were issued filed objections. Still there are 5,987 cases pending at different levels involving an area of 1,29,858 acres (Table 4.6).

The progress of land ceiling programme in Uttar Pradesh has been shown in Table 4.6. Till September 1991 only 3,34,189 acres could be declared surplus out of the expected surplus land of 8,00,985 acres. Possession could be taken of only 3,03,272 acres out of which 39,596 acres or 13 per cent of area were found unfit for cultivation. In nearly two decades only 2,19,668 acres of land has been distributed to 2,39,850 landless labourers in the state.

The limited impact of the land redistribution programme in Uttar Pradesh can be judged from the fact that hardly 0.5 per cent of the operated area in the state could be redistributed so far among only 4.6 per cent of the 52 lakh agricultural labourers in the state. Even the limited number of beneficiaries to whom the surplus land was distributed could not gain much from it due to the small size and poor quality of lands distributed as well as lack of adequate resources to bring the land under cultivation. In a recent survey

Table 4.6
Progress of Ceiling Operations under Revised Ceiling Act in Uttar Pradesh as on 31.9.1991 by Item

Item	Area in acres
1. No. of notices issued	66,829
2. Area proposed to be acquired	8,00,985
3. No. of notices against which objections filed	58,935
4. No. of cases pending at different levels	5,987
5. Area involved in pending cases	1,29,858
6. Land declared surplus	3,34,189
7. Declared land surplus over which state government has taken possession	3,03,272
8. Surplus land allotted:	
(a) Number of allottees	2,39,850
(b) Area allotted	2,19,668
9. Area unfit for cultivation vested in gaon sabha	39,596
10. Land transferred to govt. departments	8,971
11. Total area of settled land	2,74,494
12. Area of land balance of settlement	28,778

Source: Board of Revenue, UP.

of 32 land allottees in five villages of Sultanpur district, we found that 25 per cent allottees were not able to get physical possession and only one-third of the allottees with physical possession of land were found to be cultivating the allotted land (Singh et al., 1991).

Changes in Land Distribution Pattern and Agricultural Development

As we have seen above, the total area involved in land redistribution programme was too small to have a significant impact on the structure of land holding in the state. However, the threat of land ceilings has an indirect impact on land distribution pattern as it led to large scale transfer of land in the names of relatives, friends, servants, etc. A close look at the changes in the land distribution pattern over time tends to support this hypothesis (Table 4.7). Thus, we find that the rate of change in the land distribution pattern was much more pronounced during the decade 1961–1971, which saw a sharp decline in the share of medium and large holdings in the number of households as well as in area owned accompanied by a sharp increase in the share of marginal holdings in number of households as well as area owned. The land distribution pattern for 1961 and 1981 does not reveal such pronounced changes over the previous period. Thus much of the change in land distribution pattern observed between 1961–1971 is more apparent than real. The Gini coefficient, in fact shows a slight increase from 0.606 in 1961–1962 to 0.6075 in 1971–1972 and further to 0.6114 in 1982.

Table 4.7

Changes in the Distribution of Ownership Holding in UP between 1953–1954 and 1981–1982

Size category (hectares)	1953–1954	1961–1962	1971–1972	1981–1982	% change 1981–1982 over 1953–1954
A. Per cent of households					
1. Marginal (Up to 1.0)	60.0	60.0 (0.0)	65.6 (+9.3)	68.0 (+3.7)	+13.3
2. Small (1.0–2.0)	18.4	19.2 (+4.3)	18.6 (–3.1)	17.4 (–6.5)	–5.4
3. Semi-medium (2.0–4.0)	14.3	13.6 (–4.9)	10.8 (–20.6)	10.2 (–5.6)	–28.7
4. Medium & large (Above 4.0)	7.3	7.2 (–1.4)	5.0 (–30.6)	4.4 (–12.0)	–39.7
B. Per cent of area					
1. Marginal (Up to 1.0)	12.5	12.8 (+2.4)	17.5 (+36.7)	19.4 (+10.9)	+55.2
2. Small (1.0–2.0)	18.9	20.3 (+7.4)	24.7 (+21.7)	24.4 (–1.2)	+29.1
3. Semi-medium (2.0–4.0)	29.6	27.9 (–5.7)	27.9 (0.0)	28.5 (+0.4)	–3.7
4. Medium & large (Above 4.0)	39.0	39.0 (0.0)	29.9 (–23.3)	27.7 (–7.4)	–29.0

Source: Calculated from NSS (8th, 17th, 26th and 37th) rounds.

Note: Figures in parenthesis show per cent change over previous period.

Though the impact of land reforms on agrarian structure in the state was minimal, one observes a gradual shift in area in favour of marginal and small holdings mainly due to increasing population pressure and splitting up of holdings among family members. According to NSS data, the share of these two categories in area owned went up from 31.4 per cent in 1953–1954 to 43.8 per cent in 1982.

According to the Agricultural Census, 1980–1981, the average size of operational holding has shrunk to 1.01 ha. In as many as 27 districts the figure is below this. Marginal and small holdings accounted for 48.3 per cent of the operated area in Uttar Pradesh in 1980–1981. The alarming extent of the process of marginalisation of the holdings in the state is evidenced by the fact that in 31 districts the share of marginal and small holdings in operated area exceeded 50 per cent. In some districts of Eastern Uttar Pradesh and Hill region over two-thirds of operated area is now under this category.

The inter-district variation in agrarian structure basically reflects variation in the land–man ratio. Thus, the correlation coefficient between population density and average size of operational holdings at the district level is found to be –0.48. On the other hand, 'the correlation between population density and per cent area under marginal and small holdings is +0.46.

In the light of this grim scenario of agrarian structure, it would be instructive to examine the relationship between agrarian structure and agricultural development. We have tried to study this relationship through a cross-section analysis of 42 districts of Uttar Pradesh plains. The districts in the Hill and Bundelkhand Region were excluded from the analysis in view of their peculiar geographical features.

We have taken average yield of foodgrains per hectare as the indicator of agricultural development. The results of the correlation analysis have been shown in Table 4.8. The Gini coefficient of holding does not reveal any significant correlation with agrarian structure or agricultural development.

Other features of agrarian structure like size of operational holding and pattern of land distribution, however, show a clear relationship with agricultural development. Thus, average yields are positively and significantly correlated with average size of holding as well as proportion of area under holdings above two hectares. On the other hand, proportion of area under holdings below two

Table 4.8

Relationship between Agrarian Structure and Agricultural Development in Uttar Pradesh at the District Level

Variable	Average yield of foodgrains 1968–1971 1983–1986	Rate of growth of foodgrain output 1968–1986	Per cent area irrigated	Per hectare fertiliser consumption
	Correlation coefficient with			
1. Gini coefficient of holding	0.1175 0.1518	0.0463	0.0513	0.1470
2. Average size of holding	0.5158* 0.5019*	0.0975	0.5296*	0.0122
3. Per cent of operational holdings area under				
(a) Marginal holdings	−0.6140* −0.6198*	−0.1575	−0.6671*	−0.1508
(b) Small holdings	−0.3718** −0.4302*	−0.1477	−0.2379	−0.1874
(c) Marginal & small holdings	−0.5116* −0.5371*	−0.1301	−0.4381*	−0.0486
(d) Semi-medium holdings	0.6683* 0.5955*	0.0520	0.7208*	0.0872
(e) Medium holdings	0.5821* 0.5640*	0.0900	0.5397*	0.0741
(f) Large holdings	−0.364 −0.0121	−0.0387	−0.0549	−0.1150
(g) Bigger holdings (d + e + f)	0.5318* 0.5050*	0.0556	0.5184*	0.0375

Notes: *Significant at 1 per cent level.
　　　　**Significant at 5 per cent level.

hectares shows a significant negative association with agricultural productivity. The major handicap of the smaller holdings is their inability to make investments on irrigation facilities, where capital requirement is large. This is evidenced by the negative association between area under marginal and small holdings and per cent of irrigated area. In case of fertiliser use, however, the coefficients of correlation are not significant, though the sign is in the expected direction. The same is true for the rate of growth of agricultural

Table 4.9

Results of Regression Analysis on Per Hectare Foodgrain Output across Districts in Uttar Pradesh, 1980s

Variable	Eq. 1	Eq. 2	Eq. 3	Eq. 4	Eq. 5
Constant term	19.1953	9.5922	9.4901	8.1261	2.6439
X_1 Per cent of area under holdings above 2 ha	1.8693* (0.4968)			0.0444** (0.0332)	0.1340* (0.0272)
X_2 Per cent of net irrigated area		0.1234* (0.0172)		0.1095* (0.0120)	
X_3 Fertiliser consumption per hectare			4.3803* (0.8926)		0.0833* (0.0139)
R square	0.2614	0.5639	0.3758	0.5830	0.6153

Notes: 1. Number of observations 42.
2. Figures in parenthesis show standard error of the coefficient.
3. * Significant at 1 per cent level
4. ** Significant at 10 per cent level.

output during the period 1968–1971 to 1983–1986. Large holdings (i.e., above 10 ha.) are also not making efficient use of land.

The results of regression analysis shown in Table 4.9 also demonstrates that agrarian structure is affecting the level of agricultural development. However, technological factors like irrigation and fertiliser seem to be playing a greater role.

Conclusion

To sum up, the tenurial reforms in Uttar Pradesh taken up soon after Independence were successful in abolishing the intermediary rights on land and creating an agrarian structure primarily based on peasant proprietorship. This together with the land consolidation measures taken up during the subsequent period, had a positive impact on agricultural development and laid the foundations of technological transformation of agriculture in the state.

The story of land ceiling operations in Uttar Pradesh is, however, one of pious intentions rather than real achievements. During the two rounds of land ceiling legislation hardly 4.5 lakh acres of land or about one per cent of the operated area in the state could be distributed to 6–7 per cent of the agricultural labourers. Thus, land distribution programme had a minimal impact on the agrarian structure and rural poverty due to lack of strong political will.

According to the Census of Agriculture 1980–1981, there were 72,000 holdings in Uttar Pradesh which are above 10 hectares in size accounting for about 11 lakh hectares of operated area. Our analysis has indicated that holdings above 10 hectares are not making the most efficient use of land, which strengthens the economic argument for land ceilings. A more determined effort to unearth the surplus land held under *benami* possession along with removal of various exemptions granted under ceiling legislation can still release a fair amount of land for redistribution among landless labourers to give them some economic security.

The major challenge for accelerating agricultural development and removing rural poverty in our view is that of increasing productivity on the large number of non-viable marginal and small holdings, which now account for the overwhelming proportion of holdings in the state. The situation calls for a major organisational effort on the part of the government to provide necessary technological, infrastructural and input support to marginal and the small farmers to raise agricultural productivity along with efforts to diversify the economy to generate more income and employment opportunity.

References

Agarwal, S.K. (1971), *Economics of Land Consolidation in India*, Sultan Chand, New Delhi.

Directorate of Evaluation, Uttar Pradesh Government (1971), *Impact of Ceilings on Land Holdings Act, 1960: A Case Study in Gorakhpur District*, Lucknow.

P.E.O., Planning Commission, Government of India (1969), *Report on the Evaluation of Consolidation of Holdings Programmes*, New Delhi.

Planning Commission, Government of India (1965), *Implementation of Land Reforms*, New Delhi, p. 129.

Revenue Department, Uttar Pradesh Government (1975), *Report of the Uttar Pradesh Land Settlement Enquiry Committee*, Lucknow.

Singh, A.K. (1987), *Agricultural Development and Rural Poverty* (Chapter VII), Ashish Publishing House, New Delhi.

Singh, A.K. (1989), 'Land Ceiling Legislation in UP: An Assessment,' in Planning Commission, Government of India, *Proceedings and Papers of the Seminar on Land Reforms: A Retrospect and Prospect*, New Delhi.

Singh, A.K., D.K. Bajpai and P.S. Garia (1991), *Socio-Economic Survey of Selected Villages in Sultanpur District*, Giri Institute of Development Studies, Lucknow (Mimeo).

Singh, B. and S. Misra (1964), *A Study of Land Reforms in Uttar Pradesh*, Oxford Book Co., New Delhi.

5

Agrarian Structure and Agricultural Development: An Inter-district Analysis

Richa Singh

Introduction

Agricultural productivity is influenced by technological and institutional factors. The introduction of new technology is itself dependent on the agrarian structure. Agrarian structure is thus a critical element in the development of the agricultural sector. Different aspects of agrarian structure, such as nature of land ownership, land distribution, tenancy rights, rental levels and land size, have a bearing on the conditions in which farming activities are carried out and affect the capacity as well as willingness of the farmers to adopt modern technology and invest in the development of land. Security of tenure and farm size are thus of crucial importance in investment and productivity growth in agriculture.

Since Independence, the Government of India has assigned high priority to land reform, which aimed at removing the exploitative and parasitic intermediary class, giving 'land to the tiller' and preventing land concentration through ceiling of landholdings. Poor implementation and lack of political thwarted the gains from the land reforms. Nevertheless, the tenurial reforms helped in removing the unproductive intermediaries, establishing a uniform land tenure system throughout the country, providing security of tenure and regulating rental levels and contributed to the emergence of a capitalist peasantry that carried out the Green Revolution in the country. All this helped India transform itself over time from a food-deficit to a food-surplus economy.

A central feature of agrarian structure in India has been the small and declining size of landholding. Agrarian structure in India has been characterised by an increasing predominance of marginal and small holdings, in terms of both the number and area due to continuously growing pressure of population and slow progress in the diversification of the rural economy. Decline in joint family system, high rural indebtedness and defective inheritance laws further contributed to this tendency. The small size of holding has posed a major constraint on the development of agriculture in the country. Generation of agricultural surplus has remained confined to a small number of medium and large farmers. A large number of holdings remain economically non-viable due to their small size. Farming on small holdings has largely remained subsistence oriented and prevented diversification of agriculture. As a result, income and productivity levels have remained low, contributing to widespread rural poverty.

The main objective of this chapter is to study the impact of agrarian structure on agricultural productivity from the perspective of the size–productivity relationship. This relationship has been examined with the help of a cross-section study of districts in UP. The chapter seeks to investigate whether the process of marginalisation of holding has led to a decline in productivity and thwarted agricultural development in the state.

The chapter has six sections. Section titled 'The Farm Size–Productivity Debate' examines the farm size–productivity debate in the literature on agricultural economics. Section titled 'Objective and Hypothesis' spells out the hypothesis, the data and the methodology used. Section titled 'Landholding Pattern in UP—Some Descriptive Statistics' presents some descriptive statistics on the pattern of landholdings in UP. In Section titled 'Agrarian Structure and Agricultural Development: A District-level Correlation Analysis' a correlation analysis is carried out to examine whether there is any relationship between landholding size structure and key indicators of agricultural growth. In the section titled 'Multiple Regression Analysis: The Relationship between Farm Size and Agricultural Productivity', we test the hypothesis of the relationship between farm size and agricultural productivity. Section titled 'Conclusion' concludes the study.

The Farm Size–Productivity Debate

In this context, it would be appropriate to refer to the long-standing debate on farm size and agricultural productivity. The debate was initiated by Amartya Sen in the early 1960s (Sen, 1962, 1964).

Sen hypothesised an inverse relationship between land size and productivity. His contention was supported by leading economists like Deepak Majumdar (1963), Hanumantha Rao (1966) and G.R. Saini (1969, 1979). The basic contention of these economists was that the small farmers use family labour, while large farmers rely on hired labour. The small farmers with surplus family labour substitute other factors, which they cannot buy, by a more intensive use of labour. A.K. Sen argued that cost of labour was higher and managerial and supervisory diseconomies were greater on large farms. On the other band, there was more intensive use of inputs by the small farmer along with efficient management. Cropping and irrigation intensity were also higher on these farms.

Some other economists like Krishna Bhardwaj (1974), A.P. Rao (1967) and Ashok Rudra (1968) opposed the above generalisation regarding the inverse relationship between farm size and productivity. In their opinion, holding size has no effect on productivity. Rudra pointed out that the small farmers' capacity to apply capital and monetised inputs is lower compared to the large farmers. Hence, the new agricultural strategy, which was capital intensive, was likely to provide greater benefit to large farmers.

Rudra's arguments were supported by the experience of the Green Revolution. The new technology, though size neutral, was not resource neutral. Being capital intensive, it largely benefited the large farmers. Mechanisation and use of modern inputs were limited on small farms. Large farmers also had the capacity to invest in irrigation, which was a necessary precondition for the use of new HYV technology. Hanumantha Rao too highlighted the weakening and even disappearance of the inverse relationship between farm size and output during the Green Revolution period.

The broad conclusion of the size–productivity debate was that a negative relationship between land size and productivity was a common phenomenon in India, particularly in the pre–Green Revolution period when traditional technology prevailed, but the spread of new technology has since largely reversed this relationship.

Objective and Hypothesis

The basic hypothesis of our study is that agricultural productivity at the district level is inversely related to the proportion of area under small and marginal holdings and positively related to the proportion of area under medium and large holdings as well as the average size of holdings.

Our basic contention is that the small and marginal holdings suffer from a basic resource constraint and are unable to invest in modern inputs to the optimum extent. Although these holdings have an advantage over large holdings in terms of availability of free family labour and managerial and supervisory capacities, these cannot fully substitute the requirement of modern inputs. The access of the small farmers to institutional credit and support from government agencies in terms of input supply, extension, etc., is also relatively limited. In other words, we hypothesise the existence of an inverted U-type relationship between farm productivity and land size.

Data and Methodology

The study is primarily based on analysis of secondary data. The dataset used in this study includes statistics on land distribution over different farm size categories and selected indicators of agricultural development at the district level in UP. The main data sources used include the Bulletin of Agricultural Statistics, UP, the Agricultural Census conducted by the Revenue Board of Uttar Pradesh, District Level Development Indicators compiled by the Planning Department, UP Government and other official publications. Most of the data set related to the mid-1990s.

The methodology used is based on a correlation analysis across the district level between farm size and land distribution on the one hand and the indices of agricultural development, e.g., per hectare output, yields of major crops, migration, credit, mechanisation and use of inputs such as fertilisers on the other. Similar methodology has been used by Singh earlier to examine the impact of agrarian structure on agricultural development in UP (Singh, 1992). This is supplemented by a multiple regression analysis with agricultural productivity as the dependent variable and land distribution and selected input levels as the independent variables. We begin with a brief discussion of the pattern of landholdings in UP, our study area.

Landholding Pattern in UP—Some Descriptive Statistics

Agriculture is a state subject and thus policy for land reforms has differed across the country, though it bas been guided by common national objectives. The success and impact of land reform measures have also varied across the states. UP, along with the rest of the states in the country, initiated the land reform measures soon after Independence. The measures included abolition of intermediaries, consolidation of fragmented holdings and redistribution of land through land ceiling laws.

The impact of these reforms on tile rural economy of UP has been mixed. Abolition of *zamindari* provided an incentive for the peasant to invest in agriculture. The exploitative intermediaries were removed and the cultivator was brought in direct contact with the government. A necessary prerequisite for agricultural development was thus provided. Consolidation of landholdings has been by far the most successful land reform measure in UP. It greatly contributed to the high growth rate in the 1970s. Land ceiling and redistribution of land, however, failed to provide the desired results, that of an equitable distribution of land. Only a small proportion of acquired land was redistributed and that too was of poor quality and paltry size (Singh, 1992).

The foremost outcome of the land reform process in UP was a sharp decline in the share of medium and large holdings and a relative increase in the share of marginal holdings in terms of both the number of households and the area owned. Over time, this tendency has been intensified. The increasing population pressure, slow growth of non-agricultural employment opportunities, sub-division of land and break-up of joint family system all contributed to the process of 'miniaturisation' of holdings in the state (Singh, 1987, 1992). By the turn of the century, the problem had acquired an alarming proportion.

The average size of holding in UP has been reduced to a highly uneconomical size of below 1 ha. As per the Agricultural Census 1990–1991, nearly three-fourths of the holdings in UP are below 1 ha. and over half below half hectare (Table 5.1). Holdings below 1 ha. now account for almost one-third of the

Table 5.1
Distribution of Agricultural Holdings by Size Category in UP, 1990–1991

Size category in hectares	No. of holdings		Area of holdings	
	Number in '000	Per cent	Area in '000 hectares	Per cent
Below 0.5	10,461.3	52.1	2,556.0	14.2
0.5–1.0	4,358.0	21.7	3,097.4	17.2
1.0–20	3,118.5	15.6	4,390.7	24.4
2.0–3.0	1,059.5	5.3	2,555.9	14.2
3.0–4.0	483.0	2.4	1,649.9	9.2
4.0–5.0	257.7	1.3	1,141.1	6.3
5.0–10.0	290.8	1.4	1,900.9	10.6
Above 10.0	45.2	0.2	694.0	3.9
All holdings	20,074.0	100.0	17,985.9	100.0

Source: Agricultural Census Uttar Pradesh, 1990–1991, Board of Revenue, UP.

holding area. Around one-fourth area is under holdings between 1.0 and 2.0 ha. Only one-tenth of the total holdings in the state are above 2 ha., although they account for about one-third of the total holding area.

Table 5.2 brings forth the predominance of small and marginal holdings in UP at the district level. Thus, in 30 out of the 50 districts of UP plains selected for study, more than 55 per cent of the operated area is under small and marginal holdings, i.e., below 2 ha. In 16 of these districts, small and marginal holdings account for over 65 per cent of the operated area and in 7 districts over 75 per cent of the area is under such holdings. Thus, the agrarian structure of the state is predominated not only by small farmers but also by small farms.

There is little doubt that majority of holdings in UP have become economically non-viable. Such holdings have little surplus to invest on the farms. This has important implications for the rate of capital formation in agriculture, productivity levels and growth of the agricultural sector in the state. In the following section, we propose exploring the impact of the agrarian structure on the productivity levels and input use with the help of a cross-section study at the district level.

Table 5.2
Distribution of Districts by Per cent Area under Marginal and Small Holdings in UP, 1990–1991

Below 45%		Between 45% and 55%		Between 55% and 65%		Above 65%	
Mathura	35.4	Mirzapur	45.6	Bareily	56.3	Unnao	65.6
Sonebhadra	36.2	Bulandshahr	46.1	Allahabad	56.9	Mau	66.3
Saharanpur	38.4	Meerut	46.3	Etah	56.9	Gorakhpur	66.5
Aligarh	39.4	Kanpur Dehat	50.3	Hardoi	57.0	Bahraich	66.7
Agra	40.6	Moradabad	51.0	Badaun	57.9	Mainpuri	68.6
Hardwar	41.2	Ghaziabad	51.3	Ballia	59.2	Maharajganj	68.7
Ferozabad	41.4	Pilibhit	51.6	Kanpur.Nagar	59.7	Basti	71.2
Bijnor	42.2	Rampur	51.7	Etawah	59.8	Barabanki	72.3
Muzaffarnagar	43.8	Fatehpur	52.0	Kheri	60.4	Faizabad	74.3
		Shahjahanpur	54.5	Sitapur	62.6	Azamgarh	75.0
				Siddharthnagar	63.2	Deoria	75.0
				Ghazipur	64.0	Rae-Bareily	75.2
				Gonda	64.3	Sultanpur	75.3
				Farrukhabad	64.5	Varanasi	76.4
				Lucknow	64.9	Jaunpur	77.2
						Pratapgarh	80.9

Source: Calculated from Census of Agricultural Holdings Uttar Pradesh, 1990–1991, Board of Revenue, UP.

Agrarian Structure and Agricultural Development: A District-level Correlation Analysis

To study the impact of agrarian structure on agricultural development, a correlation analysis has been carried out at the district level. The analysis is carried out for the 50 districts of UP plains, which share common agro-climatic conditions. The districts falling in the hill region (now under Uttaranchal) and Bundelkhand have been excluded from analysis because of their peculiar geographic and agrarian features.

For the purpose of analysis, we have selected 10 indicators of agricultural development reflecting productivity levels, input use and extent of modernisation of agriculture. These indicators have been correlated with the proportion of area under different farm size categories. As explained earlier, data have been collected from different official publications of the Government of UP. The coefficient of correlation results is presented in Table 5.3.

Table 5.3 shows that gross value of output per hectare of net sown area increases as the size of holding increases. For farm size below 2 ha., this relationship is found to be negatively correlated. For holdings between 2 and 3 ha. the correlation is positive and highly significant. Gross value of output per worker as well as per person too shows a similar and statistically much stronger relationship with size of holdings. Average yield of food grains shows a similar positive and significant correlation for holdings above 2 ha. and a negative relation with holdings below 2 ha. Similar results are found for yield of sugarcane, the major commercial crop of the state. These results bring forth the strong link between farm size and agricultural productivity as hypothesised by us.

Our findings confirm Rudra's contention that a major cause of low productivity of small holdings is the incapacity of the small and marginal farmers to generate surplus for reinvesting on their holdings. Use of modern technology is thus inhibited. Percentage of area under irrigation and fertiliser consumption per hectare shows a negative correlation for area under holdings below 1 ha., whereas the correlation is significant and positive for area under holding between 2 and 3 ha.

The scope for market-oriented and capital-intensive cultivation is greater on holdings above 2 ha. This is evident from the positive

Table 5.3

Value of Coefficient of Correlation between Area under Different Land Size Categories and Indicators of Agricultural Development at the District Level in UP: Mid-1990s

Sl. No.	Indicators	Up to 1 ha.	1–2 ha.	2–3 ha.	Above 3 ha.
1.	Gross value of output per ha. of net sown area (1990–1993)	–0.2117	–0.1120	0.3797***	0.1718
2.	Gross value of output per agricultural worker (1990–1993)	–0.6115***	–0.1394	0.7001***	0.5352***
3.	Gross value of output per rural person (1990–1993)	–0.5879***	–0.4352***	0.6923***	0.4891***
4.	Average yield of foodgrains per ha. (1992–1995)	–0.3836***	–0.0701	0.5204***	0.3223**
5.	Average yield of sugarcane per ha. (1992–1995)	–0.5031***	–0.1647	0.5948***	0.5196***
6.	Area under commercial crops as % of gross cropped area (1993–1994)	–0.6180***	–0.2615*	0.6016***	0.5867***
7.	% of gross irrigated area to gross sown area (1993–1994)	–0.2489*	0.1662	0.3859***	0.1390
8.	Fertiliser consumption per ha. of gross cropped area (1993–1994)	–0.0981	–0.0881	0.2586*	0.0679
9.	No. of tractors per 1,000 ha. of gross sown area	–0.4797***	–0.2302*	0.4355***	0.4785***
10.	Loans by primary agricultural societies per ha. of gross cropped area (₹)	–0.5662***	–0.2222	0.4924***	0.4824***

Source: Author's calculations. Data on land distribution has been taken from the Census of Agricultural Holdings Uttar Pradesh, 1990–1991, Board of Revenue, UP, and data on indicators of agricultural development have been taken from District Level Development Indicators for various years published by the Department of Planning, Government of UP.

Notes: *Significant at 10%.
**Significant at 5%.
***Significant at 1%.

and highly significant correlation between area under commercial crops and size of holding above 2 ha. The degree of mechanisation, as represented by the number of tractors per thousand hectares of gross sown area, is also positively and significantly correlated with area under holding above 2 ha. Access to institutional credit facilities is also higher for farmers with holding above 2 ha., as brought out by the significant and positive sign of correlation co-efficient. As is well known, the medium and large farmers corner bulk of institutional credit due to their political clout. Thus, state policy has failed to compensate for the handicaps faced by the small farmers.

The inverse relationship hypothesised between land size and productivity has also been proved to be invalid in the present scenario. With the introduction of the new technology that lays emphasis on investment in land, irrigation, mechanisation and greater use of inputs, the viability of small and marginal holdings has been adversely affected. We may, therefore, conclude that the extreme 'miniaturisation' of holdings in UP has depressed the productivity levels and has been operating as a major constraint on agricultural development in the state.

Another important conclusion emerging from our analysis is that a holding between 2 and 3 ha. seems to be of an optimum size. Area under this category of land size shows a positive and highly significant correlation with all the 10 indicators of agricultural development used in the analysis. It is thus a holding size that per-mits the most efficient use of available resources. Holdings above 3 ha also show a positive relationship with all the development indicators, but the values of correlation coefficients are lower and statistically insignificant in 3 out of 10 cases.

We have further probed this relationship by correlating the aver-age size of holding at the district level with selected indicators of agricultural development. The results have been given in Table 5.4. All the 10 indicators of agricultural development show a positive relationship with the average size of holding at the district level as hypothesised by us. The value of 'R' is significant at 1 per cent level in four cases and 5 per cent level in six cases. Only in one case, that is fertiliser consumption, the relationship is statistically insignificant though positive.

The correlation analysis clearly indicates that the agrarian structure, as reflected in the average size of holding and pattern of land distribution, is exercising a clear influence on the level of agricultural development in UP. Our findings are similar to the earlier findings by Singh for the 1980s (Singh, 1992).

Table 5.4

Value of Coefficient of Correlation between Average Size of Holding and Indicators of Agricultural Development at the District Level in UP: Mid-1990s

Sl. No.	Indicators	Value of 'R'
1.	Gross value of output per ha. of net sown area (1990–1993)	0.2514*
2.	Gross value of output per agricultural worker (1990–1993)	0.6404**
3.	Gross value of output per rural person (1990–1993)	0.5980**
4.	Average yield of foodgrains per ha. (1992–1995)	0.4274**
5.	Average yield of sugarcane per ha. (1992–1995)	0.6093**
6.	Area under commercial crops as % of gross cropped area (1993–1994)	0.6803**
7.	% Of gross irrigated area to gross sown area (1993–1994)	0.2536*
8.	Fertiliser consumption per ha. of gross cropped area (1993–1994)	0.1658
9.	No. of tractors per 1,000 ha. of gross sown area	0.5724**
10.	Loans by primary agricultural societies per ha. of gross cropped area (₹)	0.2230*

Source: Author's calculations. Data on land distribution has been taken from the Census of Agricultural Holdings Uttar Pradesh, 1990–1991, Board of Revenue, UP, and data on indicators of agricultural development have been taken from District Level Development Indicators for various years published by the Department of Planning, Government of UP.

Notes: *Significant at 5% level.
**Significant at 1% level.

Multiple Regression Analysis: The Relationship between Farm Size and Agricultural Productivity

We have also carried out a multiple regression analysis to further probe the impact of farm size on agricultural productivity. Value of agricultural output per hectare has been taken as the dependent variable, and average size of holding/proportion of area under holdings below 2 ha., proportion of irrigated area and fertiliser consumption per ha. have been taken as the independent variables. The first variable represents agrarian structure and the latter two variables represent technological factors. The results have been shown in Tables 5.5 and 5.6.

Table 5.5
Results of Multiple Regression Analysis—Dependent Variable: Value of Output

Independent variables	Unstandardised coefficients		Standardised coefficients	T	
	B	*Std. Error*	*Beta*	*Statistics*	*Sig.*
Constant	8,005.662	3,040.250		2.633	.011
Area under holdings below 2 ha.	–39.657	36.329	–119	–1.092	.261
% Irrigated area	54.017	30.814	234	1.753	.086
Fertiliser consumption per ha.	59.908	15.860	497	3.777	.000

Source: Author's calculations. Data on land distribution has been taken from the Census of Agricultural Holdings Uttar Pradesh, 1990–1991, Board of Revenue, UP, and data on indicators of agricultural development have been taken from District Level Development Indicators for various years published by the Department of Planning, Government of UP.
Note: $R^2 = 0.4770$.

Table 5.6
Results of Multiple Regression Analysis—Dependent Variable: Value of Output

Independent variables	Unstandardised coefficients		Standardised coefficients	T	
	B	*Std. error*	*Beta*	*Statistics*	*Sig.*
Constant	4,289.109	2,045.755		2.097	.042
Average size of holding	1,624.307	1,621.923	.111	1.001	.322
% Irrigated area	53.804	31.003	.233	1.735	.089
Fertiliser consumption per ha.	59.335	15.894	.492	3.733	.001

Source: Author's calculations. Data on land distribution has been taken from the Census of Agricultural Holdings Uttar Pradesh, 1990–1991, Board of Revenue, UP, and data on indicators of agricultural development have been taken from District Level Development Indicators for various years published by the Department of Planning, Government of UP.
Note: $R^2 = 0.4750$.

Both the regressions explain around 50 per cent of the variation in agricultural productivity. As hypothesised by us, the sign of the coefficient of area under holdings below 2 ha. turns out to be negative, whereas the sign of the coefficient of average size of holding is positive, indicating that agrarian structure does influence agricultural productivity. However, the value of the coefficients is not statistically very significant, as indicated by T statistics. Technology variables seem to play a greater role. Thus, it would appear that if the resource constraints of the small holdings are removed through adequate government support, the handicap posed by the small size of holdings can be overcome to a great extent.

Conclusion

One of the major challenges for accelerating development of the agricultural sector is that of increasing the productivity of the large number of non-viable marginal and small holdings. Given the level of technology, the potential of generating agricultural surplus and its investment is highly limited on the small holdings. Credit and marketing systems too work in favour of the large farmers as against the small and marginal ones. Any attempt directed towards agricultural development must pay foremost attention to a reorganisation of the agrarian structure. This reorganisation would help in overcoming the serious handicap posed by the non-viability of the small and marginal holdings, towards agricultural development.

The programme of land redistribution should be taken up in all sincerity through a more effective implementation of the ceilings laws and apportioning of surplus land in favour of the small and marginal farmers. The laws should be made more realistic by plugging the various loopholes to minimise the possibility of manipulation by the big and powerful landlords. Attempt should be made to prevent legal delays, which have posed the biggest obstacle in the implementation of land ceiling laws. This would, however, require a strong political will, which is not forthcoming. Relaxation of ceiling limits in the present circumstances is not advisable as argued by economists like Vyas (2001). Corporate farming is also unsuitable in the Indian context.

Consolidation of uneconomic holdings into cooperative farms is another desirable option. Though introduced during the Second Five Year Plan, the scheme failed to gain popularity because of the strong attachment of farmers to their land and lack of a cooperative spirit. However, cooperative principle in some form is a useful means to overcome the size constraint and to secure better access to crucial inputs like seeds, fertilisers, irrigation and credit. It would make agriculture more organised and integrated and help in securing economies of scale in production, marketing and processing.

The government has followed a policy of providing support to the small and marginal farmers through a number of programmes. The most extensively used option has been that of subsidisation of agricultural inputs. Though subsidies led to an increase in the use of the modern inputs by the small and marginal farmers, they resulted in a mounting fiscal deficit. Besides, the large farmers cornered the concessions meant for the small farmers. Marginal and Small Farmers' Development Agency, Regional Rural Banks, Integrated Rural Development Programme, all these schemes were conceived to assist the small and marginal farmers. Though integral to the development of the agricultural sector, these agencies more often than not played into the hands of the large farmers, who cornered most of the gains meant for the small and marginal farmers. Institutional support thus has to be made more oriented towards the target group.

The major cause of marginalisation of holdings has been excessive population pressure on agriculture as a source of livelihood and employment. Despite the transformation of the Indian economy, still nearly two-thirds of the work force is employed in this sector. This causes sub-division and fragmentation of holdings and aggravates the problem of disguised unemployment. Rapid diversification of the rural economy is therefore urgently required. Development of non-agricultural activities including animal husbandry and other allied activities along with small and cottage industries in the rural areas is needed to reduce pressure on agriculture.

To prevent further subdivision of holdings, inheritance laws need to be reviewed. Fixation of a minimum floor of cultivation units is required. This would help bring to a halt the process of continuous splitting and miniaturisation of holdings. However, social acceptance of the needed measures is likely to be low.

Some economists have strongly pleaded for the freeing of the lease market (Vaidyanathan, 2000; Vyas, 2001). Relaxing tenancy laws will enable those owning small and marginal holdings to supplement their holdings by leasing in land and making them more viable. This will also help some of them to leave agriculture and find more productive modes of employment elsewhere. With certain safeguards that ensure secure returns or compensation for costs borne on development of land, as also security of ownership, unfreezing of the lease market could help improving the viability of the small farm units.

Economists like V.S. Vyas (2001) have suggested that the second phase of land reforms should contribute to increasing the viability of small holdings. High value addition cultivation, such as vegetable and horticulture cultivation, needs to be encouraged through adequate institutional support. Contract farming and vertical integration of production, marketing and processing activities can help overcome the handicaps posed by the small size of landholdings and ensure higher incomes to the marginal and small farmers.

To sum up, the large number of small and non-viable holdings constitutes one of the most serious problems that ails Indian agriculture, which is responsible for low investment, low productivity and inefficiency in the agricultural sector. This can be overcome only through a bold programme of agrarian reorganisation covering several dimensions including change of inheritance laws, freeing of lease market and strict enforcement of ceiling laws. The government would have to provide necessary technological, infrastructural and input support to marginal and small farmers to raise agricultural productivity. This needs to be complemented by an effort to diversify the rural economy in order to generate more income and employment opportunities and reduce dependence on land. Thus, improving the viability of small holdings is a major challenge for development of the agricultural sector and removal of rural poverty.

References

Bhardwaj, K. (1974), 'Notes on Farm size and Productivity', *Economic and Political Weekly*, IX (13).

Majumdar, D. (1963), 'On the Economics of Relative Efficiency of Small Farmers', *Economic Weekly* (Special Number), pp. 1259–1263.

Rao, A.P. (1967), 'Size of Holding and Productivity', *Economic and Political Weekly*, 2 (44), pp. 1989–1991.

Rao, C.H. (1966), 'Alternative Explanation of the Inverse Relationship Between Size and Output Per Acre', *Indian Economic Review*, 1 (2 [October]), pp. 1–12.

Rudra, A. (1968), 'Farm Size and Yield Per Acre', *Economic and Political Weekly*, 3 (Special Number), pp. 1041–1044.

Saini, G.R. (1969), 'Farm Size Productivity and Returns to Scale', *Economic and Political Weekly*, XIV.

Saini, G.R. (1979), *Farm Size Resource Use, Efficiency and Income Distribution*, Allied Publishers, New Delhi.

Sen, A.K. (1962), 'An Aspect of Indian Agriculture', *Economic Weekly*, V.

Sen, A.K. (1964), 'Size of Holding and Productivity', *Economic Weekly*, XVI.

Singh, A.K. (1987), *Agricultural Development and Rural Poverty*, Ashish Publishing House, New Delhi.

Singh, A.K. (1992), 'Impact of Land Reforms on Agrarian Structure and Agricultural Growth in Uttar Pradesh', *IASSI Quarterly*, 10 (3), pp. 48–60.

Vaidyanathan, A. (2000), 'India's Agricultural Development Policy', *Economic and Political Weekly*.

Vyas, V.S. (2001), 'Perspectives: Agriculture: Second Round of Economic Reforms', *Economic and Political Weekly*.

PART III

Land Access and the Marginalised

earnings from our labour for the *zamindars*. We would slave all day long for them and then get to eat a handful of grain at night. Our *zamindars* were Thakurs. There were three Thakur families who controlled this village. They shared ownership of the entire village and its lands. They were rich and powerful people. They had about 800 acres of land between them.

Because of the *zamindari* system, we had no land at that time. Everything was in the control of the *zamindars*. Everyone used to work for them. Even the land on which we built our houses was theirs. The administration was theirs, the land was theirs, everything was theirs.

Each of the *zamindars* had groups of people dependent on them, and they would either give us land to plough as sharecroppers or give us work as field labourers. We were bonded by tradition. We were like slaves, we would only work for one family. They gave us loans and then made sure that we were never free of the debt.

At that time we were giving the *zamindars* ₹10 for renting a half-acre field for the year. My family could sometimes afford to rent an acre or so. What would we earn? Nothing! There was no irrigation and productivity was low.

But the *zamindars* would pay just quarter of a rupee in rent to their overlords—the *zamindars* of Rajapur and Rampur—on a half-acre, even though we paid ₹10 to them. They would give us land on either rent or on a sharecropping basis. The terms were up to their whims. They would give it to you for a year or two and then they would take it back, saying that they wanted to cultivate it themselves.

Zamindari Abolition, the 1950s

Ram Dass spent much of his early adulthood working in Bombay, the years from 1949 to 1962. But in 1952 and 1953 he lived back in Baba ka Gaon. In his first months back he witnessed the legal abolition of the *zamindari* system, under an act passed by the UP legislative assembly a year earlier.

This is what he has to say of those tumultuous, heady times.

We always thought that *zamindari* would end with Independence. Most of us thought that the *zamindars* would leave with the British and go to England!

The movement to abolish *zamindari* started much before Independence. We poor people didn't know very much earlier, we didn't even go to the market very much, we stayed around the village, but around the 1940s we started to learn that *zamindari* was to be abolished by the Congress. We used to hear about this in public announcements and meetings. Local officials like the patwari used to tell us that *zamindari* would be abolished.

I had come back to the village in 1952 from Bombay. This was the time when *zamindari* was finally abolished. In the market place of Pratapgarh town, the public cryer had beaten the drum and when there was silence he shouted, "The system of *zamindari* has been ended ...." I heard this because I was in the bazaar. The Thakurs in the village were very upset, saying that their rule had been finished.

Ram Dass witnessed the formal abolition of *zamindari* in 1952, but it was while he was away in Bombay for another decade that the changes legislated by the abolition bill actually affected Baba ka Gaon.

He says,

People in the village told me that in 1954 the government officials first came and did a survey of the land and how much there was, whom it belonged to and who was renting it, and then they left. They came with some other people, who were not officials, and started measuring the land like people possessed! They were here for only a few days. They stayed at the village headman's house.

The process of giving title to tenants who possessed stable occupancy tenure—called *maurusi*—was completed in 1956 in Baba ka Gaon. The village Thakurs were not much affected by this process as very little of their land had been given out under stable tenancy rights. But they fought fiercely against the second phase in which the sub-tenants or subordinate cultivators—known as *shikmi*—were to be given title, as most of their land was worked by tenants-at-will and sharecroppers. As the *Zamindari* Abolition Act recognised the claims of these sub-tenants, the Thakurs risked losing ownership of this land.

Ram Dass says,

The shikmi was in 1959. There was a lot of tension at this time. Either you agreed to leave your land, or if you decided to stay you had to fight against the Thakurs. Much of the land that was supposed to go to the tenants didn't go. We couldn't retain possession of the land. The Yadavs got the most land and the Mauryas somewhat less but us Pasis the least. It so happened that the Yadavs were cultivating the Thakurs' land slightly far away from the village but the Mauryas and Pasis were cultivating land close to here. The Thakurs managed to keep most of their land here, though they lost some to the richest Mauryas, but the Yadavs managed to wrest the land that was at a distance because the Thakurs went there very little.

Only those people who already had some land fought, as they had the means to live! Whoever didn't have the means to fight left the land and just depended on God. There were no physical fights in our villages, though it did happen in other villages.

If you decided to fight, the nayab came with the papers. He would tell people that your case was filed and would be heard at this time. People were asked if they wanted to compromise, which could be done here and now; and if not they could fight it out. The nayab used to collect all the people from the village. He would explain to everyone, "Don't fight unnecessarily, you will waste your money if you do, only people who know they are in the right should fight the case."

No one from the scheduled castes fought against the Thakurs. We were too poor and too scared. And only two scheduled caste people got land in these years. My maternal uncle was one of them. Two acres were put in his name. But he lost most of this land later because he was blind and the Thakurs cheated him.

Though his family's poverty did not diminish one whit as a result of *zamindari* abolition, Ram Dass says he was not disappointed. Just the legal ending of *zamindari* was sufficient for him. He says, *Maybe we didn't get any land from the ending of zamindari, but at least we escaped from slavery!*

Land Ceilings, the 1960s

In contrast to their strong and informed views about *zamindari* abolition and its impact, Ram Dass and others have nothing to say about the Congress' major redistributive effort of the early 1960s — specifically, the imposition of ceilings on agricultural land and redistribution to favour the poor. Their silence is the most powerful indicator that this effort did not have an appreciable impact on their well-being. Specifically, the Land Ceiling Act that came into force in UP in 1960 was so mild and so riddled with exemptions that in Baba ka Gaon no land at all was redistributed to the poor. On the contrary, the village Thakurs secured for themselves title to all the degraded land around the village — about 30 acres — as well as the rights for fish farming in the large pond outside the village!

Garibi Hatao, the 1970s

Ceilings on agricultural land were a major thrust of the *Garibi Hatao* strategy. Though the central government's recommendations were less generous to landowners than those issued under Nehru a decade ago, they were still so rife with exemptions as to be incapable of real transformational impact.

Ram Dass comments:

> There were some small improvements. A little land was distributed to the poor. Till then of the 80 families in the village only about 10 owned land. Almost none amongst the scheduled castes had any land. This did change because of Indira Gandhi's Garibi Hatao. But till today, it is only the Thakurs and some of the middle castes that have enough land. The rest don't even have enough to feed their families from.
>
> Poor people were supposed to get enough land to live on. At a minimum they were to get enough land to make full use of a plough and pair of bullocks. This was about 3 acres. But in practice, people got two-thirds or one-third of an acre or even less. My family got one-third of an acre.
>
> All the landless people in the village got titles to land, but some were never able to take possession and others were able to take possession of only a little bit of the land allotted to them. The Thakurs threatened that they would cut us into pieces if we tried to take possession! They harassed anyone who protested. And they filed legal cases against our taking over the plots, and we poor people were ensnared in these cases for years. Many of the poorer people just gave up sooner or later. Some of them don't even know till today where the land is that they had been allotted!
>
> Even with the allotments made from the village land, the *pradhans*, who were always Thakur or Brahmin, put the land in the name of their own relatives!
>
> Three landless families in Baba ka Gaon have land on paper, but they will never get possession. One is a Pasi and another two from

middle castes. The law is that whoever has title should be given possession. The laws are very clear and strong to say that action should be taken if people aren't allowed to take control of the land given to them. But who is going to enforce this, who is going to take action? No officials came to ensure that things were being done properly. The ones who are supposed to implement are the ones who benefit from the law not being implemented! For all her promises, Indira Gandhi was always so busy visiting hundreds of countries that she never had time to see the poverty at home or to see whether her laws were working!

The 1980s—'Poverty Alleviation' in Lieu of Land Reform

The 1980s was a decade of inaction in UP on land reform, certainly when seen from the perspective of Ram Dass, his family and other Dalits in Baba ka Gaon and the other villages in which I conducted interviews. Indeed, this is an accurate reflection of the political and policy levels too, because after the Emergency, the Janata Government and then Mrs Indira Gandhi and Rajiv Gandhi turned away from even the rhetoric of land redistribution.

Of course, some of the momentum of land reform from the 1970s spilled into the early 1980s. Thus, it was only in 1982 that Ram Dass and his family finally got possession of the one-third of an acre that had been allocated to them under the *Garibi Hatao* effort.

However, there were no fresh initiatives on land reform in the 1980s, and this decade really saw only the expansion of poverty alleviation programmes sponsored by the central government, several of which had been started during the *Garibi Hatao* effort.

The 1990s—Dalit Parties Ignore Land Reform

In Baba ka Gaon, in 1997, during India's 50th anniversary of independent rule, the extent of land ownership continued to be the prime determinant of a family's economic well-being. Tragically, however, the manifest failures on land reform, decade after decade, meant that the vast majority of Dalits and other oppressed castes and communities remained 'functionally landless' and hence deeply impoverished.[1] Of the village's 100-plus households, roughly two-thirds were still deeply impoverished. At least 50 were so poor that they fell well below the official poverty line, with the poorest 5–10 of these families' destitute. These desperately poor 50 families owned no more than two-third of an acre each, almost all of it infertile. Of these, five families owned just one-sixth of an acre each. Three had no land at all. About half of these 50 impoverished families were from the scheduled castes, a slightly smaller number were from the lower ranks of the middle castes, with the remainder made up by all seven of the village's scheduled tribe families.

Ram Dass says:

> Nearly everyone in the village has very little land. All the people who got land from land reform got very little land. Some have one-third of an acre, others have two-thirds. Very few got more than two-thirds of an acre from the land reform, even though the government had said they would be given 3 acres each. But they just gave these little bits of land, not what they had promised. And the land given to most families was so bad that it is of no use to them.

Another 10 households were middle-ranking in terms of income and well-being in 1997, ranging from those who were just above the official poverty threshold to a few who had relatively ample incomes, sufficient land to feed themselves and just the right number of able-bodied adults. This small group comprised a large number from the middle castes and the better-off scheduled caste families, including Ram Dass'. The middle-ranking families in Baba ka Gaon typically owned between 1.25 and 3 acres. Ram Dass' extended family of 13 adults and 4 children owned 2.5 acres, but the household's finances were bolstered by his son Shrinath's salary as a government primary-school teacher.

Above this handful of middle-ranking families were about 30 comparatively well-off households. This group essentially comprised 20 Thakur families who are descendants of the 3 Thakur families that originally controlled Baba ka Gaon, 3 Brahmins and

---

[1] The situation in Baba ka Gaon accords with Trivedi's assessment that though "the number of absolute landless among Dalits in Uttar Pradesh is not so high, the number of functional landless is still very high" (Trivedi, 2014).

about 5 of the higher–middle-caste families. The most prosperous families in Baba ka Gaon were the 20 Thakur families. At a level of wealth equal to that of the less prosperous of the Thakurs were the three Brahmin families. About five of the higher–middle-caste families were also relatively prosperous in terms of the amount of land they own, but still do not approach the Thakurs in terms of other assets, such as the size of their homes or monetary savings.

Primarily because the three original Thakur families have branched out into 20 smaller families, none of the Thakurs individually own more than about 35 acres and about an acre of orchards. While the two largest landholders in the village would by national standards be classified into the top bracket of landowners—and also be violating UP's land ceiling laws—the remaining Thakur families on average own about 10 acres each, which ranks them as large holders by current Indian and UP standards.

But though their individual holdings are no longer on the scale of their undivided families, the amount of land owned by Baba ka Gaon's Thakurs as a group has not greatly diminished since the abolition of *zamindari*. Moreover, of the land sold by them in the past 50 years, the bulk was bought by the higher-middle castes, with only a small amount purchased by the few scheduled caste families—including Ram Dass'—who have improved their economic position. The rest of the families in Baba ka Gaon have simply been too impoverished to purchase any land.

Summing all this up, Ram Dass says:

Apart from the Thakurs everyone was poor before *zamindari* abolition. Some of the Banias did have money from business. The middle castes were also poor, though not as poor as us Harijans. And even up to now, the richest are the Thakurs, then the middle castes and the poorest are the Harijans!

The Thakurs had all the advantages earlier—they were rich, they were educated, they had land, and they had us Harijans to be their slaves. So it is not surprising that till today they are the lords and we are still poor.

Mata Prasad, another Pasi man, comments:

All the Thakur families in the village are much richer than the middle castes and scheduled castes. Now there are 20 houses of the three *zamindars*. Because of this their holdings have become less. But they still have more land than families of other castes. They have more money. And in each of their families there is someone with a job. They have government jobs — one is a professor, another is in the police, someone in the army. The poorest Thakur has 3.5 acres and quite a lot of money. He sold a lot of his land. The richest, the former *pradhan*, has more than 35 acres, and he is alone, no brothers. Another of the richest lives near Rae Bareli. He supervises the work on the land he owns here and then leaves. He is a businessman, he has a brick kiln and lots of land in other villages.

Strikingly, land reform has become a dead letter in UP despite the rise of political parties, such as the Bahujan Samaj, representing the Dalits and other impoverished groups who would gain from land reform. Shrinath Pasi, Ram Dass' older son, a schoolteacher, says: "To my knowledge, only two, three or four people have got agricultural land from the government in the last ten years. Most of the land has been allotted very far away, and not much of it is fertile."

He comments:

These new parties like the SP and BSP are better than the Congress. But in all of them the malpractices of the politicians continue. No party talks about land reform except the communists, who believe in equality. The other parties are full of people who are well off and they do not want to make laws under which they themselves will suffer. The communists contest the elections but they are never successful. They only get 20 or 22 seats in the whole of UP, and because people know they can never form a government they don't vote for them. Otherwise more of us poor people would vote for them. All the stuff the other parties do is just a lot of show! *Nautanki!* All they do is make tall promises and claims on radio and television. All the laws that they make are laws to benefit themselves. Nothing changes for the poor.

Durbhe, a younger relative of him, says:

We would be happy if there was a political party that would distribute all the *benami* land. We would vote for them. But the politicians don't want to do anything about land reform because they will have to give up their own land. All they do is that just before the elections, their leaders come and promise you a lot of things but this is all talk. All the politicians from the scheduled castes and middle castes only talk about reservations. But reservations in colleges are of no use to people who don't have the money to study, and reservations in government jobs are no use when you're not educated enough to get government jobs. Even these politicians support the rich, not the poor. We poor people would never speak frankly even to the scheduled-caste politicians if they came here and talked to us.

The 21st Century—Stasis

In UP, the stasis in land reform that was evident by the 1990s has continued through the first decade of the 21st century despite the many years of rule by the BSP. The upshot in Baba ka Gaon is that despite the passing of 65 years since India's independence, poverty amongst the Dalits remains intense and widespread. Ram Dass, aged in his late-70s, is categorical in his pronouncement: *The cause of poverty among the chote varg is only this: they don't have land.*

He relates the area of cultivable land a family has to its poverty:

If a family has less than 5 *bighaa*, then they are definitely below the poverty line. If there is at least 5 *bighaa* land, a family can meet his needs. If someone has more than 5 *bighaa*, then they are above the poverty line.

Shrinath, his son, adds: "All the bandmaanush households are people who don't have land of their own, they work as labourers in others' fields. It can be said that they are totally 'below the poverty line.'"

The egregious consequences of being functionally landless extend beyond poverty to matters of power and dependence. Land-poor people from the scheduled castes and tribes and 'lower backward' castes remain dependent on the village's landowning households, almost all from the Savarna castes. Kulla Mushara, a 65-year-old woman says, "If you don't do their work, they won't let you enter their fields and land. Not for cutting grass for your use or for wood. Which is why we give in and follow their commands."

Shrinath says: "All those who are below the poverty line remain linked in some way or the other with someone of the forward castes. So year-round they keep working in the fields of the forward castes."

Totally 65 years from India's independence, and over 90 years since the Awadh revolt, Baba ka Gaon's Dalits and scheduled tribes remain by far the worst off in the local agrarian order. The lack of political will to undertake land reform has condemned them to decade after decade of extreme poverty. The continuing strength of the linkages between land ownership and caste hierarchies has also proved to be rural UP's most intractable barrier to collective action and equitable development. The failures on land reform manifest in Baba ka Gaon are even more inexcusable in light of the Indian state's demonstrated commitment to giving land to private-sector business and industry, for urban and industrial use. Although the trade-offs between the needs of the rural poor and the national project of industrial development date back decades, the speed with which this trade-off is being implemented has accelerated with economic liberalisation and rapid economic growth. The governments of UP and other states have time and again used the colonial-era land acquisition law to acquire land for corporates at far below market prices, often forcibly evicting vast numbers of farmers and tribals who join the ranks of the landless impoverished. There could be no more damning indictment of these governments' failure to respond to the felt needs of Dalits and other impoverished rural communities.

References

Pandey, G. (1982), 'Peasant Revolt and Indian Nationalism', in R. Guha (ed.), *Subaltern Studies I*, Oxford University Press, New Delhi.

Trivedi, P.K. (2014), 'Land Reforms and Dalits', in A.K. Singh and S. Mehrotra (eds.), *Land Policies for Equity and Growth: Transforming the Agrarian Structure in Uttar Pradesh*, SAGE Publications, New Delhi.

7

Land Reforms and Dalits*

Prashant Kumar Trivedi

Land reforms, the 'forgotten agenda', is once again surfacing. Perhaps it is because the discourses around land acquisition for industries and consequent protest movements have once again forced the social scientists to revisit it. Naxalite movement and movement on land issues by left parties, for instance recently in Andhra Pradesh, also attracted people's attention towards these issues. Besides, nowadays voices for land reform are coming from a very strange corner, the World Bank. It would have impressed even those who, till recently in their euphoria of double-digit growth rate of Indian economy, considered it as something that belongs to the past. There are other fundamental reasons for which land reforms cannot be either bypassed or sidelined. It keeps coming up like an 'unfinished agenda'.

Studies have also shown the relationship between untouchability and violence against Dalits and land ownership. Households having no land or very small piece of land are forced to work as wage labour on fields generally owned by the landed class or provide services demanded by the privileged. This dependence of Dalits on non-Dalits further weakens their relative position and leaves very little room for Dalits to oppose the discrimination practised against them. In this kind of situation where social and cultural discrimination is also rooted in land relations, land becomes a crucial asset for Dalits.

The chapter is organised as follows. Section titled 'Abolition of *Zamindari*' discusses the abolition of *zamindari* and its impact and

*Paper presented at Seminar on Land Reforms in Uttar Pradesh: Retrospect and Prospects, 12–13 August 2008, Giri Institute of Development Studies, Lucknow. The author is thankful to Prof. K.B. Saxena and other participants of the seminar for their comments on the earlier draft of this paper. This text has been edited for typographical errors, stylistic consistency and sequential organisation in order to make it suitable for inclusion in this book.

caste-wise ownership as it emerged after the abolition. Section titled 'Redistribution of Ceiling Surplus Land' examines how effectively ceiling surplus land was distributed. Section titled 'Tenancy Reforms and Consolidation of Land' examines the third major dimension of tenancy reform, and the other important dimension of consolidation of fragmented landholdings. In both first and third sections the caste dimension of land ownership is analysed. Section titled 'Inputs from the Field' reports the findings of a small field survey, focusing on 300 Dalit households. The chapter concludes by spelling out the challenges for future land reform.

Abolition of *Zamindari*

UP was among the first states that initiated the land reforms programme soon after Independence. Enactment of 'Uttar Pradesh Zamindari Abolition Act, 1950' was a major step towards this end. Though statutory status and role of *zamindars* in revenue collection were abolished, very lengthy and time-consuming process and loopholes in the legislation gave them enough opportunity to save their land. The bill was widely debated for many years and then the act was struck down by the High Court of UP as *ultra-vires*. It was only after inclusion of the act in Ninth Schedule following the first constitutional amendment in 1951 that the act became enforceable. During this period *zaminadars*, *talukdars* and other intermediaries got enough time either to transfer their land to relatives or family-controlled trusts, temples etc. or to sell it off. *Benami* transaction was another means applied at a large scale to save the landed property (Das, 2000). Added to this, the prolonged process of *zamindari* abolition extending from 1946 to 1955 was utilised by the *zamindars* to forcefully evict tenants from the land. Many studies (Singh and Mishra, 1964; Srimali, 1981) have noticed sudden increase in the area under *sir* and *khudkast* in the period immediately before *zamindari* abolition. In fact, at the time of *zamindari* abolition, 10,235,000 acres of land was recorded as *sir* and *khudkast* of landlords, of which around two-third was grabbed by the *zamindars* by evicting tenants applying legal and extra-legal means. These 'legal means' included large-scale falsification of land record by the bureaucracy that had close interface with the rural landed elite. Finally, *zamindars* managed to secure around 80 per cent of their *sir* and *khudkast* (Hasan, 1989).

The way this act was conceptualised also helped *zamindars*, for instance engagement with manual labour was not a put as a precondition to define 'cultivator'. Hasan (1989, p. 157) notes that

Owing to the considerations of social status which prohibit high castes from engaging in certain kinds of manual work, performance in manual labour was not considered necessary for designation as cultivator. This ancient argument bolstered the position of higher caste *zamindars* who were allowed to retain their *sir*, *khudkast* and grove land. Two million *zamindars* were thus transformed into a privileged class of landowners.

Not only this, but *zamindars* were offered compensation for the loss of their intermediary rights and tenants were asked to pay 10 times the annual rent for their land with the Zamindari Abolition Fund to convert their *sirdari* status into *bhumidari* status. This scheme again worked against the interests of poor peasants because only rich tenants mainly among jats, ahirs, gurjars, kurmis and lodhas could raise required fund to purchase ownership rights. Besides, it seems that apprehensions regarding the stability of their *bhumidari* rights, especially in *zamindari* stronghold areas, also prevented them from making their contribution to the Zamindari Abolition Fund (Hasan, 1989).

In this process, 13.5 million superior tenants — occupancy tenants, hereditary tenants and ex-proprietary tenants — got free-hold occupation on admissible land, but inferior tenants — sharecroppers, tenants at will, contract farmers — engaged in cultivating *khudkast* (personal cultivation) land simply lost access to it. "Due to conferment of *Bhumidhari* right (free hold) upon superior tenants the latter [ex-intermediaries] got physical hold on land under personal cultivation, while the legal ban on leasing out land for cultivation meant that the inferior tillers lost access to cultivable land" (Das, 2000). Sharma (2005) notes, "The spurt in the number of agricultural workers in the wake of the first phase of land reforms was a manifestation of this reality." This comment was made in the context of Bihar but it indicates development in UP too.

Another glimpse of this changed scenario could be seen in the comparison of share of *zamindari* with that of control over

Figure 7.1

Share in Population and Land After Zamindari Abolition

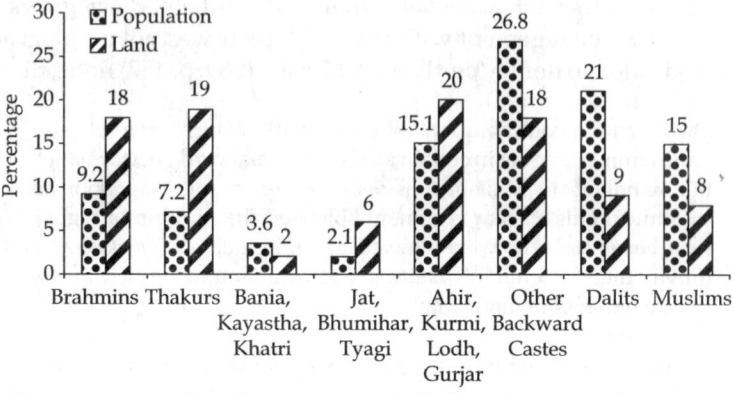

Source: N.C. Saxena (1985) cited in Hasan (1989).

total land in post-Independence India (Figure 7.1). According to Saxena (1985) Thakurs lost a substantial part of their land in the post-Independence period but even then they remained big land-owners. Before Independence, they controlled 34 per cent of the *zamindari* rights but their share in total land came down to 19 per cent in the post-Independence period. Brahmins increased their share slightly from 17 to 18 per cent. These figures clearly indicate that both these communities still had larger land compared to their proportion in the population that stands at 7.2 per cent and 9.2 per cent, respectively, for Thakurs and Brahmins. Maximum part of the land lost by Thakur *zamindars* went to the four major backward castes of Yadavs, Kurmis, Lodhas and Gujars. Their share in the land increased from 6 per cent to 20 per cent. As per Census 1931 these castes constitute 15.1 per cent of the state's population. The total share of OBCs in post-Independence UP reached 38 per cent from 8 per cent of *zamindari* rights controlled by them before Independence. Part of land controlled by Muslims came down to 8 per cent from 20 per cent. Share of Dalits in land reached to 9 per cent from 1 per cent. These figures might give the impression that Dalits gained a lot from *zamindari* abolition but keeping in view the proportion of their population that stands at 21 per cent, they emerge as the most disadvantaged section of the society. Besides, this impression is partly due to the fact that they start with a very low base as their share in land in the pre-Independence period was almost negligible (Saxena, 1985). This scenario also reveals a strong correlation and thick overlap between class and caste.

It would be appropriate to conclude this discussion with the quote from Daniel Thorner's writing that captures the picture on the ground in following words:

> UP Zamindari Abolition Act has provided for a new hierarchy of tenure holders in place of old, but the new one is too reminiscent of the old. Zamindars have officially disappeared but the same persons have been rechristened landholders of very substantial and very high quality tracts of land. For the bulk of peasantry classified as sirdars, tenure remains virtually the same and so does the rent collected by the government rather than the zamindars. At the bottom remain the mass of landless and cropsharers. (Thorner and Thorner, 1973, p. 27, cited in Hasan, 1989, p. 159)

Redistribution of Ceiling Surplus Land

As discussed earlier, without imposition of land ceiling and redistribution of surplus land, agrarian relations and land inequality were not changed substantially through only *zamindari* abolition. Pressure from the peasantry that reasserted it during the 1950s and the 1960s in many parts of the country strengthened discourse around land redistribution. In 1957, the National Development Council directed state governments to enact land ceiling laws by the end of March 1959 and implement them within a period of 3 years. Following this, in UP, the Land Ceiling Act of 1960 was enacted, which set a high ceiling of 16–32 ha. (40–80 acres). The experience of enforcement of this act was similar to *zamindari* abolition in more than one way. Again, the landed elite was pre-informed and prepared to save its land. Newell (1972, pp. 90–94) points that land transfers that took place just before the enactment of the Ceiling Act reduced the potential surplus land from 688,000 acres to 437,000 acres and even then only 20,000 acres of land was actually distributed. This was a complete failure of the land ceiling and redistribution programme.

During the late 1960s, widespread rural unrest and food crisis again forced the Indian establishment to rethink its failure on the land reform front. This led to lowering of the land ceiling in 1972. The scene was not so different again. Perhaps by now, ex-landlords and big farmers had mastered the skill of avoiding confiscation of their land by applying time-tested methods of *benami* transactions, dividing the land between family members, bogus sale, formation of cooperatives, family-controlled trusts and temples, and so on. Bureaucracy was of course by their side, like in earlier similar occasions. As per the estimates of Newell (1972, ़ 96), another four lakh acres should have become available under the modified ceiling if the above-mentioned transactions had not taken place, but altogether only 200,000 acres could be redistributed (Das, 2000; Hasan, 1989).

As of now, UP government applies a ceiling of 7.3 ha., 10.95 ha. and 18.25 ha. on irrigated with two crops, irrigated with one crop and dry land, respectively. Implementation of ceiling laws and distribution of surplus land could not yield desired results in UP. In the state, only 3,69,362 acres of land was declared surplus, and around 70 per cent of it was distributed among the landless. It is really interesting to note that government agencies provide data on ceiling surplus land in acres instead of in hectares. In fact, only 1,05,290 ha. ceiling surplus land was distributed and as per the Agricultural Census of 2001, total operated area in UP stands at around 180 million ha. These data reveal the total failure of the ceiling surplus programme, because merely 0.58 per cent of the total operated area was distributed (Table 7.1).

Programme of distribution of 'Gram Samaj' land was started in UP in 1975–1976 and its performance up to March 2008 is given in Table 7.2. As part of these reforms, *Gram Sabha* land was distributed among the landless households. Compared to the distribution of ceiling surplus land, the programme of distribution of land vested

Table 7.1
Distribution of Ceiling Surplus Land in UP up to September 2006 (Acres)

Area declared surplus	3,69,362
Area taken possession of	3,39,385
Area distributed	2,63,225
Total no. of beneficiaries	3,03,867
SC beneficiaries	2,07,450
Area distributed among SCs	1,84,808

Source: Annual Report, Ministry of Rural Development, 2006–2007.

Table 7.2
Distribution of Arable 'Gram Samaj' Land in UP up to March 2008

Category	No. of beneficiary	Area of land distributed (hectares)
SCs	20,76,874	6,43,513
STs	3,059	1,886
OBCs	9,46,216	3,35,488
Others	6,56,559	1,87,452
Ex. service men	87	155
Total	36,82,795	11,68,496

Source: Board of Revenue, Uttar Pradesh, Lucknow.

with *Gram Sabha*s has been fairly extensive. Land allotment of over 11,68,496 ha. was made to 36,82,795 households. Of the total number of beneficiaries, 56.4 per cent were SCs, 25.7 per cent were OBC and 17.8 per cent belonged to other castes. Significantly, the allotted land amounted to 6.5 per cent of area in operated holdings in 2000–2001 and the beneficiary holdings were 17 per cent of the total holdings in the state.

Besides allotting *Gram Sabha* land to Dalits, ownership rights of land occupied by Dalits but not owned by them were also vested in them. In addition to agricultural land, steps were taken to provide land for house site to Dalits. For this, if a Dalit household had occupied a piece of land, not owned by them for their housing needs, they were provided with legal ownership of that land. Measures were also taken to check land alienation from Dalits. It includes pre-approval of land transfer from Dalit to non-Dalit by district collectors. But this loophole in this law has also been exploited to the maximum possible limit as pre-approval became just another formality. This resulted in large-scale land alienation.

Tenancy Reforms and Consolidation of Land

In many parts of the state, the tiller–owner model became operational and leasing the land was declared illegal except in rare cases. Even after these regulations as per the 59th round of NSS, proportion of tenant holding in the total holding of UP in 2002–2003 is 11.7 per cent and these tenant holdings operate 9.5 per cent of the total operated area. Tenancy being declared illegal in many states including UP, it is possibly underreported in NSSO data as indicated by some studies. In the neoliberal era, stances of reverse tenancy are also coming into light where many marginal and small farmers are leasing out their land to rich farmers. Field experiences indicate that reverse tenancy is more common in cash crop area and in cases of well-irrigated land capable of growing cash crops. In these cases, rent is more likely to be paid in cash as against the dominant form of sharecropping, where a fixed share of produce is paid.

Implementation of land reforms and its impact varies across the regions of the state. UP could achieve comparatively better performance in terms of land consolidation. This achievement laid the foundation for the success of Green Revolution in western UP, where a large part of land is owned by cultivating castes like the Jats and Gujars. Up to November 2005, 587.66 lakh acres of land was consolidated in the state. In many parts of the state the second round of land consolidation process is going on.

Changes in Land Ownership Pattern

The way these reforms were designed and carried out brought out a change from cumulative inequality into dispersed inequality and linkage between caste and landownership never broke down totally, as upper caste *zamindars* continued to be the biggest land owners, tenants who purchased land or benefited from land reforms were mostly OBCs and a section of Dalits remained functionally landless agricultural labour.

It is not being argued here that the land ownership patterns remain the same in the last six decades. The state policies and market transactions mentioned in the previous section have impinged upon it. Though only some amount of land has been transferred through market transaction, the upper caste Hindus and Muslims emerge as net sellers and OBCs as net purchasers, followed by Dalits and Sikh cultivators (Lieten and Srivastava, 1999). The recent period has also seen stances of land alienation as a number of farmers have sold out their land.

Table 7.3 reveals that the bottom castes have far less land possession than others do. More than 70 per cent Dalit households

Table 7.3

Percentage Distribution of Households by Size Class of Land Possessed for Rural UP (Hectares)

Social category	Landless	0.001–0.004	0.005–0.40	0.41–1.00	1.01–2.0	2.01–4.0	4.01 and above
ST	0.0	28.2	37.8	8.6	17.1	6.3	2.0
SC	1.9	11.3	57.5	20.1	7.1	1.8	0.3
OBC	1.3	7.1	42.5	27.9	13.5	6.0	1.7
Others	1.4	8.9	32.8	24.0	18.2	10.6	4.2
All	1.5	8.7	44.7	24.9	12.7	5.8	1.8

Source: NSSO, 61st round, 2004–2005.

possess less than 0.4 ha. of land. Comparable figures for OBCs and Others are 50.9 and 43.1 per cent, respectively. It has been pointed out that this dataset underreports landlessness and inequality of land possession. NSS conceives a household landless if it possesses neither land for housing site nor agricultural land. This data fails to capture landlessness in terms of productive agriculture land as a source of livelihood. To capture this dimension, NSS provides another dataset that gives ownership pattern of operational land-holding. Still a gap remains as in some cases poor households use part of their homestead land for marginal crop production and this constitutes a substantial part of their livelihood.

Table 7.4 once again demonstrates that after the 1980s, distribution of land among Dalits has virtually stopped. During the 1980s, share of Dalits in the number of operational holdings went up from 14.77 per cent to 16.40 per cent and their share in total operated area increased from 9.24 per cent to 10.50 per cent. This still was not a satisfactory situation as the proportion of Dalits in the population is 21 per cent. After the 1980s both the indicators

Table 7.4

Share of Dalits in the Number of Operational Holdings and Total Operated Area

Year	1980–1981	1990–1991	2000–2001
No. of operational holdings[a]	14.77	16.40	17.01
Share in total operated area	9.24	10.50	10.86

Source: Agricultural census.

Note: [a] Percentage share of total holding.

Figure 7.2

Average Land Holding (Dalits, Non-Dalits and Total)

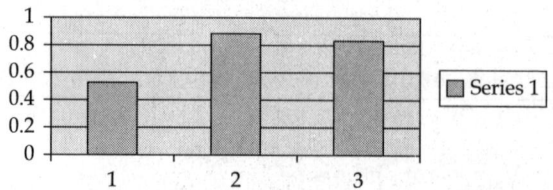

have remained stagnant. Data from agricultural census also reveal stark inequality between Dalits and non-Dalits. In UP, the average size of landholding for all social groups is 0.83 ha., for Dalits it is only 0.53 ha., whereas for non-Dalits it stands at 0.89 ha. (Figure 7.2).

Absolute landlessness among Dalits in UP is not so high, but functional landlessness is still very high. Two-third landholdings belonging to Dalits are less than 0.5 ha. The average size of land-holding in this category is only 0.23 ha. If we have a look on the less than 1-ha. category, we find that 87 per cent of the total Dalit holdings fall in this category. Sudha Pai (2000, pp. 412–413) too notes that although total land possessions by SC households have slightly gone up, but their share in operational holdings declines with rise in size category. This rise in land possession is mainly due to the state's policy of distribution of 'Gram Samaj' (village community) land among the landless and SC farmers. So, the above note should be seen with Mata Prasad's (1995, pp. 66–68) observation that around one-fifth of beneficiaries of land allotment do not get possession on that.

Inputs from the Field

This fieldwork was conducted in 2005 for a broader project on social development to ascertain changes in social development of Dalit women. For this purpose, 300 Dalit women were interviewed in five villages of the BKT block of Lucknow district. It reveals a change in the land-owning pattern among Dalits.

Data collected and qualitative observation findings are discussed in the following sub-sections.

Land Ownership and Land Distribution

- Landless Dalit families, benefited with the state's land distribution policy, have increased their landholding to an extent. Of the total respondents, more than 41 per cent got *land patta*.
- Physical possession on *patta* remains a big roadblock for Dalits. Only 33 per cent of the total households got physical possession on it. In some cases, the matter hangs in litigation for years and physical possession remains with the landed elite.
- Mostly *patta*s were on infertile land. In village Kathwara many of them were on low-lying land near the river Gomati and in other villages it was on infertile or un-irrigated land far away from the main village.
- Distant location of *patta*s makes them inaccessible for even daily needs like relieving themselves and Dalits remain dependent on non-Dalits for this.
- Some of the plots are so small that farmers don't even get government assistance for tube well. Dalits lack capital for cultivation. This situation is compounded by the fact that around two-third Dalit respondents find it difficult to take loan from the bank and around half of them feel that cooperative societies practice discrimination against them. In this situation, only those Dalit families can avail benefit of *patta* land of which at least one member is employed in the non-agricultural sector and income from that source is invested in agriculture.

Labour Wages

- Agricultural wages are still very low and women face discrimination in the labour market. For men, daily wage ranges between ₹50 and ₹70, whereas for women it ranges between ₹25 and ₹35. On an average, an agricultural labour gets 1–2 months' work a year.
- Agricultural labours from the same village get lesser wages than labour from the labour market because the former depend on landed gentry for leasing-in land as well as credit in emergency.

- Agricultural wages vary with distance from urban area, agricultural seasons and nature of work to be done. Dalits feel that even tiny land plots have enhanced their bargaining power.

Land Consolidation

- In the studied area, the second round of land consolidation drive was going on. The researcher witnessed a number of protest demonstration by middle and small peasants against prevalent corruption in the consolidation process. Dalits feel that they loose land in this process and often get inferior land without any source of irrigation located far from the village.

Tenancy

- Inspite of ban, tenancy is prevailing in UP. Terms of tenancy differ in different areas. Owner of the land shares 50 per cent of the expenses on irrigation, fertilisers and threshing. Rest of the expenses and labour are borne by the tenants. Produce is equally divided between both of them.
- Land on annual rent is also leased out. Rent could be paid in terms of either a fixed quantity of grain or cash.

Social Development and Employment Scenario

- Proportion of Dalit families solely dependent on agriculture has also gone down due to their increasing representation in other employment sources. One or more members of a land-less family have migrated to nearby towns or to distant places like Delhi in search of alternative sources of employment. Mostly these people get employment in industrial units, construction sites, brick kilns, shops, hotels and restaurants, etc. They also work as rickshaw pullers, security guards and domestic help.

• Some families got land *patta* in the 1970s and the 1980s. Their social development indicators are higher than those of other families. Educational attainment of these families is higher than that for the rest of the families. Due to education percentage of Dalit families having one of their members having a white collar job in any government or private institution has gone up.

Land Reforms: Challenges and Road Blocks

At the level of implementation, land reform measures faced stiff resistance from bureaucracy that had close interface with semifeudal social and agrarian structure in the countryside. Large-scale manoeuvring was done with land records by corrupt government officials on the behest of rural landed elite. In many cases, allotment of land remained on papers and Dalits were not given physical possession of the land.

Land reforms in India were a response to the mounting pressure from the peasantry. Mohanty (2001, p. 3859) has rightly pointed out that "When the magnitude of resistance of deprived people challenges the existing order or shows signs of potential threat, the resultant change provokes reform measures." These reform measures necessarily leave loopholes and lacuna in the laws that can be utilised by the dominant interests. The same happened with land reforms too. Furthermore, the state apparatus is also dominated by the upper caste that controls landed property in the countryside. Sharma (2005) notes that "ownership of land and other assets, caste dominance, political power structure, and the oligarchies that control the state apparatus and their resources all overlap in a way which is by no means unique to Bihar, but which takes a particularly entrenched form here." Again, this comment was made in the context of Bihar but holds ground in the context of UP too.

Besides other factors, demographic composition too contributed to the maintenance of status quo. Proportion of so-called upper caste population in UP is much higher than that in the western and southern states. Supporting this point, Mehrotra (2006) notes "... the sheer size of the upper caste population in UP makes its social structure more resistant to change than in the rest of the country ...."

Another point that comes up again and again in the land reform discourse is the role of peasant movement. "Land reform policy being fundamentally a political issue, the state passes the legislation only to pacify and neutralise the agrarian tension. In order to monitor the implementation of such measures, the existence of strong social movements is crucial." Bandyopadhay (2002, p. 5179) too supports the idea that the "real impact would depend upon correlations of political and class forces at any given time in any country". He refers to the significantly important role played by Kisan Sabhas led by CPI (M) and CPI in West Bengal. In UP, the situation is entirely different. During the freedom struggle, peasant movement in some parts of the state raised this issue but after Independence it could not maintain its momentum. Left parties are weak in the state and, as discussed earlier, backward parties, in the interest of their following, are opposed to any idea of further rupturing of agrarian relations. Bahujan Samaj Party, the Dalit party, has never taken interest in these issues of substantial import for its following. It seems that absence of a strong movement for the implementation of land reforms too would have helped the landed elite to save their land.

Field experiences and secondary sources suggest that the social development pattern of Dalits has shown a secular upward move but it seems that the relative distance between Dalits and non-Dalits has not been narrowed in many aspects of social development except for education. It is not being argued here that land reforms did not positively affect Dalit life but its scope remained limited. Only a tiny section of the upwardly mobile section of Dalits could take advantage of it. One can say that it kick started the process by setting them free from the bondages of *zamindari* system and giving some of them the capacity to capitalise benefits from rural development schemes and the policy of positive discrimination in government employment and education. Availability of opportunities in non-agricultural employment sources is another important factor that sets the Dalits free from traditional agrarian structure. All these developments gave rise to an educated middle class among the rural Dalit masses. It is this class that provides leadership to Dalits for political assertion.

However, land reform measures have, to a degree, done away with large inefficient landholdings. The peasant castes, i.e., the so-called backward castes, have specially gained from this development. It is this social structural transformation of rural India that has been the major achievement of the land reform measures. At the same time, these emerging new rural elite have joined the traditional elite in opposing further implementation of land reforms because restructuring of land ownership may lead to restructuring of socio-political scenario and they might lose their dominant socio-economic status in the emerging rural caste-class-power dynamics.

Overall land reforms have facilitated transition from 'cumulative inequality' to 'dispersed inequality' but have excluded the functionally landless strata of rural India. The latter continue to be by and large left outside the purview of land ownership. In this sense, land reforms have succeeded in the replacement of old elite and facilitated the emergence of new ones. They have failed to really transfer the land to the 'true tiller' and curb land inequality. The rural strata, which are at the bottom of resource ownership and caste hierarchy, continue to be exploited by the old and the new elite, and are often the victims of violent land conflicts. Thus, for the landless Dalits, land reform remains an 'unfinished agenda'.

Policy Suggestions

In the light of this discussion it can be suggested for further discussion that with increasing productivity of arable land, land ceiling should be further lowered down, especially in irrigated areas. As per the government records, irrigation facilities have been extended in many new areas in the years followed by Land Ceiling Act and now more than three-fifth of the area is irrigated area. In all these areas ceiling of irrigated land should be applied. Needless to say that strict implementation of ceiling laws coupled with distribution of surplus land among the landless Dalits must be ensured. It is often argued by the governments that there is no land available for distribution. Balagopal (2007, p. 3829) has rightly commented that

> And so suddenly governments, which till yesterday pretended that while it may be desirable to give the poor land for cultivating food or putting up huts, they were helpless and properly sorry about it because there was no land available and the poor should try breeding less instead, now discovered that there was any amount of land available to be put at the disposal of the corporates for investment, and the rich in general for building nice big nests for themselves.

A back-of-the-envelop calculation would give an idea that still there is enough scope to implement land ceiling laws if the political establishment shows same kind of vigour that they have shown in the case of SEZs. For making this calculation easier, it is presumed that uniform ceiling is implemented all over. It is not so vague too, as the government itself claims that more than 80 per cent of the land is covered by irrigation facilities. A closer look at the landholding pattern in the state reveals that there are 88,000 landholdings in the more than 7.5-ha. category covering an area of 9,60,000 ha. The average size of these holdings is around 11 ha. and applying a ceiling of 7.5 ha. would fetch more than 3 lakh ha. of surplus land. And if we bring down the ceiling limit to 5.0 ha. like West Bengal, we find that 2,73,000 holdings cover an area of 2,077,000 ha. In this case, the amount of ceiling surplus land would be more than 7 lakh ha. This is seven times higher than the total ceiling surplus land distributed so far.

Recent land reform discourse centres on World Bank advocated policy of land distribution through market. From the Dalit standpoint, land reform is not just transfer of an economic asset in their favour but it also involves upsetting the existing socio-political structure.

> Land being socially valued asset, its unequal distribution helps maintain the hierarchical structure and strengthen the basis of dominance of the privileged groups by perpetuating inequality and deprivation in various socio-economic spheres. Seen from this point, the idea of fair distribution of land directly strikes at the root of such social relations. (Mohanty, 2001, p. 3858)

Land reform through market skips this crucial element. Bandyopadhyay (2002, p. 5180) comments: "Land reform means disempowerment of the powerful top landowning households and empowerment of the landless and the land poor through assured access to the redistributive land and tenurial security." Referring to dangers of market mechanism, he concludes by saying, "Buying land at a fairly high price from big landholders through credit is no land reforms. It enriches the rich and impoverishes the poor."

References

Balagopal, K. (2007), 'Ceiling Surpluses and Public Lands', *Economic and Political Weekly*, 42 (38), pp. 3829–3833.

Bandyopadhay, D. (2002), 'The Forgotten Agenda', *Economic and Political Weekly*, 37 (52).

Das, S. (2000), 'A Critical Evaluation of Land Reforms in India', in B.K. Sinha and Pushpendra (eds.), *Land Reforms in India*, vol. 5, An Unfinished Agenda, pp. 29–44, SAGE Publications, New Delhi.

Hasan, Z. (1989), 'Power and Mobilization: Patterns of Resilience and Change in Uttar Pradesh Politics', in F. Frankel and M.S.A Rao (eds.), *Dominance and State Power in Modern India*, vol. 1, p. 108, Oxford University Press, Delhi.

Lieten, G.K. and R. Srivastava (1999), *Unequal Partners-Power Relations, Devolution and Development in Uttar Pradesh*, pp. 38–82, SAGE Publications, New Delhi.

Mehrotra, S. (2006), 'Well Being and Caste in Uttar Pradesh: Why UP Is not like Tamilnadu', *Economic and Political Weekly*, 7 October.

Mohanty, B.B. (2001), 'Land Distribution among Scheduled Castes and Tribes', *Economic and Political Weekly*, pp. 3857–3867.

Newell, R.S. (1972), 'Ideology and Realities: Land Distribution in UP', *Pacific Affairs*, XLV, p. 220.

Pai, S. (2000), 'Changing Socio-Economic and Political Profile of Scheduled Castes in Uttar Pradesh', *Journal of Indian School of Political Economy*, 12 (3/4), pp. 405–422.

Prasad, M. (1995), *Anusuchit Jatiyan aur Bhoomi Vyavastha Sudhar in Uttar Pradesh Ki Dalit Jatiyon Ka Dastavez*, pp. 64–69, Delhi Kitabghar, New Delhi.

Saxena, N.C. (1985), 'Caste and Zamindari Abolition in UP', *Mainstream*, 23 (42), pp. 15–19.

Shankar, K. (1999), 'Tenancy Reforms: Rhetoric and Reality', *Economic and Political Weekly*.

Sharma, A.N. (2005), 'Agrarian Relations and Socio-Economic Change in Bihar', *Economic and Political Weekly*.

Singh, B. and S. Mishra (1964), *A Study of Land Reforms in UP*, Oxford Book Company, Calcutta.

Srimali, P.D. (1981), *Agrarian Change, Agrarian Tensions, Peasant Movements and Organisation in Uttar Pradesh*, Department of Economics, University of Lucknow, mimeographed.

Thorner, D. and A. Thorner (1973), *Agrarian Prospect in India*, 2nd ed., Allied Publishing House, Delhi.

8

Asset Ownership and Terms of Tenancy Contracts: Caste and Class in a Village in Western UP

*Partha Saha**

Introduction

Economic well-being of a household in an agrarian economy is crucially linked to ownership of assets. Assets can not only be deployed in household enterprises, they can be used as collateral, sold in the markets and can be rented out. In an agrarian economy, for example, it is common to find rental markets for land and machinery. Furthermore, ownership of assets, most importantly of land, is an important determinant of the location of a household in the system of agrarian relations. Whether workers in a household sell their labour power or deploy it in their own household enterprise depends crucially on the extent to which they own various means of production.

Ownership of means of production varies across households, which necessarily implies that agricultural production is organised in different ways by different categories of households.[1] Moreover, households with different resource endowments will enter into different types of relations with each other in the process of agricultural production. Such relations can vary from village to village depending on various socio-economic factors.

*The author would like to thank Vikas Rawal for his extensive overall guidance, comments and suggestions on earlier versions of this paper. This work is a part of Project on Agrarian Relations in India (PARI) initiated by Foundation for Agrarian Studies in Kolkata. The author would also like to thank Prof. V.K. Ramachandran and Prof. Madhura Swaminathan for their guidance all throughout the work.

[1] For a detailed analysis of ownership of means of production in rural India, and in particular rural Uttar Pradesh, please refer to Saha (2009).

This chapter provides a case study from Harevli, a village in Bijnor district of western UP, about the impact of ownership of means of production on the nature of tenancy relations.[2] Also, this chapter illustrates how caste and class position of a household is intrinsically related to the ownership of assets, and thereby influences the outcome of tenancy contracts.

Section titled 'The Survey' provides a brief description of the survey. Section titled 'Basic Features of Economy and Society in Harevli' provides basic features of economy and society of the village. Section titled 'Ownership of Productive Assets in the Village' discusses very briefly the pattern of ownership of productive assets in the village. Section titled 'Land Relations in Harevli' analyses different types of tenancy contracts in Harevli. The last section provides some concluding remarks.

The Survey

A census survey of all households in the village was done during May–June 2006 as a part of the study titled 'Project on Agrarian Relations in India (PARI)' undertaken by the Foundation for Agrarian Studies, Kolkata. The PARI surveys are household-level surveys. For the purpose of these surveys, a household was defined as a group of persons who normally lived together and took food from a common kitchen.[3] The data were collected by a team of about 25 investigators. Questions were primarily addressed to the head of the households, although, if required, information was also collected from other members of the households. The detailed questionnaire canvassed in the survey included questions on demographic variables, landholdings, cropping pattern, crop production and sale, use of inputs, ownership of means of production and other assets, labour days employed on operational holdings, pattern of agricultural and non-agricultural labouring out, non-agricultural sources of income, household amenities

---

[2] According to the Census, 2001, the name of this village was Herwali. However, locally this village was known as Harevli, and this local name will be used for the present purpose.

[3] NSS uses a similar definition for the household.

and indebtedness.[4] The reference period for this study was the agricultural year 2005–2006 (i.e., June 2005 to May 2006).

Basic Features of Economy and Society in Harevli

Harevli is about 4 kilometres away from the nearest town, Mandavli, and about 14 kilometres away from the *tehsil* headquarters at Najibabad. In the absence of all-weather roads, connectivity — particularly during the monsoon season — was a major cause of concern for the people of this village. The residential area was segregated into different clusters, each inhabited by households belonging to a particular social group.

Population

There were 112 households and 658 persons in Harevli at the time of the survey (Table 8.1).

Tyagi was the dominant caste in the village. Dalit and Muslim households were often subjected to various forms of social and

---

[4] In the PARI survey schedule, data on assets were collected separately for landholdings, animal resources, other means of agricultural production and all other assets. In the section on landholdings, detailed data were collected on different types of land owned and operated by the household, on the extent of irrigation on agricultural land and on leases and mortgages. In the section on animal resources, data were collected on number and value of different types of animals owned by the household. In the section on other means of agricultural production, data were collected on agricultural machinery and implements owned by the household. Finally, in the last section of the survey schedule, data on all other assets owned by the household were collected. This section included a long list of assets including household durables. The respondents were asked, one by one, if they owned each of these assets. For the assets they owned, they were asked the number of items owned and the price they are likely to get for it if they sold it in the market. It is noteworthy that the assets have been valued at current market prices. Care was taken not to use either the original price at which the assets were purchased or the price at which a similar asset could be purchased. The respondents were asked to report the price at which assets could be sold. The valuation of the assets was done by the respondents keeping in view the markets for such assets.

Table 8.1
Caste Composition of Population, Harevli, 2006

Social group	Caste	Number of people	% share in total population
Dalit		239	36.3
	Chamar	221	33.6
	Balmiki	18	2.7
Muslim		68	10.3
OBC		148	22.5
	Dheemar	145	22.0
	Carpenter	3	0.5
Other Caste Hindu		203	30.9
	Tyagi	202	30.7
	Brahmin	1	0.2
All social groups		658	100.0

Source: Survey data.

economic oppression by households belonging to Tyagi caste.[5] Dalit and Muslim households occupied the lowest positions in the social hierarchy. They mostly worked as agricultural labourers and tenants for their livelihood.

[5] The harassment of Dalits (particularly the economically vulnerable ones) in the villages of Western UP has been reported in several village-level studies. These studies have documented incidents of exploitation of Dalits by upper castes, which were largely the consequences of the relationship of dependence. Singh (1992), based on village studies in Meerut district, pointed out to the existence of two types of dependence viz., one-sided dependence and mutual dependence. One-sided dependence represented the dependence of rural poor (mostly belonging to lower castes) on the rural rich (belonging to the upper castes). However, the concentration of means of production (particularly land) in the hands of the upper castes resulted in "one-sided dependence [being] more extensive, numerically larger than the relationship of mutual dependence". The author pointed out that "cases of harassment and oppression such as molestation and rape of women belonging to the rural poor of lower castes by the men of rural rich were not uncommon". Lieten and Srivastava (1999), based on their study of two villages in Muzaffarnagar district of Western Uttar Pradesh, observed that the dominance of Jats was unchallenged, which was extended to both Dalits and Muslims in the villages and false implications against Dalits and Muslims were not uncommon.

Economic Classification of Households

The most common indicator used for the purpose of classification of rural households is the size of landholding. The advantages of classifying households based on size classes lie in its easy applicability and uniformity across all the regions of the country. However, except for a very rough approximation of class status, such a measure is a very unsatisfactory one because it presupposes homogeneity in the productive potential of all types of land. As Ramachandran (1990) observed, "a single size category of land holding may conceal wide variations in the physical qualities of land — variations, for instance, in the irrigation and drainage facilities available to the land".

The economic classification of households in the study village was done on the basis of ownership of assets, principal source of income and whether the members of the households participated in any manual operation on their operational holding. The households were categorised into 11 economic classes (landlord, rich peasant, upper middle peasant, lower middle peasant, small peasant, manual labour, artisans, households whose main sources of incomes were from business activities other than direct crop production, households whose major earnings were from salaried employment [private or government], households whose main incomes were from remittances, pensions and scholarships, and households whose main incomes were from rent or money lending).

It may be noted that the caste and class status of households in the village were strongly correlated. Table 8.2 presents a class-caste matrix for the village. The table shows that Dalit, OBC and Muslim households were mainly concentrated in small peasant and manual worker classes. On the other hand, Other Caste Hindu households were concentrated in rich and upper middle peasant categories. The landlords, of course, belonged to the Tyagi caste.

Main Economic Activity

Agriculture was the mainstay of economy of Harevli. Income from crop production, rental income from agricultural land and orchards and income from wage labour in agriculture together

Table 8.2
Distribution of Household Belonging to Different Caste and Class, Harevli, 2006

	Dalit	OBC	Muslim	Other Caste Hindu	All social groups
Landlord	0	0	0	2	2
Rich peasant	0	1	0	9	10
Upper middle peasant	0	0	2	13	15
Lower middle peasant	5	3	3	6	17
Small peasant	15	11	2	0	28
Manual labour	18	4	4	0	26
Artisans	0	0	0	2	2
Business/self-employment	3	0	1	0	4
Households primarily dependent on salary	3	1	0	0	4
Households primarily dependent on remittances/pensions	1	0	1	0	2
Households primarily dependent on rent/money lending	1	0	0	1	2
All economic classes	46	20	13	33	112

Source: Survey data.

accounted for about 64 per cent of average household income in the village.[6]

Ownership of agricultural land in Harevli was highly unequal, with 73 per cent land being owned by the top 16 per cent of households while 33 per cent of households did not own any agricultural land (Table 8.3). Distribution of operational holdings was also highly unequal. About 26 per cent household did not operate any land, while another 26 per cent households operated a total of about

[6] Household income refers to the total income accruing to the household and aggregate earnings of the members of the household. The measurement of income in the study villages was associated with several difficulties primarily because of the fact that most rural households were simultaneously involved in production, consumption and investment and none of the households maintained any accounts of the transactions undertaken during the reference period. As a result, income had to be derived through a complex process of calculation based on detailed information (collected through household survey) on values of output produced and costs incurred in the economic activities during the reference period. For details of the methodology involved in calculation of household income, please see Rawal (2008), http://www.agrarianstudies.org.

Table 8.3
Size Class Distribution of Ownership of Agricultural Land, Harevli, 2006

Size class (acre)	% of households	% of area owned
Landless	33.0	0.0
Less than 0.50	21.4	2.4
0.50–1.00	4.5	0.9
1.01–2.00	7.1	3.3
2.01–4.00	12.5	11.3
4.01–6.00	5.4	9.0
Above 6.00	16.1	73.1
All size classes	100.0	100.0

Source: Survey data.

5 per cent of land. In contrast, top 19 per cent of operational holdings accounted for about 65 per cent of the total operated area (Table 8.4). The average size of operational holding in the village was 3.7 acres.

Cropping Pattern

An important feature of agriculture in Harevli was the availability of good irrigation facilities. The village came under the command area of Eastern Ganga Canal Project and was 100 per cent canal irrigated. In addition to canal, ground water, extracted using diesel

Table 8.4
Size Class Distribution of Operational Holding, Harevli, 2006

Size class (acre)	% of households	% of area operated
Landless	25.9	0.0
Less than 0.50	5.4	0.5
0.50–1.00	20.5	4.4
1.01–2.00	7.1	3.2
2.01–4.00	12.5	9.0
4.01–6.00	9.8	13.5
Above 6.00	18.8	69.4
All size classes	100.0	100.0

Source: Survey data.

or electric pumps, was also used extensively for the purpose of irrigation. The depth of ground water varied across different regions in the village with depth being 25–30 feet on the eastern side, while it varied between 40 and 60 feet on the west.

Sugarcane was by far the most important crop grown in the village and it accounted for about 53 per cent of gross cropped area. Sugarcane was an annual crop sown in January–February. After harvesting the first planted sugarcane crop, a ratoon sugarcane crop was harvested after 9–10 months (or, in other words, after 20–21 months after sowing). Cultivation of wheat accounted for about 21 per cent of the gross cropped area. Rest of the gross cropped area was cultivated with paddy and fodder crops (berseem, jowar, bajra). Mustard was cultivated as an inter-crop with wheat. Paddy was a kharif crop sown in June and harvested in October–November. Along with paddy, fodder (jowar and bajra) was also grown in the kharif season. After harvesting the kharif crop, land was prepared either for wheat or for sugarcane cultivation. Wheat was primarily grown for household consumption and only a small part (less than one-fifth) of the total village produce was sold to the grain merchants. Sugarcane was the principal cash crop and it was sold to the cane crushers and sugar mills situated outside the village.

Ownership of Productive Assets in the Village

Productive assets owned by the households in this village can be broadly classified as agricultural land and orchards, other means of agricultural production including draught animals and animal resources.

Ownership of Land

Concentration of land in the hands of Tyagi households was the fundamental feature of landownership in the village. The average value of crop land owned by Tyagi households was 20 times that of Dalit households, and 10 times that of Muslim and OBC households (Table 8.5). The difference across social groups was much more pronounced in case of ownership of orchard land.

Table 8.5

Average Value of Land (in ₹) and Proportion of Households Owning (%), by Social Groups, Harevli, 2006

Land type	Dalit		Muslim		OBC		Other Caste Hindu	
	Average	% of households owning	Average	% of households owning	Average	% of households owning	Average	% of households owning
Crop land	85,984	54.3	183,654	46.1	175,125	65.0	1,764,242	91.0
Orchard land	5,000	4.3	3,077	7.7	2,900	5.0	149,091	24.2

Source: Survey data.

Table 8.6
Distribution of Agricultural Land, by Size Class of Ownership Holding, by Social Groups, Harevli, 2006

Size class (acres)	Number of households				
	Dalit	*OBC*	*Muslim*	*Other Caste Hindu*	*All social groups*
Not owning any agricultural land	21	7	7	3	38
Less than 0.50	16	6	1	0	23
0.50–2.00	3	5	2	2	12
2.01–4.00	6	1	2	6	15
4.01–6.00	0	0	1	5	6
6.01–10.00	0	0	0	7	7
10.01 and above	0	1	0	10	11
All households	46	20	13	33	112

Source: Survey data.

Across size classes of agricultural land, Other Caste Hindu households were located at the higher-size classes, while large numbers of Dalit, Muslim and OBC households were either landless or owned small plots of land (Table 8.6). The incidence of landlessness was most pronounced among Muslim households in this village.

In fact, 30 per cent of Other Caste Hindu households owned more than 10 acres of agricultural land. Among Dalit households, 45 per cent did not own any agricultural land at all, while another 35 per cent owned less than 0.5 acre.

Ownership of Animal Resources

In Harevli, the value of animal resources constituted 1.5 per cent of the total value of assets. Like most other assets, Tyagi households accounted for the bulk of animal resources in the village. A feature of animal holdings in the village was that Tyagi households owned bulk of the bovines while relatively low-value animals like goats and poultry were commonly owned by Muslim households. From Table 8.7, we observe that there were substantial differences in the average values of household holdings of milch cows and

Table 8.7

Average Value (in ₹) of Animal Resources and Proportion of Households Owning (%), by Social Groups, Harevli, 2006

Type of livestock	Dalit		Muslim		OBC		Other Caste Hindu	
	Average value	% of households owning	Average value	% of households owning	Average value	% of households owning	Average value	% of households owning
Milch cow	321	8.7	1,230	7.7	1,700	25.0	4,269	42.4
Milch buffalo	4,173	32.6	2,346	30.8	6,680	65.0	2,3227	78.8
Calf	889	45.6	1,684	30.8	3,770	75.0	2,552	66.7
Others	504	15.2	1,603	46.1	0	0.0	0	0.0

Source: Survey data.

milch buffaloes as well as the proportion of households owning them across social groups in the village. As many as 78.8 per cent of Other Caste Hindu households owned milch buffaloes, and the average value was 5.6 times the average value for Dalit households, 9.9 times the average value for Muslim households and 3.5 times the average value for OBC households.

Ownership of Other Means of Agricultural Production

Other means of agricultural production include hand implements, powered machines (e.g., tractor and accessories, diesel pump, electric pump, trolley, thresher, disc plough and power tiller) and draught animals. In general, the prices of hand implements are much lower than those of powered machines and draught animals. In this section, the focus will be on ownership of powered machines and draught animals.

Rental markets for powered machines and draught animals are common in rural India. However, for a cultivator, ownership of machines and draught animals holds certain advantages over depending on the rental market to avail them. First, the cost of using the machine is typically lower for owners than for those who hire them. Second, ownership of machines and draught animals also ensures that they are at the disposal of their owners at all times. The owners can use them at the most appropriate time while those who hire machines/draught animals may have to schedule their use depending upon their availability. Third, owners of these assets often not only use them on their own operational holdings but also rent them out to those who do not own them. This gives them additional income.

Renting tractors and irrigation equipment was common in the village. An important feature of ownership of other means of agricultural production was that they were owned by those households that owned agricultural land. In other words, ownership of other means of agricultural production was conditional on the ownership of agricultural land. The primary motivation for the ownership of other means of agricultural production was not renting them out, but rather for own use. Therefore, the ownership of other means of agricultural production was related to the ownership of agricultural land. Moreover, items like tube wells were not portable and were fixed on a particular plot of land. Hence, ownership of tube wells was tied up with landownership, and investment in tube wells could only be made by the landowners.

The concentration of ownership of other means of agricultural production in Harevli was extremely high, and it was true for all major items in the category (Table 8.8). Of the various major items under this category, inequality was the lowest for draught animals and highest for tractors and accessories.

The most important agricultural machinery owned by the households in Harevli were irrigation equipment, and tractor and accessories. In addition to these, a few households also owned threshers.[7] In the present context, threshers have been considered as a part of other agricultural machinery.

Across social groups, the average values of other means of agricultural production and the proportion of households owning them were the highest for Other Caste Hindu households. Except for draught animals, the average values and the proportion of households owning them were the lowest among Dalit households (Table 8.9).

The lack of ownership of other means of agricultural production among Dalit, Muslim and OBC households was most glaring in the case of ownership of agricultural machinery. No Dalit household owned a tractor and only one Dheemar (OBC) and one Muslim household owned one. In contrast, there were 12 Tyagi households that owned tractors. Two among these owned two tractors each. Households owning a tractor also, typically, owned

Table 8.8

Concentration of Other Means of Agricultural Production (Gini Coefficient), Harevli, 2006

Item of means of production	Gini coefficient
Tractor and accessories	0.91
Irrigation equipment	0.79
Draught animals	0.65
All means of production	0.82

Source: Survey data.

[7] In Harevli, there were four households that owned a thresher. In addition to threshing their own crop, they rented out their threshing machines.

Table 8.9

Average Value of Other Means of Agricultural Production (in ₹) for Households Owning Them and Proportion of Households Owning (%), by Social Groups, Harevli, 2006

Item of means of production	Dalit		Muslim		OBC		Other Caste Hindu	
	Average value	% of households owning	Average value	% of households owning	Average value	% of households owning	Average value	% of households owning
Draught animals	9,598	26	7,690	31	8,980	65	11,817	70
Irrigation equipment	20,164	15	18,226	23	24,150	40	36,071	82
Tractor and accessories	0	0	216,337	8	358,800	5	144,986	36
Other machinery	0	0	0	0	14,770	10	12,717	30

Source: Survey data.

several accessories for use with it. These included different types of ploughs and tractor trolleys. In all, about 85 per cent of Other Caste Hindu households owned at least one powered machine or draught animals. In contrast, among Dalits, only 33 per cent households owned at least one item in this category.

The pattern of ownership of means of production in this village was characterised by a high degree of concentration within Other Caste Hindu (Tyagi) households belonging primarily to landlords and rich peasant economic classes, and lack of ownership of means of production among Dalit, Muslim and OBC households belonging primarily to small peasant and manual labour economic classes.

Land Relations in Harevli

Tenancy was an important institution in Harevli and it played a major role in the village economy. A large number of households (69 per cent) in Harevli accessed land through different forms of tenancy. Different types of tenancy contracts that existed in Harevli could be broadly classified as: (1) share rent contract where a share of crop output was paid as rent and (2) fixed rent contract where rent was fixed in advance, independent of the crop output.

Incidence of Tenancy

An interesting feature of land tenancy in Harevli was the presence of some households simultaneously as tenants and lessors in the lease market (Table 8.10).

This phenomenon of simultaneously leasing-in and leasing-out was absent among Muslim households, and was most commonly seen among Other Caste Hindu households. More than a quarter of Other Caste Hindu households (landlords, rich peasants and upper middle peasant classes) participated in the lease market simultaneously as tenants and as lessors. As lessors, they leased out small plots of land on seasonal share rent to Dalit, and OBC households, and as tenants they leased in large plots of land (at least larger than 1 acre) from Other Caste Hindu households,

Table 8.10
Percentage of Households by Tenancy Status, by Social Groups, Harevli, 2006

Social group of household	Only leasing in	Only leasing out	Both leasing in and leasing out	Neither leasing in nor leasing out	All households
Dalit	50	17	9	24	100
Muslim	23	15	0	62	100
OBC	60	5	5	30	100
Other Caste Hindu	0	45	27	28	100
All social groups	34	23	12	31	100

Source: Survey data.

most of whom resided outside the village. Among Dalit, OBC and Muslim households, participation as tenants in the lease market was more predominant, while Other Caste Hindu households were the dominant lessors. Dalit and OBC households, which were both tenants and lessors simultaneously in the lease market, leased in land from Other Caste Hindu (Tyagi) households on seasonal share rent for cultivation of paddy. The share of Dalit and OBC tenants in such cases was one-third of crop output. As landowners, Dalit and OBC households leased out land to households belonging to these two social groups on seasonal share rent as well as annual fixed rent.

Tenancy in Harevli took various forms and the only common feature in all lease contracts was the fact that labour was provided entirely by the tenants (whether it was the labour of the family members of the tenants' household or the casual labourers hired in by the tenants). It has already been pointed out that in Harevli both share tenancy contracts and fixed tenancy contracts existed. Between the two broad classifications of tenancy contracts, share tenancy was clearly the predominant form and the incidence of share tenancy was twice that of fixed-rent tenancy. Within the category of share contracts, several patterns of crop sharing and sharing of input were possible, and, to a very large extent, it depended on the socio-economic status of landowners and tenants. In fixed rent contracts, although in most cases rent was paid in cash, payment in crop was not totally absent. Table 8.11 depicts information about incidence of tenancy across social groups and economic classes.

Table 8.11

Incidence of Tenancy by Social Groups and by Class, Harevli, 2006

Classification of households	Leasing in				Leasing out			
	Proportion of households leasing in annually	Annually leased in area as proportion of operated area	Proportion of households seasonally leasing in	Seasonally leased-in area as proportion of operated area	Proportion of households leasing out annually	Annually leased out area as proportion of owned area	Proportion of households seasonally leasing out	Seasonally leased-out area as proportion of owned area
By Social Group								
Dalit	15	13	46	37	22	15	4	5
OBC	30	43	50	21	10	12	0	0
Muslim	0	0	31	21	7	3	7	4
Other Caste Hindu	27	21	0	0	9	3	67	19
By Class								
Landlord	50	19	0	0	0	0	100	13
Rich peasant	40	8	0	0	20	4	90	20
Upper middle peasant	20	35	0	0	0	0	73	25
Lower middle peasant	47	39	18	5	18	10	18	5
Small peasant	18	24	78	56	4	5	4	4
Manual labour	0	0	31	100	15	77	0	0
All Households	20	22	30	7	13	4	23	17

Source: Survey data.

Note: Partial leasing implies leasing in/out for one crop season and not for the whole year.

Leasing in cropland was more common as compared to leasing out in the case of Dalit, Muslim and OBC households, while leasing out land was predominant among Other Caste Hindu households. Among Dalit, Muslim and OBC households, the proportion of households leasing in land for one season (which implies partially leasing in land) was higher than the proportion of households leasing in land annually. From Table 8.11, it can be observed that 46 per cent of Dalit households, 50 per cent of OBC households and 31 per cent of Muslim households leased in land for one season on share-rent contract, while Other Caste Hindu households never leased in land on a seasonal contract basis. Households seasonally leasing in land belonged to the lowest classes, namely small peasant and manual labour. Although seasonal leasing-in existed in the case of lower middle peasantry as well, it was more prevalent among small peasant and manual labour households. In fact, manual labour households could lease in land only on a seasonal share contract basis. Other Caste Hindu households (landlords, rich peasant and upper middle peasant households) in the village leased in land only on annual fixed-rent contracts.

In case of leasing-out, Dalit and Muslim households leased out both on annual contracts and on seasonal contracts. As far as leasing-out was concerned, manual labour households owned very little land (1.75 acres in all), and most of it was leased out on annual contract, and the households depended on wage income from agricultural labouring out. On the other hand, seasonal leasing-out predominated among Other Caste Hindu households, although annual leasing-out was not totally absent. The Other Caste Hindu households belonging to landlords, rich peasants and upper middle peasant classes leased out land to Dalit, Muslim and OBC social groups for one crop season on a share rental basis.

It may be recalled that in Harevli, there was a strong congruence between caste and class. Dalit, Muslim and OBC households, belonging to small peasant and manual labour classes, could lease in land only for one season on a crop-sharing basis. As lessors, they leased out within their social groups on an equal crop-sharing basis. On the other hand, Other Caste Hindu households, belonging to upper classes, leased in land only on annual contract. As lessors, they leased out land for one crop season (paddy) to Dalit, Muslim

Table 8.12

Distribution of Lessors, Tenants, Leased-out Area and Leased-in Area, by Size Class of Ownership Holding, Harevli, 2006

Size class of land ownership (acre)	Number of households			% share in total leased out area	% share in total leased in area
	Lessors	Tenants	All households		
Landless	na	17	37	na	12.7
Up to 0.50	10	18	27	4.8	22.5
0.51 – 2.00	3	5	10	9.3	35.2
2.01 – 4.00	7	7	14	11.9	7.4
4.01 – 6.00	5	1	7	6.4	2.4
6.01 – 10.00	4	1	6	9.5	2.9
Above 10.00	11	4	11	58	16.8
All size classes	40	53	112	100	100

Source: Survey data.
Note: 'na' implies not applicable.

and OBC households. When households were classified according to size class of ownership holding, it was observed that one-third of the tenants were landless and another one-third of the tenants owned less than 0.5 acre of land (Table 8.12). In other words, two-third of tenant households owned less than 0.5 acre of land, all belonging to Dalit, Muslim and OBC social groups, and leasing in land for one crop season only.

The lessors were concentrated at the two extreme size classes of land ownership. All households owning more than 10 acres of cropland were lessors along with more than one-third of the households owning less than 0.5 acre of land. Households belonging to the lowest size class owning cropland and the highest size class together constituted more than half of the households leasing out agricultural land. The area leased out by the highest size class constituted 58 per cent of total leased out area. Lessors at the lower size class of land ownership belonged to Dalit and OBC households, leasing out land within these two social groups on an equal crop-sharing basis. On the other hand, lessors at the higher size classes of land ownership belonged to Other Caste Hindu households, leasing out land to Dalit, Muslim and OBC households only for paddy cultivation.

Types of Tenancy Contracts

As already mentioned, tenancy contract in the village was predominated by the existence of share tenancy. Within the two broad categories of tenancy contracts (fixed and share), a lot of variations were observed. This was particularly true in the case of share tenancy where different combinations of sharing of crop outputs and inputs existed. The complication was not only the result of multiple crop sharing and input sharing arrangements that existed in the village, but was also because of the fact that households belonging to the same socio-economic groups participated in the lease market both as tenants and as lessors, and in a few cases, the same households participated simultaneously both as lessors and as tenants (already observed in Tables 8.10 and 8.11). In all tenancy contracts, socio-economic status of households and patterns of ownership of means of production were important factors determining the specific forms of tenancy contracts. In Harevli, the different types of tenancy contracts could be broadly classified under four different types. In what follows, these four different types of tenancy contracts are analysed.

Fixed-rent Tenancy between Non-resident Tyagi Lessors and Resident Tyagi Tenants (Type 1)

A large amount of land in the village was owned by non-resident Tyagi households, which had migrated to Delhi and other urban areas for non-agricultural businesses and salaried jobs. Such Tyagi non-resident landowners leased out their land to resident Tyagi households and typically had kinship ties with the tenants. In such cases, the tenants belonged to landlord, rich peasant and upper middle peasant classes and owned substantial means of production. In addition to non-resident Tyagis, there were two lessor households in which resident members were too old to cultivate land and the working-age members had migrated from the village. These two Tyagi households also leased out their entire land to other Tyagi households in the village.

These tenancy contracts were fixed-rent contracts payable in cash. While the rent was paid annually, the tenancy contracts were renewed year after year and most tenants had been cultivating the land for a substantial number of years. In a number of cases, half of the rent was paid at the beginning of the crop year and the remaining after the crop harvest.

Sugarcane was the main crop cultivated on land leased under such contracts. The average rental income of the landowners from such tenancy contracts was ₹6,206 per acre; this constituted about 26.6 per cent of the gross value of output from the land. On the other hand, the net income of the tenants was ₹2,113 per acre; this constituted 9.3 per cent of the gross value of output.

It is noteworthy that the tenants who cultivated land under such contracts themselves owned enough means of production including large amounts of land. The tenants belonged mostly to the rich peasantry and upper middle peasantry and, in addition to land, they owned substantial amount of other means of production, particularly agricultural machinery. The tenancy contracts only added to the process of accumulation for such tenant households. All the tenant households in such contracts owned irrigation equipment (diesel or electric pump sets in addition to other equipment) and the average value was ₹32,700; 50 per cent of households owned tractor and accessories with an average value of ₹1,53,812 and 75 per cent of households owned draught animals with an average value of ₹9,792 (Table 8.13). The 25 per cent of households that did not own draught animals owned tractor and accessories instead. In addition to owning large plots of irrigated land themselves (10.4 acres on average), these tenant households leased in substantial amounts of land (7.6 acres on average) for cultivation of sugarcane.

It is also noteworthy that the lessors in such cases were long-term migrants who were unlikely to return to the village and resume self-cultivation. The landowners were interested in retaining control over the land for as long as possible, getting substantial returns from the land and keeping the land within the extended family and caste. In addition to the motivation to keep the land within the family, another factor that resulted in land being leased only to Tyagi tenants was that only Tyagi households had financial resources and means of production required for cultivating irrigated crops like sugarcane.

The fixed-rent contract in these cases suited both the tenants and the lessors. Under a fixed-rent contract, the lessors did not have to supervise cultivation at all. On the other hand, being rich peasants themselves, the tenants took land under a fixed-rent contract

Table 8.13
Household Characteristics of Tenant Households in Type 1 Tenancy Contract, Harevli, 2006

Number of tenants		8	
Caste			
Tyagi		8	
Class			
Landlord		1	
Rich peasant		3	
Upper middle peasant		4	
Extent of land (acre)	*Minimum*	*Average*	*Maximum*
Leased-in	1.0	7.6	30.0
Owned	1.8	10.4	34.0
Rent as proportion of gross value of output	13.0	35.0	26.6
Ownership of other means of agricultural production	*Number of households owning*		*Average value (₹) for households owning*
Draught animals	6		9,792
Irrigation equipment	8		32,700
Tractor and accessories	4		153,812

Source: Survey data.

in which the rent, as a share, constituted only about one-fourth of the value of produce. Given that irrigated crops were cultivated on the land, the production risk was relatively low.

SHARE TENANCY CONTRACTS BETWEEN NON-RESIDENT TYAGI LESSORS AND DALIT/OBC TENANTS (TYPE 2)

This type of tenancy contracts involved non-resident Tyagi land-owners leasing out land to Dalit or OBC households. Unlike the non-resident Tyagi landowners in Type 1 contract, the non-resident Tyagi landowners in this case lived in nearby towns and villages, and visited the village frequently during the course of agricultural operations. Although they were engaged in various kinds of salaried employment and businesses, they were not totally detached from agriculture. Of the tenants, six households were Dalit (Chamar) and the other seven belonged to Dheemar caste (OBC). In terms of class status, seven belonged to lower middle peasant class, five to small peasant class and one household was primarily dependent on salaried employment (Table 8.14).

The terms and conditions of such tenancy contract involved equal crop sharing between landowners and tenants. In addition to half of the crop share, the tenants retained the entire by-product. However, all inputs—material inputs as well as labour—were provided by the tenants. The contracts were annual and sugarcane was the most commonly cultivated crop.

On average, rent in these contracts constituted 47 per cent of gross value of output. It is clear that Dalit and OBC households

Table 8.14
Household Characteristics of Tenant Households in Type 2 Tenancy Contract, Harevli, 2006

Number of tenants		13	
Caste			
Chamar		6	
Dheemar		7	
Class			
Lower middle peasant		7	
Small peasant		5	
Households primarily dependent on salary		1	

Extent of land (acre)	*Minimum*	*Average*	*Maximum*
Leased-in	0.3	2.3	9.4
Owned	0.0	1.1	2.1
Rent as proportion of gross value of output	25.0	47.1	57.0

Ownership of other means of agricultural production	*Number of households owning*	*Average value (₹) for households owning*
Draught animals	13	9,356
Irrigation equipment	8	18,125
Tractor and accessories	1	265,000

Source: Survey data.

who leased in land under annual contracts paid a share rent, which in terms of its value was considerably higher than the fixed rent paid by Tyagi households who leased land for cultivation of crops like sugarcane (under Type 1 contracts). At the same time, it is interesting to examine how a few Dalit and OBC households were able to get land for cultivation of crops like sugarcane. The explanation for this lies in the fact that, unlike most Dalit and OBC households, these households owned certain means of production. More than half of the tenant households (62 per cent) who cultivated land under Type 2 contracts owned more than 1 acre of agricultural land (Table 8.14). All these households owned draught animals. More than half of the households (62 per cent) owned irrigation equipment and one household even owned a tractor. It is clear that these Dalit or OBC households got access to irrigated land for cultivation of sugarcane and other profitable crops because of ownership of means of production.

SEASONAL SHARE-RENT TENANCY CONTRACTS BETWEEN DALIT AND OBC HOUSEHOLDS (TYPE 3)

In this type of contract, a Dalit or OBC landowning household that did not have enough working capital or means of production leased out to another Dalit or OBC household on a share tenancy contract. Under these contracts, the lessor and the tenant shared the produce equally. Typically, the lessor also provided an equal share in some or all of the costs of material inputs. This type of tenancy arrangement was mainly done for cultivation of wheat. It may be noted that wheat was primarily an irrigated crop in the village, while sugarcane and paddy were sown during the monsoon season (though both required supplementary irrigation). As a result, access to irrigation and ownership of irrigation equipment was crucial for wheat cultivation.

The caste profile of lessors and lessee households under this type of contract shows that lessors came primarily from the Chamar caste, while the tenants came both from Chamar and Dheemar castes. In terms of the class status, lessors belonged to lower middle peasant and small peasant classes. One household depended on salaried employment, while one household belonged to manual labour class. An interesting point in Type 3 tenancy contract was that Dheemar households did not lease out land to Chamar

Table 8.15
Caste Matrix of Lessor and Lessee in Type 3 Tenancy Contract, Harevli, 2006

	Lessee	
Lessor	Chamar	Dheemar
Chamar	3	2
Dheemar	0	1

Source: Survey data.

households (Table 8.15). Asset position of Chamar households in the village being weaker, Dheemar households always leased out land to other Dheemar households under Type 3 tenancy contracts.

The average net rental income of households that leased out land under such contracts was only ₹1,945 per annum (₹4,452 per acre per annum). The rents in this type of tenancy contract were much lower than that in Type 1 and Type 2 contracts. The crop grown under this type of contract was wheat, while under Type 1 and Type 2 contracts it was primarily sugarcane. It is noteworthy that lessors in this type of tenancy arrangements were asset-poor households. Of the six lessor households of this type in the village, five of them owned below 0.5 acre of land, three of them owned draught animals, only one household owned irrigation equipment and none of them owned tractor (Table 8.16). Clearly then, undertaking crop production, particularly in the *rabi* season, was difficult for such households.

SEASONAL SHARE TENANCY CONTRACTS BETWEEN RESIDENT TYAGI LESSORS AND DALIT/MUSLIM/OBC TENANT HOUSEHOLDS (TYPE 4)

This type of tenancy contract was the most widespread in the village. It not only depicted the economic relation between the landowner and the tenant, but also clearly highlighted the position of dominance of Tyagi households in the socio-economic hierarchy in this village. They owned 85 per cent of the total value of land and 68 per cent of the total value of non-land means of production in the village. In this type of tenancy contract, resident Tyagi households belonging to landlord, rich peasant and upper middle peasant economic classes were the lessors. Tenants belonged to Dalit, Muslim and OBC households, belonging primarily to small peasant and manual labour classes, and owning no agricultural land at all or small plots of land (less than 0.5 acre). Ownership of

Table 8.16
Household Characteristics of Lessor Households in Type 3 Tenancy Contract, Harevli, 2006

Number of lessors		6	
Caste			
Chamar		5	
Dheemar		1	
Class			
Lower middle peasant		2	
Small peasant		2	
Manual labour		1	
Households primarily dependent on salary		1	
Extent of land (Acre)	*Minimum*	*Average*	*Maximum*
Leased-out	0.2	0.4	0.8
Owned	0.3	1.0	3.4
Rent received (₹)			
Total rent	400	1,945	6,000
Rent per acre	2,000	4,452	7,500
Ownership of other means of agricultural production (₹)	*Number of households owning*		*Average value (₹) for households owning*
Draught animals	3		11,333
Irrigation equipment	1		3,000
Tractor and accessories	0		0

Source: Survey data.

any non-land means of production for such tenant households was extremely rare, and they had to depend on manual labour, mainly in agriculture, for their survival.

The resident Tyagi households, being landowners in such tenancy contracts, leased out land to Dalit, Muslim and OBC households on share rent for a period of one season for paddy cultivation. The tenants could only retain one-third of the crop output, whereas the landowner took two-third of crop output along with the entire by-product. Landowners generally shared a part of the input cost. In most of the cases, the landowners ploughed the field with his tractor before handing over the land to the tenants. In general, the landowners shared a greater part of costs of material inputs when the land was leased out for a season to one of their long-term workers.

The Dalit, Muslim and OBC tenants entering into such tenancy contracts owned very little land and other means of production. Out of 29 tenant households under such contract, 14 did not own any agricultural land, while the remaining 15 owned not more than 0.5 acre. The average size of agricultural land owned by such tenant households was 0.2 acre (Table 8.17). Only three households owned some irrigation equipment, and eight of them owned draught animals, out of which five of them owned only one draught animal. The ownership of single draught animal meant that the households had to share them with other households for the purpose of ploughing. In addition to ploughing the fields through sharing arrangements, the draught animals were also used for transporting, which was a source of rental income for the households.

Clearly, the lack of ownership of means of production by Dalit, Muslim and OBC households resulted in their dependence on wage employment for survival. The tenants worked on the land cultivated by the landowners as wage labourers, which could only be assured to them if they accepted the seasonal share rental contract for the cultivation of paddy. Thus, the linkage between the tenancy market and labour market was established through this relation of dependence. In other words, Tyagi households, owning the bulk of agricultural land and other non-land means of production, provided wage employment to Dalit, Muslim and OBC households conditional on their acceptance of the seasonal share rental contract. The motive for Dalit, Muslim and OBC households in accepting such onerous terms of contracts was the assurance of wage employment on the operational holdings of the landowners. Most commonly, land was given by these landowners for paddy cultivation in the *kharif* season to their long-term workers. The tenants also had to provide un-paid or under-paid labour services to their landowners. The various forms of labour services involved working at the employer's house during some ceremonies, cleaning the employer's house every morning before working in the field, and doing various kinds of animal husbandry work like feeding animals, milking and cleaning dung.

The lack of ownership of the means of production by Dalit, Muslim and OBC households provided the Tyagi households with the opportunity to exploit them by appropriating, on average, about

Table 8.17
Household Characteristics of Tenant Households in Type 4 Tenancy Contract, Harevli, 2006

Number of tenants		29	
Caste			
Chamar		20	
Muslim		3	
Dheemar		6	
Class			
Small peasant		20	
Manual labour		8	
Business/self-employment		1	
Extent of land (acre)	*Minimum*	*Average*	*Maximum*
Leased-in	0.1	0.8	4.6
Owned	0.0	0.2	0.5
Rent as proportion of gross value of output	50.4	65.2	84.9
Ownership of other means of agricultural production	*Number of households owning*		*Average value (₹) for households owning*
Draught animals	8		8,250
Irrigation equipment	3		5,067
Tractor and accessories	0		0

Source: Survey data.

65 per cent of the gross value of output. The exploitation of these tenants was extended through the inter-linkage between tenancy contracts and wage employment, which also included labour services. The situation was that of compulsive market participation for the asset-poor Dalit, Muslim and OBC households on extremely onerous terms for sheer survival.

Concluding Remarks

Ownership of assets is an important determinant, along with other socio-economic factors, of where a household is situated in the system of production relations in an agrarian economy. Asset base of a household plays a crucial role in determining its nature of participation in agrarian markets. This chapter provides a case study from Harevli to illustrate how participation in tenancy relations and the terms of tenancy contracts were influenced by ownership of means of production.

This village on the one hand was characterised by a high degree of concentration of means of production (in particular land and agricultural machinery) within Other Caste Hindu (Tyagi) households belonging primarily to landlord and rich peasant economic classes, and on the other it was characterised by lack of ownership of means of production among Dalit, Muslim and OBC households belonging primarily to small peasant and manual labour economic classes. This asymmetry in ownership of means of production across households belonging to different castes and economic classes had its impact on the tenancy relations in the village.

Tenancy was an important institution in the system of agricultural production in Harevli. About 69 per cent of households were involved in tenancy contracts. There were four different types of tenancy contracts in Harevli. Households belonging to different castes and having different asset base participated in different types of tenancy contracts.

Some rich and upper middle peasants belonging to Tyagi caste leased in large plots of land from non-resident Tyagi landowners on annual fixed-rent basis for the cultivation of sugarcane. Such tenant households owned sufficient means of production of their own. On average, these tenants paid ₹6,206 per acre rent for the leased-in land.

In contrast, relatively asset-poor OBC households leased land from Tyagi landowners living in nearby villages and towns on share contracts. These tenants came from small and lower-middle peasant backgrounds and paid, on average, ₹9,223 per acre rent on land.

The most oppressive tenancy contracts were those under which landlords and rich peasants belonging to Tyagi caste leased land to the most asset-poor Dalit households. These lands were leased on seasonal contracts for paddy cultivation. The tenants in these contracts were, most commonly, persons who also worked as long-term workers for the landlords. These tenant-cum-long-term workers had to provide various kinds of unpaid labour services to the landowners. These tenants paid, on average, a rent of ₹9,498 per acre for cultivating the land in one season.

In contrast with asset-wealthy landowners, poor Dalit landowners who did not own complementary means of production or have access to finance for cultivation leased out land on low rent to other Dalit or OBC households. Such landowners got the lowest (on average, ₹4,452 per acre) rent on the land.

Successful implementation of land reform programmes and, in particular, tenancy reform programmes can make way for bringing an end to the subjugation of Dalit, Muslim and OBC households by Tyagi households.

This chapter argued that along with the social disparities associated with caste system, a skewed distribution of land and other productive assets resulted in a differential access of households to the tenancy markets. The asset-poor Dalit, Muslim and OBC households obtained land under extremely oppressive terms. On the other hand, asset-rich Tyagi households extracted substantial rent as lessors and extracted unpaid labour services through interlinked tenancy and wage labour contracts. As lessors, they paid modest rent on land leased in from non-residents and used it for profitable sugarcane cultivation.

In the context of the study village (Harevli) it can be argued that if tenancy in agricultural land is legalised, it will benefit the land-scarce Dalit, Muslim and OBC households, which have no protection against the landowning Tyagi households and have to accept lease contracts on extremely onerous terms and conditions.[8] If tenancy is legalised and tenancy acts have sufficient security for the tenants like in the West Bengal Land Reform Act (1977), then it can reduce the threat of being evicted for not accepting the extremely onerous terms and conditions of the contract.[9] However, the issue of political will and grass root mobilisation of the peasantry for the effective implementation of land reforms still remains a big question mark.

---

[8] There are a lot of variations in tenancy legislations across different states in India. In some states it is completely banned (Kerala, Jammu and Kashmir), while in others a lot of restrictions are put in place. In Uttar Pradesh, leasing is prohibited except in case of widows, unmarried women, student and PHC person (Mehrotra, 2008).

[9] According to the West Bengal Land Reform Act (1977), the burden of proving that the sharecropper is not a sharecropper lies with the landowner.

References

Lieten, G.K. and R. Srivastava (1999), *Unequal Partners: Power Relations, Devolution and Development in Uttar Pradesh*, SAGE Publications, New Delhi.

Mehrotra, S. (2008), 'Land Relations — A 11th Plan Perspective', paper presented at National Seminar on Land Reforms in Uttar Pradesh: Retrospect and Prospects, 12–13 August.

Saha, P. (2009), 'Land Relations and Asset Holdings: A Study Based on Village-Level Evidence from Uttar Pradesh', unpublished Ph.D. thesis submitted to Jawaharlal Nehru University, New Delhi.

Singh, J. (1992), *Capitalism and Dependence: Agrarian Politics in Western Uttar Pradesh, 1951–1991*, Manohar Publishers, New Delhi.

Ramachandran, V.K. (1990), *Wage Labour and Unfreedom in Agriculture: An Indian Case Study*, Clarendon Press, Oxford.

Rawal, V. (2008), 'Estimation of Rural Household Incomes in India: Selected Methodological Issues', paper presented at Studying Village Economies in India: A Colloquium on Methodology, 21–24 December 2008.

9

The Unfinished Agenda of Land Reforms: A Qualitative Assessment

Kripa Shankar

This chapter argues that every stage of what has been called 'land reform' in UP has enlarged the bigger landowners, in terms of their both political and economic power, whether it was the *zamindari* abolition of 1951 (section titled '*Zamindari* Abolition'), the Land Ceiling Act that followed soon after (section titled 'Ceiling') or the spread of tenancy (section titled 'Tenancy') that resulted from the extreme inequality of landholding that was, in turn, created by the *zamindari* abolition and the ineffective implementation of land ceiling laws.

Zamindari Abolition

The UP Zamindari Abolition Committee Report, which is supposed to be the most radical among such reports of other states where *zamindari* was abolished, was wholly opposed to any land redistribution despite the fact that it had noted that less than 2 per cent of the *zamindars* in UP owned nearly 58 per cent of the land. It had found that the top 9,000 *zamindars* owned above 100 acres of land each and that their *sir* and *khudkast* land alone constituted one-fourth of the agricultural land. Still the Report observed that "... we do not think that the result achieved (through land redistribution) would be commensurate with the discontent and hardship resulting from it. We, therefore, recommend that no limit be placed on the maximum area held in cultivation." (Government of UP, 1948, p. 389). It further observed that land distribution would "increase the difficulty of *zamindars* in adjusting them to change conditions". And further it opposed distribution of land on the strange logic that "the dismemberment of large holdings would have the result of displacing a large number of agricultural labourers" (Government of UP, 1948, p. 389). The UP Zamindari and Land Reforms Act that was passed in 1950 follows the recommendations of the Committee and did not envisage any redistribution of land. The Act was enforced only in July 1952 and gave ample time to *zamindars* to grant *patta* of *gram samaj* and other lands to influential persons on payment of *Nazrana*. The poor were nowhere in the picture. The Act had vested all cultivable wasteland, pastures, etc. to the *Gram Sabha* (GS), which amounted to about 93 lakh acres, which could be given on *patta* to the landless as also to farmers with holdings up to 3.125 acres through the Land Management Committee (LMC), which was to be constituted in every GS with the *Pradhan* as president and *Lekhpal* as secretary. The two were all-in-all as the LMC only existed on paper. They allotted the GS land to those who were close to them, were members of their own family or sometimes in their own name or those who greased their palms. It alarmed the government, which legislated that approval of SDM was necessary. It was only a formality and even if a complaint was made, the latter would refer to the *Tehsildar* for enquiry, who in turn will ask the same *Lekhpal* to enquire. The latter would report that allotment has been done according to rules. The Bhoomi Vyawastha Janch Samity (Government of UP, 1974), popularly known as Mangaldev Vishrad Committee, expressed its grave dismay over the distribution of GS land to ineligible persons.

Ceiling

The UP Imposition of Ceiling of Land Holding Act, 1960, provided a high ceiling of 40 acres for fair-quality land and if the family was of more than five members it could go up to 64 acres. It provided for various exemptions and the large landowners took full advantage of it. Hardly 2 lakh acres of land could be declared surplus. The Act was amended and the UP Land Ceiling (Amendment) Act, 1972, reduced the ceiling limit to 7.3 ha. The ceiling could go up to 13.3 ha. if the family had more than five members. Certain exemptions were withdrawn. There had been a spate of fictitious transfers ever since ceiling measures were talked about. The amended act significantly recognised as valid all transfers made prior to January 1971. The landowners invariably approached the courts challenging the notices issued to them. According to Annual Report of Ministry of Rural Development, Government of India 2006–2007 as regards UP out of 369,362 acres of land declared as ceiling surplus land, 339,385 acres had been taken possession, out of which only 263,225 acres had been distributed. The fact that only 70 per cent of the land declared as surplus could be distributed so far speaks volumes about the 'success' of the ceiling measures. This constitutes slightly more than 0.7 per cent of the net sown area in the state and is generally the most inferior land. The landowners have the option to declare land of their choice as surplus ceiling land and naturally they declare the worst land as surplus, which may be even unfit for cultivation. They have currently 14 lakh acres of land that is barren and unfit for agriculture. At the time of imposition of ceiling, they had nearly 30 lakh acres as barren and unfit for cultivation. Obviously it was this land out of which land for ceiling was surrendered. Similar is the case with cultivable waste land.

When ceiling surplus land is allotted to a beneficiary, the latter cannot take possession until the same is demarcated by the *Lekhpal*, who mints money in the process. On account of *cordiale entente* between large landowners and the *Lekhpal*, the latter would not like to go against the former. Even if the *Lekhpal* demarcates, it the owner who may refuse to vacate the land. He may say that this part of the plot has not been allotted as usually the plot is much larger in area from which land is allotted for redistribution. Can the poorest person who often depends on the same landlord for his livelihood come one fine morning with his plough and bullock and begin tilling the land and ask the landlord to get out of the land? How many of the allottees are actually cultivating the land distributed to them and to what extent it has been distributed in favour of landless and other poor who are entitled to it are moot questions. Periodic drives by the state government to give possession to beneficiaries of the land distributed show that land distribution has been mostly done on paper (Shankar, 1990).

Developmental process has resulted in shifting of the agricultural population to non-agricultural activities primarily to industries in the developed countries over the years. But the experience in India and in its various states has been different. Although an overwhelmingly large part of the investment is going to the non-agricultural sector, adequate jobs are not being created on account of its being highly capital intensive in the first instance and whatever job opportunities are being created are skill intensive, which the rural poor lack. As only 5 per cent of the investment goes in rural areas, very few job opportunities are coming up there although there is vast possibility of job creation in the rural areas in infrastructural development, particularly construction of roads, water harvesting structures, storages, etc. Extension of irrigation leads to more intensive agriculture, thereby creating more jobs in that sector. Labour use per unit of land in countries like China, Korea, Japan, etc., has a much higher level of irrigation, but with the much lower irrigation intensity in UP the possibility of employing more persons in agriculture hardly exists. The rising rural labour force is forced to continue with agriculture even with very low incomes as there is no alternative. In UP the growth of marginal holdings of less than 1 ha. is shown in Table 9.1.

Average size of a marginal holding is 0.40 ha. and average size of a holding in UP is 0.83 ha. The number of marginal holdings in UP is rising annually by over 2 lakh. Sub-marginal holding of less than 0.5 ha. is rising even faster.

There is no doubt that there is great disparity in the ownership of land as the area held by the top 1 per cent of the rural house-holds is equal to the area held by the bottom nearly 60 per cent of the households. But any measure to acquire land without any compensation will witness great resistance.

The acquisition of ceiling surplus land and its distribution are beset with great difficulties as landowners wield political and social power in the villages. They provide wage employment and con-sumption loans to the poor. The lower rung of revenue bureaucracy comes from this class and would not go against them. For example the *Lekhpal* is required to record all the land that is leased out by landowners but no *Lekhpal* ever does so and no DM, *Tehsildar* or

Table 9.1
Growth of Marginal Holdings (Less than 1 ha.) in UP

	Lakh	%
1985–1986	137.8	72.6
1990–1991	150.0	73.8
1995–1996	155.7	75.6
2000–2001	166.6	76.9

Source: Board of Revenue, UP, *Agricultural Census* (various years).

SDM bothers to ask them to do so. Now the same *Lekhpal* is enjoined to demarcate the surplus land. And even if he demarcates the land, can the poorest of the poor who depends on the landowner for his livelihood one fine morning ask him to vacate his land? Can he dare come forward and prevent the landlord from ploughing the field for which he is permitted under the Act until actual possession is given to the allottee. He can do so only when the landlord agrees to allow him to cultivate the demarcated plot.[1]

The government is promoting the policy of Special Economic Zones by facilitating the acquisition of even highly fertile agricultural land as when farmers get a very high price they sell the land. The banks are providing huge finance to the real estate sector. The poor have no access to bank finance. Under these circumstances, government intervention should be to directly purchase land at market price for redistribution to the poor.

In this connection, the government can also intervene in the land market. It has been estimated that 0.1 per cent of the agricultural land is being purchased and sold every year. The Panchayats should be empowered to negotiate such deals and provided with funds to purchase such land to be distributed to the poor.

The failure of the land distribution programme has largely been due to the fact that it was an expropriatory one. The World Bank (2001) is also emphasising it. As even a much higher rate of growth of the economy is not likely to lessen the burden on agriculture, the only option is that the government should purchase land from bigger landowners at market price and distribute the same to the poor through the Panchayats.

Tenancy

If there is large landlessness at the bottom of the land distribution pyramid along with extreme concentration of land at the top, then leasing will continue to exist clandestinely even if it is illegal. This

[1] Surplus land to be demarcated for distribution is small and the plot out of which it has to be demarcated is large. The *Lekhpal* puts no boundary indication on the actual plot to be distributed and mints money in the process from allottees for demarcating the actual area. Even after the demarcation the landlord may turn away the allottee saying that this is not the portion that he had surrendered.

has been the case in UP ever since leasing was made illegal when *zamindari* was abolished more than five decades ago. The number of landless and small farmers is increasing, with no decline in the concentration ratio. As the trend is likely to continue in the foreseeable future, providing security of tenure and increasing the share of the lessees have been the concerns of all but cannot be implemented in the context of increasing pressure on land. As leasing is illegal no statutory measure can be undertaken to provide greater security raising the share. The first step should be to make it legal so that the lessors may not frequently change the lessees and thus some degree of security may be provided in an indirect manner. But the lessors cannot countenance any increase in the share of the produce for in that case they may opt for fixed produce and now fixed money is proving to be more attractive as it absolves them from any risk of cultivation. If there is any loss the lessees will have to bear it.

In UP in the village *Khatauni* maintained by the Lekhpal there is no record of leasing activity.

Hence officially there is no land under lease. National Sample Survey provides data on leased land, but there is considerable under-reporting because lessors do not want such a phenomenon to be recorded. According to the 48th round of NSS 1992 data, nearly 6 per cent of the rural households lease out land and nearly 17 per cent lease in land. The data show that nearly 8 per cent of leased-in area was under fixed money, 19 per cent was on fixed produce, 56 per cent of the area was on share of produce together with other terms, 7 per cent was on share of produce with no specified terms, 7 per cent from relatives and so on.

Given the assertion of Dalits in UP politics the lessors are apprehensive and in order to pre-empt any measure to benefit the lessees they are increasingly moving towards fixed money as in that case its becomes a contractual arrangement as opposed to a share cropping one. It will be outside the ambit of any law to provide greater share or security to the lessees if the land is given on fixed money.

Concluding Remarks

In the given situation, it is meaningless to talk about greater security or for that matter increasing the share of the lessees. On the other hand, the strategy should be to create massive job opportunities in the non-crop-producing sector both in rural and in urban areas so that the surplus rural population may be absorbed in these activities and the new entrants in the rural labour force may also find an opening there. If this happens there will be few to lease-in land and the lessees then may be in a better position to dictate for greater share and greater security. But it is easier said than done. It requires a thorough change in the policies that have failed to utilise the vast manpower potential. Conservation and augmentation of soil, water and forest resources and creation of infrastructure itself is highly labour intensive and has the potential to absorb the idle labour force provided the village community is enjoined to undertake these activities with popular participation, transparency and accountability instead of relying on largely a corrupt bureaucracy. For financing such schemes, additional resources should be mobilised from the richer sections who are cornering the benefits of development and are resorting to speculative activities for their further aggrandisement. The Centre has command over the resources and through greater resource mobilisation it should finance such programmes.[2]

References

Board of Revenue, UP (various years), *Agricultural Census*, Lucknow.
Government of UP (1948), *Report of the Zamindari Abolition Committee*, Vol. I, Government of UP Press, Allahabad.
Government of UP (1974), Bhoomi Vyawastha Janch Samitee (Land Settlement Enquiry Committee), Department of Revenue, Government of UP, Lucknow.
National Sample Survey Organisation (1992), Report on the 48th Round of NSS, New Delhi.
Shankar, K. (1990), *Land Transfers*, Gian Publishers, New Delhi.
World Bank (2001), *World Development Report*, pp. 93–94, Washington, D.C.

[2] Tax GDP ratio in India at nearly 12 is one of the lowest and is half of what it is in many developed countries. The annual tax exemptions given to richer classes are over ₹4 lakh crore. The subsidies on petrol, diesel and power are largely enjoyed by them, amounting to nearly ₹4 lakh crore. Rather than taxing the rich the government has relied on borrowings.

PART IV

Land Reforms: Findings from a Primary Survey

10

Land Reforms: A Farmer Perspective*

Ajit Kumar Singh

Introduction

During the recent decades land reforms had receded from the political agenda of the state governments. But today land issues are
emerging again all over the country, forcing back attention to the
important question of land. Often the debate about land reforms
is conducted among economists and policy-makers without taking
into account the views of the basic stakeholders, i.e., the farmers
and the landless agricultural labourers. This chapter based on a
primary survey carried out in 2008 in rural UP presents the views
of the farmers on various issues related to land reforms like consolidation of holdings, land ceilings and land lease.

The chapter is organised as follows. The first section gives details
of the sample design and characteristics of the sample farmers. We
then discuss farmers' views on land consolidation and its impact.
This is followed by a discussion of the farmers' views on land ceiling and its effects. The next section presents their views on land
leasing and tenancy. Last section summarises the findings.

The Sample

The chapter is based on a survey of 280 farmers of Uttar Pradesh
selected through a carefully designed survey. One district was selected from each of the main agro climatic region of the state, namely,

*This chapter was previously published in "Land Policies for Inclusive
Development", edited by T. Haque and published by Concept. This text has been
edited for typographical errors, stylistic consistency and sequential organisation
in order to make it suitable for inclusion in this book.

Etah (Western UP), Hardoi (Central UP), Lakhimpur Khiri (UP Tarai), Sultanpur (Eastern UP) and Jhansi (Bundelkhand). These districts were purposely selected on the criterion of the extent of land distributed to the landless under different programmes. From each district we selected the tehsil where maximum land was distributed. In the next state one block in the tehsil was selected on the same criterion. From each selected block two villages were selected where maximum land was distributed. In the final stages we selected 25–30 farming households randomly. The sample details are given in Table 10.1.

Out of the 280 sample farmers 80 per cent were Hindus, 19 per cent were Muslims and 1 per cent were Sikhs. About 10 per cent farmers belonged to Scheduled castes, about 75 per cent to OBCs and remaining 14.3 per cent to upper castes. A little less than 75 per cent farmers were in the middle age group (25–60 years). 28.6 per cent farmers were illiterate, nearly 50 per cent were literate or

Table 10.1
Details about the Respondents

Details	Lakhimpur		Hardoi		Sultanpur		Etah		Jhansi		Total	
	Nos.	%	Nos.	%	Nos.	%	Nos.	%	Nos.	%	Nos.	%
1. Religion												
Hindu	34	58.6	43	71.7	47	78.3	50	100.0	50	96.2	224	80.0
Muslim	21	36.2	17	28.3	13	21.7			2	3.8	53	18.9
Sikh	3	5.2	–		–		–		–		3	1.1
Total	58	100.0	60	100.0	60	100.0	50	100.0	52	100.0	280	100.0
2. Caste												
SC	13	22.4	7	11.7	1	1.7	4	8.0	1	1.9	26	9.3
OBC	43	74.1	47	78.3	35	58.3	38	76.0	51	98.1	214	76.4
General	2	3.4	6	10.0	24	40.0	8	16.0	–		40	14.3
Total	58	100.0	60	100.0	60	100.0	50	100.0	52	100.0	280	100.0
3. Age group (year)												
Below 25	5	8.6	–		–		4	8.0	1	1.9	10	3.6
25–45	24	41.4	21	35.0	16	26.7	16	32.0	19	36.5	96	34.3
45–60	16	27.6	30	50.0	20	33.3	20	40.0	23	44.2	109	38.9
60+	13	22.4	9	15.0	24	40.0	10	20.0	9	17.3	65	23.2
Total	58	100.0	60	100.0	60	100.0	50	100.0	52	100.0	280	100.0

(Table 10.1 Continued)

(*Table 10.1 Continued*)

Details	Lakhimpur		Hardoi		Sultanpur		Etah		Jhansi		Total	
	Nos.	%	Nos.	%	Nos.	%	Nos.	%	Nos.	%	Nos.	%
4. Education												
Illiterate	23	39.7	15	25.0	6	10.0	12	24.0	24	46.2	80	28.6
Literate	3	5.2	8	13.3	5	8.3	6	12.0	5	9.6	27	9.6
Up to Elementary	22	37.9	22	36.7	26	43.3	18	36.0	19	36.5	107	38.2
High school/ Intermediate	4	6.9	12	20.0	22	36.7	8	16.0	3	5.8	49	17.5
Graduate and above	6	10.3	3	5.0	1	1.7	6	12.0	1	1.9	17	6.1
Total	58	100.0	60	100.0	60	100.0	50	100.0	52	100.0	280	100.0

Source: Field survey.

educated up to elementary level, while 17.5 per cent were educated up to high school or intermediate and 6 per cent were graduates. The average size of sample households was large—around 8.5.

The average size of land owned was 4.09 acres and varied between 2.53 acres in Hardoi to 5.19 acres in Jhansi (Table 10.2). The size of the operational holding was 3.29 acres. In Lakhimpur Khiri, Sultanpur and Etah the holdings were fully irrigated. Lowest irrigated area was found in Jhansi.

Agriculture was the primary occupation of 76.8 per cent households. 5.7 per cent were engaged in business and 6.7 per cent in service (Table 10.3). About 8.5 per cent worked as labourers and 2 per cent were engaged in animal husbandry. Majority of households were also occupied in some secondary activity mostly animal husbandry and rural labour.

Views about Land Consolidation and Its Impact

Land consolidation measures were introduced in the state in the mid fifties following the UP. Consolidation of Holdings Act, 1953 which provided for compulsory consolidation. One-round of consolidation has been completed in most parts of the state, while second round of consolidation was introduced in selected tehsils since the Sixth Five Year Plan. In all the districts surveyed by us

Table 10.2
Size of Land Owned and Operated on Sample Farms

Land owned/leased	Lakhimpur		Hardoi		Sultampur		Etah		Jhansi		Total	
	Total	Irrigated	Total	Irrigated	Total	Irrigated	Total	Irrigated	Total	Irrigated	Total	Irrigated
Own land	3.65	3.65	2.91	2.91	3.88	3.48	5.15	5.15	5.19	3.74	4.09	3.74
Leased in	0.03	0.03	0.04	0.04	0.03	0.03	0.06	0.06	0.02	0.02	0.04	0.04
Leased out	0.34	0.34	0.42	0.42	0.74	0.65	1.16	1.16	0.47	0.47	0.61	0.59
Total operated land	3.34	3.34	2.53	2.53	3.17	2.86	4.04	4.04	4.74	3.29	3.52	3.19

Source: Field survey.

Table 10.3
Primary and Secondary Occupation of Respondents

District	Primary/Secondary occupation	Agriculture	Animal husbandary	Ag-labour	Non-ag-labour	Business	Service	Total
Lakhimpur	Primary	50	1	2	4	1		58
	%	86.21	1.72	3.45	6.90	1.72	0.00	100.00
	Secondary	5	23	2	7	2		39
	%	12.82	58.97	5.13	17.95	5.13	0.00	100.00
Hardoi	Primary	50	3		1	5	1	60
	%	83.33	5.00	0.00	1.67	8.33	1.67	100.00
	Secondary	9	21		15		1	46
	%	19.57	45.65	0.00	32.61	0.00	2.17	100.00
Sultanpur	Primary	49				1	10	60
	%	81.66	0.00	0.00	0.00	1.67	16.67	100.00
	Secondary	11	14	6	16	6	7	60
	%	18.33	23.33	10.00	26.67	10.00	11.67	100.00
Etah	Primary	44	2			1	3	50
	%	88.00	4.00	0.00	0.00	2.00	6.00	100.00
	Secondary	5	35	1	2	4	1	48
	%	10.42	72.92	2.08	4.17	8.33	2.08	100.00

(Table 10.3 Continued)

(Table 10.3 Continued)

District	Primary/Secondary occupation	Agriculture	Animal husbandary	Ag- labour	Non- ag-labour	Business	Service	Total
Jhansi	Primary	22			17	8	5	52
	%	42.31	0.00	0.00	32.69	15.38	9.62	100.00
	Secondary	26	12	1	11		2	52
	%	50.00	23.08	1.92	21.15	0.00	3.85	100.00
Total	Primary	215	6	2	22	16	19	280
	%	76.79	2.14	0.71	7.86	5.71	6.79	100.00
	Secondary	56	105	10	51	12	11	245
	%	22.86	42.85	4.08	20.82	4.90	4.49	100.00

Source: Field survey.

consolidation was done many years ago except in case of Jhansi, which is yet to be covered by consolidation process.

Only 17.1 per cent of our sample farmers reported owning less than two plots before consolidation. About 12 per cent farmers had their holdings spread over 2–4 plots and another 12 per cent had holdings spread over 4–6 plots. Almost 60 per cent had their land ownership distributed over 6 plots. In nearly one-third cases number of plots owned were over 10, indicating the severe problem of land fragmentation. The situation is reported to have improved dramatically after consolidation (Table 10.4). 52.2 per cent

Table 10.4
Number of Plots Before and After Consolidation

Details	Lakhimpur		Hardoi		Sultanpur		Etah		Total	
	Nos.	%	Nos.	%	Nos.	%	Nos.	%	Nos.	%
No. of plots before consolidation										
Less than 2 acres	24	41.38	15	25.00	—	0.00	—	0.00	39	17.11
2–4	16	27.59	10	16.67	1	1.67	—	0.00	27	11.84
4–6	9	15.52	12	20.00	5	8.33	1	2.00	27	11.84
6–8	4	6.90	6	10.00	14	23.33	5	10.00	29	12.72
8–10	1	1.72	10	16.67	13	21.67	11	22.00	35	15.35
10–12	4	6.90	5	8.33	11	18.33	5	10.00	25	10.96
12+	—	0.00	2	3.33	16	26.67	28	56.00	46	20.18
Total	58	100.00	60	100.00	60	100.00	50	100.00	228	100.00
No. of plots after consolidation										
Less than 2 acres	44	75.86	51	85.00	18	30.00	6	12.00	119	52.19
2–4	10	17.24	7	11.67	21	35.00	11	22.00	49	21.49
4–6	4	6.90	2	3.33	8	13.33	11	22.00	25	10.96
6–8	—		—		7	11.67	11	22.00	18	7.89
8+	—		—		6	10.00	11	22.00	17	7.46
Total	58	100.00	60	100.00	60	100.00	50	100.00	228	100.00
Quality of land allotted										
Good	18	31.03	26	43.33	23	38.33	12	24.00	79	34.65
Average	32	55.17	26	43.33	35	58.33	25	50.00	118	51.75
Poor	8	13.79	8	13.33	2	3.33	13	26.00	31	13.60
Total	58	100.00	60	100.00	60	100.00	50	100.00	228	100.00

Source: Field survey.
Note: Consolidation has not been carried out in Jhansi.

farmers reported that the number of plots was reduced to 1 or 2 and another 21.5 per cent reported the number of plots between 2 and 4. However, about one-fourth farmers reported holdings spread over more than 4 plots. Thus, the problem of fragmentation, though considerably reduced, has not been fully eliminated.

Majority of farmers were satisfied about the quality of land allotted after consolidation. About one-third reported that the quality of allotted land was good and about half reported it to be satisfactory. Only 13.6 per cent said that poor quality land has been allotted to them. The proportion of farmers reporting poor quality of land was relatively more in Etah district.

Table 10.5 shows the response of the sample farmers about the changes in investment and productivity after consolidation. 86.4 per cent farmers reported improvement in their productivity after

Table 10.5
Change in Productivity and Investment After Consolidation

Description	Lakhimpur		Hardoi		Sultanpur		Etah		Total	
	Nos.	%	Nos.	%	Nos.	%	Nos.	%	Nos.	%
1. Did productivity increase after consolidation?										
Yes	50	86.21	52	86.67	58	96.67	37	74.00	197	86.40
No	8	13.79	8	13.33	2	3.33	13	26.00	31	13.60
Total	58	100.00	60	100.00	60	100.00	50	100.00	228	100.00
2. If yes, to what extent?										
Below 10%	8	16.00	38	73.08	8	13.79	6	16.22	60	30.46
10–20%	31	62.00	11	21.15	35	60.34	21	56.76	98	49.75
20–30%	11	22.00	3	5.77	13	22.41	7	18.92	34	17.26
30%	—	—	—	—	2	3.45	3		5	2.54
3. Has investment increased after consolidation?										
Yes	31	62.00	32	61.54	25	43.10	13	35.14	101	51.27
No	19	38.00	20	38.46	33	56.90	24	64.86	96	48.73
Total	50	100.00	52	100.00	58	100.00	37	100.00	197	100.00
4. If yes, on which item?										
1. Irrigation	7	22.58	18	56.25	17	68.00	3	23.08	45	44.55
2. Mechanisation	12	38.71	6	18.75	2	8.00	7	53.85	27	26.73
3. Fertiliser seeds	12	38.71	8	25.00	6	24.00	3	23.08	29	28.71

Source: Field survey.

consolidation. Out of them about 30 per cent reported an improvement of upto 10 per cent, while 50 per cent reported improvement between 10 and 20 per cent and the remaining 17 per cent reported an improvement of over 20 per cent. Slightly over 50 per cent reported that their investment on land increased after consolidation mainly on irrigation, mechanisation and fertilisers. These findings should be treated as indicative of the gains rather than their exact measurement as they are based on a long recall period. However, these are in line with the findings of the earlier studies as well (Agarwal, 1971; PEO, 1969).

The major gains of consolidation are in terms of reduced work time and reduction in drudgery. Over two-thirds of the farmers reported that consolidation reduced their drudgery and saved time on going to work on farm (Table 10.6). About 60 per cent reported saving in work period by 10–20 per cent and about 17 per cent reported saving in time of more than 20 per cent. Only 22.6 per cent felt that saving in time was less than 10 per cent.

Forty per cent farmer did not report any type of problem faced during consolidation process (Table 10.7). However, remaining complained of various problems like too much delay in the process (17.5 per cent), discriminatory attitude of revenue officials (7.5 per cent), payment of bribe (5.7 per cent) and running around block and tehsil offices (10.36 per cent). About 10 per cent reported litigation

Table 10.6
Impact of Consolidation on Work Time and Drudgery of Work

Description	Lakhimpur Nos.	%	Hardoi Nos.	%	Sultanpur Nos.	%	Etah Nos.	%	Total Nos.	%
Has consolidation reduced time and drudgery of work?										
Yes	46	79.31	51	85.00	37	61.67	21	42.00	155	67.98
No	12	20.69	9	15.00	23	38.33	29	58.00	73	32.02
If yes, extent of to which work time has reduced										
0–10%	13	28.26	8	15.69	11	29.73	3	14.29	35	22.58
10–20%	23	50.00	42	82.35	16	43.24	13	61.90	94	60.65
20–30%	8	17.39	1	1.96	7	18.92	3	14.29	19	12.26
30%	2	4.35	0	0.00	3	8.11	2	9.52	7	4.52
Total	58	100.00	60	100.00	60	100.00	50	100.00	228	100.00

Source: Field survey.

Table 10.7

Problems Faced during Consolidation

Type of problem	Lakhimpur		Hardoi		Sultanpur		Etah		Total	
	Nos.	%	Nos.	%	Nos.	%	Nos.	%	Nos.	%
1. No problem	32	55.17	30	50.00	20	33.33	29	58.00	111	39.64
2. Too much time	17	29.31	9	15.00	12	20.00	11	22.00	49	17.5
3. Discrimination by revenue officials	7	12.07	2	3.33	7	11.67	5	10.00	21	7.5
4. Had to pay bribe	2	3.45	3	5.00	9	15.00	2	4.00	16	5.71
5. Frequent visits to offices	—	—	16	26.67	10	16.67	3	6.00	29	10.36
6. Other	—	—	—	—	2	3.33	—	—	2	0.71
Did consolidation lead to litigation?										
Yes	1	1.72	1	1.67	17	28.33	9	18.00	28	10.00
No	57	98.28	59	98.33	43	71.67	41	82.00	200	71.43
Total	58	100.00	60	100.00	60	100.00	50	100.00	228	81.43
Has the case been decided?										
Yes	1	100.00	1	100.00	15	88.24	8	88.89	25	8.929
No	—	—	—	—	2	11.76	1	11.11	3	1.071
If no, how many years have lapsed?										
More than 20 Years	—		—		2	100.00	1	100.00	3	100.00

Source: Field survey.

over consolidation involving time and money. Three cases are still pending in spite of a gap of 20 years.

Overall 75 per cent of farmers feel that consolidation is a necessary measure and there is no need to repeal the Act (Table 10.8). However, majority of those who supported consolidation want it to be made voluntary.

The main suggestions given by the farmers for improving the consolidation process are:

(a) There should be no discrimination against anybody by consolidation officials.

(b) The total size of land should not be reduced.

Table 10.8

Respondents' Views Regarding Consolidation

Views about consolidation	Lakhimpur		Hardoi		Sultanpur		Etah		Total	
	Nos.	%	Nos.	%	Nos.	%	Nos.	%	Nos.	%
Do you feel consolidation is necessary?										
Yes	38	65.52	46	76.67	46	76.67	42	84.00	172	75.44
No	20	34.48	14	23.33	14	23.33	8	16.00	56	24.56
Total	58	100.00	60	100.00	60	100.00	50	100.00	228	100.00
Suggestion for improving the process of consolidation?										
No discrimination	9	23.68	11	23.91	25	54.35	10	23.81	55	31.98
No reduction in plot size	14	36.84	8	17.39	10	21.74	15	35.71	47	27.33
Consolidation within stipulated time	21	55.26	13	28.26	29	63.04	22	52.38	85	49.42
Consolidation under supervision of officials	13	34.21	21	45.65	13	28.26	14	33.33	61	35.47
Should Consolidation Act be repealed?										
Yes	20	34.48	14	23.33	14	23.33	8	16.00	56	24.56
No	38	65.52	46	76.67	46	76.67	42	84.00	172	75.44
Total	58	100.00	60	100.00	60	100.00	50	100.00	228	100.00
If no, should it be made voluntary?										
Yes	28	73.68	18	39.13	37	80.43	35	83.33	118	68.60
No	10	26.32	28	60.87	9	19.57	7	16.67	54	31.40

Source: Field survey.

(c) Consolidation process should be completed within stipulated time.

(d) Consolidation should be carried out under the supervision of senior officials.

Views about Land Ceilings

Land Ceiling Act in UP was first passed in 1960. It provided for a ceiling of 40 acres of 'fair quality land' for a family. Not only the Act fixed a very liberal ceiling, it allowed for a large number of exemptions and contained many loopholes, which defeated the purpose of the act. Hence in 1972 the Land Ceiling Act in UP was amended removing some of the exemptions. It also reduced the ceiling to 18 acres of irrigated land for a family. The various loopholes that remained in the act coupled with its lackadaisical implementation rendered it practically ineffective measure of agrarian change as various studies have shown (Government of UP, 1971 and 1975; Singh, 1989). Even the limited land that was declared surplus could not be distributed fully due to various problems.

Only 5 farmers out of 280 surveyed by us reported that their land was taken away under the Ceiling Act. Only one-fifth of the sample farmers were opposed to ceiling legislation on the ground that they have sentimental attachment for ancestral land (29.6 per cent), their holdings will be reduced in size (29.6 per cent), and smaller holdings will reduce their income (Table 10.9). However, it is important to note that almost 80 per cent farmers are in favour of ceiling legislation.

Table 10.9
Respondents' Views about Abolition of Ceilings Act

	Lakhimpur		Hardoi		Sultanpur		Etah		Jhansi		Total	
Opinion	No.	%	No.	%	No.	%	No.	%	No.	%	No.	%
Should the Ceiling Act be repealed?												
Yes	7	12.1	5	8.3	13	21.7	6	12.0	23	44.2	54	19.39
No	51	87.9	55	91.7	47	78.3	44	88.0	29	55.7	226	80.7
Total	58	100.0	60	100.0	60	100.0	50	100.0	52	100.0	280	100.0
If yes, give your reasons												
Ancestral land has a sentimental value	3	42.8	1	20.0	2	15.4	1	16.7	9	39.1	16	29.6
Land holding size is reduced	2	28.5	3	60.0	3	23.1	4	66.7	4	17.4	16	29.6
Smaller land holding reduces income	2	28.5	1	20.0	8	61.5	1	16.7	10	43.5	22	40.7
Total	7	100.0	5	100.0	13	100.0	6	100.0	23	100.0	54	100.0

Source: Field survey.

When asked what should be the size of the land ceiling almost half of the respondents felt that it should be below 10 acres of irrigated land (Table 10.10). About 30 per cent favoured a ceiling between 10–12 acres and about 20 per cent a ceiling of over 12 acres of irrigated land. Our respondents feel that for unirrigated land ceiling should be little higher with majority indicating a ceiling between 12 and 16 acres. Around one-fifth would like ceiling to be higher than this.

Thus, it appears that the large majority of farmers think that the present ceiling of 18 acres of irrigated land in the state should be reduced. It needs to be mentioned that majority of our respondents are small and marginal farmers, who think that a reduction in ceiling can make more land available for them.

About 85 per cent farmers felt that the Ceiling Act has been beneficial for the poor as it has improved their income levels as well as their educational and social status (Table 10.11). It had a beneficial impact on their livelihood through greater access to credit and taking up activities like animal husbandry.

About 62 per cent farmers support land ceiling and redistribution as a poverty eradication strategy. However, over half of

Table 10.10
Respondents' Views about Maximum Land Holding Size

Type of land (acres)	Lakhimpur		Hardoi		Sultanpur		Etah		Jhansi		Total	
	Nos.	%	Nos.	%	Nos.	%	Nos.	%	Nos.	%	Nos.	%
Irrigated land												
Below 8	12	20.69	13	21.67	5	8.33	8	16.00	7	13.46	45	16.07
8–10	31	53.45	7	11.67	41	68.33	4	8.00	9	17.31	92	32.86
10–12	12	20.69	25	41.67	5	8.33	19	38.00	24	46.15	85	30.36
12+	3	5.17	15	25.00	9	15.00	19	38.00	12	23.08	58	20.71
Total	58	100.00	60	100.00	60	100.00	50	100.00	52	100.00	280	100.00
Unirrigated land												
Below 12	9	15.517	12	20.00	5	8.333	11	50.00	7	13.46	44	15.71
12–14	29	50.00	26	43.33	20	33.33	19	50.00	9	17.31	103	36.79
14–16	13	22.41	14	23.33	21	35.00	7	50.00	24	46.15	79	28.21
16+	7	12.07	8	13.33	14	23.33	13	50.00	12	23.08	54	19.29
Total	58	100.00	60	100.00	60	100.00	50	100.00	52	100.00	280	100.00

Source: Field survey.

Table 10.11

Views of the Respondents about Benefits of Ceiling Act

Details	Lakhimpur Nos.	%	Hardoi Nos.	%	Sultanpur Nos.	%	Etah Nos.	%	Jhansi Nos.	%	Total Nos.	%
Is Ceiling Act helpful for the poor?												
Yes	46	79.31	52	86.67	55	91.67	43	86.00	43	82.69	239	85.36
No	12	20.69	8	13.33	5	8.33	7	14.00	9	17.31	41	14.64
Total	58	100.00	60	100.00	60	100.00	50	100.00	52	100.00	280	100.00
If yes, in which way (multiple response)?												
Education has improved	17	36.96	12	23.08	9	16.36	11	25.58	13	30.23	62	25.94
Social status has gone up	21	45.65	19	36.54	11	20.00	12	27.91	16	37.21	79	33.05
Income has increased	12	26.09	23	44.23	16	29.09	9	20.93	24	55.81	84	35.15
Taking loan has become easy	6	13.04	2	3.846	9	16.36	14	32.56	7	16.28	38	15.90
Assisted in animal husbandry	9	19.57	17	32.69	5	9.09	8	18.61	3	6.98	42	17.57
Helped to construct houses	7	15.22	6	11.54	2	3.64	13	30.23	4	9.30	32	13.39

Source: Field survey.

Table 10.12
Respondents' Views about Ceilings and Poverty

Details	Lakhimpur		Hardoi		Sultanpur		Etah		Jhansi		Total	
	Nos.	%	Nos.	%	Nos.	%	Nos.	%	Nos.	%	Nos.	%
Do you think allotment is a useful method for reducing poverty?												
Yes	40	68.97	44	73.33	25	41.67	24	48.00	41	78.85	174	62.14
No	18	31.03	16	26.67	35	58.33	26	52.00	11	21.15	106	37.86
If no, what should be done?												
Provide employment	9	50.00	6	37.5	22	62.86	8	30.77	3	27.27	48	45.28
Provide loan for self-employment	6	33.33	9	56.25	12	34.29	14	53.85	6	54.55	47	44.34
Implement govt. programmes such as NREGA	11	61.11	13	81.25	8	22.86	13	50.00	7	63.64	52	49.06

Source: Field survey.

them feel that other programmes like loans for self-employment or employment generation programmes like NREGA should be adopted (Table 10.12).

Views about Land Leasing

Sub letting of land is prohibited under the Zamindari Abolition Act of UP except for certain categories of handicapped persons like widows, physically handicapped, serving in armed forces, etc. However, in practice leasing out continues as the NSS surveys have shown. About 28 per cent farmers in our survey reported that they had leased out land, while 3 per cent reported leasing in of land (Table 10.13). No case of simultaneous leasing in and leasing out was reported.

Land leasing is being prasticed mostly among the small and marginal farmers. In half of the cases the land leased out was small being less than 2 acres, in 36 per cent cases it was 2–4 acres and only in 11.5 per cent cases land leased out exceeded 4 acres (Table 10.14).

The most common term of leasing out is 50–50 per cent sharing of paid out costs (irrigation and fertilisers only) and output.

Table 10.13

Distribution of Respondents by Type of Leasing

Details	Lakhimpur No.	%	Hardoi No.	%	Sultanpur No.	%	Etah No.	%	Jhansi No.	%	Total No.	%
Only leasing in	1	1.73	2	3.33	2	3.34	2	4.00	1	1.93	8	2.86
Only leasing out	10	17.24	24	40.00	17	28.33	16	32.00	11	21.15	78	27.85
Neither leasing in or leasing out	47	81.03	34	56.67	41	68.33	32	64.00	40	76.92	194	69.29
Total respondents	58	100.00	60	100.00	60	100.00	50	100.00	52	100.00	280	100.00

Source: Field survey.
Note:　No cases of lease in–lease out were reported.

Table 10.14

Details Regarding Leasing Out of Land

Details about leasing	Lakhimpur No.	%	Hardoi No.	%	Sultanpur No.	%	Etah No.	%	Jhansi No.	%	Total No.	%
Have you leased out land?												
Yes	10	17.24	24	40.00	17	28.33	16	32.00	11	21.15	78	27.86
No	48	82.76	36	60.00	43	71.67	34	68.00	41	78.85	202	72.14
Total	58	100.00	60	100.00	60	100.00	50	100.00	52	100.00	280	100.00
If yes, how much (acres)?												
Below 1	1	10.00	10	41.67	1	5.88	1	6.25	—		13	16.67
1 to 2	3	30.00	12	50.00	6	35.29	—		7	63.64	28	35.90
2 to 3	3	30.00	2	8.33	5	29.41	5	31.25	1	9.09	16	20.51
3 to 4	3	30.00	—		2	11.76	5	31.25	2	18.18	12	15.38
4+	—		—		3	17.65	5	31.25	1	9.09	9	11.54
Total	10	100.00	24	100.00	17	100.00	16	100.00	11	100.00	78	100.00
Average land leased out	2.00		1.04		2.49		3.63		2.95		2.20	

Source: Field survey.

Nearly 80 per cent farmers reported leasing out on sharing of cost and output basis (Table 10.15). However, in about one-fifth cases no sharing in cost was done, while half of the produce was shared. Only 2.5 per cent farmers reported giving land on cash basis. The prevailing rate is around ₹4,000 per acre. Incidentally all the cases where land is leased out on cash basis or without sharing costs were reported from Sultanpur district, where population pressure is more and landlessness is higher.

In nearly 58 per cent cases the terms of tenancy were based on the common practice prevailing in the district (Table 10.16). However, about 18 per cent farmers leasing out reported that they fixed the terms of lease, while in 24 per cent cases the tenant decided the term. The proportion of the latter was relatively higher in Etah and Jhansi districts. Thus, the landowners are not a definite dominant position as far determination of conditions of lease is concerned.

The main reasons for giving out land on lease were high cost of production (58 per cent) and low incomes from agriculture (20.5 per cent). Only 7.7 per cent reported leasing out due to non-availability

Table 10.15
Terms of Leasing Out

Terms for leasing out	Lakhimpur		Hardoi		Sultanpur		Etah		Jhansi		Total	
	No.	%	No.	%	No.	%	No.	%	No.	%	No.	%
50% sharing of cost of production & total produce	10	100.00	24	100.00	—		16	100.00	11	100.00	61	78.21
50% sharing of produce only	—		—		15	88.24	—		—		15	19.23
Fixed amount ₹4,000/ acre	—		—		2	11.76	—		—		2	2.56
Total	10	100.00	24	100.00	17	100.00	16	100.00	11	100.00	78	100.00

Source: Field survey.

Table 10.16
Who Fixes the Condition for Leasing

Details	Lakhimpur		Hardoi		Sultanpur		Etah		Jhansi		Total	
	No.	%	No.	%	No.	%	No.	%	No.	%	No.	%
Self	3	30.00	5	20.83	2	11.76	3	18.75	1	9.09	14	17.95
Tenant	2	20.00	1	4.17	2	11.76	7	43.75	7	63.64	19	24.36
Common practice	5	50.00	18	75.00	13	76.48	6	37.50	3	27.27	45	57.69
Total	10	100.00	24	100.00	17	100.00	16	100.00	11	100.00	78	100.00

Source: Field survey.

of labour. About one-fifth said that they have leased out as they have taken up non-agricultural activity (Table 10.17).

All the reported cases of tenancy were oral tenancy since leasing out is legally prohibited (Table 10.18). Around one-fourth lessors reported that they engaged their tenants for work without payment or on lower wages, indicating a kind of dependency on the lessors. However, in three-fifths of cases no such dependency was

Table 10.17
Reasons for Leasing Out Land

Reasons	Lakhimpur		Hardoi		Sultanpur		Etah		Jhansi		Total	
	No.	%	No.	%	No.	%	No.	%	No.	%	No.	%
Engaged in non-agricultural activity	3	30.00	4	16.67	1	5.88	0	0.00	0	0.00	8	10.26
High cost of cultivation	5	50.00	9	37.50	7	41.18	3	18.75	5	45.45	29	37.18
Low income from agriculture	2	20.00	9	37.50	8	47.06	11	68.75	6	54.55	36	46.15
Non-availability of agricultural labourers	0	0.00	2	8.33	1	5.88	2	12.50	0	0.00	5	6.41
Total	10	100.00	24	100.00	17	100.00	16	100.00	11	100.00	78	100.00

Source: Field survey.

Table 10.18
Type of Tenancy and Changes in Tenants

Details of tenancy	Lakhimpur No.	%	Hardoi No.	%	Sultanpur No.	%	Etah No.	%	Jhansi No.	%	Total No.	%
Type of tenancy												
Oral	10	100.00	24	100.00	17	100.00	16	100.00	11	100.00	78	100.00
In writing	–	–	–	–	–	–	–	–	–	–	–	–
Other work taken from tenant												
Work without payment	–		3	12.50	2	11.76	1	6.25	2	18.18	8	10.26
Work on low wages	2	20.00	3	12.50	1	5.88	4	25.00	1	9.09	11	14.10
No work taken	8	80.00	18	75.00	14	82.35	11	68.75	8	72.73	59	75.64
Change in the leasing system over last 5 years												
No changes	10	100.00	19	79.17	11	64.71	16	100.00	8	72.73	64	82.05
Payment in advance	–		5	20.83	6	35.29	–		3	27.27	14	17.95

Source: Field survey.

reported, which is suggestive of the fact that leasing is largely a market driven process (Table 10.15).

Over four-fifth farmers reported that there has been no change in the system of tenancy during the past five years. However, about one-fifth reported that practice of advance cash payment is emerging (Table 10.19).

A little over one-third farmers reported that they have not changed in tenants during the last five years. However, about three-fourth respondents reported that they had changed the tenant during the last 5 years (Table 10.19). The main reasons for changing the tenant were low productivity (30.5 per cent), demand of more share in cost by lessee (49.2 per cent), non-utilisation of money given for cost sharing (13.6 per cent) and quarrelsome nature of the tenant (6.8 per cent).

About 70 per cent of the farmers leasing out land reported that they have not made any investment on the leased out land. Lack of funds and infertile nature of land were cited as the main reason for not making investment. However, about 30 per cent did report

Table 10.19

Details of Change in Tenants over Last Five Years

	Lakhimpur		Hardoi		Sultanpur		Etah		Jhansi		Total %	
Details	No.	%	No.	%	No.	%	No.	%	No.	%	No.	%
Change in tenants												
Yes	7	70.00	15	62.50	12	70.59	12	75.00	7	63.64	53	67.95
No	3	30.00	9	37.50	5	29.41	4	25.00	4	36.36	25	32.05
Total	10	100.00	24	100.00	17	100.00	16	100.00	11	100.00	78	100.00
If yes, reasons for change												
Low productivity	1	14.29	8	53.33	6	50.00	4	33.33	4	57.14	23	43.4
Not utilising money for input use	2	28.57	3	20	0	0.00	2	16.67	1	14.29	8	15.09
Demanding more share in cost	3	42.86	3	20	6	50.00	4	33.33	2	28.57	18	33.96
Tenant is quarrelsome	1	14.29	1	6.667	0	0.00	2	16.67	0	0.00	4	7.55
Total	7	100.00	15	100	12	100.00	12	100.00	7	100	53	100.00

Source: Field survey.

making investment of leased out land in activities like levelling of field, bunding and irrigation (Table 10.20).

Over two-thirds of the farmers who reported leasing out land favoured the view that leasing should be legalised (Table 10.21). The main reason for supporting legalisation of lease was that it will make the process easier (42.3 per cent), will allow retention of land ownership (21.8 per cent) and will allow fair sharing of costs and outputs (35.9 per cent). However, about one-third of lessors were opposed to legalisation of lease as they feared that it will result in loss of ownership of land and may lead to corruption and malpractices by revenue officials. About 15 per cent of farmers not leasing out land at present also supported the view that leasing should be legalised. The remaining respondents were apprehensive that it is likely to result in loss of ownership of land. On the whole, 30 per cent farmers surveyed by us were in favour of legalisation of tenancy.

Table 10.20
Investment Made on Leased-out Land

Type of tenancy	Lakhimpur No.	%	Hardoi No.	%	Sultanpur No.	%	Etah No.	%	Jhansi No.	%	Total No.	%
Investment made on leased out land												
Yes	6	60.00	8	33.33	2	11.76	1	6.25	6	54.55	23	29.49
No	4	40.00	16	66.67	15	88.24	15	93.75	5	45.45	55	70.51
Total	10	100.00	24	100.00	17	100.00	16	100.00	11	100.00	78	100.00
If yes, in what												
Levelling of land	2	33.33	5	62.50	–		1	100.00	2	33.33	10	43.48
Bunding	1	16.67	–		–		–		3	50.00	4	17.39
Irrigation	3	50.00	3	37.50	2	100.00	–		1	16.67	9	39.13
If no, reason												
Lack of fund	1	25.00	4	25.00	9	60.00	7	46.67	2	40.00	23	41.82
Land is infertile	3	75.00	12	75.00	6	40.00	8	53.33	3	60.00	32	58.18

Source: Field survey.

Table 10.21
Perception of Respondents Regarding Tenancy

Details	Lakhimpur No.	%	Hardoi No.	%	Sultanpur No.	%	Etah No.	%	Jhansi No.	%	Total No.	%
Should tenancy be legalised?												
Yes	7	70.00	16	66.67	11	64.71	10	62.50	9	81.82	53	67.95
No	3	30.00	8	33.33	6	35.29	6	37.50	2	18.18	25	32.05
Total	10	100.00	24	100.00	17	100.00	16	100.00	11	100.00	78	100.00
If yes, reasons												
Procedure will become easy	2	28.57	6	37.5	4	36.36	3	30.00	2	22.22	17	32.08
Land will remain with owner	2	28.57	4	25.00	2	18.18	3	30.00	3	33.33	14	26.42

(Table 10.21 Continued)

(Table 10.21 Continued)

Details	Lakhimpur		Hardoi		Sultanpur		Etah		Jhansi		Total	
	No.	%	No.	%	No.	%	No.	%	No.	%	No.	%
Fair sharing of cost & production	3	42.86	6	37.5	5	45.45	4	40.00	4	44.44	22	41.51
If no, reasons												
Owners monopoly will end	1	33.33	5	62.5	4	66.67	3	50.00	1	50.00	14	56.00
Corruption might increase	2	66.67	3	37.5	2	33.33	3	50.00	1	50.00	11	44.00

Source: Field survey.

About 18 per cent felt that the period of lease should be up to 3 years; while as many as 47 per cent felt it should be five years and 35 per cent felt it should be even longer (Table 10.22). Around

Table 10.22
Views about the Term and Conditions of Lease

Details	Lakhimpur		Hardoi		Sultanpur		Etah		Jhansi		Total	
	No.	%	No.	%	No.	%	No.	%	No.	%	No.	%
What should be the duration of tenancy?												
Three years	6	60.00	11	45.83	6	35.29	5	31.25	6	54.55	34	43.59
Five years	2	20.00	9	37.50	7	41.18	8	50.00	3	27.27	29	37.18
Above five years	2	20.00	4	16.67	4	23.53	3	18.75	2	18.18	15	19.23
Total	10	100.00	24	100.00	17	100.00	16	100	11	100.00	78	100.00
What should be the conditions of tenancy?												
Cash	2	20.00	5	20.83	3	17.65	3	18.75	2	18.18	15	19.23
50% share of production	3	30.00	3	12.5	4	23.53	3	18.75	4	36.36	17	21.79
Equal sharing of cost and produce	5	50.00	16	66.67	10	58.82	10	62.50	5	45.45	46	58.97
Total	10	100.00	24	100.00	17	100.00	16	100	11	100.00	78	100.00

Source: Field survey.

38 per cent who favoured leasing preferred leasing on cash basis, while 62 per cent desired leasing on the basis of sharing of output and costs on 50–50 basis.

Conclusion

Our study based on a field survey of 280 farmers from 5 districts representing different economic and agro-climatic regions shows a general positive response of farmers to the land reform measures introduced in the state. The major findings may be summed up as follows:

(i) Consolidation of holdings is one of the most successful land reform measures. It has reduced time and drudgery of farmers on moving one field to another and enabled them to make investment on development of land. It has a clear favourable impact on agricultural productivity. There is an overwhelming support among the farmers to consolidation measures. However, there are some procedural problems and malpractices associated with the process which need to be removed.

(ii) Land ceilings did not affect the majority of our sample farmers directly. However, by and large they favour land ceiling measures as it has a positive impact on the economic and social status of the land allottees. In fact, a good proportion of farmers feel that the land ceiling size may be further reduced to below 10 acres of irrigated land. The majority of our respondents are small and marginal farmers, who think that a reduction in ceiling can make more land available for them as well as the landless labourers.

(iii) Though sub-letting of land is prohibited under the Zamindari Abolition Act of UP except for certain categories of handicapped persons, the practice of oral lease is quite common. Land leasing is being practiced mostly among the small and marginal farmers and is a mechanism to make adjustment in their investment and income requirements. The most common term of leasing out is 50–50 per cent sharing of paid out costs and output. However, the practice of advance cash payment is emerging in some parts. The survey also indicates that the landowners are not a dominant position in the land lease market which is largely determined by market forces of demand and supply of land. Over two-thirds of the farmers who reported leasing out land favoured the view that leasing should be legalised as they felt that it will make the process easier, will allow retention of land ownership and will allow fair sharing of costs and outputs. Overall our study lends support to the view that land leasing should be allowed as it will increase access of marginal farmers and the landless labourers to land and improve their economic condition.

References

Agarwal, S.K. (1971), *Economics of Land Consolidation in India*, Sultan Chand, New Delhi.

Directorate of Evaluation, UP Government (1971), *Impact of Ceilings on Land Holdings Act, 1960: A Case Study in Gorakhpur District*, Lucknow.

P.E.O., Planning Commission, GOI (1969), *Report on the Evaluation of Consolidation of the Holdings Programmes*, New Delhi.

Revenue Department, Government of UP (1975), *Report of the Uttar Pradesh Land Settlement Enquiry Committee*, Lucknow.

Singh, A.K. (1989), 'Land Ceiling Legislation in U.P.: An Assessment', in Planning Commission, GOI, *Proceedings and Papers of the Seminar on Land Reforms: A Retrospect and Prospect*, New Delhi.

11

Status of Tenancy: Some Facts from the Field*

Introduction

Tenancy has been traditionally considered as an exploitative form of cultivation, negatively impacting farm productivity and equity. As a result soon after Independence most states in India enacted tenancy legislation, which imposed either blanket ban or put significant restrictions and regulations on tenancy. The tenants in different parts of the country acquired ownership or secured rights on the land cultivated by them. On the other hand, such controls had a most damaging consequence on the livelihood of a large number of erstwhile tenants who were dispossessed of land traditionally cultivated by them. The tenants became unprotected by the law and vulnerable to eviction. One estimate points out that such eviction took place on about 30 per cent of the operated area and these evictions took place even in the states that benefited large numbers of tenants with ownership or ownership-like rights (Appu, 1997).

The fact remains that tenancy in its various forms has shown no sign of extinction, despite the legislative regulations and restrictions imposed on tenancy. The National Sample Survey (NSS) 37th round (1981–1982) put the figure of tenancy at 6–7 per cent of the operated area, which was considered as gross underestimation. Several micro studies have indicated that incidence of tenancy varies from 15 to 35 per cent of the operated area (Cherian, 2004; John, 2004; Latha and Madhusudan, 2004; Nair et al., 2004; Veron, 1999).

* This chapter was previously published in *Journal of Rural Development*, 2012. This text has been edited for typographical errors, stylistic consistency and sequential organisation in order to make it suitable for inclusion in this book.

[†]The author is thankful to Prof. A.K. Singh, Director, Giri Institute of Development Studies, for sanctioning funds for this study and providing valuable insights for analysis of data.

One section of the scholars believes that tenancy runs under exploitative terms and is based mostly on oral contracts without any security of lease. An opposite view has also emerged among the scholars that tenancy is an effective means of increasing land access to the poor, redistributing the gains of agricultural development, empowering tenants and improving their bargaining power. Thus, the tenancy has been recognised as an important mechanism for increasing the income of the poor and alleviating them from poverty.

In the light of the above conflicting views about tenancy, it is important to empirically examine the issue in its various dimensions and the views of the affected parties at the ground level. The present study based on a field survey of tenants in Uttar Pradesh is a modest attempt in this direction. First section presents the objectives and methodology of the sample survey in four districts, one each from the four economic regions of UP. Second section analyses the National Sample Survey data from various rounds on tenancy in UP. Third section discusses the profile of the tenants — their family composition, caste, religion, age, occupation and income. Fourth section examines the farm characteristics of tenant households: land size, crops cultivated, cost of cultivation, and investment on leased land. Fifth section examines the characteristics of tenancy, e.g., sources of area leased-in, whether the tenant is also owner of land, or a pure tenant, the land size leased-in and the reasons for leasing-in. Sixth section examines the lessor: his caste and occupation. Seventh section discusses whether the contract of tenancy was oral or written, terms and tenure of leasing and the relationship between tenant and lessor. The final section summaries the findings and offers policy suggestions.

Objectives

The major objectives of the study are:

1. To study the status of tenancy in Uttar Pradesh
2. To examine the socio-economic profile of tenants
3. To study the farming characteristics of tenant households
4. To find out the terms and conditions of tenancy in UP
5. To suggest measures to reform the tenancy system

Methodology

The study is based on a field survey of tenants in UP. First, from each of the four economic regions of the state, one district was selected where largest area was distributed under the different land distribution programmes. On this criterion, Hardoi district from the Central Region, Sultanpur district from the Eastern Region, Etah district from the Western Region and Jhansi district from the Bundelkhand Region were selected. In addition, Lakhimpur Kheri district was also selected from the *tarai* region (sub-mountain) which presents a distinct agro-climatic situation.

In the second stage, one *tehsil* was selected from each sample district on the basis of criteria as followed in the selection of sample districts. Thereafter, two villages were selected randomly from each tehsil. From each sample village 10 per cent of tenants were selected randomly for the interview. On the whole, 43 tenants in Lakhimpur district, 56 tenants in Hardoi district, 60 tenants in Sultanpur district, 50 tenants in Etah district and 49 tenants in Jhansi district were selected. A detailed schedule was developed to collect primary data from the tenants. The names of sample districts, *tehsils* and villages with number of tenants interviewed have been shown in the following Table 11.1.

Table 11.1
Details of the Study Sample

Sample districts	Sample tehsils	Sample villages	Number of sample tenants
Lakhimpur	Lakhimpur Sadar	Saidapur-Devkali Safipur	23
			20
Hardoi	Sandila	Begumganj	30
		Sahgaon	26
Sultanpur	Sultanpur Sadar	Jajjaur	30
		Saiffullaganj	30
Etah	Etah Sadar	Killermau	25
		Pura	25
Jhansi	Jhansi Sadar	Khailar	24
		Saiyar	25
Total (nos.)	5	10	258

Source: Field survey.

Status of Tenancy in Uttar Pradesh

The Uttar Pradesh Zamindari Abolition Act, 1951, prohibited sub letting of farm land except by certain exempted categories of persons such as widows, minors, and members of the armed forces. However, in actual practice tenancy continued to prevail in all parts of the state as the various rounds of National Sample Survey have shown.

Table 11.2 presents details of operational holdings in UP and India based on NSS surveys. The percentage share of leased-in holdings in total holdings was found to be higher in UP as compared to all India average during all the NSS rounds. However, the proportion of leased-in holdings has steadily declined over

Table 11.2
Characteristics of Operational Holdings: UP and India (Rural)

		Round			
		26th	37th	48th	59th
Item	UP/India	(1970–1971)	(1981–1982)	(1991–1992)	(2002–2003)
No of operational	UP	11.1	13.1	17.0	18.03
holdings (million)	India	57.1	71.0	93.5	101.27
Total area operated	UP	17.2	16.8	17.1	13.87
(million ha.)	India	125.7	118.6	125.1	107.65
Average area	UP	1.5	1.3	1.0	0.77
operated (ha.)	India	2.2	1.7	1.3	1.06
Percentage of operational holdings with party or wholly					
(a) Owned land	UP	98.6	97.8	97.4	90.08
	India	95.6	92.9	96.2	95.33
(b) Leased-in land	UP	–	20.1	15.5	11.7
	India	24.7	15.2	11.0	9.9
In total area operated, percentage share of					
(a) Area owed	UP	87.0	88.1	88.5	87.5
	India	89.3	91.1	90.4	92.7
(b) Area leased-in	UP	–	10.2	10.5	9.5
	India	10.6	7.2	8.5	6.5

Source: NSS reports.

the past three decades. During 59th round (2002–2003), share of number of leased-in holdings in total holdings was 11.7 per cent in UP and 9.9 per cent at the all India level. About 10 per cent of operated land was under leasing-in farming in UP against 6.5 per cent in India.

The percentage of households who have reported leasing-out constituted around 5 per cent in UP as against 3 per cent in the country as a whole (Table 11.3). On other hand, the households reporting leasing-in were 13 per cent and 12 per cent in UP and India respectively. It was also reported that the average area leased-in per household was 0.51 ha. in UP as against 0.44 ha. in the country as a whole. Leased-in area constituted 10.52 per cent of their total area in UP as against 7.05 per cent in the India as a whole.

Among different terms of leasing-in of land being practiced, sharing of produce is most prevalent followed by fixed money and fixed produce (Table 11.4). The sharing of produce is followed in about 53 per cent of tenancies in UP in comparison with 40 per cent in India.

Table 11.3
Incidence of Tenancy in UP and India (2002–2003)

State/Country	Percentage of households reporting		Average area leased in per reporting household (in hectare)	Leased in area as per cent of total area owed
	Leasing out	Leasing in		
UP	5.36	12.78	0.51	10.52
India	2.80	11.52	0.44	7.05

Source: NSS 59th round.

Table 11.4
Percentage Distribution of Area Leased-in According to Terms of Leasing: UP and India (2002–2003)

State/Country	Fixed money	Fixed produce	Share of produce	From relatives	Other	All
Uttar Pradesh	23.8	12.9	52.9	5.0	5.4	100.0
India	29.5	20.3	40.3	4.0	5.9	100.0

Source: NSS 59th round.

Table 11.5
Percentage Distribution of Area Leased-out by the Terms of Leasing (2002–2003)

State/Country	For fixed money	For fixed produce	For share of produce	Other items	All
UP	14.48	21.18	51.93	12.00	100.00
India	31.04	15.30	39.55	14.11	100.00

Source: NSS 59th round.

Sharing of produce is also reported as the dominant form of leasing-out followed by fixed produce in UP. However, at the all India level fixed money is a more popular form of leasing out as compared to UP (Table 11.5).

Socio-Economic Profile of Tenants

In order to study the present status of tenancy in UP and to know the views of the tenants about making leasing legal a sample study of 258 tenant farmers was carried out. In this section, we present the findings of the field survey.

Family Details

Average family size of the sample households is 6.55 persons varying from 5 to 7 persons in the sample districts. A notable feature is that the sex ratio is 902 females per 1,000 males (Table 11.6). In case of Jhansi district, an area of high out-migration, sex ratio is as low as 779.

Caste, Religion and Gender

Other Backward Castes (OBCs) constituted around 78 per cent of all tenants in the sample (Table 11.7). The share of OBC tenants is found to be particularly high in the districts of Sultanpur,

Table 11.6
Family Composition and Sex Ratio of Tenant Households

District	Male (adult)	Female (adult)	Male (child)	Female (child)	Average family size	Sex ratio
Lakhimpur	86 (32.09)	70 (26.12)	55 (20.52)	57 (21.27)	6	901
Hardoi	114 (29.09)	94 (23.98)	93 (23.72)	91 (23.21)	7	894
Sultanpur	112 (26.99)	118 (28.43)	95 (22.89)	90 (21.69)	7	959
Etah	85 (24.57)	90 (26.01)	93 (26.88)	78 (22.54)	7	944
Jhansi	71 (27.52)	59 (22.87)	74 (28.68)	54 (20.93)	5	779
All	478 (28.30)	431 (25.52)	410 (24.27)	370 (21.91)	7	902

Source: Field survey.
Note: Figures in brackets show percentages.

Table 11.7
Caste-wise Distribution of Sample Tenants

Caste/Religion	Lakhimpur	Hardoi	Sultanpur	Etah	Jhansi	All
General	2 (4.65)	–	–	–	–	2 (0.77)
OBC	21 (48.84)	45 (80.36)	56 (93.33)	33 (66.00)	45 (91.84)	200 (77.52)
SC	20 (46.51)	11 (19.64)	4 (6.67)	17 (34.00)	4 (8.16)	56 (21.71)
Total	43 (100.00)	56 (100.00)	60 (100.00)	50 (100.00)	49 (100.00)	258 (100.00)

Source: Field survey.
Note: Figures in brackets show percentages.

Jhansi and Hardoi. The scheduled castes constituted the second largest group of tenants. Their share is higher in the districts of Lakhimpur and Etah. Less than 1 per cent of tenants were from the general castes.

Table 11.8
Age Profile of the Sample Tenants

Age group	Lakhimpur	Hardoi	Sultanpur	Etah	Jhansi	All
15–30	10(23.25)	10(17.86)	4(6.67)	9(18.00)	15(30.61)	48(18.60)
30–45	16(37.21)	24(42.86)	26(43.33)	26(52.00)	27(55.10)	121(46.90)
45–60	12(27.91)	16(28.57)	14(23.33)	14(28.00)	5(10.21)	65(25.19)
60+	5(11.63)	6(10.71)	1(1.67)	1(2.00)	2(4.08)	24(9.31)
Total	43(100.00)	56(100.00)	60(100.00)	50(100.00)	49(100.00)	258(100.00)

Source: Field survey.
Note: Figures in brackets show percentages.

Age of Tenants

The age structure of sample tenants showed that about 19 per cent were in the young age group of 15–30 years and another 47 per cent in the age group of 30–45 years (Table 11.8). A little less than 10 per cent belonged to older age group.

Education Level among Tenants

Table 11.9 shows the level of education of the tenants. Almost half of the tenants were illiterate. Around 40 per cent has education up to primary or upper primary level. The remaining 12 per cent tenants had education up to high school or above (Table 11.9).

Table 11.9
Education Level of Sample Tenants

Caste	Lakhimpur	Hardoi	Sultanpur	Etah	Jhansi	All
Illiterate	22	36	30	15	19	122
	(51.16)	(64.29)	(50.00)	(30.00)	(38.78)	(47.29)
Below primary	5	5	3	4	14	31
	(11.63)	(8.93)	(5.00)	(8.00)	(28.57)	(12.02)
Primary	6	7	8	7	6	34
	(13.95)	(12.50)	(1.33)	(14.00)	(12.24)	(13.18)

(Table 11.9 Continued)

(*Table 11.9 Continued*)

Caste	Lakhimpur	Hardoi	Sultanpur	Etah	Jhansi	All
Upper primary	7 (16.28)	5 (8.93)	13 (21.67)	7 (14.00)	7 (42.29)	39 (15.12)
High school	2 (4.65)	2 (3.57)	4 (6.67)	9 (18.00)	2 (4.08)	19 (7.36)
Intermediate	–	1 (1.79)	1 (1.67)	4 (8.00)	–	6 (2.33)
Technical diploma	–	–	–	–	1 (2.04)	1 (0.39)
Graduate	–	–	1 (1.67)	3 (6.00)	–	4 (1.55)
PG	1 (2.33)	–	–	1 (2.00)	–	2 (0.78)
Total	43 (100.00)	56 (100.00)	60 (100.00)	50 (100.00)	49 (100.00)	258 (100.00)

Source: Field survey.
Note: Figures in brackets show percentages.

Main Occupation of Tenants

About 60 per cent of tenants reported agriculture as their prime occupation. About 20 per cent were engaged in non-agricultural activities (Table 11.10). Surprisingly, less than 3 per cent tenants reported agricultural labour as their primary occupation. A relatively small proportion was also engaged in other low income activities like animal husbandry and trade. Some variations across districts were also observed. Thus, in Lakhimpur district 81.4 per cent tenants were agriculturists, but in Sultanpur district only 35 per cent reported agriculture as their primary occupation. In the latter district, 30 per cent tenants were engaged in animal husbandry.

Secondary Occupation of Tenants

Over 42 per cent of tenants were employed as labour generally in non-agricultural activities as far their secondary occupation

Table 11.10

Main Occupation of Sample Tenants

Occupation	Lakhimpur	Hardoi	Sultanpur	Etah	Jhansi	All
Agriculture	35	39	21	30	26	151
	(81.40)	(69.64)	(35.00)	(60.00)	(53.06)	(58.53)
Agriculture labour	3	1	1	2	–	7
	(6.98)	(1.79)	(1.67)	(4.00)		(2.71)
Non-agriculture labour	4	11	4	15	17	51
	(9.30)	(19.64)	(6.67)	(30.00)	(34.69)	(19.77)
Animal husbandry	–	1	18	–	–	19
		(1.79)	(30.00)			(7.36)
Trade	1	3	10	–	3	17
	(2.32)	(5.35)	(16.66)		(6.12)	(6.59)
Services	–	–	3	3	2	8
			(5.00)	(6.00)	(4.09)	(3.10)
Artisan	–	1	3	–	1	5
		(1.39)	(5.00)		(2.04)	(1.94)
Total	43	56	60	50	49	258
	(100.00)	(100.00)	(100.00)	(100.00)	(100.00)	(100.00)

Source: Field survey.

Note: Figures in brackets show percentages.

was concerned while about one third reported agriculture as their secondary occupation (Table 11.11). Over one-fifth of tenants were also engaged in animal husbandry as their secondary occupation.

Income of Sample Tenants

The average annual income per household of tenants has been estimated to be ₹23,116. This amounted to a per capita income of about ₹3,300. As shown in Table 11.12, the contribution of income from the leased-in land in total income is highest (22.3 per cent), closely followed by the income from the non-agricultural labour (21.2 per cent) and income from owned land (20.2 per cent) and animal husbandry (16.5 per cent).

Tenants in Jhansi and Sultanpur districts have much higher income level as compared to other sample districts. In Jhansi

Table 11.11
Secondary Occupation of Tenants

Occupation	Lakhimpur	Hardoi	Sultanpur	Etah	Jhansi	All
Agriculture	6	17	31	11	21	86
	(13.95)	(32.08)	(51.67)	(22.00)	(42.86)	(33.73)
Agriculture labour	7	3	–	11	–	21
	(16.28)	(5.66)		(22.00)		(8.23)
Non-agriculture	15	28	6	14	24	87
labour	(34.88)	(52.83)	(10.00)	(28.00)	(48.98)	(34.11)
Animal husbandry	14	5	18	13	4	54
	(32.56)	(9.43)	(30.00)	(26.00)	(8.16)	(21.18)
Trade	1	–	2	–	–	3
	(2.33)		(3.33)			(1.18)
Artisan	–	–	3	1	–	4
			(5.00)	(2.00)		(1.57)
Total	43	53	60	50	49	255
	(100.00)	(100.00)	(100.00)	(100.00)	(100.00)	(100.00)

Source: Field survey.
Note: Figures in brackets show percentages.

district non-agriculture labour contributed as much as 37.6 per cent in household income, while in Sultanpur district income from animal husbandry and services and pension made a significant contribution to family's income. The contribution of income from leased in land varied from a low of 13.9 per cent in Sultanpur district to a high of 38.3 per cent in Lakhimpur district (Table 11.12).

Farm Characteristics of Tenant Households

Several scholars have considered tenancy as an inefficient form of farming. The argument has been given that since the tenants get only a part of the output they produce or pay a higher fixed rent in cash, they have less incentive to put in required efforts and inputs to realise as much production as could be possible. Without ownership right with fear of eviction any time, they do not make investment on the land which prohibits realising the higher productivity gains. In this section, the status of farming under tenancy is examined to analyse this aspect.

Table 11.12
Average Net Annual Income Per Sample Household by Source (₹)

Sources	Lakhimpur	Hardoi	Sultanpur	Etah	Jhansi	All
Owed land	1,919	5,149	5,935	6,508	3,108	4,669
	(10.32)	(25.71)	(19.55)	(43.34)	(10.35)	(20.20)
Leased-in land	7,134	5,290	4,213	2,406	7,267	5,163
	(38.38)	(26.42)	(13.88)	(16.02)	(24.20)	(22.34)
Animal husbandry	3,799	1,418	7,075	1,978	4,476	3,820
	(20.44)	(7.08)	(23.31)	(13.17)	(14.91)	(16.53)
Agriculture labour	1,628	450	438	192	604	623
	(8.76)	(2.25)	(1.44)	(1.28)	(2.01)	(2.70)
Non-agriculture labour	3,465	5,834	2,740	1,512	11,290	4,918
	(18.64)	(29.13)	(9.03)	(10.07)	(37.60)	(21.28)
Trade	209	1,214	3,317	160	1,429	1,372
	(1.12)	(6.06)	(10.93)	(1.07)	(4.76)	(5.94)
Construction		500		102		128
	–	(2.50)	–	(0.68)	–	(0.55)
Artisan		170	1,350	400	714	564
	–	(0.85)	(4.45)	(2.66)	(2.38)	(2.44)
Service	279		1,600	840	1,143	798
	(1.50)	–	(5.27)	(5.59)	(3.81)	(3.45)
Remittances			583			136
	–	–	(1.92)	–	–	(0.59)
Pension	153		3,100			747
	(0.82)	–	(10.21)	–	–	(3.23)
Total	18,586	20,025	30,351	15,015	30,030	23,116
	(100.00)	(100.00)	(100.00)	(100.00)	(100.00)	(100.00)

Source: Field survey.
Note: Figures in brackets show percentages.

Land Size

The average operated area of agricultural land per tenant household comes to 2.45 acres, varying from 1.63 acres in Hardoi district to 4.07 acres in Jhansi district (Table 11.13). Average leased in land per tenant was 1.61 acres, which was higher than owned land per household (1.19 acres). Only in Etah district average area owned per household is higher than the average area leased-in by

Table 11.13
Land Owned and Leased in Per Tenant Household (in Acres)

District	Lakhimpur	Hardoi	Sultanpur	Etah	Jhansi	All
Owed land						
(a) Average per household	0.82	0.68	0.65	1.90	1.72	1.19
(b) Percentage of irrigated land	100.00	100.00	91.50	100.00	27.68	77.56
Leased land						
(a) Average per household	1.70	1.22	1.24	1.37	2.77	1.61
(b) Percentage of irrigated land	100.00	100.00	92.18	100.00	96.69	97.52
Total land						
(a) Average per household	1.89	1.63	1.76	3.08	4.07	2.45
(b) Percentage of irrigated land	100.00	100.00	91.85	100.00	74.63	70.64

Source: Field survey.

all households. In Lakhimpur, Hardoi and Etah districts, entire leased-in and owned land was irrigated. In Jhansi district, which is generally drought prone, leased in area was almost fully irrigated even though only 28 per cent of owned area was irrigated.

Crop Production

Table 11.14 presents farm characteristics of the sample households. Tenants have reported that they use major part of their cultivated area for foodgrain cultivation. It indicates that leasing-in of land is mainly to meet their food requirement. Wheat and Paddy are the dominant crops cultivated both on owned and leased-in land. The percentage of irrigated area in leased-in land is also higher than that of owned land. Productivity level of all the crops grown on leased-in land is found to be higher than the productivity realised on the owned land. All this indicates that tenants are cultivating leased-in land more efficiently than their owned land and they are realising better productivity from the leased-in land as compared

Table 11.14

Characteristics of Crop Production on Owned and Leased-in Land on Sample Farms

Crop	Percentage of gross cropped area		Percentage of irrigated area under crop		Yield quintal/acre (irrigated)		Yield quintal/acre (unirrigated)	
	Owned	Leased-in	Owned	Leased-in	Owned	Leased-in	Owned	Leased-in
Wheat	69.56	85.45	89.39	99.86	8.86	9.50	4.00	4.00
Paddy	96.05	74.09	100.00	100.00	12.36	12.43	–	–
Barley	1.88	1.32	100.01	100.00	7.08	8.70	–	–
Maize	10.26	4.32	43.10	89.70	4.81	5.26	1.76	4.81
Potato	11.01	2.57	100.00	100.00	36.75	38.33	–	–
Vegetable	0.68	0.92	100.00	100.00	32.99	33.50	–	–
Pulses	14.66	15.82	17.82	76.27	2.19	2.90	1.00	1.30
Groundnut	19.92	29.83	50.00	95.06	2.46	3.08	1.06	1.07
Mustard	16.99	10.46	24.41	100.00	3.10	3.61	0.92	–
Sugarcane	–	58.53	–	100.00	–	38.33	–	–

Source: Field survey.

to their own land. This may be due to the fact that the quality of leased-in land is superior to quality of owned land and irrigation facilities are available on leased in land.

Cost of Cultivation on Owned and Leased-in Land

Cost of various inputs applied in the cultivation of different crops on the leased-in land is more or less same as used in the cultivation of owned land. It has been calculated that the cost of inputs amounts to 40–50 per cent of the value of production of different crops (Table 11.15).

Investment on Leased-in Land

It is generally presumed that tenants have no incentive to make investment on development of the leased-in land as they have no security of tenure. This assumption is supported by the result of

Table 11.15

Crop-wise Per Acre Cost of Cultivation on Owned and Leased-in Land (in ₹)

Crop	Seed		Fertiliser/Pesticide		Irrigation		Others		Total	
	Owned	Leased -in	Owned	Leased -in	Owned	Leased -in	Owned	Leased -in	Owned	Leased -in
Wheat	860	797	1,239	1,158	1,747	1,788	1,319	1,447	5,634	5,190
Paddy	440	369	1,362	1,471	1,554	1,502	1,554	1,060	4,910	4,402
Maize	103	104	166	217	214	197	288	273	771	791
Potato	3,175	3,160	1,208	1,342	941	907	1,292	1,290	6,616	6,699
Vegetable	546	480	850	760	1,418	1,600	713	1,180	3,527	4,020
Pulses	253	412	239	324	234	417	385	445	1,111	1,598
Mustard	138	163	353	310	206	197	366	477	1,063	1,147
Groundnut	980	841	293	290	315	489	785	859	2,373	2,479

Source: Filed survey.

Table 11.16
Tenants Reporting Investment on the Leased-in Land

Type of lease	Lakhimpur	Hardoi	Sultanpur	Etah	Jhansi	All
Yes	9	12	7	14	4	46
	(20.93)	(21.43)	(11.67)	(28.00)	(8.16)	(17.83)
No	34	44	53	36	45	212
	(79.07)	(78.57)	(88.33)	(72.00)	(91.84)	(82.17)
Total	43	56	60	50	49	258
	(100.00)	(100.00)	(100.00)	(100.00)	(100.00)	(100.00)

Source: Field survey.
Note: Figures in brackets show percentages.

our field data, which shows that more than 82 per cent of sample tenants did not make any investment on the land leased-in by them (Table 11.16). The proportion of tenants making some investment on the leased-in land is relatively higher in Lakhimpur, Hardoi and Etah districts as compared to Sultanpur and Jhansi districts.

Levelling of land is the main item of investment of tenants. Around 65 per cent of tenants reported to have made investment in land levelling, while about 20 per cent reported investment in irrigation (Table 11.17). A small number had also spent money on soil testing. It looks that tenants who get inferior quality of land on lease do try to improve its quality through land levelling, irrigation, etc., to increase its productivity.

Table 11.17
Type of Investment Made on the Leased-in Land

Item of investment	Lakhimpur	Hardoi	Sultanpur	Etah	Jhansi	All
Land levelling	5	7	7	10	3	32
	(55.55)	(58.33)	(100.00)	(71.43)	(75.00)	(69.56)
Irrigation	3	4	–	2	–	9
	(33.33)	(33.33)		(14.29)		(19.57)
Soil testing	1	1	–	2	1	5
	(11.12)	(8.34)		(14.28)	(25.00)	(10.87)
Total	9	12	7	14	4	46
	(100.00)	(100.00)	(100.00)	(100.00)	(100.00)	(100.00)

Source: Field survey.
Note: Figures in brackets show percentages.

Characteristics of Tenants

In this section we present the findings relating to the characteristics of tenancy such as ownership of leased-in land from relatives and non-relatives, caste of lessors and the length of lease, terms and type of lease, sharing of inputs costs, lessor–lessee relationship and the views of the tenants about tenancy.

Sources of Area Leased-in

Around 92 per cent of all sample tenants have reported that they have leased-in farm land from non-relatives and the percentage of area thus leased-in constituted more than 95 per cent in total area leased-in at the level of aggregate sample. This trend is more or less similar across all the sample districts (Table 11.18).

Table 11.18
Source of Area Leased-in by the Tenants

Items	Lakhimpur	Hardoi	Sultanpur	Etah	Jhansi	All
Relatives						
No. of households	2	3	5	8	5	23
	(4.65)	(5.36)	(8.33)	(16.00)	(10.20)	(8.91)
Land area (acre)	12.00	4.30	10.25	23.10	29.5	79.15
	(5.47)	(2.46)	(3.38)	(7.52)	(4.53)	(4.79)
Non-relatives						
No. of households	41	53	55	42	44	235
	(95.35)	(94.64)	(91.67)	(84.00)	(89.80)	(91.90)
Land area (acre)	207.21	170.79	293.10	283.00	621.25	1,575.35
	(94.53)	(97.54)	(96.62)	(92.48)	(95.42)	(95.21)
Total						
No. of households	43	56	60	50	49	258
	(100.00)	(100.00)	(100.00)	(100.00)	(100.00)	(100.00)
Land area (acre)	219.21	175.09	303.35	306.10	650.75	1,654.50
	(100.00)	(100.00)	(100.00)	(100.00)	(100.00)	(100.00)

Source: Field survey.
Note: Figures in brackets show percentages.

Type Owner Tenant or Pure Tenant?

Tenancy may be divided into two broad categories. One is the pure tenants and the other is owner tenants. The pure tenants are those who have no land of their own for cultivation and the owner tenants are those who have some own land but also take others' land on rent. The survey has revealed that 30 per cent of total sample tenants are pure tenants, leasing-in 35 per cent of the total area leased-in (Table 11.19). The owner tenants are 70 per cent and they lease-in 75 per cent of total leased-in area. In Lakhimpur district, the proportion of pure tenants is higher (77 per cent), while in Etah district, owner tenants are relatively large in number (90 per cent). On the whole, owner tenants have been found to be in majority.

Distribution of Tenants According to Land Size

Analysis of tenants by size of holding shows that nearly half of the tenants had taken less than one acre land on lease and another

Table 11.19
Type of Tenants by Ownership of Land

District	Pure tenants		Owner tenants	
	No.	*Area leased in*	*No.*	*Area leased in*
Lakhimpur	33	64.69	10	8.44
	(76.74)	(88.46)	(23.26)	(11.54)
Hardoi	15	25.98	41	37.95
	(26.79)	(40.64)	(73.21)	(59.36)
Sultanpur	12	19.85	48	54.35
	(20.00)	(26.75)	(20.00)	(73.25)
Etah	5	5.70	45	62.70
	(10.00)	(8.33)	(90.00)	(91.67)
Jhansi	12	27.50	37	108.25
	(24.50)	(20.26)	(75.50)	(79.74)
Total	77	143.72	181	271.69
	(29.84)	(34.60)	(70.16)	(65.40)

Source: Field survey.
Note: Figures in brackets show percentages.

Table 11.20

Distribution of Tenants According to Land Size

Area (acres)	Lakhimpur		Hardoi		Sultanpur		Etah		Jhansi		All	
	No	%	No	%	No	%	No	%	No	%	No	%
0.00–0.50	5	11.63	10	17.86	5	8.93	5	10.00	1	2.04	26	10.24
0.50–1.00	16	37.21	28	50.00	27	48.21	24	48.00	3	6.12	98	38.58
1.00–1.50	8	18.60	9	16.07	11	19.64	9	18.00	3	6.12	40	15.75
1.50–2.00	6	13.95	7	12.50	6	10.71	8	16.00	15	30.61	42	16.54
2.00–2.50	–	–			4	7.14	–		–		4	1.57
2.50–3.00	4	9.30	2	3.57	1	1.79	2	4.00	18	36.73	27	10.63
3.00–3.50	–	–			1	1.79	–		–		1	0.39
3.50–4.00	2	4.65	–		1	1.79	1	2.00	6	12.24	10	3.94
4.00–5.00	1	2.33	–		–		1	2.00	–		2	0.79
5.00+	1	2.33	–		–		–		3	6.12	4	1.57
Total	43	100.00	56	100.00	56	100.00	50	100.00	49	100.00	254	100.00

Source: Field survey.

one third between one and two acres (Table 11.20). Less than 4 per cent tenants had taken 3 acres or more land on lease.

Reasons of Leasing-in of Land

The survey also probed the reasons for leasing-in of land. The majority of respondents (45 per cent) reported that they leased-in land for their livelihood. In Sultanpur and Lakhimpur districts about 93 per cent and 49 per cent of all sample tenants respectively reported leasing-in of land as a means of livelihood (Table 11.21). The second main reason was the small size of own farm land. About one-fourth of the tenants referred to small size of their holding as the main reason for leasing in. In Hardoi and Etah districts over 40 per cent tenants mentioned this reason. On the whole, it appears that leasing-in of land is resorted for getting greater access to land for increasing income and better livelihood.

Table 11.21
Reasons for Leasing-in of Land

Reasons	Lakhimpur	Hardoi	Sultanpur	Etah	Jhansi	All
As a means of livelihood	21 (48.84)	13 (23.21)	56 (93.33)	11 (22.00)	14 (28.57)	115 (44.57)
Small size of own land	8 (18.60)	26 (46.43)	4 (6.67)	21 (42.00)	7 (14.29)	66 (25.58)
Full utilisation of bullocks	2 (4.65)	3 (5.36)	–	4 (8.00)	1 (2.04)	10 (3.88)
For additional income	2 (4.65)	7 (12.50)	–	12 (24.00)	1 (2.04)	10 (3.88)
To repay the debt	–	–	–	–	4 (8.16)	4 (1.55)
Other reasons*	10 (23.26)	7 (12.50)	–	2 (4.00)	22 (44.90)	41 (15.89)
Total	43 (100.00)	56 (100.00)	60 (100.00)	50 (100.00)	49 (100.00)	258 (100.00)

Source: Field survey.
Notes: *Landlessness, own land un-irrigated, other personal needs.
Figures in brackets show percentages.

Characteristics of Lessors

The study has also probed the characteristics of farmers leasing out their land based on the responses of the tenants. The findings are reported below.

Caste of Lessors

The tenants have reported that among all land owners who leased-out their land, around 60 per cent were OBCs, followed by general castes (24.26 per cent). About 16 per cent of lessees belonged to scheduled castes (Table 11.22). In Jhansi and Hardoi districts, proportion of OBC lessees was quite high. The percentage of lessees of general castes in Sultanpur district and scheduled castes in Lakhimpur district was much higher than the average share of these lessees in the aggregate sample.

Table 11.22
Caste of Landlords Who Have Leased-out Land

Caste	Lakhimpur	Hardoi	Sultanpur	Etah	Jhansi	All
General	–	11	35	15	5	66
		(18.33)	(57.38)	(28.85)	(9.44)	(24.26)
OBC	29	45	13	33	43	163
	(63.04)	(75.00)	(21.31)	(63.46)	(81.13)	(59.93)
SC	17	4	13	4	5	43
	(36.96)	(6.67)	(21.31)	(7.69)	(9.43)	(15.81)
Total	46	60	61	52	53	272
	(100)	(100)	(100)	(100)	(100)	(100)
Average land owned (acres)	5.05	2.92	5.33	6.73	12.94	6.61

Source: Field survey.
Note: Figures in brackets show percentages.

Comparing the caste composition of the lessees and the lessors, we find that while 24.3 per cent of lessees belonged to general caste, less than one per cent reported leasing in land. The dominant players in the lease market were the OBCs, both among lessees and lessors. A significant proportion of lessees as well as lessors belonged to SCs.

Most of the lessees in our sample belonged to the category of small and medium farmers. Thus, average size of land ownership among lessees was 6.61 acres, though it varied from 2.92 acres in Hardoi to 12.96 acres in Jhansi district (Table 11.23). The size of land owned among lessors was much smaller across all the districts, hardly 1.19 acres.

Table 11.23
Average Size of Land Owned by Lessees and Lessors

Average size of land owned (acres)	Lakhimpur	Hardoi	Sultanpur	Etah	Jhansi	All
Lessees	5.05	2.92	5.33	6.73	12.94	6.61
Lessors	0.82	0.68	0.65	1.90	1.72	1.19

Source: Field survey.

Main Occupation of Tenants

It has been reported by the sample tenants that agriculture was the main occupation of around 50 per cent of all lessees. About one-fourth lessees were engaged in services and another 17 per cent were doing some trade (Table 11.24). In Lakhimpur and Etah districts, a higher proportion of lessees have agriculture as their main occupation. Thus, it looks that landowners generally lease out land due to problems faced in self cultivating. Nearly one–fourth of them were the absentee land owners.

Type, Terms and Tenure of Leasing

In this section we have probed the type, terms and duration of leasing.

TENANCY: ORAL OR WRITTEN?

Since sub-letting of land is prohibited in UP, we find that all tenancies reported in our survey were oral without any written or legal

Table 11.24
Main Occupation of Lessees

Occupation of lessee	Lakhimpur	Hardoi	Sultanpur	Etah	Jhansi	All
Agriculture	3.5	20	22	35	19	131
	(81.40)	(35.72)	(36.67)	(70.00)	(38.78)	(50.78)
Trade	1	14	13	5	11	44
	(2.32)	(25.00)	(21.67)	(10.00)	(22.45)	(17.05)
Service	7	18	12	10	14	61
	(16.28)	(32.14)	(20.00)	(20.00)	(28.57)	(23.64)
Other activities	–	4	13	–	5	22
		(7.14)	(13.66)		(10.20)	(8.53)
Total	43	56	60	50	49	258
	(100)	(100)	(100)	(100)	(100)	(100)

Source: Field survey.
Note: Figures in brackets show percentages.

agreement. Thus, the tenants were having no security over the leased in land and were in constant threat of eviction at any time by the land owners.

TERMS OF LEASING

The dominant form of leasing was the sharing of produce and cost (mainly irrigation and fertiliser costs) in most of the districts surveyed. However, some regional variations were observed. In Sultanpur district, landlords did not share in cost. This may reflect the weak bargaining power of the tenants in the district where landlessness and poverty were high. As a result, tenants have little options except to lease-in on the land owners terms. In Jhansi district where sharing of produce and cost is generally prevalent, few cases of fixed cash rent (₹4,000/- per acre) and fixed produce (3 quintals per acre) were also reported.

Majority of tenants has said that their land owners shared the cost of cultivation. Around one-fourth of sample tenants have reported that their landlords did not share the cost of cultivation. Variations across districts were evident. In three districts namely Lakhimpur, Hardoi and Etah all the respondents have reported cost sharing by the landlords. In Sultanpur district, no practice of cost sharing was reported between the lessee and lessor while in Jhansi district, 94 per cent tenants have reported the practice of cost sharing.

The pattern of sharing of input costs varies across different districts. In Lakhimpur and Hardoi districts, cost of fertiliser and irrigation was shared on 50–50 per cent basis between lessors and lessees in case of wheat, paddy and sugarcane crops. In Sultanpur district, tenants have reported that there was no practice of cost sharing between the tenants and landlords in the cultivation of any crop. However, in the districts of Etah and Jhansi, each of the inputs was shared on 50–50 per cent basis between the tenants and landlord except the cost of hired labour, which was totally borne by the tenants.

TENURE OF LEASE

Tenancy contracts are generally for short duration. Around 20 per cent of all tenancy contracts were of less than one year duration and

Table 11.25
Duration of Tenancy

Duration of lease	Lakhimpur	Hardoi	Sultanpur	Etah	Jhansi	All
Less than 1 year	19 (44.19)	1 (1.79)	6 (10.00)	22 (44.00)	3 (6.12)	51 (19.77)
1–2 Years	10 (23.26)	35 (62.50)	12 (20.00)	7 (14.00)	35 (71.43)	99 (38.37)
2–3 Years	8 (18.60)	7 (12.50)	22 (36.67)	9 (18.00)	7 (14.29)	53 (20.54)
3–4 Years	3 (6.98)	3 (5.36)	12 (20.00)	6 (12.00)	3 (6.12)	27 (10.47)
4 Years and above	3 (6.97)	10 (17.85)	8 (13.33)	6 (12.00)	1 (2.04)	28 (10.85)
Total	43 (100)	56 (100)	60 (100)	50 (100)	49 (100)	258 (100)

Source: Field survey.
Note: Figures in brackets show percentages.

38 per cent were for the period of 1–2 years duration (Table 11.25). Another 20 per cent contracts were for the period of 2–3 years. Thus, around 90 per cent of all leased-in land was contracted for the period of less than 4 years. Short term tenancy contracts were more prevalent in the districts of Lakhimpur and Etah as compared to Hardoi, Jhansi and Sultanpur districts.

Who Decides the Terms of Leasing?

The tenants were asked to give information on who decided the terms of leasing. More than half of the respondents reported that terms were decided as per practices of leasing prevalent in the area (Table 11.26). About one-third respondents reported that the terms were dictated by the landlords, while in about 10 per cent cases the tenants laid down the conditions of lease. However, remarkable differences in lease decisions were observed across the districts. In Lakhimpur and Hardoi districts more than 50 per cent respondents have reported that landlords decided the terms, while in Sultanpur and Jhansi districts less than 10 per cent reported that terms were decided by the landlords.

Table 11.26
Distribution of Respondents by Decision Maker about the Terms of Leasing

Decision maker	Lakhimpur	Hardoi	Sultanpur	Etah	Jhansi	All
Tenant	5	3	3	8	5	24
	(11.63)	(5.36)	(5)	(16.0)	(10.20)	(9.30)
Landlord	26	28	5	19	4	82
	(60.47)	(50)	(8.33)	(38.0)	(8.16)	(31.78)
General practice	12	25	49	23	34	143
	(27.91)	(44.64)	(81.67)	(46.0)	(69.39)	(55.43)
Mutual understanding	–	50	3	–	6	9
			(5)		(12.24)	(3.49)
Total	43	56	60	50	49	258
	(100.00)	(100.00)	(100.00)	(100.00)	(100.00)	(100.00)

Source: Field survey.

Place of Sharing the Produce After Harvesting

The place of sharing of produce is likely to affect the proportion in which output is to be shared between tenants and landlords. It may be argued that if the produce is kept at the place of landlord after harvesting for sharing between the tenant and landlord, chances are there that landlord may take away greater share than what was decided upon. The analysis of our survey data showed that in most cases (63.2 per cent) tenants kept the produce in the field after harvesting. In around 22 per cent cases produce was kept at the place of tenants. The practice of keeping the produce at the place of landlords was reported by only 8 per cent of all tenants (Table 11.27). In Jhansi district the produce was shared at the field, while in Sultanpur district it was kept at the tenants place in more than 50 per cent cases. Thus, it can be said that the produce was shared between tenants and landlord amicably.

Recent Changes in Tenancy Pattern

We also tried to probe whether there have been changes in any aspect of tenancy during the past five years. The majority of sample

Table 11.27
Place of Sharing the Produce After Harvesting

Place of sharing	Lakhimpur	Hardoi	Sultanpur	Etah	Jhansi	All
In field	32 (74.42)	50 (89.29)	10 (16.67)	24 (48.00)	47 (95.92)	163 (63.18)
At tenants' place	5 (11.63)	2 (3.57)	31 (51.67)	16 (32.00)	2 (4.08)	56 (21.71)
At landlords' place	4 (9.30)	4 (7.14)	7 (11.66)	5 (10.00)	–	20 (7.75)
Any other place	2 (4.65)	–	12 (20.00)	5 (10.00)	–	19 (7.36)
Total	43 (100.00)	56 (100.00)	60 (100.00)	50 (100.00)	49 (100.00)	258 (100.00)

Source: Field study.
Note: Figures in brackets show percentages.

tenants (62 per cent) have reported there has been no change of any form in the tenancy during the last five years (Table 11.28). The remaining tenants reported change in tenancy in respect of choice of crop (16 per cent), terms of lease (14 per cent) and sharing in cost (8 per cent).

Table 11.28
Changes Reported in Tenancy during Last Five Years

Changes	Lakhimpur	Hardoi	Sultanpur	Etah	Jhansi	All
Type of lease	19 (44.19)	1 (1.78)	4 (6.67)	5 (10.00)	8 (16.33)	37 (14.34)
Sharing in cost	3 (6.98)	5 (8.93)	–	7 (14.00)	5 (10.20)	20 (7.75)
Selection of crops	4 (9.30)	12 (21.43)	–	24 (48.00)	–	40 (15.50)
Others (timely payment)	2 (4.65)	–	–	–	–	2 (0.78)
No change	15 (34.88)	38 (67.86)	56 (93.33)	14 (28.00)	36 (73.47)	159 (61.63)
Total	43 (100.00)	56 (100.00)	60 (100.00)	50 (100.00)	49 (100.00)	258 (100.00)

Source: Field survey.
Note: Figures in brackets show percentages.

There were differences in pattern of response in different districts. A relatively higher proportion reported no change in tenancy system in Sultanpur, Jhansi and Hardoi district. However, 44 per cent tenants reported change in terms of lease in Lakhimpur, while 48 per cent reported change in selection of crops in Etah district.

Relation of Tenants with Landlords

The study also probed the nature of relations between tenants and landlords. Hardly 2 per cent of tenants reported that there has been any dispute with the landlords.

Decision about Cropping Pattern

About 60 per cent of tenants have reported that the decision about cropping pattern was taken jointly in majority of cases (Table 11.29). Around 28 per cent of tenants expressed the view that landlords took such decisions. This proportion was higher in Hardoi and Etah districts, 53.6 and 36.0 per cent respectively. About 13 per cent of tenants took decision themselves about cropping pattern.

Table 11.29
Decision about Cropping Pattern

Decision taken by	Lakhimpur	Hardoi	Sultanpur	Etah	Jhansi	All
Tenant	6	1	13	11	3	34
	(13.95)	(1.79)	(21.67)	(22.00)	(6.12)	(13.18)
Landlord	10	30	13	18	1	72
	(23.26)	(53.57)	(21.66)	(36.00)	(2.04)	(27.91)
Jointly	27	25	34	21	45	152
	(62.79)	(44.64)	(56.67)	(42.00)	(91.84)	(58.91)
Total	43	56	60	50	49	258
	(100.00)	(100.00)	(100.00)	(100.00)	(100.00)	(100.00)

Source: Field survey.
Note: Figures in brackets show percentages.

Table 11.30

Tenants Reporting Taking Loan from the Landlord

Purpose of loan	Lakhimpur	Hardoi	Sultanpur	Etah	Jhansi	All
Production	–	2	8	5	8	23
		(3.57)	(13.33)	(10.00)	(16.33)	(8.92)
Consumption	–	–	3	2	7	12
			(5.00)	(4.00)	(14.29)	(4.65)
Total	–	2	11	7	15	35
		(3.57)	(18.33)	(14.00)	(30.61)	(13.56)

Source: Field survey.

Loan Taken from Landlords

In the sample, 14 per cent tenants reported to have taken loan from the landlords. About 9 per cent tenants had taken loan for production purpose while 5 per cent of took the loan for consumption purpose (Table 11.30). The proportion of tenants taking loan both for production and for consumption purposes was relatively higher in Jhansi district.

Undue Favours Taken by Landlords

One-fourth of total tenants have reported that the landlords seek undue favour from them. In majority of cases, landlords ask them to work at lower wage rates and on their terms. The percentage of such tenants who reported undue favour sought by the landlords is lower in Lakhimpur district as compared to other districts (Table 11.31).

Problems Faced by Tenants

The tenants were also asked about the problems they faced as tenants. Nearly one-third tenants complained about insecurity of tenancy. Over one-fourth of the tenants mentioned non

Table 11.31
Tenants Reporting Undue Favours Taken by Landlords

Undue favours	Lakhimpur	Hardoi	Sultanpur	Etah	Jhansi	All
Labour on unfavourable terms	1 (4.65)	3 (5.36)	5 (8.33)	3 (6.00)	3 (6.12)	15 (5.81)
Labour at lower rates	1 (4.65)	7 (12.50)	7 (11.67)	11 (22.00)	11 (22.45)	37 (14.34)
Demand to work as permanent servant	–	1 (1.79)	6 (10.00)	4 (8.00)	1 (2.04)	12 (4.65)
Total	2 (4.65)	11 (19.64)	18 (30.00)	18 (36.00)	15 (30.61)	64 (24.81)

Source: Field survey.
Note: Figures in brackets show percentages.

availability of institutional credit as a problem. Over one-fifth faced problem of lack of equipment and machinery for cultivation. Exploitation by landlord was reported by about one-sixth of the tenants (Table 11.32).

Table 11.32
Problems Faced by the Tenants

Problems	Lakhimpur	Hardoi	Sultanpur	Etah	Jhansi	All
Insecurity of tenancy	6 (13.96)	16 (21.62)	43 (38.39)	8 (16.00)	37 (52.11)	110 (31.42)
Non-availability of institutional credit	15 (34.88)	16 (21.62)	38 (33.93)	1 (2.00)	23 (32.39)	93 (26.57)
Non-availability of machinery & equipment	9 (20.93)	33 (44.60)	3 (2.68)	32 (64.00)	1 (1.41)	78 (22.29)
Exploitation by landlord	13 (30.23)	8 (10.81)	19 (16.96)	7 (14.00)	10 (14.09)	57 (16.29)
Non-sharing of cultivation cost	–	1 (1.35)	9 (8.04)	2 (4.00)	–	12 (3.43)
Total	43 (100.00)	74 (100.00)	112 (100.00)	50 (100.00)	71 (100.00)	350 (100.00)

Source: Field survey.
Note: Figures in brackets show percentages.

Table 11.33
Opinion of Tenants about Legalisation of Tenancy

Opinion about legalisation of tenancy	Lakhimpur	Hardoi	Sultanpur	Etah	Jhansi	All
Agree	37	39	42	32	45	195
	(86.05)	(69.64)	(70.00)	(64.00)	(91.84)	(75.58)
Disagree	6	17	18	18	4	63
	(13.95)	(30.36)	(30.00)	(36.00)	(8.16)	(24.42)
Total	43	56	60	50	49	258
	(100.00)	(100.00)	(100.00)	(100.00)	(100.00)	(100.00)

Source: Field survey.
Note: Figures in brackets show percentages.

Views of Tenants on Legalisation of Tenancy

As mentioned earlier tenancy is illegal in UP although it is prevalent in all parts of the state in a concealed form. The respondents were asked whether in their view tenancy should be legalised. More than 75 per cent of the tenants reported that tenancy should be legalised (Table 11.33). While an overwhelming majority of tenants in Lakhimpur and Jhansi districts wanted legalisation of tenancy, about one-third of tenants were not in favour of its legalisation in the districts of Hardoi, Sultanpur and Etah. It may be observed that in the former two districts land inequity is greater and the proportion of large holdings is also greater. On the other hand, in the other three districts holdings are smaller and land pressure is more. Thus, tenants of latter districts fear that if tenancy is legalised landlords may not be willing to give their land on lease.

Conclusions and Suggestions

The major findings of the study are summarised below:

1. Despite the legislative regulations and restrictions on the tenancy, it is being widely practiced in UP as well as in India. The NSS figures show that percentage of tenant holdings

was 20.5 per cent in UP during 1980–1981 which declined to 11.7 per cent in 2002–2003. The percentage of leased-in area in total area has remained around 10 per cent in UP during 1980–1981 to 2002–2003.

2. The socio-economic conditions of the sample tenants have revealed that majority of them belonged to backward castes followed by scheduled castes, while very few tenants were from upper castes. Agriculture was the main occupation of about 60 per cent of tenants, while about 20 of them were rural labourers.

3. Average land leased-in per household was 1.61 acres, which was higher than the land owned per household (1.19 acres).

4. The main reason for leasing-in of land is better livelihood.

5. The leased-in land did provide an average annual income of ₹5,163 per household, which accounted for 22.34 per cent of average annual income per household.

6. The majority of landlords who rented out their land also belonged to Other Backwards Castes (OBCs) and around half of them were engaged in agriculture and rest were in service and trade professions.

7. All lease agreements are oral. The length of lease was generally of short duration. In most of the cases duration of lease was of 1–2 years.

8. The terms of lease were generally decided according to the prevalent lease practices in the area. The dominant form of leasing was based on the sharing of produce and cost on 50:50 basis. Generally the cost of fertilisers and irrigation was shared on 50–50 per cent basis between tenants and landlords. The practice of leasing-in on the basis of cash payment was also found to be emerging in some districts.

9. Insecurity of lease contract was the most serious problem perceived by tenants.

10. About one-third of tenants have reported taking loan from the land owners for production or consumption purposes.

11. One-fourth of the tenants have reported that their land owners sought undue favour in lieu of leasing-in of land to them in the form of payment of lower wages for labour.

12. The majority of tenants who were interviewed expressed the view that tenancy should be legislated.

To conclude, leasing-in of land is a livelihood strategy adopted by landless labourers and farmers with small holdings to augment their income. It is an effective measure for increasing the access of poor to land without imposing ceiling on agricultural land for its redistribution among the land less people. As the Tenth Five Year Plan has rightly observed in this connection:

> The prohibition of tenancy has not really ended the practice. This, in turn, also depresses employment opportunities for the landless agricultural labourers. The ban on tenancy, which was meant to protect tenants, has only ended up hurting the economic interests of the tenants as they are not even recognised as tenants. As a result, they are denied the benefits of laws that provide security of tenure and regulate rent.

Our field study in Uttar Pradesh provides support to the above observations. Liberalisation of lease market has become essential in the present circumstances for improving the performance of agriculture and generation of income and employment opportunities for the poor. It is high time that the state government should take necessary steps to legalise tenancy and formulate an appropriate policy balancing the interests of the tenants and the landlords. Such policy framework should insure fixity of tenure for a given period and the right of lessors over land. A five year renewable contract may be provided for. Land leasing should be permitted within the land ceiling limit. As a precautionary measure leasing-in by large landholders from small and marginal farmers should not be allowed. The government may indicate the maximum rent to be realised by the landlord, but within that limit it is better to leave the terms of contract to be decided by the market. A simple format of agreement may be provided for, which may be registered with the village Panchayat or tehsil office. The policy should also spell out mechanism to organise the contract between the lessors and lessees. Making available the relevant information on the availability of farm land for lease, its quality etc. to potential tenants should be the integral part of the plan of land lease liberalisation. The Panchayats should maintain details of land available for lease with details of its quality, irrigation facility, etc. All the tenant cultivators should be recorded and they should also be made eligible for the institutional loans.

The reform in tenancy laws on the above lines will be mutually beneficial to all parties concerned and will certainly promote the ends of equity and growth.

References

Appu, P.S. (1997), *Land Reform in India: A Survey of Policy, Legislation and Implementation*, Vikas Publishing House, New Delhi.

Cheriyan, O. (2004), *Changes in the Mode of Labour Due to Shift in the Land use Pattern*. Discussion Paper No. 81, Centre for Development Studies, Thiruvanantapuram.

Deshpande, R.S. (2008), 'Contract Farming and Tenancy Reforms: Entangled without Tether', Manohar Publishers & Distributors, New Delhi.

Haque, T. (2001), *Impact of Tenancy Reforms on Productivity Improvement and Socio-Economic Status of Poor Tenants*, National Centre for Agricultural Economics and Policy Research, Vikas Publishing House, New Delhi.

Haque, T., Pushpendra and B.K. Sinha (1999), 'Some Aspects of Tenancy Debate: Implications for Policy Reforms', in papers for National Workshop on 'Whither Tenancy?', Centre for Rural Studies, LBSNAA, Moussoorie.

Government of India (1997), *Policy Relating to Sharecropping and Leasing*, Department of Rural Development, New Delhi.

Government of India (1999), *Concept Note on Legalizing Leasing of Agricultural Land*, Prime Minister's Office, New Delhi.

Latha, A. and C.G. Madhusoodhanan (2004), *Sustainability of Commercial Banana Production in Watershed Based Agricultural Development: A Case Study of Two Micro Watersheds*. Discussion Paper No. 95, Centre for Development Studies, Thiruvanantapuram.

Nair, K.N. and V. Menon (2005), *Lease Farming in Kerala: Findings from Micro level Studies*, Working Paper No. 378, Centre for Development Studies, Thiruvanantapuram.

Shankar, K. (1980), *Concealed Tenancy and its Implications for Equity and Economic Growth: A Study of Eastern Uttar Pradesh*, Concept Publishing Company, New Delhi.

Tripathi, R.N. (1985), *Tenancy and Efficiency of Farming in a Developing Economy*, Mittal Publications, New Delhi.

Veron, R. (1999), *Real Markets and Environmental Change in Kerala, India: A New Understanding of Crop Markets on Sustainable Development*, Ashgate Publishing Ltd., Farnham, Surrey, United Kingdom.

12

Impact of Land Distribution on the Rural Poor: A Field Study

Ajit Kumar Singh and Pratap Singh Garia

Introduction

Distribution of land to the landless and rural poor is an important strategy for poverty alleviation and rural development as several studies have shown (Haque and Parthasarathy, 1992; Planning Commission, 2007; Sharma et al., 1993; Singh et al., 1993). The first phase of land reforms in post-Independent India started with the abolition of intermediaries. UP also passed the Zamindari Abolition and Land Reforms Act in 1950. In the second phase of land reforms the imposition of land ceilings and redistribution of surplus land to the rural poor was taken up. The UP Imposition of Land Ceiling Act was passed in 1960. The Act put the ceiling limit at 40 acres. It defined family in a liberal manner and allowed a large number of exemptions. The provisions of the Act were widely misused and its implementation was lackadaisical, with the result that the Act hardly made an impact on the land distribution situation in the state.

The shortcomings of the land ceiling acts in different states led to a fresh thinking about the provisions of the land ceiling acts and need for amendment in the Act was felt. As a follow-up, UP amended its Land Ceiling Act in 1973. The amended Act brought down the ceiling limit and removed many of the exemptions given in the earlier act. According to the revised ceiling act, the ceiling was fixed at 7.3 ha. of irrigated land for a family of five. An additional 2-ha. area was allowed for every additional family member. Land ceiling for a single cropped irrigated area was kept at 10.95 ha. and for unirrigated area it was kept at 18.25 ha.

Even the amended Land Ceiling Act of UP failed in its basic objectives as by that time big landlords had also distributed their land in several names to escape the provisions of the Act.

Table 12.1
Surplus Land under Amended Land Ceiling Act Distributed in UP till 31 March 2008

	Total	
Details	*No.*	*Area*
No. of landholders against whom ceiling proceedings were launched	48,466	793,474
Cases filed before the designated authority	83,852	1,024,102
Cases decided by the prescribed authority	50,334	504,154
Cases pending	421	1,516
Surplus land yet to be settled		13,243

Source: Board of Revenue, UP.

A large number of cases were also filed by the landholders to whom notices were issued under the ceiling Act. Till 31 March 2008 an area of 7.93 lakh ha. was declared surplus and notices were issued to 48,466 landholders. However, 83,853 cases were filed before the designated authority, out of which 50,334 cases were decided till 31 March 2008 (Table 12.1). Still about half of the area to be acquired is under dispute.

Till 31 March 2008 only 244,524 ha. of land was distributed to 2.89 lakh beneficiaries. This amounts to hardly 1.36 per cent of the operational area of 179.8 lakh ha. in the state. Thus, land ceiling legislation failed to bring about any noticeable change in the structure of land distribution in the state. Nearly 69 per cent of distributed land was given to scheduled castes (SCs) and about 31 per cent to other categories (Table 12.2). Very little land was distributed to scheduled tribes (STs), who constitute a very nominal proportion of state population.

The successive state governments have been following the policy of distribution of *Gram Samaj* land to the landless. Surplus

Table 12.2
Surplus Land Distributed in UP till 31 March 2008 by Category

Category	*Persons (no.)*		*Area (ha.)*	
SC	199,453	168,443	68.9	68.9
ST	505	985.4	0.17	0.4
Others	89,434	75,095	30.92	30.9
Total	289,392	244,524	100	100

Source: Board of Revenue, UP.

land available in a village is distributed by the Sub-Divisional Magistrate of the *tehsil* on the recommendation of the Village Land Management Committee. The eligible categories include landless, SC and ST, persons below the poverty line, agricultural labourers and artisans living in the village. Minimum land distributed is 1.26 acres. For homeless people 100–150 sq. yard land is given to build a house.

The total area of *Gram Samaj* land distributed by the government is much larger than that distributed under the Land Ceiling Act. Till March 2008 a total of 11.68 lakh ha. of *Gram Samaj* land was distributed to 36.83 lakh persons in the state (Table 12.3). Per person allotted land comes to 0.32 ha. Of the total land allottees in the state 56.0 per cent belonged to SC, 0.08 per cent to ST, 26.0 per cent to OBC and 16 per cent to other categories.

The chapter is organised as follows. Section titled 'Objectives of the Study and Sample Design' outlines the objectives of the study and the sample design of the primary survey. Section titled 'Land Distribution in Selected Districts and Villages' presents details of the ceiling surplus and the *Gram Sabha* land distributed. Section titled 'Social, Demographic and Economic Characteristics of Allottees' describes the social, demographic and income characteristics of the allottees. Section titled 'Details of Own and Allotted Land' presents

Table 12.3

Category-wise Cumulative Gram Sabha *Land Allotted in UP during 1975–1976 and 31 March 2008*

Category	Land allotted		Possession	
	No.	*Area (ha.)*	*No.*	*Area*
Scheduled caste	2,076,874 (56.39)	643,513.6 (55.07)	99.92	99.92
Scheduled tribe	3,059 (0.08)	1,866.11 (0.16)	100.00	100.00
OBC	946,216 (25.69)	335,488.96 (28.71)	99.77	99.90
Others	656,646 (17.83)	187,607.62 (16.06)	99.90	99.87
Total	3,682,795 (100.00)	1,168,496.3 (100.00)	99.88	99.91

Source: Board of Revenue, UP.
Note: Figures in brackets show percentage to total.

the findings in regard to owned and allotted land of the families surveyed. Section titled 'Problems in Obtaining Land *Patta* and Possession' discusses the problems faced by allottee households in obtaining ownership title and actual physical possession of the land. Section titled 'Utilisation of Allotted Land and Problems in Cultivation' reveals the problems the allottee households faced in actually cultivating the land allotted to them. Section titled 'Impact of Land Allotment on Allottees' discusses the impact on the allottees in terms of net income, employment and yield from the allotted land. Section titled 'Opinion of land Allottees about the Process of Land Allotment' presents the opinion of land allottees on the process of land allotment. The final section summarises the findings.

Objectives of the Study and Sample Design

This chapter presents the findings of a field study carried out by the Giri Institute of Development Studies to examine the impact of the land distribution programme on the rural poor in 2008. The objectives of the study included the following:

1. To examine the land allotment process in the state
2. To verify whether possession of land has been handed over to the allottees or not
3. To study the pattern of utilisation of the allotted land
4. To study the impact of land allotment on the socio-economic conditions of the allottees
5. To obtain the views of the allottees for improvement in the land allotment process

Sample Design

It was decided to carry out the fieldwork in five districts of the state representing the different agro-economic regions, namely, eastern region, western region, central region, Bundelkhand and *tarai* region. From each region one district was selected where the highest amount of land was distributed. The five selected districts were Etah from western region, Hardoi from central region, Sultanpur from eastern region, Lakhimpur Khiri from Tarai region and Jhansi from Bundelkhand. From the selected districts, one *tehsil* was selected where maximum land has been distributed. From each *tehsil* two villages were selected where maximum land has been distributed. Finally from each village a minimum of 25 land allottees were selected randomly for detailed interview. Thus, our sample consisted of 5 districts, 5 *tehsils*, 10 villages and 279 beneficiaries. Details of the sample and names of selected villages have been provided in Table 12.4.

Land Distribution in Selected Districts and Villages

Distribution of Land Ceiling Act Surplus Land

Table 12.5 shows details of land distribution in the surveyed villages. The survey revealed that 1,204 ha. land was distributed to

Table 12.4
Details of the Sample Design

District	Tehsil/block	Village	Beneficiaries		
			Male	*Female*	*Total*
Lakhimpur	Lakhimpur				
	1. Lakhimpur	1. Saidapur Deokali	28	1	29
	2. Phool Beha	2. Safipur	25	2	27
Hardoi	Sandila		29	1	30
	1. Sandila	1. Begumganj	26	1	27
	2. Bharawan	2. Sehgavan			
Sultanpur	Sadar		28	2	30
	1. Dhanpatganj	1. Jhajaur	22	3	25
	2. Kudebhar	2. Saifullaganj			
Etah	Sadar		30	–	30
	1. Sheelatpur	1. Pura	30	–	30
		2. Kilarmau			
Jhansi	Sadar	1. Kailar	24	2	25
	1. Babina	2. Saiyyar	23	2	25
Districts 5	*Tehsils* 5 Blocks 8	*Villages* 10	265	14	279

Table 12.5
Details of Ceiling Land Distributed in the Selected Villages

District/caste	No.	Area (ha.)	Average Area (ha.)	No.	Area (ha.)	No.	Area (ha.)	No.	Area (ha.)
		Land allotted		Possession not handed over		Land sold by allottees		Non-eligible beneficiaries	
Lakhimpur	97	171.38	1.77	1	.60	13	19.73	1	0.47
Hardoi	98	91.36	0.93	–	–	6	7.63	–	–
Sultanpur	156	102.87	0.66	6	6.36	25	21.61	28	9.43
Etah	477	546.95	1.15	8	19.80	1	0.50	–	–
Jhansi	105	298.03	2.81	6	11.20	6	20.89	–	–
Total	933	1,204.59	1.29	21	37.96	51	70.36	29	9.898

Source: Computed from revenue records of the villages.

933 persons in the surveyed villages. Per person land distributed comes to 1.29 ha. However, it varied from 0.66 ha. in Sultanpur to 2.81 ha. in Jhansi. Twenty-one allottees (2.25 per cent) could not get possession of their allotted land so far. Fifty-one allottees (5.5 per cent) had sold the land allotted to them. About half of these allottees belong to Sultanpur district where land allotted per person was very small. Twenty-nine allottees (3.1 per cent) were found to belong to non-eligible category.

Distribution of Gram Samaj Land

Table 12.6 shows the total *Gram Samaj* land distributed in the sample districts till 31 March 2008. Total land distributed amounted to 40,048 ha. in Lakhimpur Khiri, 49,000 ha. in Hardoi, 22,531 in Sultanpur, 44,110 in Etah and 34,374 ha. in Jhansi. The number of allottees was 119,140; 128,160; 122,733; 84,710 and 49,092 in the five districts, respectively. Average land allotted comes to 0.34, 0.38, 0.18, 0.52 and 0.70 ha., respectively. Proportion of SC allottees varies from 37.66 per cent in Lakhimpur and 63 per cent in Hardoi. Similarly, the proportion of OBC allottees varies from 44.3 per cent in Lakhimpur to 19.3 per cent in Sultanpur.

Table 12.6

Category-wise Cumulative Gram Sabha Land Allotted in Selected Districts during 1975–1976 and 31 March 2008

	Scheduled caste		Scheduled tribe		OBC		Others		Total	
	No.	Area	No.	Area	No.	Area	No.	Area	No.	Area
Lakhimpur										
	44,871	21,040.98	413	319.68	52,775	9,363.22	21,081	9,324.17	119,140	40,048.06
	37.66	52.54	0.35	0.80	44.30	23.38	17.69	23.28	100.00	100.00
Hardoi										
	80,955	27,747.39	–	–	32,576	14,536.47	14,629	6,716.67	128,160	49,000.48
	63.17	56.63			25.42	29.67	11.41	13.71	100.00	100.00
Sultanpur										
	75,997	14,108.79	–	–	27,963	4,354.72	18,773	4,067.34	1,22,733	22,530.87
	61.92	62.77			22.78	19.25	15.29	17.98	100.00	100.00
Etah										
	42,681	23,643.17	–	–	24,810	11,744.46	17,219	8,722.57	84,710	44,110.21
	50.38	53.60			29.29	26.63	20.33	19.77	100.00	100.00
Jhansi										
	27,067	23,573.50	–	–	16,968	8,234.69	5,057	2,665.73	49,092	34,373.92
	55.14	68.58			34.56	23.96	10.30	7.46	100.00	100.00
Uttar Pradesh										
	2,076,874	643,513.60	3,059	1,866.11	946,216	335,488.96	656,646	187,607.62	3,682,795	1,168,496.29
	56.39	55.07	0.08	0.16	25.69	28.71	17.83	16.06	100.00	100.00

Source: Board of Revenue, UP.

Note: Figures in brackets show percentage to total.

Social, Demographic and Economic Characteristics of Allottees

Table 12.7 shows the social and demographic characteristics of the respondents. Of respondents, 46.3 per cent belonged to SC, 47.7 per cent to OBC and 4 per cent to ST category. Only 1.4 per cent belonged to other social groups. Of respondents 87 per cent were Hindu and 13 per cent Muslim.

Table 12.7

Distribution of Beneficiaries by Caste and Religion

Caste/religion	Lakhimpur	Hardoi	Sultanpur		Jhansi	Total
A. Caste						
Scheduled caste	46	12	22	25	26	131
	(82.14)	(21.05)	(40.00)	(41.67)	(50.98)	(46.95)
Scheduled tribe	—	—	—	—	11	11
					(21.57)	(3.95)
OBC	9	43	32	35	14	133
	(16.07)	(75.44)	(58.18)	(58.33)	(27.45)	(47.67)
Others	1	2	1	—	—	4
	(1.79)	(3.51)	(1.82)			(1.43)
Total	56	57	55	60	51	279
	(100.0)	(100.0)	(100.0)	(100.0)	(100.00)	(100.0)
B. Religion						
Hindu	52	40	43	57	50	242
	(92.86)	(70.18)	(78.48)	(95.00)	(98.04)	(86.74)
Muslim	4	17	12	3	1	37
	(7.14)	(29.82)	(21.82)	(5.00)	(1.96)	(13.26)

Source: Field survey.
Note: Figures in parentheses show percentage to total.

About 45 per cent of the land allottees were below 45 years of age, 34 per cent were in the age group of 45–60 years and remaining 23 per cent were above 60 years (Table 12.8).

The average size of the family of sample households was 6.66. It varied from 5.96 in Jhansi district to 7.69 in Sultanpur district (Table 12.9).

Table 12.8
Distribution of Respondents by Age

Age group (years)	Lakhimpur	Hardoi	Sultanpur	Etah	Jhansi	Total
Below 25	1 (1.79)	—	2 (3.64)	1 (1.67)	2 (3.92)	6 (2.15)
25–45	20 (35.7)	27 (47.37)	14 (25.45)	31 (51.66)	24 (47.06)	116 (41.58)
45–60	16 (28.57)	21 (36.84)	17 (30.91)	25 (41.67)	15 (29.41)	94 (33.69)
Above 60	19 (33.93)	9 (15.79)	22 (40.00)	3 (5.00)	10 (19.61)	63 (22.58)
Total	56 (100.0)	57 (100.0)	55 (100.0)	60 (100.0)	51 (100.00)	279 (100.0)

Source: Field survey.
Note: Figures in brackets show percentage to total.

Table 12.9
Average Size of Respondent Household

Sex	Lakhimpur	Hardoi	Sultanpur	Etah	Jhansi	Total
Male	1.89	1.96	2.53	2.02	1.82	2.05
Female	1.73	1.61	2.02	1.77	1.61	1.75
Boys	1.43	1.61	1.80	1.42	1.33	1.52
Girls	1.43	1.21	1.35	1.50	1.20	1.34
Total	6.48	6.40	7.69	6.70	5.96	6.66

Source: Field survey.

Table 12.10 shows the distribution of respondents by level of education; 52.3 per cent of respondents were illiterate. The proportion of illiterate varied from 23.3 per cent in Etah to 64 per cent in Lakhimpur. About 9 per cent of the allottees were simply literate and 29.4 per cent had received education up to the upper primary level. About 7.5 per cent respondents were educated up to the middle level and 1.4 per cent had done graduation.

Occupation and Household Income of the Allottees

Table 12.11 shows the occupational distribution of the allottees. The majority of the allottees (42.7 per cent) were working as

Table 12.10
Distribution of Respondents by Level of Education

Educational level	Lakhimpur	Hardoi	Sultanpur	Etah	Jhansi	Total
Illiterate	36	33	35	14	28	146
	(64.29)	(57.89)	(63.64)	(23.33)	(54.90)	(52.33)
Literate	5	4	5	6	6	26
	(8.93)	(7.03)	(9.09)	(10.00)	(11.76)	(9.32)
Up to upper	15	16	15	24	12	82
primary level	(26.78)	(28.07)	(27.27)	(40.00)	(23.53)	(29.39)
Up to middle	—	3	—	14	4	21
level		(5.26)		(23.33)	(7.85)	(7.53)
Graduate and	—	1	—	2	1	4
above		(1.75)		(3.34)	(1.96)	(1.43)
Total allottees	56	57	55	60	51	279
	(100.0)	(100.0)	(100.0)	(100.0)	(100.00)	(100.0)

Source: Field survey.

non-agriculture labour. The other main beneficiary category was that of farmers (41 per cent). However, in Sultanpur and Jhansi very few allottees were following agriculture as their primary occupation. A surprising finding is that very few agricultural labourers were allotted land. About 9 per cent allottees were engaged in self-employment and about 3 per cent in services.

Table 12.12 shows the household income of allottees by different sources. Total household income of the allottees from all sources was estimated at ₹28,598 per year. Per capita income came to ₹4,294 only. Income levels were quite low in Lakhimpur and Etah district. Agriculture contributed about 43 per cent of household income. But its share was much lower in Sultanpur district (26 per cent). Income from cultivation of the allotted land was reported at ₹6,588 or 23 per cent of the total household income. But its contribution ranged from as little as 12.3 per cent in Sultanpur to 46 per cent in Lakhimpur. About 37 per cent of household income was derived from working as non-agricultural labour. In Jhansi the share of income from this source was as high as 71 per cent. The contribution of other sources taken together was hardly about 20 per cent.

The analysis of household income data suggests that most of the respondents were living near or below the poverty line. Income from cultivation on allotted land helps in their subsistence, but it is far from adequate for survival and has to be supplemented by other sources of livelihood.

Table 12.11

Primary and Secondary Occupation of the Allottees

Occupation	Lakhimpur		Hardoi		Sultanpur		Etah		Jhansi		Total	
	Main	Secondary	Main	Secondary	Main	Secondary	Main	Secondary	Main	Secondary	Main	Secondary
Agriculture	34 (60.71)	20 (38.46)	31 (54.39)	30 (57.69)	4 (7.27)	25 (48.08)	43 (71.67)	20 (33.33)	2 (3.92)	29 (60.42)	114 (40.86)	124 (46.97)
Agricultural labour	3 (5.36)	12 (23.08)	—	2 (3.85)	8 (14.55)	10 (19.23)	—	9 (15.00)	—	15 (31.25)	11 (3.94)	48 (18.18)
Non-agricultural labour	18 (32.14)	19 (36.54)	14 (24.56)	18 (34.62)	29 (52.73)	16 (30.77)	15 (25.00)	31 (51.67)	43 (84.32)	4 (8.33)	119 (42.66)	88 (33.33)
Self-employed	—	1 (1.92)	11 (19.30)	2 (3.84)	11 (20.00)	1 (1.92)	—	—	3 (5.88)	—	25 (8.96)	4 (1.52)
Service	1 (1.79)	—	1 (1.57)	—	3 (5.45)	—	2 (3.33)	—	3 (5.88)	—	10 (3.58)	—
Total	56 (100.0)	52 (100.0)	57 (100.0)	52 (100.0)	55 (100.0)	52 (100.0)	60 (100.0)	60 (100.0)	51 (100.0)	48 (100.0)	279 (100.0)	264 (100.0)

Source: Field survey.

Table 12.12
Annual Household Income of the Allottees by Source (in ₹)

Source of income	Lakhimpur	Hardoi	Sultanpur	Etah	Jhansi	Total
Agriculture on own	3,505	6,471	4,400	5,423	–	5,612
land	(16.2)	(23.57)	(13.9)	(25.11)	–	(19.62)
Agriculture on	9,949	6,953	3,894	8,221	5,123	6,588
allotted land	(45.95)	(25.33)	(12.3)	(38.06)	(14.37)	(23.04)
Total agriculture	13,454	13,424	8,294	13,644	5,123	12,200
	(62.15)	(48.9)	(26.2)	(63.17)	(14.37)	(42.66)
Animal husbandry	152	2,074	827	266	–	674
	(0.7)	(7.55)	(2.61)	(1.23)	–	(2.36)
Agricultural labour	2,204	196	3,124	126	1,198	1,344
	(10.18)	(0.71)	(9.87)	(0.58)	(3.36)	(4.7)
Non-agricultural	5,428	6,674	10,196	7,154	25,246	10,616
labour	(25.07)	(24.31)	(32.2)	(33.12)	(70.82)	(37.12)
Own business	89	3,774	5,704	–	608	2,024
	(0.41)	(13.74)	(18.01)	–	(1.71)	(7.08)
Service	257	1,316	2,509	410	3,331	1,512
	(1.19)	(4.79)	(7.92)	(1.9)	(9.34)	(5.29)
Other sources	64	–	1,011	–	141	228
	(0.3)	–	(3.19)	–	(0.4)	(0.8)
Total income	21,648	27,458	31,665	21,600	35,647	28,598
	(100)	(100)	(100)	(100)	(100)	(100)
Per capita income	3,341	4,290	4,118	3,224	5,981	4,294

Source: Field survey.

Details of Own and Allotted Land

Table 12.13 gives details of own and allotted land of the respondents. Average land owned by the allottees was 0.21 acres and average land allotted was 1.41 acres. Allotted land varied from 0.77 acres in Sultanpur to 2.53 acres in Jhansi. About two-thirds of the allotted land was irrigated. Proportion of irrigated land was, however, very low in Jhansi and Sultanpur. On average land cultivated per allottee is 1.48 acres. Allotted land as per cent of total land was 86.6 per cent. Allottees could not get possession of about 6 per cent land allotted to them. This was mainly due to the fact that the land allotted was a flood-affected area near the river

Table 12.13
Details of Own and Allotted Land per Allottee (in Acres)

Details	Lakhimpur	Hardoi	Sultanpur	Etah	Jhansi	Total
Own land	0.03	0.32	0.05	0.58	0.00	0.21
Allotted land	1.37	1.04	0.77	1.43	2.53	1.41
Irrigated land	1.37	1.04	0.28	0.97	0.36	0.92
Per cent irrigated	100.00	100.00	36.36	67.83	14.23	65.25
Land under possession	1.25	1.04	0.68	1.43	2.53	1.33
Percentage of allotted land to total landholding	97.99	76.30	93.03	70.96	100.00	86.56
Land not given possession	0.11	0.00	0.09	0.01	0.38	0.08
As percentage of allotted land	8.32	0.17	11.50	0.46	14.85	5.58
Allotted land cultivated	1.23	1.03	0.59	1.42	2.13	1.27
As percentage of allotted land	97.95	99.83	86.96	99.53	84.35	95.42
Total cultivated land	1.25	1.36	0.64	2.01	2.13	1.48
Average size of holding	1.28	1.36	0.73	2.01	2.53	1.54

Source: Field survey.

bed. In some cases land was under possession of other persons and could not be handed over to the allottees. Almost 95 per cent of allotted land was reported under cultivation.

Source, Size and Period of Distributed Land

Details of allotted land like source of land, size of allotted land and place of allotment have been given in Table 12.14.

Nearly 88 per cent allotted land was *Gram Samaj* land and only 12 per cent land was ceiling surplus land. In Sultanpur no ceiling surplus land was distributed to our sample allottees at all. Land

Table 12.14
Source, Purpose, Size and Period of Allotted Land

Details	Lakhimpur		Hardoi		Sultanpur		Etah		Jhansi		Total	
	No.	%	No.	%	No.	%	No.	%	No.	%	No.	%
1. Source of allotted land												
Land ceiling surplus	18	32.14	2	3.51	–	–	5	8.33	9	17.65	34	12.19
Gram Samaj land	38	67.86	55	96.49	55	100.0	55	91.67	42	82.35	245	87.81
Total	56	100.0	57	100.0	55	100.0	60	100.0	51	100.0	279	100.0
2. Purpose of land allotted												
Agriculture	56	100.0	57	100.0	55	100.0	60	100.00	51	100.0	279	100.0
3. Size of land distributed (acre)												
Less than 0.50	18	32.14	19	33.33	17	30.91	6	10.00	2	3.92	62	22.22
0.50–1.00	9	16.07	19	33.33	23	41.82	19	31.67	3	5.88	73	26.16
1.00–2.00	13	23.22	12	21.06	15	27.27	28	46.67	25	49.02	93	33.33
2.00–3.00	16	28.57	7	12.28	–	–	6	10.00	6	11.76	35	12.55
Above 3.00	–	–	–	–	–	–	1	1.66	15	29.42	16	5.74
4. Period elapsed since allotment (years)												
Less than 5	–	–	3	5.26	17	30.90	–	–	15	29.41	35	12.54
5–10	7	12.50	4	7.02	–	–	10	16.67	–	–	21	7.53
10–15	–	–	24	42.11	–	–	29	48.33	–	–	53	19.00
15–30	–	–	12	21.05	19	34.55	19	31.67	–	–	50	17.92
More than 30	49	87.50	14	24.56	19	34.55	2	3.33	36	70.59	120	43.01

Source: Field survey.

allotment was only for cultivation purpose. Against the policy of distributing minimum 1.5 acre land to allottees, about 22 per cent of the allottees were given less than 0.5 acre of land, while 26 per cent allottees were given between 0.5 and 1 acre of land. About one-third allottees received 1–2 acres of land and only 18 per cent above 2 acres.

Most of the land allotment was made in the 1970s and the 1980s. About 19 per cent allottees were given land 10–15 years back; 18 per cent got land 15–30 years back and 43 per cent got land over 30 years back. Only 13 per cent allottees were given land during last 5 years and about 13 per cent during the last 5–10 years.

Under the rules land allotment notice is given through drum beating in the village. But only 42 per cent of the sample allottees said this was so. Over half (54 per cent) of the allottees were informed about allotment by the *Pradhan* and 4 per cent by *Lekhpal* (Table 12.15). Rules require that *Lekhpal* will give the *patta* to the allottee by visiting his house. Only 25 per cent allottees were delivered *pattas* at their home. Sixty-four per cent of sample allottees mentioned that they were given *patta* by the *Pradhan* in a *Gram Sabha* meeting. About 11 per cent allottees had to go to the *tehsil* office to get their land *patta* (Table 12.15).

Problems in Obtaining Land *Patta* and Possession

Majority of allottees did not report harassment in obtaining *patta*. Nearly 90 per cent allottees said that they could get the *patta* by meeting the *Lekhpal* once or twice. About 7 per cent had to run to *Lekhpal* from three to five times and about 3 per cent had to make numerous turns to *Lekhpal* or the *tehsil* to obtain the *patta* (Table 12.16).

Nearly 80 per cent allottees could get the *patta* within 2 months of allotment as provided under the rules. However, 13 per cent allottees said that they had to wait for *patta* from 2 to 6 months and 7 per cent had to wait between 6 and 12 months (Table 12.16).

Over half (55 per cent) of the allottees were handed over vacant land identified for them. Another 36 per cent were given possession by removing unauthorised possession by others. However, 10 per cent allottees could not get possession of the land so far (Table 12.16).

Table 12.15

Source of Information and Place of Receiving Patta

Details	Lakhimpur		Hardoi		Sultanpur		Etah		Jhansi		Total	
	No.	%	No.	%	No.	%	No.	%	No.	%	No.	%
1. Source of information about allotment												
Through drum beating	26	46.43	50	87.72	–	–	40	66.67	–	–	116	41.58
By *Pradhan*	23	41.07	5	8.77	55	100.00	18	30.00	51	100.0	152	54.48
By *Lekhpal*	7	12.50	2	3.51	–	–	2	3.33	–	–	11	3.94
2. Place of receiving *patta*												
Gram Sabha meeting	20	35.71	30	52.63	36	65.45	51	85.00	42	82.35	179	64.16
By *Lekhpal*	34	60.72	17	29.83	19	34.55	–	–	–	–	70	25.09
Tehsil office	2	3.57	10	17.54	–	–	9	15.00	9	17.65	30	10.75

Source: Field survey.

Table 12.16
Problems Faced in Receiving Patta

Type of problems	Lakhimpur		Hardoi		Sultanpur		Etah		Jhansi		Total	
	No.	*%*	*No.*	*%*	*No.*	*%*	*No.*	*%*	*No.*	*%*	*No.*	*%*
1. Running to officials												
1–2 times	54	96.42	50	87.72	50	90.91	55	91.67	42	82.35	251	89.96
3–5 times	1	1.79	6	10.53	5	9.09	3	5.00	5	9.80	20	7.17
More than 5 times	1	1.79	1	1.75	&	&	2	3.33	4	7.85	8	2.87
Total	56	100.0	57	100.0	55	100.0	60	100.0	51	100.0	279	100.0
2. Time taken in getting *patta*												
1 month	11	19.64	37	64.91	43	78.18	41	68.33	5	9.80	137	49.10
1–2 months	17	30.36	12	21.05	7	12.73	13	21.67	36	70.59	85	30.47
2–6 months	13	23.21	5	8.77	4	7.27	5	8.33	10	19.61	37	13.26
More than 6 months	15	26.79	3	5.27	1	1.82	1	1.67	–	–	20	7.17
3. How land was given possession												
By showing the allotted land	30	53.57	12	21.05	25	45.45	37	61.67	48	94.12	152	54.48
By removing unauthorised possession	25	44.64	43	75.44	10	18.18	20	33.33	2	3.92	100	35.84
Possession not given	1	1.79	2	3.51	20	36.37	3	5.00	1	1.96	27	9.68

Source: Field survey.

Quality of Allotted Land and Problems Faced in Getting Possession

About 69 per cent respondents reported that they were allotted cultivable land. In 12 per cent cases the allotted land was sodic land. Gypsum was distributed to the allottees who had sodic land (sodic soil has high levels of sodium in the soil, and can be offset by the use of gypsum to ameliorate such soil). In 19 per cent cases the allotted land was not level, wasteland, waterlogged or sandy land not suitable for cultivation (Table 12.17).

Of the total allottees, 40 allottees (14.3 per cent) reported that they had to face problems in getting possession of land. The main reasons given were that the land was under possession of powerful people of the village, demand of bribe by government officials and lack of support from government functionaries. Three per cent of the total allottees complained that either the possession of full land was not given or the allotted land was not at one place (Table 12.18).

There is no provision of government assistance to land allottees. About 80 per cent allottees said they have not received any assistance from government for cultivation. However, about 20 per cent allottees received assistance in the form of cash fertilisers, seed and gypsum. Details are given in Table 12.19.

Utilisation of Allotted Land and Problems in Cultivation

Table 12.20 shows the details of land use of the allotted land. The survey revealed that 90 per cent land allottees are cultivating the land allotted to them. But 7 per cent of the allottees were not cultivating the land as the land allotted was *usar* or wasteland. Majority of such cases were found in Sultanpur district. In a few cases the whole or part of the allotted land has been sold by the allottees.

The land allottees are facing many problems in cultivating the allotted land. Over three-fifth of the allottees (63 per cent)

Table 12.17
Quality of Allotted Land

Quality of allotted land	Lakhimpur		Hardoi		Sultanpur		Etah		Jhansi		Total	
	No.	%	No.	%	No.	%	No.	%	No.	%	No.	%
Suitable for cultivation	54	96.42	45	78.95	37	67.20	31	51.67	25	49.02	192	68.81
Sodic land	–	–	12	21.06	–	–	21	35.00	–	–	33	11.83
Wasteland, sandy, waterlogged	2	3.57	–	–	18	32.80	8	13.33	26	50.98	54	19.36
Total	56	100.0	57	100.0	55	100.0	60	100.0	51	100.0	279	100.0

Source: Field survey.

Table 12.18

Problems in Getting Possession of Land

Quality of allotted land	Lakhimpur		Hardoi		Sultanpur		Etah		Jhansi		Total	
	No.	*%*	*No.*	*%*	*No.*	*%*	*No.*	*%*	*No.*	*%*	*No.*	*%*
Running to officials			2	50.00			2	22.22			4	10.53
Demand of bribe					4	44.44	4	22.22			8	15.79
Unlawful possession by others	9	75.00					1	11.11	2	50.00	12	31.58
Lack of official support	2	16.67	2	50.00			3	33.31			7	18.42
Only part of land given possession	1	8.33			5	55.56	1	11.11	2	50.00	9	23.68
Total	12	100.0	4	100.0	9	100.0	11	100.0	4	100.0	40	100.0

Source: Field survey.

Table 12.19
Details of Government Assistance Given to Land Allottees

Details	Lakhimpur		Hardoi		Sultanpur		Etah		Jhansi		Total	
	No.	%	No.	%	No.	%	No.	%	No.	%	No.	%
1. Whether assistance given by government for cultivation												
Yes			17	29.82			34	56.67			51	18.28
No	56	100.0	40	70.18	55	100.0	26	43.33	51	100.0	228	81.72
2. Type of assistance and amount												
Cash (₹)			550	32			1,300	38			1,850	81
Fertilisers in kg			1,455	86			970	29			2,425	11
Seed in kg			327	19			638	19			965	4
Gypsum in kg			31,950	1,879			29,350	863			61,300	269

Source: Field survey.

Table 12.20

Status of Land Use of Allotted Land

Details of land use	Lakhimpur		Hardoi		Sultanpur		Etah		Jhansi		Total	
	No.	%	No.	%	No.	%	No.	%	No.	%	No.	%
Under cultivation	55	98.22	57	100.0	35	63.63	60	98.33	51	90.19	253	90.68
Land lying fallow					15	27.27			5	9.81	20	7.17
Constructed house	1	1.78									1	0.36
Sold whole or part of land					5	9.09					5	1.79
Total	56	100.0	57	100.0	55	100.0	60	100.0	51	100.0	279	100.0

Source: Field survey.

mentioned problems related to irrigation such as irregular power supply, absence of government tube well, high charge of water, etc. Nearly three-fifth (58 per cent) allottees complained about the lack of availability of seed and fertiliser and their high prices. Some respondents (14 per cent) complained about problems in ploughing or threshing. About 10 per cent faced problems due to uneven surface of the allotted land (Table 12.21).

Respondents were asked to give their suggestions for improvement in agriculture. Their responses are given in Table 12.22. Of allottees 59 per cent wanted better irrigation facilities and 56 per cent wanted supply of seed and fertilisers at reasonable prices. Twenty-nine per cent wanted credit facilities. About 17 per cent wanted levelling of land and help in making tractor and thresher available.

Impact of Land Allotment on Allottees

In view of the fact that the land allotment in most of the cases was done 20–30 years back, it is not possible to directly assess the impact of land distribution on agricultural productivity and incomes. Therefore, we have tried to assess the impact of land allotment by examining the difference in the productivity and income from own land and allotted land. The analysis did not include Jhansi as all the allottees in the district were landless with no land of their own earlier to facilitate comparison.

Table 12.23 shows the net agricultural income derived from own land and allotted land. Net agricultural income per allottee came to ₹12,000 per year, out of which 56 per cent was contributed by allotted land and 43 per cent by own land.

Table 12.24 shows per acre yield of wheat and rice on own and allotted land in the districts surveyed. Average yield of both the crops was higher on own land in Hardoi and Sultanpur district, while reverse was the case in Lakhimpur and Etah. These differences reflect the difference in the quality of own and allotted land and availability of irrigation. Also we find that average yields are higher in Lakhimpur district, where soils are more fertile.

Table 12.25 shows the number of days of employment before and after land allotment. The employment days have more than

Table 12.21
Problems Faced in Cultivation on Allotted Land

Problems in cultivation	Lakhimpur		Hardoi		Sultanpur		Etah		Jhansi		Total	
	No.	%	No.	%	No.	%	No.	%	No.	%	No.	%
Lack of agricultural implements	8	14.28	28	49.12	16	39.09	38	63.33	6	11.76	40	14.34
Problem of irrigation	22	39.28	45	78.95	34	61.82	35	58.33	40	78.43	176	63.08
Problem in obtaining seed and fertilisers	21	37.50	37	64.91	36	65.45	43	71.67	26	50.98	163	58.42
Problem of uneven land	2	3.57			3	5.45	8	13.33	15	29.41	28	10.03
Waterlogged land	3	5.36									3	1.07
Total	56	100.0	57	100.0	55	100.0	60	100.0	51	100.0	279	100.0

Source: Field survey.

Table 12.22
Suggestions for Improvement in Agriculture

Suggestions	Lakhimpur		Hardoi		Sultanpur		Etah		Jhansi		Total	
	No.	%	No.	%	No.	%	No.	%	No.	%	No.	%
Irrigation facilities	35	62.50	27	47.37	32	58.18	27	45.00	43	84.31	164	58.78
Supply of seed and fertiliser	31	55.36	42	73.68	37	67.27	38	63.33	8	15.68	156	55.91
Credit facility	16	28.57	7	12.28	35	63.64	17	28.33	8	15.69	81	29.03
Levelling of land	2	3.57			20	36.36			28	54.90	50	17.92
Supply of machinery	6	10.71	19	33.33				33.33			45	16.13
Total	56	100.0	57	100.0	55	100.0	60	100.0	51	100.0	279	100.0

Source: Field survey.

Table 12.23
Net Income from Cultivation from Allotted and Own Land Per Household

District	Net income (in ₹)		Net income from cultivated land (in ₹)
	Own land	Allotted land	
Lakhimpur	4,204 (33.5%)	8,348 (66.5%)	12,547 (100.0%)
Hardoi	6,312 (43.5%)	8,205 (56.5%)	14,517 (100.0%)
Sultanpur	4,073 (49.2%)	4,209 (50.8%)	8,282 (100.0%)
Etah	6,701 (46.0%)	7,877 (54.0%)	14,578 (100.0%)
Jhansi	–	5,239 (100.0%)	5,239 (100.0%)
Grand total	5,323 (42.7%)	7,158 (57.3%)	12,481 (100.0%)

Source: Field survey.

Table 12.24
Per Acre Yield of Wheat and Paddy on Own and Allotted Land in Quintal

District	Wheat		Rice	
	Own land	Allotted land	Own land	Allotted land
Lakhimpur	11.14	12.01	13.86	14.21
Hardoi	10.50	9.06	12.20	11.09
Sultanpur	10.12	9.34	11.47	7.53
Etah	10.08	11.21	10.15	12.31
Jhansi	–	9.12	–	6.37
All districts	10.46	10.15	11.92	10.30

Source: Field survey.

doubled, from 84 days to 181 days. It may also be observed that while number of days of employment in non-agricultural activities has declined, in agriculture it has increased as the allottees now have more land to cultivate. Employment days of the family members in non-agricultural activities show an increase.

Table 12.26 shows the extent of impact on the quality of life of the land allottees. All allottees reported positive impact on various dimensions of life, though the extent of impact varied. Three out of five (60 per cent) respondents reported a large impact on social prestige. Nearly 90 per cent found it easier to obtain credit. The allottees reported that they were able to construct a *pucca* house after land allotment. Keeping milch animal became easier for them.

Table 12.25
Impact of Land Allotment on Employment (Days/Year)

District	Before allotment			After allotment		
	Agriculture	Non-agriculture	Total	Agriculture	Non-agriculture	Total
Lakhimpur						
Self	83	160	243	160	102	262
Family members	50	103	153	84	100	184
Hardoi						
Self	90	132	222	201	69	270
Family members	30	100	130	90	129	219
Sultanpur						
Self	54	200	254	180	123	303
Family members	40	88	128	69	170	239
Etah						
Self	109	123	232	180	120	300
Family members	38	65	103	65	180	145
Jhansi						
Self	—	250	250	182	100	282
Family members	—	150	150	70	150	220
All districts						
Self	84	173	257	181	123	304
Family members	32	101	133	76	146	222

Source: Field survey.

Table 12.26

Qualitative Impact on Various Dimensions of Life of the Allottees

Type of impact	Lakhimpur		Hardoi		Sultanpur		Etah		Jhansi		Total	
	To some extent	To large extent	To some extent	To large extent	To some extent	To large extent	To some extent	To large extent	To some extent	To large extent	To some extent	To large extent
Social prestige	12 (21.43)	42 (75.00)	23 (40.35)	34 (59.65)	47 (85.45)	8 (14.55)	22 (36.67)	38 (63.33)	4 (7.84)	47 (92.16)	108 (38.71)	169 (60.57)
Self-confidence	16 (28.57)	38 (67.87)	18 (31.58)	39 (68.42)	27 (49.09)	28 (50.91)	35 (58.33)	25 (41.67)	40 (78.43)	11 (21.57)	136 (48.75)	141 (50.54)
Reduction in oppression	36 (64.29)	18 (32.14)	35 (61.40)	22 (38.60)	54 (98.18)	1 (1.82)	21 (35.00)	39 (65.00)	27 (52.94)	24 (47.06)	173 (62.01)	104 (37.28)
Access to credit	39 (69.64)	15 (26.79)	16 (28.07)	41 (71.93)	40 (72.73)	15 (27.27)	23 (38.33)	37 (61.67)	17 (33.33)	34 (66.67)	135 (48.49)	142 (50.90)
Promoted animal husbandry	15 (26.79)	39 (69.64)	17 (29.82)	40 (70.18)	40 (72.73)	15 (27.27)	43 (71.67)	17 (28.33)	40 (78.43)	11 (21.57)	155 (55.56)	122 (43.73)
Pucca house	13 (23.21)	41 (73.21)	36 (63.16)	21 (36.84)	55 (100.0)	&	18 (30.00)	42 (70.00)	43 (84.31)	8 (15.69)	165 (59.14)	112 (40.14)
Health	40 (71.43)	14 (25.00)	29 (50.88)	28 (49.12)	51 (92.73)	4 (7.27)	35 (58.33)	25 (41.67)	32 (62.75)	19 (37.25)	187 (67.03)	90 (32.25)
Education of children	23 (41.07)	31 (55.36)	30 (52.63)	27 (47.37)	53 (96.36)	2 (3.64)	38 (63.33)	22 (36.67)	21 (41.18)	30 (58.82)	165 (59.14)	112 (40.14)

Source: Field survey.

Reduction in harassment by local goons was also reported. A good proportion reported significant improvement in health status and education of children. Thus, the benefits of land allotment were not confined to improvement in income and employment but also significant improvement in the quality of life.

Opinion of Land Allottees about the Process of Land Allotment

We also sought the opinion of the allottees about different aspects of land allotment. The responses are shown in Table 12.27.

About 8 per cent respondents said that land has been allotted to non-eligible persons. This proportion was higher in Lakhimpur district. About 16 per cent respondents were critical of the working of the Land Management Committee. About 22 per cent respondents said that the land has been sold by allottees. This proportion was much higher in Lakhimpur and Hardoi districts. Thus, deficiencies in the implementation of the programme are found at the field level. Moreover, in some districts the implementation deficiencies are found to be higher. This shows that the functioning of the official machinery at the lower level has an impact on the effectiveness of the land distribution programme.

The respondents have given suggestions for improving the programme of land distribution.

- About 45 per cent respondents were of the view that good-quality land suitable for cultivation should be distributed. The proportion of these respondents was much higher in Sultanpur and Jhansi districts where the quality of land distributed was not good.
- About 47 per cent respondents were of the view that possession of land should be ensured at the time of giving *patta*, as the allottees fail to get possession of land even after getting the *patta*.
- Nearly half of the respondents said that there is need to keep a check on the working of the Land Management Committee as the *Pradhans* misuse their position to distribute land to their favourites. A high proportion felt that the presence of

Table 12.27

Opinion of Allottees on Different Aspects of Land Allotment

Opinion about land allotment	Lakhimpur		Hardoi		Sultanpur		Etah		Jhansi		Total	
	No.	%	No.	%	No.	%	No.	%	No.	%	No.	%
1. Has the land been allotted to eligible persons?												
Yes	48	85.71	53	92.98	51	92-73	58	96-67	47	92-16	257	92.11
No	8	14.29	4	7.02	4	7-27	2	3-33	4	7-84	22	7.89
2. Does land management committee discriminate?												
Yes	16	28.57	14	24.57	8	14-55	3	5.00	4	7.84	45	16.13
No	40	71.43	43	75.43	47	85-45	57	95.00	47	92.16	235	83.87
3. Have the allottees sold their land?												
Yes	15	26.79	19	33.33	21	38.18	5	8.33	2	3.92	62	22.22
No	41	73.21	38	66.67	34	61.82	55	91.67	49	96.08	217	77.78
4. What are your suggestions for improving the system of land allotment?												
Land suitable for cultivation should be distributed	16	28.57	10	17.54	34	61.82	29	48.3	37	72.55	126	45.16
Physical possession should be given along with *pattas*	33	50.93	26	45.61	37	27.27	18	30.00	16	31.37	130	46.59

(Table 12.27 Continued)

(Table 12.27 Continued)

Opinion about land allotment	Lakhimpur		Hardoi		Sultanpur		Etah		Jhansi		Total	
	No.	%	No.	%	No.	%	No.	%	No.	%	No.	%
Higher officials should be present at the time of selection of allottees	21	37.50	21	36.84	30	54.55	23	38.33	17	33.33	112	40.14
Discriminatory policy of LMC should be checked	27	48.21	20	35.09	30	54.55	38	63.33	21	41.18	136	48.75
Support should be given for cultivation	12	21.43	19	33.33	17	30.91	26	43.33	32	62.75	106	37.99
Land should be allotted at one place	18	32.14	12	21.05	7	12.73	9	15.00	30	58.82	76	27.24
Corruption should be checked	9	16.07	29	50.88	43	78.18	16	26.67	18	35.29	115	41.22
Only eligible people should be given land	23	41.07	31	54.39	20	36.36	16	26.67	20	39.22	110	39.43
There should be restriction on sale of land by allottees	10	17.86	12	21.05	8	14.55	9	15.00	12	23-53	51	18.28

Source: Field survey.

higher-level officials at the time of selecting the beneficiaries would ensure proper distribution of land.

- About 27 per cent allottees want that allotted land should be given at one place rather than as scattered plots. Nearly 40 per cent want that government should provide assistance for cultivation of land through irrigation facilities and distribution of seeds, gypsum, etc.
- It was found during the field visit that *Pradhan* and *Lekhpal* take money ranging from ₹2,500 to ₹5,000 from the land allottees for giving *patta*. Such complaints were more common in Hardoi and Sultanpur districts. No wonder 41 per cent allottees demand that corruption related to land distribution should be checked.
- Around 40 per cent allottees demand that land should be given only to the eligible persons and around one-fifth want control on sale of land by the allottees.

Conclusion and Suggestions

Our analysis shows that land distribution to the landless labourers and marginal farmers is an effective instrument of social justice and rural development. Land distribution programme had a posi tive impact on the economic and social status of the allottees and has brought about qualitative change in their life and contributed to better health and education of children. At the same time several deficiencies in the implementation of the programme have been observed, which reduce the impact of the programme. Major deficiencies noted by us related to the selection of non-eligible persons, discriminatory attitude of Land Management Committee, delay in getting possession of land, distribution of poor quality of land, demand for illegal payment, lack of government assistance for cultivation, etc.

We suggest the following to remove the deficiencies in the implementation of the programme:

1. Normally land suitable for cultivation should be allotted. If degraded land is acquired for distribution, government

should make the land cultivable by measures like levelling, treatment of sodic soil, creation of irrigation facilities, etc.

2. Early possession of land to the allottees should be ensured by the government officials by removing the adverse possession by village strongmen.

3. Land allotted to a person should be in the form of a single plot rather than scattered plots.

4. *Tehsil* and district-level officials should exercise effective supervision in the identification of beneficiaries and working of the Land Management Committee.

5. The process of land distribution should be transparent and hassle-free.

6. Resale of land by the allottee should be prohibited.

7. Government should provide adequate support in terms of inputs, equipment, credit, etc., to enable the land allottees to properly cultivate the land.

References

Haque, T. and G. Parthasarathy (1992), 'Land Reforms and Rural Development: Highlights of a National Seminar', *Economic and Political Weekly*, XXVII (8).

Planning Commission (2007), *Uttar Pradesh Development Report, Vol. II*, Planning Commission, Government of India, New Delhi.

Sharma, R.K., A. Kumar and S.K. Chauhan (1993), 'Impact of Land Reform on Farm Production', *Kurukshetra*, XLI (5).

Singh, A.K., D.K. Bajpai and P.S. Garia (1993), 'Allotting Gaon Sabha Land for Poverty Alleviation', *Kurukshetra*, XLI (5).

PART V

Emerging Issues

13

Land Use Scenario in Uttar Pradesh

Vasant W. Ambekar and R.K. Singh

Introduction

Owing to increasing pressure of population, there is excessive demand for more land both for agricultural and for non-agricultural use. Land is a scarce resource and there is competing demand for it. The demand for land for grazing, forestry, wildlife, tourism and urban development is greater than the land resource available. This has resulted in decrease in per capita cultivable land besides causing ecological imbalances. Our basic needs of food, water, fuel, clothing and shelter must be met from the land that is in limited supply.

On the other hand, the area under wasteland—degraded/eroded, saline, sodic, waterlogged, deserted—is increasing. In UP, the estimated area under wastelands is 16.98 lakh ha., which is 7.05 per cent of the state's geographical area (Wasteland Atlas, 2005). Major types of soil degradation in the state result from erosion, salt accumulation, water logging, depletion of nutrients, destruction of vegetative cover and non-judicious land use and its management.

Any attempt towards land reforms involves a systematic assessment of land and water potential and to select and put in to practice those land uses that will meet the needs of the people while safeguarding resources for the future. The driving force in planning is the need for change, the need for improved management or the need for a quite different pattern of land use desired by changing circumstances. The land-use planning should be based on assigning present and future needs and systematically evaluating the land's ability to supply them. Land should ensure the individual land user greater return for the capital and labour invested or greater benefits from the least cost. With growing population and limited land resources, the relevance of land-use planning is obvious. Land has limited carrying capacity, beyond which there will be degradation and loss in productivity due to excessive use. In order to meet the various demands of the growing population, land degradation has to be checked.

Over the years, different types of degraded lands have established particular cropping systems, which are not remunerative. Hence, it is quite imperative to develop crop models for different degraded lands like sodic, ravine, waterlogged, *diara* and eroded lands. These crop models should be economically viable, technically feasible, environment friendly and acceptable to farmers.

In the context of talking about land reforms, it is necessary to look into the land-use pattern of the state for the last six decades. However, with the formation of Uttarakhand in the year 2000 there were substantial changes not only in the reporting area but also in other factors. Particular change observed is considerable reduction in the forest area both in absolute and in percentage term. The land-use pattern for UP from 1950–1951 to 2009–2010 is given in Table 13.1 in two parts, first for combined UP up to 2000–2001 and second for reconstituted UP from 1990–1991 to 2009–2010.

Reporting Area

Reporting area during 1950–1951 to 2000–2001 varies from 292.58 lakh ha. to 297.93 lakh ha. However, in 1970–1971, the area reported was 298.06 lakh ha. and thereafter it is around 297 lakh ha. Thus, there is no significant difference in the reporting area during this 50-year span. In the year 1990–1991 the total reporting area of UP was 297.93 lakh ha. Of this 244.32 lakh ha. relates to the remaining portion of the state after formation of Uttarakhand state. However, with the transfer of Haridwar district from UP to Uttarakhand, the total reporting area of UP ranges between 241.7 and 242.44 lakh ha., say on an average, 242 lakh ha., indicating a decrease of around 56 lakh ha. after the formation of Uttarakhand. It is unchanged at 241.70 lakh ha. from 2006–2007 to 2009–2010.

Reconstituted UP has four economic regions, viz., western, central, Bundelkhand and eastern. The number of districts in eastern and western regions each is 27 whereas that in Bundelkhand region it is 7 only and the central region has 10 districts. The reporting area of the eastern region is the highest at 86.32 lakh ha. in 2009–2010, followed in the second place by the western region with 80.36 lakh ha. The central region stood third with 45.41 lakh ha. and Bundelkhand

Table 13.1
Land Utilisation Statistics of Uttar Pradesh (Area in lakh hectares)

Year	Reporting area	Forests	Barren & uncultivable land	Land put to non-agricultural uses	Culturable wasteland	Permanent pasture & other grazing land	Land under miscellaneous tree crops & groves not included in net area sown	Current fallow	Other fallow	Net area sown
A. Combined UP and Uttarakhand										
1950–1951	292.58	31.94	28.87	18.53		0.49	14.15	10.78	2.91	162.31
1960–1961	294.95	37.94	25.91	19.12	16.40	0.44	8.93	1.74	12.60	171.88
1970–1971	298.06	49.53	14.18	20.34	13.45	0.77	12.60	8.70	5.45	173.05
1980–1981	297.39	51.29	11.41	22.80	11.48	2.96	6.39	11.70	7.16	172.21
1990–1991	297.93	51.62	10.35	24.47	10.34	3.03	5.45	10.84	8.84	172.99
2000–2001	295.92	51.54	6.48	25.88	9.20	2.99	5.92	10.86	7.10	175.95
B. Reconstituted UP										
1990–1991	242.44	16.94	7.37	22.96	7.14	0.75	3.28	12.42	6.49	165.09
2000–2001	242.01	16.89	6.17	24.36	5.35	0.70	3.40	10.48	6.41	168.25
2001–2002	242.02	16.89	5.95	25.14	5.18	0.71	3.55	10.26	6.24	168.12
2003–2004	242.01	16.86	5.48	25.94	4.68	0.66	3.59	11.37	5.94	167.50
2005–2006	242.01	16.54	5.15	27.00	4.39	0.65	3.76	12.70	5.50	166.33
2007–2008	241.70	16.58	5.07	27.61	4.40	0.65	3.74	14.08	5.40	164.17
2009–2010	241.70	16.62	4.94	28.01	4.31	0.65	3.59	12.32	5.37	165.89

Sources: (1) Uttar Pradesh ke Krishi Ankade (Agricultural Statistics of UP) of different years, a publication of Directorate of Uttar Pradesh.
(2) Souvenir, 2008–2009, State Land Use Board, Planning Department, Government of UP.

region had the least area of 29.62 lakh ha. Naturally, these differences are mainly due to the variation in the number of districts in these regions. However, it is interesting to note that the regions having the highest reporting area (eastern) and the lowest reporting area (Bundelkhand) are comparatively backward than the western and central regions on different parameters, viz., production and productivity and many other factors. The western region being near to the National Capital Region (NCR) is much ahead of the other regions.

Forest and Miscellaneous Tree Cover

These two categories of land uses have been grouped together due to the reason that the requirement under National Forest Policy that forest cover in UP should at least be 20 per cent permits inclusion of trees outside forest (TOF).

Forest

Reported forest area in 1950–1951 was 31.94 lakh ha. and gradually it increased to 51.54 lakh ha. over a period of 50 years. Significant jump is observed from 31.94 lakh ha. in 1950–1951 to 49.53 lakh ha. in 1970–1971. Thereafter the increase was insignificant. Probably the forest areas with *zamindars* were earlier not included in reporting the areas under forest, which may be the reason for the increase in forest area.

The figures for UP for 1990–1991 (for the area that remained in UP after its bifurcation into two states) available show that the area under forest is 16.94 lakh ha. Thereafter from 2000–2001 (year of actual bifurcation) to 2009–2010 it fluctuated between 16.54 and 16.89 lakh ha. For the year 2009–2010 it is 16.62 lakh ha. Thus it can be concluded that in the past around 20 years, there has been little change in the area under forest.

One point is very clear. Merely having a certain area known as forest will not serve any fruitful purpose. Present status of forest is not satisfactory. Dense and moderately dense forests are about 40 per cent of the forest area. Rest is either open or covered with scrub. The fact that about 60 per cent of forest area is under open and scrub categories poses a big challenge for environmental conservation, biodiversity, wood production and livelihoods of forest-dependent population. This area must be rejuvenated.

In physical terms, the eastern region has the highest forest area of 7.85 lakh ha. as of 2009–2010, which is 9.1 per cent of the reporting area. This is followed by Bundelkhand region, which though has only 2.45 lakh ha. under forest but it is 8.3 per cent of the reporting area. Western and central regions have 3.86 and 2.45 lakh ha. land, respectively, under forest but represent only 4.8 per cent and 5.4 per cent, respectively. Thus, all the regions — particularly western and central — have low percentage of forest area and they will have to do a lot to improve the tree cover. During the period 2000–2001 to 2009–2010, the western region increased its area under forest from 3.60 lakh ha. to 3.87 lakh ha. Other regions reported decline. The increase in the western region appears to be due to more coverage of tree planting on field boundaries in this region as farmers are getting better returns from the trees planted through ply board and paper industries. Table 13.2 presents the region-wise forestland from 2000–2001 to 2009–2010.

The most important issue is that there is no possibility of increasing the area under forest. The only remedy is to increase the area under tree cover outside the forest area. However, this aspect will get success only by providing the marketing of trees produced and

Table 13.2
Region-wise Forest Area

	Regions							
	Western		*Central*		*Bundelkhand*		*Eastern*	
Year	*Area, lakh ha.*	*% of reporting area*	*Area, lakh ha.*	*% of reporting area*	*Area, lakh ha.*	*% of reporting area*	*Area, lakh ha.*	*% of reporting area*
2000–2001	3.6	4.46	2.47	5.45	2.69	9.09	8.13	9.42
2001–2002	3.6	4.46	2.47	5.45	2.69	9.09	8.13	9.42
2003–2004	3.86	4.78	2.39	5.21	2.37	8.01	8.24	9.61
2005–2006	3.86	4.78	2.38	5.19	2.43	8.21	7.87	9.18
2007–2008	3.86	4.8	2.38	5.24	2.44	8.24	7.9	9.15
2009–2010	3.87	4.82	2.45	5.4	2.45	8.27	7.85	9.09

Sources: (1) Uttar Pradesh ke Krishi Ankade (Agricultural Statistics of UP) of different years, a publication of Directorate of Uttar Pradesh. (2) Souvenir, 2008–2009, State Land Use Board, Planning Department, Government of UP.

their processing, which needs to be promoted specially in eastern and Bundelkhand regions.

Land under Miscellaneous Tree Crops and Groves

There have been fluctuations in the figures reported during 1950–1951, 1960–1961 and 1970–1971, which were 14.15, 8.93 and 12.60 lakh ha., respectively. However, in 1980–1981, it had significantly reduced to 6.39 lakh ha. and in 1990–1991 to 5.45 lakh ha. There appears to be some policy issues regarding the reporting under this category, which may have caused this fluctuation. Out of 5.45 lakh ha., an area of 3.28 lakh ha. belonged to the portion comprising reconstituted UP.

The afore-mentioned 3.28 lakh ha. area under miscellaneous tree cover went up to 3.76 lakh ha. during the period from 1990–1991 to 2005–2006 but again declined to 3.59 lakh ha. in 2009–2010. This trend is not acceptable in view of an urgent need to increase tree cover outside forest so as to achieve the 20 per cent goal set under National Forest Policy. Over the years, large-scale fruit tree plantations were taken up but at the same time many old orchards were cut down for fuel and timber purposes. Hence, there has not been any significant change in this category of land use.

In the year 2000–2001, the eastern region had 1.87 lakh ha. followed by 0.79 lakh ha. in the central region, 0.63 lakh ha. in the western region and only 0.11 lakh ha. in Bundelkhand region. In 2009–2010 there was an increase in the area in this category by 0.22 lakh ha. and 0.19 lakh ha. in Bundelkhand and eastern regions, respectively, but a decline by 0.09 lakh ha. in the western region and 0.12 lakh ha. in the central region. This change appears to be due to orchard plantation taken up in eastern and Bundelkhand regions whereas felling of old orchards in the western and central regions may be the reason for the decline in these regions. Region-wise changes from 2000–2001 to 2009–2010 are presented in Table 13.3.

There is a need for increasing this category of areas by taking up large-scale plantation of fruit trees. This can be easily done on the lands belonging to absentee farmers. To get this done, a very systematic approach needs to be taken up to have substantial increase in these areas, which are required for increasing the tree cover in the state.

Table 13.3

Region-wise Land under Miscellaneous Tree Crops

	Regions							
	Western		Central		Bundelkhand		Eastern	
Year	Area, lakh ha.	% of reporting area	Area, lakh ha.	% of reporting area	Area, lakh ha.	% of reporting area	Area, lakh ha.	% of reporting area
2000–2001	0.63	0.78	0.79	1.74	0.11	0.37	1.87	2.17
2001–2002	0.66	0.82	0.8	1.76	0.18	0.61	1.91	2.21
2003–2004	0.56	0.69	0.77	1.68	0.4	1.35	1.85	2.16
2005–2006	0.56	0.69	0.76	1.66	0.33	1.12	2.11	2.46
2007–2008	0.56	0.7	0.74	1.63	0.33	1.11	2.12	2.46
2009–2010	0.54	0.67	0.67	1.48	0.33	1.11	2.06	2.39

Sources: (1) Uttar Pradesh ke Krishi Ankade (Agricultural Statistics of UP) of different years, a publication of Directorate of Uttar Pradesh. (2) Souvenir, 2008–2009, State Land Use Board, Planning Department, Government of UP.

Barren and Uncultivable Land and Culturable Wastelands

These two categories have been discussed together as both can usefully be converted into categories like net area sown, forest including tree outside forest and land put to non-agricultural uses. Such conversions will ultimately improve the environment and provide more land for farming.

Barren and Uncultivable Land

Area reported under barren category in 1950–1951 was 28.87 lakh ha. and this has significantly come down to 6.48 lakh ha. in 2000–2001. This is probably due to population pressure on lands and the use of such lands for urbanisation. Besides this, barren lands were developed into industrial areas in the state.

Reconstituted UP had an area of 6.17 lakh ha. in 2000–2001, which decreased to 4.94 lakh ha. in 2009–2010. This again is due to setting up of industrial estates and habitations in these areas.

Table 13.4
Region-wise Barren and Uncultivable Land

Year	Western Area, lakh ha.	Western % of reporting area	Central Area, lakh ha.	Central % of reporting area	Bundelkhand Area, lakh ha.	Bundelkhand % of reporting area	Eastern Area, lakh ha.	Eastern % of reporting area
2000–2001	1.94	2.4	1.39	3.07	1.15	3.89	1.7	1.97
2001–2002	1.88	2.33	1.27	2.8	1.14	3.85	1.65	1.91
2003–2004	1.67	2.07	1.19	2.59	1.14	3.85	1.49	1.74
2005–2006	1.56	1.93	1.09	2.37	1.1	3.72	1.4	1.63
2007–2008	1.49	1.85	1.07	2.36	1.09	3.68	1.42	1.65
2009–2010	1.42	1.77	1.05	2.31	1.07	3.61	1.4	1.62

Sources: (1) Uttar Pradesh ke Krishi Ankade (Agricultural Statistics of UP) of different years, a publication of Directorate of Uttar Pradesh. (2) Souvenir, 2008–2009, State Land Use Board, Planning Department, Government of UP.

In fact, there should be strict policy that this category of land be utilised for industrial and other uses as far as possible.

In this category, the largest area of 1.94 lakh ha. was in the western region followed by 1.70 lakh ha. in the eastern region. In central and Bundelkhand regions, it was 1.39 and 1.15 lakh ha., respectively. In a span of 9 years from 2000–2001 to 2009–2010, all the regions reduced this to some extent by putting the land under various useful categories. In 2009–2010, the respective areas are 1.42, 1.40, 1.05. and 1.07 lakh ha. (Table 13.4). A comparison with the respective reporting areas in these regions indicates that Bundelkhand region has the highest percentage of land (3.6 per cent) under this category, followed by the central (2.3 per cent), western (1.8 per cent) and eastern (1.6 per cent) regions.

Culturable Wasteland

The area under culturable wastelands was 22.62 lakh ha. in 1950–1951, which reduced to 9.20 lakh ha. in 2000–2001. Naturally, this is because of population pressures and the impact of land reclamation activities undertaken by the government. However, the population pressure is one significant factor underlying this change. Geographical area comprising the present UP after bifurcation had 7.14 lakh ha. land as culturable waste in 1990–1991. This came down to 5.35 lakh ha. in 2000–2001. The state has only 4.31 lakh ha. land under this category as of 2009–2010. This gradual reduction in culturable wasteland has been possible due to various watershed development programmes and land reclamation activities of the state.

In the year 2000–2001 the maximum area under culturable waste-lands was in the Bundelkhand region, i.e., 1.42 lakh ha. followed by 1.39 lakh ha. in the eastern region, 1.38 lakh ha. in the western region and 1.16 lakh ha. in the central region. These areas have come down in all the four regions. In the year 2009–2010 these are 1.16, 1.22, 1.05 and 0.88 lakh ha., respectively, in Bundelkhand, eastern, western and central regions as indicated in Table 13.5. In terms of percentage to the reporting area, Bundelkhand region is at the top with 3.9 per cent followed by the central (1.9 per cent), eastern (1.4 per cent) and western (1.3 per cent) regions. Bundelkhand region was at the top in respect of barren land also. The reduction in areas as afore-mentioned has been possible mainly due to the government's efforts in soil and water conservation/watershed

Table 13.5
Region-wise Culturable Wasteland

Year	Regions							
	Western		Central		Bundelkhand		Eastern	
	Area, lakh ha.	% of reporting area	Area, lakh ha.	% of reporting area	Area, lakh ha.	% of reporting area	Area, lakh ha.	% of reporting area
2000–2001	1.38	1.71	1.16	2.56	1.42	4.8	1.39	1.61
2001–2002	1.29	1.6	1.15	2.54	1.39	4.7	1.36	1.58
2003–2004	1.17	1.45	0.99	2.16	1.21	4.09	1.3	1.52
2005–2006	1.1	1.36	0.91	1.98	1.15	3.89	1.24	1.45
2007–2008	1.08	1.34	0.92	2.03	1.17	3.95	1.23	1.42
2009–2010	1.05	1.31	0.88	1.94	1.16	3.92	1.22	1.41

Sources: (1) Uttar Pradesh ke Krishi Ankade (Agricultural Statistics of UP) of different years, a publication of Directorate of Uttar Pradesh. (2) Souvenir, 2008–2009, State Land Use Board, Planning Department, Government of UP.

development activities along with farmers' efforts due to population pressure. Considering the pressure of rising population, industrialisation and infrastructure development activities, fall in net area sown will have to be arrested. Under the circumstances, these culturable wastelands need to be reclaimed in a systematic way in the coming Five Year Plans and this should come down to almost nil level by the year 2030. Necessary budgetary provision and long-term perspective plan for reclaiming these lands need to be adopted on a priority basis.

Permanent Pasture and Other Grazing Lands

It is interesting to note that the areas under permanent pastures and other grazing lands reported in 1950–1951, 1960–1961 and 1970–1971 were 0.49, 0.44 and 0.77 lakh ha., respectively. Thereafter in 1980–1981 and 1990–1991 it increased significantly to 2.96 and 3.03 lakh ha., respectively, which may be due to the change in the reporting system in Uttarakhand, which is corroborated by the fact that the divided UP had only 0.75 lakh ha. under this category in 1990–1991, which came down to 0.7 lakh ha. in 2000–2001.

From 2000–2001 to 2009–2010 there has been continuous decline in pasture land and it has reached a level of only 0.65 lakh ha. in the year 2009–2010. Keeping in view the trend reported for bifurcated UP, it is a cause of concern that the pasture lands are decreasing. This cannot be considered a good sign. In fact, there appears no possibility of increasing these lands in the coming years. The policy of allotting government and *Gram Sabha* lands to landless persons should be immediately stopped, especially when the land in question is common grazing land. As per revenue laws this category of common land cannot be allotted.

The downtrend is visible in almost all the regions. It was 0.26, 0.20, 0.19 and 0.05 lakh ha., respectively, in central, eastern, western and Bundelkhand regions in 2000–2001. In 2009–2010, these areas are 0.25, 0.17, 0.18 and 0.05 lakh ha. in these regions, respectively. Table 13.6 presents the changes in these 9 years. Percentage of this category to reporting area is maximum at 0.55 per cent in the central region. The

Table 13.6

Region-wise Permanent Pasture and Other Grazing Lands

	Regions							
	Western		Central		Bundelkhand		Eastern	
Year	Area, lakh ha.	% of reporting area	Area, lakh ha.	% of reporting area	Area, lakh ha.	% of reporting area	Area, lakh ha.	% of reporting area
2000–2001	0.19	0.24	0.26	0.57	0.05	0.17	0.20	0.23
2001–2002	0.19	0.24	0.26	0.57	0.05	0.17	0.20	0.23
2003–2004	0.18	0.22	0.25	0.54	0.06	0.20	0.18	0.21
2005–2006	0.18	0.22	0.25	0.54	0.05	0.17	0.17	0.20
2007–2008	0.18	0.22	0.25	0.55	0.05	0.17	0.17	0.20
2009–2010	0.18	0.22	0.25	0.55	0.05	0.17	0.17	0.20

Sources: (1) Uttar Pradesh ke Krishi Ankade (Agricultural Statistics of UP) of different years, a publication of Directorate of Uttar Pradesh. (2) Souvenir, 2008–2009, State Land Use Board, Planning Department, Government of UP.

other three regions hover around 0.20 per cent. Though, looking to higher-level population of cattle, there was a need to increase these areas but it appears that it may not be possible. Looking at the trends in the last six decades, the pressure on croplands for growing fodder crops will increase in the coming years.

Land Put to Non-agricultural Use

Over the years, the area put to non-agricultural use has gone up from 18.53 lakh ha. in 1950–1951 to 25.88 lakh ha. in the year 2000–2001. Thus, there is significant upward change in this category. This is due to urbanisation, industrialisation and infrastructural developments that took place during this period. However, this is a sign of overall development that has taken place during these 50 years. In any developing state, this is going to happen and this trend is likely to be higher and higher during the coming years. In these 40 years, 7.35 lakh ha. land is added to non-agricultural use.

As discussed earlier, it can be very well said that the pressure of development, urbanisation, industrialisation and infrastructure is going to have a significant impact on increase under non-agricultural use.

On the basis of the figures of reconstituted UP for 1990–1991, the area under this category was 22.96 lakh ha., which increased to 24.36 lakh ha. in 2000–2001. However, it jumped to 28.01 lakh ha. in the last 9 years, occupying 44.51 per cent of the reporting area in 2009–2010. This works out to a conversion rate of 40,000 ha. of land per year to non-agricultural uses. This shows a rising rate per year compared to only 14,000 per year in the 1990s. This is a very significant rise, which is the reason that a national land-use policy must be put in place for urban and industrial sector development without jeopardising multiple-cropped and well-irrigated land. If we take a long-term view for the last six decades it comes to about 16,000 per year.

Year-wise observation of the size of land under this category for the year 2000–2001 onwards indicates that the high rate at which the land was converted to non-agricultural uses was due to a sudden jump of 75,000 ha. in it in 2001–2002. Afterwards, the annual conversion decreased and the average up to 2007–2008 was 46,000 ha. per year. This came down to 40,000 ha. per year in 2009–2010. This can be considered a good sign.

Areas put to non-agricultural uses in 2000–2001 were 9.80 lakh ha. in the eastern region, 8.15 lakh ha. in the western region, 4.32 lakh ha. in the central region and least area of 2.11 lakh ha. in Bundelkhand. The percentage area under this category against the reported area is 11.35, 10.08, 9.52 and 7.12, respectively. In a period of 9 years, i.e., by the year 2009–2010, this area increased in all the four regions to 11.02, 9.06, 5.37 and 2.56, respectively. Thus, the highest increase was in the eastern region followed by the central region, the western region and the Bundelkhand region. However, the increased percentages in the eastern, central, western and Bundelkhand regions are 12.77, 11.83, 11.27 and 8.64, respectively, as shown in Table 13.7.

It is very clear that the areas under non-agricultural use increased in all the four regions of the state. The percentage increase in the eastern region is higher amongst the four regions and the lowest in Bundelkhand region. This is a cause of concern and this category of land use has to be controlled by having region-specific strategies.

Table 13.7
Region-wise Land Put to Non-agricultural Use

	Regions							
	Western		*Central*		*Bundelkhand*		*Eastern*	
Year	*Area, lakh ha.*	*% of reporting area*	*Area, lakh ha.*	*% of reporting area*	*Area, lakh ha.*	*% of reporting area*	*Area, lakh ha.*	*% of reporting area*
2000–2001	8.15	10.09	4.32	9.53	2.11	7.13	9.8	11.35
2001–2002	8.17	10.11	4.56	10.06	2.3	7.77	10.1	11.7
2003–2004	8.51	10.53	4.83	10.52	2.38	8.04	10.22	11.92
2005–2006	8.74	10.82	5.19	11.31	2.45	8.28	10.61	12.37
2007–2008	8.9	11.08	5.3	11.67	2.53	8.54	10.87	12.59
2009–2010	9.06	11.27	5.37	11.83	2.56	8.64	11.02	12.77

Sources: (1) Uttar Pradesh ke Krishi Ankade (Agricultural Statistics of UP) of different years, a publication of Directorate of Uttar Pradesh. (2) Souvenir, 2008–2009, State Land Use Board, Planning Department, Government of UP.

Fallow Lands and Net Area Sown

Current Fallows

Status of areas under current fallows in 1950–1951 was 10.78 lakh ha., followed by a sudden fall to 1.74 lakh ha. in 1960–1961. Probably this is due to the inclusion of the area in other fallow category in 1960–1961. This again increased to 8.70 lakh ha. in 1970–1971. Thereafter, it ranged as 11.70, 10.84 and 10.86 lakh ha. in the years 1980–1981, 1990–1991 and 2000–2001, respectively. Thus, it can very well be said that the areas under current fallows continued to be at around 10 lakh ha.

In reconstituted UP, the area under this land-use class was 12.42 lakh ha. in 1990–1991, which reduced to 10.48 lakh ha. in 2000–2001 and 10.26 lakh ha. in 2001–2002. Thereafter there has been no significant change and it remained around 12 lakh ha. in the last 8 years (Table 13.1). These are the potential areas that need special attention as to why these lands are kept fallow. Absentee landlords, drought-like situations and may be to some extent incorrect reporting might be some of the reasons for this much area being shown as current fallows.

The eastern region with 4.16 lakh ha. land in this category had the highest area in 2000–2001, followed by 2.86 lakh ha. in the central region, 2.00 lakh ha. in the western region and 1.46 lakh ha. in Bundelkhand region. There has been an increase in the area in the year 2009–2010 in all but Bundelkhand region. The eastern region has 5.47 lakh ha. followed by 3.09 lakh ha. in the central region, 2.46 lakh ha. in the western region and 1.30 lakh ha. in Bundelkhand region (Table 13.8). In Bundelkhand region, a drop of 0.16 lakh ha. was observed while the eastern, western and central regions recorded increases of 1.41, 0.46 and 0.23 lakh ha., respectively, in 8 years. Percentage-wise, the central and eastern regions have 6.80 and 6.34 per cent of reporting areas in this category. Bundelkhand and western regions have 4.39 per cent and 3.06 per cent, respectively.

Other Fallow Lands

In the year 1950–1951, the area under 'Other Fallow Lands' was 2.91 lakh ha. In 1960–1961 it went up to 12.60 lakh ha., which again came down to 5.45 lakh ha. in 1970–1971. In the year 1950–1951, the

Table 13.8

Region-wise Current Fallow Land

	Regions							
	Western		Central		Bundelkhand		Eastern	
Year	Area, lakh ha.	% of reporting area	Area, lakh ha.	% of reporting area	Area, lakh ha.	% of reporting area	Area, lakh ha.	% of reporting area
2000–2001	2.00	2.48	2.86	6.31	1.46	4.93	4.16	4.82
2001–2002	2.11	2.61	2.91	6.42	1.06	3.58	4.17	4.83
2003–2004	2.29	2.83	3.26	7.10	1.15	3.89	4.67	5.45
2005–2006	2.46	3.05	3.23	7.04	1.56	5.27	5.46	6.37
2007–2008	2.42	3.01	2.86	6.30	3.17	10.70	5.63	6.52
2009–2010	2.46	3.06	3.09	6.80	1.30	4.39	5.47	6.34

Sources: (1) Uttar Pradesh ke Krishi Ankade (Agricultural Statistics of UP) of different years, a publication of Directorate of Uttar Pradesh. (2) Souvenir, 2008–2009, State Land Use Board, Planning Department, Government of UP.

area under 'Other Fallow Lands' was 2.91 lakh ha. In 1960–1961 it went up to 12.60 lakh ha. which again came down to 5.45 lakh ha. in 1970–1971. The reason appears to be the inclusion of some area in this category from current fallows. Thereafter, it has been 7.16, 8.84 and 7.10 lakh ha. in the years 1980–1981, 1990–1991 and 2000–2001, respectively. Thus it can be concluded that it was fluctuating between 3.00 and 12.60 lakh ha. in undivided UP. In the year 1990–1991 when figures for Uttarakhand were subtracted, the area under other fallow went down to 6.49 lakh ha. This indicates that the areas under 'other fallows' are much more in Uttarakhand considering its small size.

Large chunk of areas under 'other fallows' is also a cause of worry and these areas need to be brought down to meet the likely gap in the net area sown due to the pressure of urbanisation and industrialisation.

In reconstituted UP, area under 'other fallow lands' declined from 6.49 lakh ha. in 1990–1991 to 6.41 lakh ha. in 2000–2001 and further reduced to 5.37 lakh ha. in the year 2009–2010. This issue also needs a focused study as to why such large areas are fallow. The reasons need to be probed and suitable remedial measures be taken to bring such lands under productive uses, say forest, farming, pasture or non-agriculture use like various developmental purposes.

The eastern region had maximum area in this category, 2.13 lakh ha. in the year 2000–2001. Next comes the central region with 1.83 lakh ha., followed by 1.71 lakh ha. in the western region and 0.74 lakh ha. in Bundelkhand region. However, In terms of percentage to reported area in 2009–2010, it is the highest in the central region, i.e., 3.59 followed by 2.21, 1.89 and 1.58 per cent in the eastern, Bundelkhand and western regions, respectively. These areas came down in all the regions during the 9-year period. In the year 2009–2010, the eastern region had 1.91 lakh ha. as other fallows. The central, western and Bundelkhand regions have 1.63, 1.27 and 0.56 lakh ha., respectively (Table 13.9).

Net Area Sown

A very interesting picture emerges on review of the net area sown in the last six decades. In the year 1960–1961, the net area sown jumped to 171.88 lakh ha. up from 162.31 lakh ha. in 1950–1951.

Table 13.9
Region-wise Other Fallow Land

	Regions							
	Western		*Central*		*Bundelkhand*		*Eastern*	
Year	*Area, lakh ha.*	*% of reporting area*	*Area, lakh ha.*	*% of reporting area*	*Area, lakh ha.*	*% of reporting area*	*Area, lakh ha.*	*% of reporting area*
2000–2001	1.71	2.12	1.83	4.04	0.74	2.5	2.13	2.47
2001–2002	1.62	2.01	1.82	4.02	0.72	2.43	2.08	2.41
2003–2004	1.41	1.75	1.87	4.07	0.6	2.03	2.06	2.4
2005–2006	1.33	1.65	1.68	3.66	0.59	1.99	1.9	2.22
2007–2008	1.30	1.62	1.65	3.63	0.56	1.89	1.89	2.19
2009–2010	1.27	1.58	1.63	3.59	0.56	1.89	1.91	2.21

Sources: (1) Uttar Pradesh ke Krishi Ankade (Agricultural Statistics of UP) of different years, a publication of Directorate of Uttar Pradesh. (2) Souvenir, 2008–2009, State Land Use Board, Planning Department, Government of UP.

Thereafter it remained at around 173 lakh ha. However, it reached 175.95 lakh ha. in the year 2000–2001. It can be concluded from this that the net sown area fluctuated between 171 and 176 lakh ha. This fluctuation was mainly due to drought situations during the same years, which brought down the net areas sown, resulting in not only lesser overall food grain production but also adverse impact on productivity.

It is worth mentioning that at the national level also the net area sown remained almost around 140 million ha. Thus, it can be said that UP is consistent with the national trend. The share of food grain production in UP remained around 20 per cent of the national-level production.

It is very significant to note that in case of reconstituted UP, the net sown area was 165.09 lakh ha. in 1990–1991 and went up to 168.25 lakh ha. in 2000–2001 and 168.12 lakh ha. in 2001–2002. Thereafter it remained almost in the range of 164.17 lakh ha. to 166.83 lakh ha. in the last 8 years. The fluctuation in these years may be due to the pattern of rainfall. The net sown area came down to 165.97 lakh ha. in 2002–2003 and in the year 2007–2008 it was only 164.17 lakh ha. In these years, the rainfall was much below the normal rainfall, which resulted in reduction in the net sown area. This naturally affects the overall production of food grains in the state. In the year 2009–2010, the net area sown again increased to 165.89 lakh ha.

In fact, a critical analysis of rainfall for the last 10 years from 2000–2001 to 2009–2010 clearly indicates that in the years when rainfall was less than normal by 25–35 per cent, the net sown areas came down significantly. It is observed that in the last 10 years the average rainfall was much lower than the normal rainfall. It was only in the years 1999–2000, 2003–2004 and 2008–2009 that the state received average rainfall whereas in the rest of the years the average rainfall was much lower than normal. Food grain production in normal rainfall years was 442.61 lakh metric tons in 1999–2000, 444.64 lakh metric tons in 2003–2004 and 467.31 lakh metric tons in 2008–2009. In all other years with less than normal rainfall, the production of food grains remained much lower. In fact, in the year 2002–2003 it came down to 382.79 lakh metric tons reducing the per capita availability of food grains significantly.

The western region has the highest net area sown in the year 2000–2001. It was 61.19 lakh ha. in this region followed by 56.94 lakh ha. in the eastern region, 30.28 lakh ha. in the central region and only 19.85 lakh ha. in Bundelkhand region. In terms of percentage to reporting area, it is 75.75 per cent in the western region followed by 67.08 per cent in Bundelkhand, 66.80 per cent in the central region and 65.96 per cent in the eastern region. There are yearly fluctuations in net sown area, which is mainly due to the rainfall pattern and situation. Whenever there were drought-like situation and shortage in average rainfall, the net area sown went down. In the western region the yearly fluctuation in the net area sown ranged between 60.52 and 61.27 lakh ha. In the central region it fluctuated between 29.68 and 30.64 lakh ha. in these 9 years. In Bundelkhand region, the range of net sown area is 18.27–20.34 lakh ha. This fluctuation in this region is more due to the less average rainfall and drought situation. In the eastern region, the net sown area varied from 54.85 to 56.94 lakh ha. (Table 13.10). In alluvial tracts, i.e., in the western, central and eastern regions, the areas under irrigation are more due to which in these regions the effect of rainfall on net sown areas is comparatively less than that in Bundelkhand region. The percentage of net area sown to reporting area in 2009–2010 is 75.31, 66.11, 67.96 and 63.97 in western, central, Bundelkhand and eastern regions, respectively.

Table 13.10
Region-wise Net Area Sown

	Regions							
	Western		Central		Bundelkhand		Eastern	
Year	Area, lakh ha.	% of reporting area	Area, lakh ha.	% of reporting area	Area, lakh ha.	% of reporting area	Area, lakh ha.	% of reporting area
2000–2001	61.19	75.75	30.28	66.8	19.85	67.08	56.94	65.96
2001–2002	61.27	75.85	30.10	66.4	20.04	67.73	56.71	65.7
2003–2004	61.14	75.69	30.35	66.12	20.28	68.54	55.73	64.99
2005–2006	60.99	75.5	30.41	66.25	19.94	67.39	55.00	64.14
2007–2008	60.58	75.39	30.23	66.57	18.27	61.68	55.08	63.81
2009–2010	60.52	75.31	30.02	66.11	20.13	67.96	55.22	63.97

Sources: (1) Uttar Pradesh ke Krishi Ankade (Agricultural Statistics of UP) of different years, a publication of Directorate of Uttar Pradesh. (2) Souvenir, 2008–2009, State Land Use Board, Planning Department, Government of UP.

Thus, it can very well be said that there is negligible change in the percentage of net area sown to reporting area between 2000–2001 and 2009–2010.

Conclusions

Naturally there is no significant change in the reporting area. This happened only after the formation of Uttarakhand state in 2000–2001. In the pre-bifurcation stage, the reporting area varied from 292.58 to 298.06 lakh ha. Similarly in the present UP the reporting area ranges between 241.70 and 242.44 lakh ha.

Forest

Area under forest in the early days jumped from 31.94 lakh ha. in 1950–1951 to 49.53 lakh ha. in 1970–1971. Thereafter no significant change took place and the forest area went up to 51.62 lakh ha. level in 1990-1991. After the formation of Uttarakhand the area under forest straight way came down to 16.89 lakh ha. (2000-2001) and in the past 9 years there has been no significant change. As argued earlier, rejuvenation of degraded forestland and planting of trees must be taken up on top priority basis to improve forest cover and resultantly the ecology.

Land under Miscellaneous Tree Crops

The area under this head was 14.15 lakh ha. in 1950-1951, which came down to 5.92 lakh ha. in 2000-2001. This basically was due to the cutting down of trees for fuel and cutting of old orchards to convert them for agricultural crops (may be due to pressure on land).

After the formation of Uttarakhand, the area increased from 3.40 lakh ha. in 2000-2001 to 3.60 lakh ha. in 2009-2010. This happened due to the promotion of fruit trees/orchards and plantation done under social forestry.

Barren and Uncultivable Lands

Before the formation of Uttarakhand, land under this category was 28.87 lakh ha., which came down to 6.48 lakh ha. in 2000-2001. Similarly, after the formation of Uttarakhand, this area came down to 4.94 lakh ha. in 2009-2010 from 6.18 lakh ha. in 2000-2001.

Culturable Wastelands

In the year 1950-1951, area under culturable wastelands was 22.62 lakh ha., which came down to 9.20 lakh ha. in 2000-2001. In the case of present UP, area under this category reduced from 5.35 lakh ha. in 2000-2001 to 4.31 lakh ha. in 2009-2010. This is because of the pressure of population as well as soil and water conservation/watershed development works undertaken by the government as well as farmers' efforts.

Permanent Pasture and Other Grazing Lands

This is a grey area. In 1950–1951, only 49,000 ha. area was reported in this category, which went up to around 3 lakh ha. by 2000–2001. This happened due to the Uttarakhand region. There appears to be a change in classification. Moreover, Uttarakhand has large chunks of pasturelands and pastures.

After the formation of Uttarakhand, the area came down to 0.65 lakh ha. in 2009–2010. Against this, the population of cattle is on a rising trend. This will put pressure on agriculture land for fodder crops. The policy of allotting government and *Gram Sabha* lands to landless persons should be immediately stopped, especially when the land in question is common grazing land.

Land Put to Non-agriculture Use

This is a very important grey area in the entire land-use planning. In the year 1950–1951 the area under non-agriculture use was 18.53 lakh ha. This went up to 25.88 lakh ha. in 2000–2001.

In reconstituted UP, this area reached 28.01 lakh ha. in the year 2009–2010 from 24.38 lakh ha. in 2000–2001. The growth in the last 9 years is much faster and this needs to be curbed through suitable policy decisions. The rate of non-agriculture use has gone up to 40,000 ha. per year in the last 9 years.

- For the development of the state, industrialisation needs to be promoted and population dependent on agriculture needs to be brought down.
- However, there is a good scope for curbing urbanisation by encouraging vertical growth rather than horizontal expansion of urban areas.
- Third issue in this context is promoting our ex-president's suggestion of 'PURA' concept, i.e., provision of urban facilities

in rural areas. This will bring down the rate of migration from rural to urban areas.

Current Fallows

Area under current fallows was 10.78 lakh ha. in 1950–1951. This has gone to 10.86 lakh ha. in the year 2000–2001. Even after the formation of Uttarakhand, it went up to 12.32 lakh ha. in 2009–2010 from 10.48 lakh ha. in 2000–2001.

A special probe on this issue is necessary. One of the reasons appears to be the absentee landlords. The other reasons may be occasional droughts and non-availability of irrigation and may be incorrect reporting. Serious thought should be given by the state government to give legal standing to leasing of land by farmers not able to cultivate due to some reasons including being absent.

A special study needs to be undertaken by a suitable agency like Land Use Board, Planning Department, Government of UP, by selecting a few villages in each region and field-to-field verification needs to be done to know the actual position.

Other Fallow Lands

Under this category of land use, area reported was 2.91 lakh ha. in 1950–1951, which went up to 8.84 and 7.10 lakh ha. in 1990–1991 and 2000–2001, respectively.

After the formation of Uttarakhand, the area reported is much less and it is 5.37 lakh ha. in 2009–2010, a reduction from 6.41 kh ha. in 2000–2001. It is very clear that the area under other fow lands is much higher in Uttarakhand.

In order to know the reasons for the 'other fallow la still in good hectarage. it needs to be probed. In order to me de- mands for urban, industrial and infrastructure develop it, some concrete plan is required to bring these areas under ation by removing the bottlenecks, if any. A long-term prosnder regu- required by identifying these areas and bringing th plantation. lar cultivation or by putting these lands under orc

Net Area Sown

Area reported in 1950–1951 was 162.31 lakh ha., which went up to 171.88 lakh ha. in 1960–1961. Thereafter, it remained in the range of 172–176 lakh ha. in a span of 40 years. After carving out of Uttarakhand, the net area cultivated ranged between 164.16 and 168.26 lakh ha. This fluctuation is mainly due to drought situation in the respective years.

The area under cultivation is likely to be further reduced due to pressure of urbanisation, infrastructure development and industrialisation. Naturally, in the agriculture sector, we have to promote intensive farming by increasing the cropping intensity in the coming years. This is all the more necessary due to population pressure. Moreover, UP has the responsibility of providing not only the present level of contribution but it has to increase this contribution substantively to the national kitty. There is a good scope in the state having very low productivity levels compared to many other states. However, very strong efforts have to be made to put improved technology in the field.

Reference

Department of Land Resources (2005), Wasteland Atlas of India 2005, Ministry of Rural Development, Government of India, New Delhi.

14

Forest Land: Disputes over Ownership— Case Study of Kaimur Region of UP

Ashok Choudhary and Roma Malik

Background

The forest and forestland had traditionally remained as common resources, governed by the communities for centuries. The dispute over the distribution of forest resources with the community started with the British invasion of India, when the forest resources were used to serve the imperial interests and were equated closely with capital. When the British invaded India, almost 250 years ago, they found abundant natural resource which they wanted to use for the development in their own imperialist economy. By that time they had already exhausted their own indigenous forest resources and sought to use the rich forest reserves of the Asian subcontinent through imperialist policies. The East India Company's 'empire building' efforts and the first 100 years of British rule witnessed a colossal plunder of half of India's forest resources. The endangered species of timber wood from the Himalayas was used for railways and shipyards in both India and England. They soon cleared large chunks of forests in the sensitive Himalayan zone and in other parts of the country. The forest was also cleared to settle the white planters (tea, coffee, indigo and sugarcane). To control these vast natural resources, the loyal intermediatory class was created, who became the tax collector and landlords later, in native language they were known as *zamindars*, *malguzars*, *talukdars*, etc. British took control over forest, land and water and then minerals within the first 100 years of colonisation. The *adivasis*, who had an age-old symbiotic relationship with these invaluable natural resources as part of their heritage, vehemently opposed the colonial design, which gave rise to serious conflicts and oppressions in various parts of the country, especially in Jharkhand, since the 18th century. On the other hand, the local peasant communities came into conflict with the colonial rule, which was involved in extracting more revenue from agriculture through the absentee landlord system. The first independence struggle in 1857 saw the series of peasant resistances that shook the British regime. Although all these revolts were brutally crushed by the British Empire with the help of the Indian elites who were close allies of the British, the issue of control over land, water and forest resources remained very much relevant in the socio-political scenario during the struggle for independence. This forced the colonial regime to enact various laws such as Police Act, Code of criminal procedure, Forest Act, Land Acquisition Act, etc., to protect their loot and plunder of resources against any indigenous protest.

In 1864, the first forest administration for the British Empire (Imperial Forest Service) was created in order to take control over natural resources like forest and land. In 1868 and 1878, India was 'endowed' with its first forest policy and Forest Act, which, prescribed, among other things, banishing indigenous communities from the forest and restricting forest usage by them. To protect the interests of the queen and the British Empire, the forest was declared as an 'eminent domain' by the British. The British Empire looted the forest resources ever since its invasion and during this loot it saw innumerable protests by the tribal and forest people; they found very hard to annex the forest resources and to legitimise this loot. The Indian Forest Act, 1927, came into existence by amending the 1878 Indian Forest Act. The first line of this Act reads—"An Act to consolidate law relating to forest, the transit of forest produce and duty leviable on forest, timber and other forest produce." This Act is still being followed by the Forest Department (FD) to retain its eminent domain in India and also in the South Asian countries such as Pakistan, Sri Lanka, Burma and Bangladesh. It was very clear that this Act was enacted only to generate revenue from the forest rather than to conserve them for environmental purposes. Forest land is an important resource for revenue generation since more than half of the forest area does not have forest but land, water bodies, bushes, etc. Besides timber, Minor Forest Produces (MFP) is also a major resource for state earning and it also engages a huge army of intermediatories.

Since its inception, FD created by the British had been using this Act as a tool of coercion through which people could be kept out of the forest and forest land; soon the rights got converted into concessions, then privileges and then into absolute termination of rights as the colonial legacy continued even in independent India till 2006.

This draconian Act of 1927 empowered the government to declare its intention to notify any area as a reserved or protected forest, settlement of rights such as the right to cultivate in forest land, collect minor forest produce, grazing rights, collecting fuel wood, fishing, hunting, etc., was entrusted on a forest settlement officer appointed under the provision of the Act who is an administrative officer of subdivisional magistrate (SDM) rank. A settlement of the rights in reality meant the complete termination of these rights. Thus, people who had been traditionally living in the forest area became like outsiders, and the FD declared itself the owner of these vast resources and its officials and staffs became insiders.

Post-Independence Period and Land Reform Programme

After Independence, the Constitution of India committed itself to abolishing absentee landlordism and enact legislations, supposedly to protect the rights of both the tenants and the tiller in the entire country. Since 'Land' is a state subject, the state legislations were enacted to include this spirit in the new Act by enacting new 'Land Reform Act'. In UP, the 'Zamindari Abolition and Land Reform Act' was enacted in 1950; its intention was to vest the agricultural land to the tiller by abolishing the *zamindari* system established by the British. But there were major loopholes, rather 'elephant holes', in the Act—the provision in the Act made a room for compensating the landlords. The said objective of the Land Reform Act could not be achieved after Independence and if we see the data, less than 2 per cent ceiling land is being distributed among the landless population across the country (Kripa Shankar, *Maistream*, 1999).

The irony in the forest region was that the forests were kept out of the ambit of land reforms; as a result during Independence, overnight the colonial FD was made the biggest landlord of this country. Even today, if we see the data of the vesting of the land to both revenue and forest, it is clearly visible that FD holds maximum area of the land in this country, which is around 70 million ha. of land, officially approximately 69.2 million ha.

When princely estates were merged to form modern Indian state, the forestland, which was under the control of *zamindars*, was transferred to the FD for the purpose of management of the forests. Similarly, many village forests were also taken over by the FD. It is to be noted that the transferring of these lands was not backed by any legislation or any provision of Zamindari Abolition (ZA) Act but was done through simple notifications under Gazette I of GOI. Thus in successive years till the ZA Act was fully implemented in UP (the process of implementation of the Act is still incomplete) large amounts of land were recorded as forest land. In many areas of UP, such as in the districts of Mirzapur and Varanasi, it took almost 18 years for the ZA Act to get implemented because the royal families, big landords and feudal lords opposed it. During these years, a large chunk of land was misappropriated by these groups with the help of the revenue officials. The game sanctuary, common forest that was the property of the *Gram Sabha*, was transferred to FD. The dawn of freedom from the British empire brought slavery for the vast section of forest people residing inside the forest areas because the FD had emerged as the biggest 'landlord' in independent India.

Though the lands were to be transferred to FD, the entries of these lands in the land records were made much later and in many areas the process of transfer remains incomplete. Without completing the proper legal process of the transfer according to the Indian Forest Act (IFA) 1927 into reserve forest, the land cannot be notified as part of Section 20A, which are categorised as 'reserve forest'.

It is very important to mention here that the fact that forest and forestland were kept out of the realm of land reform in our country is visible from this data. The Indian State of Forest Report 2011 states that out of the total percentage of the geographical area, 22.33 per cent is forestland, which amounts to 69.2 million ha. of land, of which 2.54 per cent of land is dense forest, 9.76 per cent is moderately dense forest, 8.75 per cent is open forest and 1.28 per cent is scrub forest. However, the report itself mentions the discrepancy of the satellite imageries such as visibility problem due to clouds, growth of weeds and grasses mistaken for the forest as reasons for the lack of accuracy.

By handing over forest areas and thousands of hectares of land used as 'nistar' by the village people to the FD, the spirit of land reform was defeated in our country. The purpose of the land reforms and the passing of the ZA Act was very much defeated over a period of time also due to the lack of political will. Instead of finding out the actual reasons for the failure of land reforms, most experts and policy-makers work in favour of the landlord lobby and the FD, sometimes in the name of increasing productivity and sometimes in the name of environmental protection. The cultural relationship between forests and the people was destroyed in a systematic way under the protection of the state and gradually all forest rights were extinguished. Further, any rights claimed were labelled as 'forest crime'. The colonial legacy of the British continued and the understanding that people, especially the tribal, Dalit, pastorals and other poor sections who had a symbiotic relationship with the forest, was totally suppressed by the government in order to protect the interest of the elites, big companies and the corporate. The alienation of local communities from the forest continued even after Independence and this had a negative impact on the status of forests in India. This is the basis of the 'historical injustice' (as mentioned in the Preamble of the Forest Right Act, 2006) meted out to the people who depend on forest and land for their livelihood. The preamble of the Forest Right Act, 2006, has aptly mentioned about this fact that

> ... the forest rights on ancestral lands and their habitat were not adequately recognised in the consolidation of State forests during the colonial period as well as in independent India resulting in 'historical injustice' to the forest dwelling scheduled tribes and other traditional forest dwellers who are integral to the very survival and sustainability of the forest ecosystem. ...

FRA and Recognition of Rights in Forestland

After Independence, the new government failed to protect the democratic rights of the tribal, Dalits and other poor sections dependent on the natural resources for their livelihood. The non-implementation of the Constitutional provisions inside the forest regions totally destroyed the community's relationship of people with the forest and the land. In most forest areas, the disputes started arising between *Village and FD, Village and revenue department and the forest and revenue department.* The crisis has deepened in such a way that the whole forest belt of India is in turmoil where forest people and tribal are being treated as anti-nationals and enemies of the forest.

It was 60 years after Independence that the first attempt was made by the Parliament of India to enact The Schedule Tribe and Other Forest Dwellers (Recognition of Forest Rights Act, 2006), under pressure exerted directly by people movements, tribal and left movements and indirectly by the armed groups to pass this new Act in order to mitigate the 'historical injustices' on the tribal and forest people. However, if the fundamental disputes of the land are not resolved, this effort will also not be able to bring favourable results for forest people and *adivasis*. Though the preamble of the Act mentions about the 'Historical injustices', the Act has not defined clearly about these historical injustices. So, the Forest Right Act in the present scenario cannot be implemented in its right spirit if these historical injustices are not understood in a proper way.

The list of the disputes in UP — 'the historical injustices' (the list of disputes are applicable to the whole of India):

- The revenue land that was not acquired under Zamindari Abolition was vested with FD under Indian Forest Act (1927) and was termed as 'forest land'. In UP, Bihar and Bengal the forest was vested under UP Private Forest Act enacted in 1948 just before our Constitution came into existence and before the enactment of Zamindari Abolition and Land Reform Act in 1950. Moreover, the notification of the ZA Act was delayed for many years in areas like Bihar and Sonbhadra. The revenue lands were appropriated by the landlords and the forestland was appropriated by the FD. The FD extinguished all rights enjoyed by the people in such forestland after Independence.
- Both forest and revenue departments claim the same land in their records, known as double entry, and have been showing separate actions in their respective land records relating to the same land for the last 50 years. Examples of such disputes

are common in Chitrakoot, Sonbhadra, Mirzapur, Chandauli, Lakhimpur Khiri, Bahraich, etc.

* In most forest areas, the disputes that arose after Independence were of a serious nature: they were between *FD and the village, revenue department and the village and the FD and the revenue department.*

After Independence, no serious work was done to prepare a proper land record in such disputed areas. These issues have been highlighted very prominently in the Mangal Dev Visharad Report of Revenue Board in 1972 and also in the 29th Report of SC/ST Commissioner by Shri B.D. Sharma, especially relating to Mirzapur, Sonbhadra and forest villages. Both these reports tried to point out the disputes on the forestland created by the revenue department by fraudulent entries in the land records in connivance with feudal, upper caste sections, administration and the FD. The Mangal Dev Visharad report talks extensively of how the land in the forest regions was appropriated in large number in Tarai region where residents of Punjab and some so-called environmentalists such as Billy Arjan Singh managed to grab thousands of hectares of land (Billy Arjan Singh till his death in 2010 used to control around 250 acres of land inside Dudhwa National Park). Serious disputes occurred in the entire Kaimur region of UP, Sonbhadra, Mirzapur and Chandauli; these areas also became the centre for armed groups later. The report also discusses the failure of implementation of the ZA Act in the state.

These wrongs need to be corrected by our parliament, judiciary and governments. Until this work is done, proper agrarian reform, which would result in the community's ownership on natural resources, can never be established. There are several issues relating to UP that needs to be discussed.

In relation to UP these land disputes have emerged in a more serious way and there has been no political will since Independence to solve this serious problem. There has been no serious effort to understand this problem and to permanently resolve these disputes so that the village society is able to become self-dependent. This will help them to protect their environment and biodiversity and live in harmony with nature. Instead, *patta*s distributed in paper and various development schemes are being floated to divert the attention from the real issues, thus demeaning the citizens as 'beneficiaries'.

Similarly, in Uttarakhand (previously UP Hills) 65 per cent of the total land is forest and in the hilly region it is 84 per cent. In the hilly regions after historic struggles, two types of forest management were being practised since the British Raj. Van Panchayats in British Garhwal areas used to manage the forest adjacent to the villages, which would provide fuel, fodder and other NTFPs for daily use. Van Panchayats were under the revenue department and not under the FD. Over the years, various amendments were done in the Van Panchayat rules and they were gradually taken over by the FD. They became virtually non-functional except in some areas where women have taken some initiatives. For the interior forest there used to be village reserve forest (VRF), managed by the communities that would provide other requirements. But in 1962 the FD took control of these VRFs and made it RF, through a government order without any consultation in the Legislative Assembly or with the communities. This had a very adverse impact on the communities since large-scale commercialisation of forest produces and commercial plantation was started. The famous Chipko movement started in the 1970s in the tribal areas of Nanda Devi to stop commercialisation in the forest. The Van Panchayat rules were never converted into an Act despite a strong movement by local residents. These rules still do not cover the reserve forests and national parks. Both the FD and the Government of Uttarakhand oppose the implementation of FRA in the hilly region saying that the Act is not needed since Uttarakhand has Van Panchayat regulation, which is not even an Act and it is still under the domain of FD. Thus, the concept of colonial eminent domain continues in the forestland.

Case Study of Kaimur Region of UP

The Kaimur region (district Sonbhadra, Mirzapur and Chandauli), although very rich in minerals and forest resources, is considered as a very backward region of UP, and it is known for its very complicated land disputes especially relating to forestland. This whole area was part of the Jharkhand–Bihar region before Independence, but after the state boundaries were demarcated this region was brought under UP for the purpose of generating the revenue. The situation of land and forest vis-à-vis the tribals and Dalits has been a complicated issue before and since Independence as most of the forestland inhabited by the *adivasis* was illegally transferred to FD under Section 4 of the Indian Forest Act 1927 for management. The Government of UP, vide memo No. 4768/XIV-695/1953 dated 10.10.1953, ordered private forest and wasteland lying south of the Kaimur range in the Mirzapur district to be handed over to the FD for management purposes wherein the existing rights of the people of the villages within the Kaimur Range shall remain. Thus, it is clear that after abolition of *zamindari* the private forests were handed over to the FD after Independence for management. The order is attached in Annexure I.

The history of appropriation of such common land is account-ed in the document of the FD only, known as 'Working Plan'. According to the working plan of FD 1950–1960, more than 8 lakh acres of revenue land was transferred under Section 4 of Indian Forest Act to the FD in district Mirzapur. This land was finally declared as reserve forest, without following the procedure laid down from Sections 5–19 of the Act, and was illegally transferred as reserve forest under Section 20 of the Act. Today more than 500 villages and their vast cultivating land have been notified as reserve forest under Section 20 A of the Indian Forest Act (1927). The Ceiling Act that was imposed on the big landlords was misappropriated to such an extent that both the revenue and the forestland remains in the illegal control of the feudal forces and rich landlords in this region. The disputes in the Kaimur region of UP have been one of the second largest disputes after Independence. These disputes were highlighted very well in the 29th SC/ST Commissioner report by Dr B.D. Sharma and also in the report 'Van Bhoomi ke vivado ka niptara — in January 1990 to initiate step to resolve these disputes by the GOI' (Annexure II). The list of these disputes was also highlighted in the orders, issued by Ministry of Environment and Forest, GOI, by the then Secretary Shri S.R. Shankaran in 1990. Six issues including disputed forestland and recognition of forest village were identified on that order on which programmes would have to be taken. But such action was never taken and disputes remained unresolved.

Kaimur region was completely disintegrated into various states without realising the fact that in the long term, it will have a deep impact on the lives of tribal residing in this region. The states' boundaries alienated the tribal identity and they were dealt like outsiders by the respective states. If Gond, Baiga, Orao, etc., were ST in Jharkhand they were SC in UP, the Agarias were ST in UP and not in Jharkhand. Such anomalies were created deliberately to disintegrate the identity of the tribal of this region completely to take over the control of vast natural resources in this area. All issues were raised consistently but even now, these issues have not been taken into consideration by the respective governments.

In 1972, these disputes were very well highlighted in 'Mangal Dev Visharad Committee Report', but recommendations of these committees were not taken seriously by the ruling class. The land disputes became more intense after the construction of hydroelectric dams and massive industrialisation took place in this area for the generation of hydro and thermal power; the issue of compensation arose after major displacement took place in these areas. As the FD had fraudulently notified many of the areas notified under Section 4 as reserve forest without following the legal procedure as laid down in IFA 1927, the houses of tribal were also considered in forestland. But after the enactment of Forest Conservation Act in 1980, the Section 4 lands were declared as reserve forest without following any legal procedure. The government record says that 433 villages came under this dispute, which was considered as forestland. But no serious political will was shown to solve these disputes; rather the process followed later on complicated the land disputes further more. In order to know the disputes that arose due to industrial expansion, two committees were set up: one by the Planning Commission in 1982 and the other by Board of Revenue in 1983. But in 1982 a writ petition was filed by one of the prominent Gandhian organisations Banwasi Sewa Ashram vs State of UP and Others on 20 November 1986 in the Supreme Court, which further complicated the land dispute in this area. The organisation filed this writ petition to basically save some 300 acres of *bhoodan* land that was illegally transferred to the organisation, which was forestland, to save it from getting converted into reserve forest (Annexure II). The Court directed to appoint five additional district judges to find the list of the disputes. Massive corruption took place during settling of these disputes. The lands were transferred to many outsiders and thus in one piece of land many claimants were created. This fact has been recorded in Maheshwar Prasad Committee Report also. The Court also appointed a board of commissioners to supervise operations and see the implementation of the direction of the Court; one of the commissioners was chief functionary of this Gandhian organisation. This order of the Supreme Court did not consider the land notified under Section 20 and gave direction only on the Section 4 lands. In this massive appropriation of land took place by the appointed functionaries. The Court in its order stated that it should also wait to see the findings of the Maheshwar Prasad Committee report and take further action accordingly.

In 1986 committee headed by the Revenue Board Chairperson Maheshwar committee report also identified 433 villages lying south of the Kaimur Range of the Mirzapur district to be relevant for the present dispute. Of those 299 were in Dudhi *tehsil* and the remaining 134 in Robertsganj *tehsil*. The area involved was 9,23,293 acres, out of which in respect of 58,937.42 acres notification under Section 20 of the Act has been made, declaring the same as reserved forest and in respect of 7,89,086 acres notification under Section 4 of the Act has been made. The Committee in its report pointed out that unauthorised occupation related to roughly 1,82,000 acres. In the same affidavit, it has been further stated that the Government by notification dated 5 August 1986 has established a special 'Kaimur Survey Settlement Agency' for survey and record operations to solve the problems of the claimants in the area. The agency was to settle the disputes in another 2 years. This agency further complicated the land disputes. It was propagated that 80 per cent of the problem has been solved and 20 per cent remains disputed land. These false figures alienated the tribal further more and by the end of the 1990s, the armed conflict started in the forest regions of Kaimur.

The pressure increased on forestland in the 1980s and the 1990s. There was a massive operation to bring all the land under the reserve category and evict the forest dwellers who were settled in those lands. An eviction drive was started in the late 1990s. Whole of the Kaimur region was considered to be very rich in forest and mineral wealth but the population who were entirely dependent on them were left without any option. This resulted in starvation deaths in recent years in regions like Sonbhadra, Naugarh and Mirzapur.

The crisis of livelihood deepened in these areas and, on the other hand, the state violence also increased unabated. Atrocities were inflicted on the poor tribal and Dalit population; there is a tendency by the state to shrink the whole democratic space in the region arising out of the land crisis. Democratic movements and the struggle for land rights are being branded as Naxalite or Maoist movements. As a result, various fake encounters have taken place and poor tribal, landless, bonded labourers were booked under the Prevention of Terrorism Act (POTA) in 2001. This phenomenon is witnessed even in the highly industrialised areas such as aluminium factory of the private sector firm, Hindalco, and the public sector-owned National Thermal Power Corporation, which has a power plant in the district. However, the issues of human rights violation were fought strongly by the National Forum of Forest People and Forest Workers in this area and a Public Hearing was organised in January 2003. This brought very good results after the matter was highlighted in the press; the then Government of UP headed by Ms Mayawati withdrew all the 42 cases of POTA and brought relief to innocent tribal and Dalits who were falsely implicated in this case.

Since the year 2000–2001 the democratic struggle for land has intensified to such an extent that the tribal and Dalits of this region have been struggling to take over the land through collective initiatives and challenged the illegal occupation by the FD and its allies. The fight has intensified more due to the corporate onslaught on the forestland. The Jay Pee Associates was transferred 1,083.23 ha. of land in the Kaimur region. The forest settlement officer went beyond his jurisdiction and de-reserved these lands and made illegal orders in favour of Jay Pee Associates. This order was confirmed by the district judge also (Ref: Additional Affidavit filed on behalf of the Union of India, in the Supreme Court of India, IA no. 2469 of 2009 in writ petition no. 202 of 1995, filed by Shri Y.K. Singh Chauhan, Conservator of Forest [Central] Regional office, Lucknow). The company has illegally constructed the Super Cement Plant in the said land that has been stayed by the Supreme Court.

In this whole region, *adivasis* started the movement of taking over the control of land, which they call reclaiming their lost space, and more than 20,000 acres of land is under the control of *adivasis* and Dalits, who are claiming that the land belonged to their ancestors, which was under cultivation since Independence. The movement has spread to more than 100 villages in Sonbhadra district and also spread to neighbouring districts like Mirzapur and Chandauli. This movement has also spread to the neighbouring states of Jharkhand, Bihar and Madhya Pradesh. Massive repression took place after forest people started asserting their rights in this manner, the district administration branded the movement as 'Maoist' and filed false cases under various sections of the Indian Forest Act and under the Indian Penal Code on 1,500 tribals, Dalits and activists. The National Security Act was implicated against the leading women activist of the organisation in August 2007. But such false cases could not stand in front of a very strong movement led by tribal women. The government had to withdraw the cases.

However, all such state repressions could not stop the tribal and forest people especially women from taking back their land that belonged to their ancestors. This movement also strengthened the Dalit and other poor sections in the entire region to launch a struggle to get land against the feudal landlords, also in whose fields they worked as agricultural workers. The forest people, peasants, agriculture workers and poor women are now geared up in collective action against the feudal and state appropriation of the land and are mobilising to expose the loot done by the feudal and capitalist forces in connivance with revenue department and FD. There is a sharp conflict in these areas *on the issue of disputed forestland* between people and state, representing the feudal and capitalist forces, *who are controlling most of the disputed forestland.*

Possible Action Programme: The Action Research Study

In order to examine these disputes in Kaimur region a preliminary study was conducted in 2000 by National Forum of Forest People and Forest Workers activists. Another study was also carried out in 2008 to understand the forestland disputes in UP and Uttarakhand by collecting the gazette notifications from 1947 onwards to 2000 from the GOI, Gazette notification Part—I for one year. In this study, data was collected to find out how forestland was acquired by the FD, under which Act, which sections and how much land was transferred. These notifications show that in one simple notification lakhs of *acres of land* was transferred to the FD starting from the British time till the 1980s. These lands were acquired u/s 4 of Indian Forest Act (1927) and later without completing the process from Section 4 to Section 19 the said land was notified u/s 20 of IFA (1927) to make it reserve forest. We could only make a rough estimate of the amount of the land illegally possessed by the FD, but in order to know the exact status a detailed study needs to be conducted. These notifications can be referred in 'Bharat sarkar ka Rajpatra, Part—I'.

After the notification of the Forest Rights Act in 2008, it was felt by the peoples' organisations that it was very important to find out how much land has been acquired by the FD after Independence under the Indian Forest Act, 1927, and also through other forest acts. Through our experience, it was found that the FD is in possession of most of the community and *Gram Sabha* lands that originally belonged to the community. Second, the *zamindari* forests where the rights of the community were recorded were also acquired by the FD through the Private Forest Act (1948) before the passing of the Zamindari Abolition and Land Reform Act in 1952 in UP. In this way a large amount of land was taken over by the FD illegally and the Indian Government was instrumental in making FD the biggest landlord in this county post Independence.

So in the forest areas, the disputes arose among the communities, FD and revenue department, which resulted in unrest in these areas, giving rise to militancy and in some areas Maoist activity.

The aspects pertaining to disputes in the land system, i.e., revenue, forest, etc., in UP need further research, but due to limited resources and without academic help the organisation could not pursue it long. Moreover, very unfortunately this kind of research has not been taken seriously by the government, policy-makers, media and academic institutions. Still a lot more needs to be investigated if resources are to be handed over to people dependent on it with political will. The following questions need to be investigated if proper implementation of FRA or land reform programme has to be carried out effectively:

- After the enactment of Zamindari Abolition Act of 1950 what changes have been brought by the revenue department in the land records (bhoo-abhilekh)?
- Similarly what actions were taken by FD after it notified the revenue lands into forestland under Section 20A of the

Indian Forest Act 1927 in the revenue records? When were these actions taken? Which actions are still pending?

- It is necessary to collect information regarding the various notifications that the revenue department and FD have, according to their own laws, announced in the government Gazette, e.g., consolidation of land, the record of rights issued by the revenue department, notifications for the settlement from time to time. Similarly, the FD has also issued notification under Section 4, Section 20 and also issued notifications relating to de-notification of forestland to convert them to revenue lands. These data needs to be collected.

- After the Zamindari Abolition Act of 1950 various amendments were brought in the revenue laws, and new rules were made. Similarly, the FD also brought various amendments and changes in the laws relating to the community/traditional/ customary rights in relation to Section 5 to Section 19 of the Indian Forest Act of 1927. There is a need to study what amendments were brought, and what new rules were made? How these amendments continued to strengthen the control of the state through the FD and revenue department.

- As pointed out earlier, after Independence the government acquired two kinds of land: first, the community land from the *malguzars, zamindars, jagirdars, mahal* and *rayatwari* regions; and second land acquired through the Ceiling Act. In both these cases it is important to know what was in the records of the revenue and what actions have been taken by the revenue department from 1950 until now?

All this information needed to be studied in great depth to ascertain as to where fraud has been committed by the various departments and the ruling class in sharpening the land disputes in the state. These issues are the burning issues of the new era of agrarian reform. Unless these issues are researched properly, acts like FRA will never be implemented in its full spirit.

On the basis of the above collected information, a proper 'village register' could be prepared in a new way to maintain a full record of the village in relation to forest, revenue and the community rights in order to identify the source of the record. This exercise will reveal the actual status of the land in the village and indicate the disputes in the village. *The formation of the village register will eventually become the document for the resolution of the disputes of land in the village.*

Conclusion

1. At the time of Independence, land reform policies were not framed with proper perspectives, i.e., the issue of social justice was not kept as a foundation of the policies and the concept of eminent domain was not abolished, resulting in the continuation of the landlordism both by the state and by the private parties.
2. FD became the largest landlord in independent India, resulting in intensification of historic injustice on forest-dwelling people, especially on the poor and landless cultivators inside the 'forest area'.
3. The development paradigm and the environmental protection policy persuaded by the Indian state to strengthen the elites created large-scale displacement of the forest people from their homestead land. In the absence of any proper rehabilitation programme, the landlessness increased and the number of the surplus labour also increased. Thus, social and political crisis became the major issue in the development process.
4. In the absence of any attempt to initiate land reform programme properly so that political and social crisis in the rural areas could be resolved, oppressive measures were used by the state against the poor, resulting in serious law and order problem in the forest areas. The fraud and hierocracy of the Indian state resulted in failure in providing environmental justice. This created a serious environmental crisis in protecting forest, land and water against the onslaught from the national and international corporate.
5. The situation demands serious investigation on the status of land and its redistribution among the forest dwellers, as per the provision of the FRA 2006.
6. Serious effort is necessary for research and the implementation process of FRA.
7. Academics and social movement should come together to complete this task so that historical injustice is totally eradicated in the forest areas.

Annexure I

1953 order: Type Copy

Appendix – 3 ga (1)

No.47/68/XIV-695/1953

From,
   Sri R.S. Mehra, B.Sc.
   Under Secretary to the Government
   Uttar Pradesh

To,
   The Chief Conservator of Forests,
   Uttar Pradesh
   Nainital

Forest Department   Dated Lucknow October 10, 1953

Subject: Vesting of private forests and waste lands lying South of Kaimur in the Mirzapur district.

Sir,
   With reference to your letter No. 1932/35-12, dated September 1953. I am directed to say that the Divisional Forest Officer, Dudhi and the Sub Divisional Officer concerned should first of all make out lists of private forests and lands which will be managed by the Forest Department and those which are given over to Gaon Samajs. In preparing the lists of private forests and the lands, which are to be managed by the Forest Department, the following guiding principles should be borne in mind:

I. In the case of private forests the principle to be observed should be that all private forests of 50 acres or more in area or small areas which are contiguous to Govt. forests or those which form compact block of 50 acres or more should be managed by the Forest Department.

II. In the case of waste lands the principle to be followed should be that the uncultivated area which is surplus to the needs of the Gaon Samajs should be taken over by the Forest

Department provided that the uncultivated area remaining with the Gaon Samajs if not less than 50 per cent of the total cultivated area of the village and secondly that the area to be excluded from vesting in Gaon Samajs should not be less than 100 acres.

2. The Collector, Mirzapur, is being requested to help the Divisional Forest Officer in Compiling these lists.

3. I am to add that in the mean time the Collector, Mirzapur is being asked to hand over all private forests to the Forest Department for management, but it should be clearly borne in mind that the existing rights of the people in those villages, are not Interfered with in any way.

Yours faithfully,
Sd/-R.S. Mehra,
Under Secretary.
No.47/68/XIV-695/1953

Copy, with a copy of the letter under reference, forwarded to the Collector, Mirzapur for necessary action with the request that all private forests lying South of Kaimur range in the Mirzapur district may, pending issue of vesting notification under section 117 of the Zamindari Abolition and Land Reforms Act, be handed over to the Forest Department for management and lists of such forests and waste lands, as indicated, should be prepared without avoidable delay.

By order,
Sd/-R.S. Mehra,
Under Secretary.

Annexure II

van bhoomi ke vivado ka niptara:

वन भूमि के विवादों का निपटारा

भारत सरकार
की पहल संबंधी दस्तावेज़

डॉ0 बी0 डी0 शर्मा
आयुक्त, अनुसूचित जाति एंव जनजाति,
नई दिल्ली
जनवरी, 1990

विषय – सूची

Annexure III

banvasi sewa ashram holding land of 250 acres:

कार्यालय तहसीलदार दुद्धी, सोनभद्र
पंत्राक : 296, / सात –र0का0–भू0अधि0अधिनियम2005 / सु0प्रे0 / 2011
दिनांक : जुलाई 21, 2011

विषय : जनसूचना अधिकार अधिनियम के तहत सूचना का प्रेषण

श्री विजय विनीत
ग्राम लखनपुरवा, पो0 घरनीपुर
जनपद सोनभद्र

कृपया सूचना अधिकार अधिनियम के तहत अपर जिलाधिकारी सोनभद्र को सम्बोधित अपने प्रार्थना पत्र का संदर्भ ग्रहण करने का कष्ट करें जिसके द्वारा सूचना अधिकार अधिनियम के तहत कतिपय बिन्दुओं पर आम क्षरा सूचना चाही गई है। उक्त के क्रम में कार्यालय जिलाधिकारी सोनभद्र के पत्रांक 562 / जनसूचना लि0 – कलेक्ट्ट / 2011 दिनांक : मई 25, 2011 द्वारा प्रार्थना पत्र में अलिलखत बिन्दुओं के सम्बन्ध में आपको सूचना उपलब्ध कराने हेतु निर्देषित किया गया है। आप क्षरा ाही गई बिन्दुवार सूचना निम्तवत् है।

बिन्दु प्रश्न	सूचना
1. बनवासी सेवा आश्रम गाविन्दपुर को सरकार ने कुल कितनी जर्मीन दी थी	250 एकड़
2. बनवासी सेवा आश्रम को जो जर्मीन दी गई वह ग्राम समाज की थी व वनविभाग की थी या भूदान यज्ञ की थी।	वनभूमि थी जो भूदान यज्ञ समिति को आश्रम की स्थापना हेतु निःशुल्क हस्तातरित की गई थी
3. दी गई जर्मीन अगर वनविभाग की थी तो वह धारा 4 की थी अथवा धारा 20 की थी	वनविभाग स्पष्ट कर सकता है कि वह भूमि उस धारा 4 अथवा धारा 20 की थी
4. वनवासी सेवा आश्रम को क्या कुछ किसानों की थी भूमि दी गई, अगर किसानों की भूमि दी गई तो उसका क्षेत्रफल क्या था। क्या किसानों ने जर्मीन दान की या रजिट्रेशन अथवा सरकार ने अधिगशहित किया	नहीं

5. वनवासी सेवा आश्रम को जो जमीन दी गई। क्या जिस उद्देश्य से जमीन दी गई वह मंशा फली भूत हो रही है	वनवासी सेवा आश्रम से सम्बन्धित है वांछित जानकारी उन्हीं से प्राप्त की जा सकती है

तहसीलदार
दुद्दी, सोनभद्र

Annexure IV

Banvasi seva ashram judgement:

Supreme Court of India

Banwasi Sewa Ashram vs State Of U.P. And Ors on 20 November, 1986

Equivalent citations: 1987 AIR 374, 1987 SCR (1) 336

Bench: Bhagwati, P.N.

PETITIONER:

BANWASI SEWA ASHRAM

Vs.

RESPONDENT:

STATE OF U.P. AND ORS.

DATE OF JUDGMENT 20/11/1986

BENCH:

BHAGWATI, P.N. (CJ)

BENCH:

BHAGWATI, P.N. (CJ)

MISRA RANGNATH

CITATION:

1987 AIR 374 1987 SCR (1) 336

1986 SCC (4) 753 1986 SCALE (2)867

ACT:

Indian Forest Act, 1927—ss. 4 and 20—Jungle lands notified and declared reserved forest—Possession of the Adivasis—Whether legal and valid.

Environmental Law:

Forests—National Asset—Important for ecological balance and economy—Schemes to generate electricity equally important and cannot be deferred.

Legal Aid

Jungle land habitated and cultivated by Adivasis—Declared reserved forest—Dispossession sought—Provision of legal aid to protect their rights.

HEADNOTE:

Consequent upon the State Government declaring a part of the jungle lands in two tehsils of the District of Mirzapur as reserved forest under s.20 of the Indian Forest Act, 1927 and notifying other areas under s.4 of the Act for final declaration as reserved forests, the forest officers started interfering with the operations of the Adivasis living for generations in those areas. Criminal cases for encroachments as also other forest offences were registered against them and systematic attempts were made to obstruct their free movement, and even steps were taken under the UP Public Premises (Eviction of Unauthorised Occupants) Act, 1972, for throwing them out of the villages raised by them, and in existence for quite some time. Their attempts to cultivate the lands around these villages, converted by them into cultivable fields and on which they had been raising crops for food, were also resisted.

On the basis of a letter received from the petitioner- Ashram, a writ petition under Art. 32 of the Constitution was registered by this Court with regard to the claims of these Adivasis to land and related rights. By its order dated August 22, 1983 the Court directed the claims of Adivasis or tribals, to be in possession of land and to regularisation of such possession, to be investigated by a high powered committee with a view to reaching a final decision. The committee has since identified 433 villages relevant for the present dispute, and roughly one lakh eighty-two thousand acres in unauthorised occupation.

On December 15, 1983 the Court directed appointment of a high powered committee consisting of a retired High Court Judge and two officers for the purpose of adjudicating upon the claims of the persons belonging to scheduled castes and backward classes. The Government by notification dated August 5, 1986 has established a special agency for survey and record operations.

While the matter had been pending before the court the Government decided to locate a super thermal power plant of the National Thermal Power Corporation (NTPC) in a part of these lands and acquisition proceedings were initiated. NTPC, now a party before the Court, is seeking dispossession of person in occupation and takeover of lands sought to be acquired for its propose. The Court gave the following directions:

1. The lands which have already been declared as reserved forest under s. 20 of the Act not to form part of the writ petition. [342 C]

2. Forest Officers to demarcate and identify the lands notified under s.4 of the Act within six weeks from 1st December, 1986. The matter to be widely publicised. Claims as contemplated under s.6(c) of the Act to be received within three months from 15th January, 1987. [342 F-343 A]

3. Adequate number of record officers to be appointed by December 31, 1986. Five Additional District Judges to be located at five notified places in the area and to exercise the powers of the Appellate Authority as provided under s. 17 of the Act. [343 C-F]

4. After the Forest Settlement Officer has dealt with the matter, the findings with the requisite papers to be placed before the Additional District Judge of the area, even though no appeal is filed. These to be scrutinised by him as if an appeal has been taken. The order of the Additional District Judge passed therein to be taken to be the order contemplated under the Act. [343 G]

5. When the Appellate Authority finds that the claim is admissible, the State Government to honour the said decision and proceed to implement the same. [344 A] 338

6. Assistance by way of legal aid to be provided to the persons seeking to raise claims and for facilitating information for lodging of claims and processing them both at the original as also the appellate stage. State Government to provide the necessary funds. [344 C]

7. The land sought to be acquired by the NTPC to be free from the ban of dispossession. However, provisions of the Land Acquisition Act to be complied with. Necessary record to be maintained, as indicated, for use in proceedings that may be

taken subsequently. Facilities to be given to land oustees as undertaken before the Court. [344 F]

8. A Board of Commissioners to supervise the operations and oversee the implementation of the directions. [345 C-D] Forests are a much wanted national asset. On account of the depletion thereof ecology has been disturbed; climate has undergone a major change and rains have become scanty. These have long-term adverse effects on national economy as also on the living process. At the same time, the court cannot lose sight of the fact that for industrial growth as also for provision of improved living facilities there is great demand in this country for energy such as electricity. A scheme to generate electricity, therefore, is equally of national importance and cannot be deferred. [342 AB]

JUDGMENT:

ORIGINAL JURISDICTION: Crl. Misc. Petition No. 2662 of 1986 IN

Writ Petition (Crl.) No. 1061 of 1982 (Under Article 32 of the Constitution of India) M.K. Ramamurthi and M.A. Krishnamurthy for the Petitioner. Dalveer Bhandari and D.D. Sharma for the Respondents. J.C. Seth, Secretary and Gen. Attorney for N.T.P.C. The Court made the following Order:

On the basis of a letter received from Banwasi Seva Ashram operating in the Mirzapur District this writ petition under Article 32 was registered. Grievance was made on several scores in that letter but ultimately the question 339 that required detailed consideration was relating to the claim of the Adivasis living within Dudhi and Robertsganj Tehsils in the District of Mirzapur in Uttar Pradesh to land and related fights. The State Government declared a part of these jungle lands in the two Tehsils as reserved forest as provided under section 20 of the Indian Forest Act, 1927 and in regard to the other areas notification under section 4 of the Act was made and proceedings for final declaration of those areas also as reserved forests were undertaken. It is common knowledge that the Adivasis and other backward people living within the jungle used the forest area as their habitat. They had raised several villages within these two Tehsils and for generations had been using the jungles around for collecting the requirements for their livelihood — fruits, vegetables, fodder, flowers, timber, animals by way of sport and fuel wood. When a part of the jungle became reserved forest and in regard to other proceedings under the Act were taken, the forest officers started interfering with their operations in those areas. Criminal cases for encroachments as also other forest of- fences were registered and systematic attempt was made to obstruct them from free movement. Even steps for throwing them out under the UP Public Premises (Eviction of Unauthorised Occupants) Act, 1972 were taken. Some of the villages which were in existence for quite some time also came within the prohibited area. The tribals had converted certain lands around their villages into cultivable fields and had also been raising crops for their food. These lands too were included in the notified areas and, therefore, attempt of the Adivasis to cultivate these lands too was resisted.

On 22.8.1983, this Court made the following order: "The Writ Petition is adjourned to 4th October, 1983 in order to enable the parties to work out a formula under which claims of adivasis or tribals in Dudhi and Robertsganj Tehsils, to be in possession of land and to regularisation of such possession may be investigated by a high powered committee with a view to reaching a final decision in regard to such claims. Meanwhile, no further encroachments shall be made on forest land nor will any of the adivasis of tribals be permitted under colour of this order or any previous order to cut any trees and if any such attempt is made, it will be open to the State authorities to prevent such cutting of trees and to take proper action in that behalf but not so as to take away possession of the land from the adivasis or tribals."

On behalf of the State of Uttar Pradesh an affidavit was filed by the Assistant Record Officer wherein it was stated: 340

It is respectfully submitted that for the information of this Court the State Government is already seized with the matter and is trying to identify claims and find out ways and means to regularise the same. To achieve this aim the Government has already appointed a High Power Committee chaired by the Chairman of Board of Revenue, U.P., Collector, Mirzapur and Conservator of Forest, South Circle, are also members of this Committee. This Committee has already held two sittings. In the last meeting held at Pipri on 16/17.8.1983 people of all shades of opinion presented their respective points of view before the Committee.

On 15.12.1983, this Court made another order which indicated that the Court was of the view that another High Powered Committee should be appointed. The relevant portion of that order was to the following effect: "... the parties will discuss the composition and modalities of the High Power Committee to be appointed by the Court for the purpose of adjudicating the various claims of the persons belonging to the Scheduled Castes and other backward classes in Robertsganj and Dudhi Tehsils of Mirzapur District. Notice will also specify, that the Court proposes to appoint a High Power Committee consisting of retired High Court Judge and two other officers for the purposes of adjudicating upon the claims of the persons belonging to Scheduled Castes and backward classes in Dudhi and Robertsganj Tehsils of their land entitlements as also to examine the hereditary and customary fights of farmers in those tehsils and to adjudicate upon the claims of tribals of their customary fights with respect to fodder fuel, wood, small timber, sand and stones for the houses, timber for agriculture implements, flowers, fruits and minor forest produce. The Uttar Pradesh Government had in the meantime indicated that the tenure of the Committee under the Chairmanship of Shri Maheshwar Prasad was to expire on December 31, 1983 and Government was awaiting the recommendations of that Committee. In that letter it was specifically stated: "In the opinion of the State Government it would be more fruitful if the Committee proposed in your letter is constituted after the recommendations and advice of the previous Committee are received. The Government have agreed in principle that the proposed Commit- tee with wide legal powers be constituted for adjudication of disputes."

341

Admittedly there had been no survey and settlement in these tehsils and in the absence of any definite record, this Court accepted the representation of the parties that it would be difficult to implement the directions of the Court. The Court, therefore, directed that survey and record operations in these Tehsils be completed. But later it was again represented on behalf of the State Government that completion of such operations within a short and limited time would be difficult and particularly, during the rainy and the winter seasons it would not at all be practicable to work. The Court thereafter did not reiterate its directions in the matter of preparation of the survey and record operations and awaited the report of the Maheshwar Prasad Committee. Intermittent directions were given on applications filed on behalf of tribals when further prosecutions were launched.

From the affidavit of Shri B.K. Singh Yadav, Joint Secretary to the Revenue Department of the State Government, it appears that the Maheshwar Prasad Committee identified 433 villages lying south of the Kaimur Range of the Mirzapur District to be relevant for the present dispute. Of those 299 were in Dudhi Tehsil and the remaining 134 in Robertsganj Tehsil. The area involved was 9,23,293 acres out of which in respect of 58,937.42 acres notification under section 20 of the Act has been made declaring the same as reserved forest and in respect of 7,89,086 acres notification under section 4 of the Act has been made. The Committee in its report pointed out that unauthorised occupation related to roughly one lakh eighty-two thousand acres. In the same affidavit, it has been further stated that the Government by notification dated August 5, 1986, has established a special agency for survey and record operations to solve the problems of the claimants in the area and a copy of the notification has also been produced.

While this matter had been pending before this Court and there has been a general direction that there should be no dispossession of the local people in occupation of the lands, Government has decided that a Super Thermal Plant of the National Thermal Power Corporation Limited (for short NTPC) would be located in a part of these lands and acquisition proceedings have been initiated. NTPC is now a party before us upon its own seeking and has made an application indicating specifically the details of the lands which are sought to be acquired for its purpose. It has been claimed that the completion of the Project is a time-bound programme and unless the lands intended to be acquired are made free from prohibitive directions of this Court, the acquisition as also the consequential dispossession of persons in occupation and takeover of possession by the Corporation are permitted, the Project cannot be completed.

342
Indisputably, forests are a much wanted national asset. On account of the depletion thereof ecology has been disturbed; climate has undergone a major change and rains have become scanty. These have long-term adverse effects on national economy as also on the living process. At the same time, we cannot lose sight of the fact that for industrial growth as also for provision of improved living facilities there is great demand in this country for energy such as electricity. In fact, for quite some time the entire country in general and specific parts thereof, in particular, have suffered a tremendous

setback in industrial activity for want of energy. A scheme to generate electricity, therefore, is equally of national importance and cannot be deferred. Keeping all these aspects in view and after heating learned counsel for the parties in the presence of officers of the State Government and NTPC and representatives of the Banwasi Seva Ashram, we proceed to give the following directions:

1. So far as the lands which have already been declared as reserved forest under section 20 of the Act, the same would not form part of the Writ Petition and any direction made by this Court earlier, now or in future in this case would not relate to the same. In regard to the lands declared as reserved forest, it is, however, open to the claimants to establish their rights, if any, in any other appropriate proceeding. We express no opinion about the maintainability of such claim.

2. In regard to the lands notified under section 4 of the Act, even where no claim has been filed within the time specified in the notification as required under section 6(c)of the Act, such claims shall be allowed to be filed and dealt with in the manner detailed below:

   I. Within six weeks from 1.12.1986, demarcating pillars shall be raised by the Forest Officers of the State Government identifying the lands covered by the notification under section 4 of the Act. The fact that a notification has been made under section 4 of the Act and demarcating pillars have been raised in the locality to clearly identify the property subjected to the notification shall be widely publicised by beat of drums in all the villages and surrounding areas concerned. Copies of notices printed in Hindi in abundant number will be circulated through the Gram Sabhas giving reasonable specifications of the lands which are covered by the notification. Sufficient number of inquiry booths would be set up within the notified area so as to enable the people

343

Of the area likely to be affected by the notification to get the information as to whether their lands are affected by the notification, so as to enable them to decide whether any claim need be filed. The Gram Sabhas shall give wide publicity to the matter at their level, Demarcation, as indicated above, shall be completed by 15.1.1987. Within three months therefrom, claims as contemplated under section 6(c) shall be received as provided by the statute.

II. Adequate number of record officers shall be appointed by 31st December, 1986. There shall also be five experienced Additional District Judges, one each to be located at Dudhi, Muirpur, Kirbil of Dudhi Tehsil and Robertsganj and Tilbudwa of Robertsganj Tehsil. Each of these-Additional District Judges who will be spared by the High Court of Allahabad, would have his establishment at one of the places indicated and the State shall provide the requisite number of assistants and other employees for their efficient functioning. The learned Chief Justice of the Allahabad High Court is requested to make the services of five experienced Additional District Judges available for the purpose by 15th December, 1986 so that these officers may be posted at their respective stations by the first of January, 1987. Each of those Additional District Judges would be entitled to thirty per cent of the salary as allowance during the period of their work. Each Additional District Judge would work at such of the five notified places that would be fixed up by the District Judge' of Mirzapur before 20th of December, 1986. These Additional District Judges would exercise the powers of the Appellate Authority as provided under section 17 of the Act.

III. After the Forest Settlement Officer has done the needful under the provisions of the Act, the findings with the requisite papers shall be placed before the Additional District Judge of the area even though no appeal is filed and the same shall be scrutinised as if an appeal has been taken against the order of the authority and the order of the Additional District Judge passed therein shall be taken to be the order contemplated under the Act 344

3. When the Appellate Authority finds that the claim is admissible, the State Government shall (and it is agreed before us) honour the said decision and proceed to implement the same. Status quo in regard to possession in respect of lands covered by the notification under section 4 shall continue as at present until the determination by the

appellate authority and -no notification under section 20 of the Act shall be made in regard to these lands until such appellate decision has been made.

4. Necessary assistance by way of legal aid shall be provided to the claimants or persons seeking to raise claims and for facilitating obtaining of requisite information for lodging of claims, actual lodging of claims and substantiating the same both at the original as also the appellate stage as contemplated, by the claimant. Legal aid shall be extended to the claimants, without requiring compliance of the procedure laid down by the Legal Aid Board. The Legal Aid and Advice Board of Uttar Pradesh and the District Legal Aid and Advice Committee of Mirzapur shall take appropriate steps to ensure availability of such assistance at the five places indicated above. For the purpose of ensuring the provision of such legal aid, State of Uttar Pradesh has agreed to deposit a sum of rupees five lakhs with the District Legal Aid Committee headed by the District Judge of Mirzapur and has undertaken to deposit such further funds as will be necessary from time to time. It shall be open to the District Legal Aid Committee under the supervision of the State Legal Aid Board to provide legal aid either by itself or through any Social Action Groups, like the Banwasi Seva Ashram.

5. The land sought to be acquired for the Rihand Super Thermal Power Project of the NTPC shall be freed from the ban of dispossession. Such land is said to be about 153 acres for Ash Pipe Line and 1643 acres for Ash Dyke and are located in the villages of Khamariya, Mitahanai, Parbatwa, Jheelotola, Dodhar and Jarha. Possession thereof may be taken after complying with the provisions of the Land Acquisition Act, but such possession should be taken in the presence of one of the Commissioners who are being appointed by this order and a detailed record of the nature and extent of the land, the name of the person who is being dispossessed and the nature of enjoyment of the land and all other relevant particulars should

345

Be kept for appropriate use in future. Such records shall be duly certified by the Commissioner in whose presence possession is taken and the same should be available for use in all proceedings that may be taken subsequently.

The NTPC has agreed before the Court that it shall strictly follow the policy on "facilities to be given to land oustees" as placed before the Court in the matter of lands which are subjected to acquisition for its purpose. The same shall be taken as an undertaking to the Court.

6. It is agreed that when a claim is established appropriate titledeed would be issued to the claimant' within a reasonable time by the appropriate authority.

7. The Court appoints the following as a Board of Commissioners to supervise the operations and oversee the implementation of the directions given:

   (i) Mr. P.R. Vyas Bhiman (I.A.S. retired), Executive Chairman of the State Board of Revenue, U.P. now residing at Lucknow;

   (ii) Dr. Vasudha Dhagamwar;

   (iii) A representative to be nominated by the Banwasi Seva Ashram.

The Committee shall be provided by the State Government with transport facilities and the appropriate infrastructure. This should be completed before 31st December, 1986.

In the affidavit filed by Shri Yadav, Joint Secretary to the State Government on November 7, 1986, certain instructions of the State Government have been detailed. To the extent the instructions are not superseded by the Court's directions in today's order the same shall remain effective.

We must express our satisfaction in regard to the cooperation shown by the parties. Mr. Gopal Subramaniam appearing for the State of Uttar Pradesh has taken considerable pains to give shape to the matter. Mr. Ramamurthi for the petitioner has also done considerable work in evolving the ambit of the

346

Guidelines which we have adopted. We hope that all parties concerned with the matter would exhibit the proper spirit necessary to successfully complete the assignment. We give liberty to parties to move for directions as and when necessary. The Board of

Commissioners shall also be at liberty to approach this Court for directions when necessary for implementing the present arrangements. P.S.S. Petition disposed of.

Annexure V

Documents needed to be studied:

1. Collection of Gazette showing the declaration of reserve forest under section 4 and under section 20 that is available in Part-I of "Bharat ka Rajpatra" from Lucknow from the period of 1947–2005.
2. The collection of forest settlement reports, working scheme and working plans from Forest Research Institute, Dehradun or Nainital in order to find out the terms of land transfer and to compare the records collected from gazettes. This will help in identifying the misappropriation of land from official forest department records
3. Collection of document Bajibularj (known as record of rights document made before independence from District Sonbhadra and Lakhimpur Khiri). This will enable us to record the rights that people enjoyed earlier and help us to re-establish those rights.
4. Information collection from Forest Settlement Officer (FSO) regarding

   a. Notification of intention for declaration of Forestland.
   b. Guidelines of demarcation of such lands.
   c. Settlement reports of these two districts.

The collection of records for the entire state can help to formulate a very authentic and solid agrarian policy for the state of UP and Uttarakhand Tarai region.

15

Land Management in Uttar Pradesh: Land Records and Property*

Ajay Kumar Singh

Introduction

Uttar Pradesh has contributed significantly to the evolution of the land records' management system in India since the pre-British days. Land, or territory, has been recognised as one of the constituent elements of state. Land administration has been, historically, a sovereign function, and a major source of taxes (land revenue) for the state. In India, well-documented history in this regard dates far back. Kautilya, in his treatise, the *Arthashastra*, written not later than 150 AD, makes detailed references of this in the days of the Nanda and Maurya dynasties. Systems of land measurement also existed in the medieval period and during Sher Shah's times. However, it was during the reign of the great Mughal king Akbar (who ruled from Agra, in the current State of UP) that remarkable work was done by one of his *navaratna*s, Raja Todar Mal, who introduced a system of land survey and settlement in 1582, known as the *bandobast* system, on which the land taxation systems of later days were based, including the *ryotwari* system introduced by Thomas Munro in the early 1800s in parts of southern India, while in the western world, Napoleon introduced the system of cadastral survey, land classification and ownership records in 1807. However, the current systems of land records and titling in India are largely based on the systems introduced by the British.

---

* *Disclaimer:* The views expressed are that of the author only and do not reflect the stand of the government on the subject.

Management of Land Records

Settlement and Records of Rights

Settlement refers to the conferring of property rights in land by the state on someone (historically, by the sovereign on the subject). During the British period, this was done generally in return for a stream of revenue. The revenue was fixed in perpetuity, as in 1793 in Bengal Presidency (permanent settlement), or revised every few years (temporary settlement). The medium of collection could be an intermediary with whom large areas of land were settled (*zamindari* system, e.g., in Bengal Presidency — now Bihar, Bengal, Orissa; parts of now UP, Central Provinces [now Madhya Pradesh], parts of Madras Presidency [now Andhra Pradesh and Tamil nadu]); or it could be directly the cultivator (*ryotwari* system, e.g., in parts of Madras and Bombay Presidencies), an agent (*mauzadari* system, e.g., in Assam, which is a variation on the *ryotwari* system) or a village body (*mahalwari* system, e.g., in Punjab, north-western provinces).

To provide a basis for revenue collection, detailed documents (records of rights, or RoRs) were prepared following cadastral surveys, and updated through revisional surveys. These records were maintained by the government, or in some areas, e.g., Bihar, by the *zamindars*. Procedures were laid down in the revenue manuals and land and revenue regulations (e.g., the Assam Land & Revenue Regulation, 1886, etc.) for updating and maintaining the records. Despite the underlying similarity in content, different regions adopted somewhat different forms for records and called them by various vernacular names (e.g., *khatian, khatauni, chitha, jamabandi, tippan*, etc.). These textual and spatial records, i.e., RoRs and maps, formed the basic land records, and are continuing throughout India to this day, with only few modifications.

Revenue collection was the primary purpose of land management for the British in India, for whom this was the biggest source of revenue. Because land records were merely an aid to revenue collection, there was less emphasis on maintaining accurate and up-to-date textual and spatial records of individual ownership. Often maps were prepared with reference to the village, and records were prepared for agricultural lands, leaving out the *abadi* (residential lands in the villages), urban and other marginal or government lands, which were not a significant source of revenue in those days, or were not assessed.

After Independence, the Constitution placed the matters related to land in the State List. Land records remained in the realm of the state governments, who were supposed to carry out survey and settlement operations periodically and to update the records and maps. In the period between such operations, the records were supposed to be kept updated by recording mutations following every change in ownership due to sale, partition, succession, gift, etc. However, land records are generally not in a fully updated state in many states, including UP.

Current Status of Land Records

Land records are poorly maintained, mainly for the following reasons: In the post-Independence period, land revenue has seen a continuous decline in importance. The costs of collection often exceed the amounts collected, and many states have abolished land revenue altogether. As a result, the revenue staff are deployed for a plethora of other duties. The policy focus on land reforms during the 1950s to the 1970s and even later, and disaster management responsibilities, also added to their regular duties. Thus, the revenue staff are left with little time for their primary work of maintaining land records. Moreover, there has been relatively low public investment for this purpose in the central and state Five Year Plans and most states have kept these works largely under the non-plan heads in their budgets.

The institutional set-up for land records' maintenance is another area of concern. Land records are handled by three to four departments in most of the states: textual records by the Revenue Department, spatial records by the Survey & Settlement or Consolidation Department (including UP), mutations and village records by the *panchayats* (in some states), property registration by the Stamps and Registration Department (which often falls under the Finance or Taxation Department, as is the case in UP) and urban property records by the municipal authorities (in many states, including UP). A person has to approach all the agencies concerned to get his/her complete records. Each department takes its own time, e.g., in registration, 12–30 years of legacy data, depending upon the local laws, have to be searched. Government interface at each stage leads to scope for rent seeking and harassment. There is no interconnectivity among these departments, and each works in a stand-alone manner. In fact, updation of records by any one of them makes the records of the others outdated. Therefore, land records are commonly out-of-date and do not reflect ground reality on a real-time basis.

The enjoyer of property rights has no access to his/her record of rights, because the records are kept with the field-level revenue functionaries such as *patwari*s. For the same reason, the records are susceptible to tampering.

Outdated survey technology, e.g., chain and tape, etc., which is widely prevalent, makes the survey work cumbersome, expensive and time-consuming. Therefore, survey, which is the cornerstone for updating of land records, is neglected, making the land records unreliable.

The state of the property registration system is unsatisfactory. Usually the registrar is under no obligation to check the veracity of claims made in any deed presented for registration, nor is he/she empowered or provided with any means for doing so. The registrar's offices do not have connectivity with the land records and cadastral map systems, and do not have access to the textual and spatial data for carrying out meaningful checks.

There is a huge backlog of mutations, and current ownership is not reflected in the records. Irrespective of the backlog, usually there is no means of indicating immediately following a transaction that the mutation is pending. In fact, even the computerised registration offices lack this vital functionality in the software and procedural routines. In such a situation, verification of the records would not prevent multiple fraudulent registration of transaction against the same property.

Cadastral records are not integrated and harmonised on a geographic information system (GIS) platform, thereby precluding their use in macro-level land-use planning, building an enterprise knowledge base supporting economic, regulatory and other activities requiring location-specific information, or making market-based purchase decisions of large areas of land.

Further, the current titling system is a major contributor to the unsatisfactory state of affairs.

The Property Titling System

The legal framework for property titling in India does not provide for registration of conclusive titles, and there is no system of title guarantee or title insurance. The Registration Act, 1908, provides for registration of deeds and documents. Deeds are instruments of conveyance, and deed registration merely creates a public record of the claimed transaction, not the validity of that transaction for transfer of title (because of the legal principle *nemo dat quod non habet*, or 'no one gives what one doesn't have'), leading thereby to only a 'presumptive' record of title, which gives scope for frauds, disputes and litigation.

This lack of title security adds significantly to market failure in respect of land and real property. In the absence of systematic accounting of land records and titles, title insurance markets fail to take root. Not only land sale markets, but also land lease markets are affected, as the owners fear for losing the property to unscrupulous lessees (although some tenancy laws that give unfair advantage to the lessees do contribute to this situation)

On the other hand, many countries that have gone for land management reforms have successfully introduced title registration, a variation on the system originally introduced in South Australia by Sir Robert Richard Torrens (with the enactment of the 'Torrens' Act, or Real Property Act, 1858), and, therefore, popularly known as the Torrens system. These countries include Australia, New Zealand, Germany, Switzerland, the United Kingdom, Singapore, Canada and the United States (with state-to-state variations), many other developed countries, and also a number of developing countries such as Kenya, Thailand, Malaysia, Uganda, Fiji, etc.

Kenya is a case in point, which shared the relevant laws with India, as the British applied the Indian Registration Act, 1908, and the Transfer of Property Act, 1882, there also. However, Kenya brought the Registered Land Act, 1963, and introduced the Torrens system. Puducherry is an interesting case from India itself. The French introduced the Torrens system there, but the Union territory had to adopt presumptive titles due to the Indian legal framework.

The Torrens System

In title registration or Torrens system, a register of titles is maintained as a public record, which serves as the primary evidence of ownership, registration is compulsory for transfer of title to be effected, mutation is automatic following registration and the title is indefeasible and a *conclusive* proof of ownership.

This system is based on certain principles: (i) the 'mirror' principle, which states that, at any given moment, land records mirror the ground reality; (ii) the 'curtain' principle, which refers to the fact that the record of title is a true depiction of the ownership status, and there is no need of probing into past title transactions; (iii) title insurance, which refers to the fact that the title is guaranteed for its correctness and the party concerned is indemnified against any loss arising because of inaccuracy in this regard; and (iv) a single agency to handle land records (including maintenance and updation of the textual records and maps, survey and settlement, registration, mutation, etc.).

At the moment, land records in India do not reflect any of these principles, although the state governments are free to seek reforms along these lines as land is a state subject under the Indian Constitution. There is no report of any legislative proposal along these lines from the state of UP, although the neighbouring Government of Delhi has drafted a property titling law.

Thus far the discussion has focused on the fundamental aspects of land records' management and property titling in India (including UP). Now follows a brief outline of the administrative arrangements in this regard in UP.

Administrative Arrangements for Land Management in UP

The administrative machinery for land management in UP includes the Revenue Department of the State Government, the Revenue Board, the Consolidation Commissioner's Organization, the Directorate of Land Acquisition, the Survey and Settlement Organization, the Revenue Courts, including those at the levels of the divisional commissioners, *janpads* and *tehsils*, the property registration offices and the *Lekhpal* training schools. Some important details about them are provided in the following sections.

The Revenue Department

The Revenue Department of the UP government is responsible for almost all the matters related to land management, including land acquisition and land reforms, but excluding property registration, which falls under the Finance Department. The important works of the Revenue Department include land records' management, land reforms, collection of land revenue, disposal of land-related disputes, removal of illegal encroachments and restoration of lands to lawful owners, identification and distribution of land for agricultural and residential purposes, collection of data related to agricultural production, computerisation of land records, survey and settlement operations, issuance of land-based certificates to the citizens, distribution of fisheries, distribution of land sites for afforestation, distribution of ceiling surplus land, distribution of home sites to agricultural labourers, rural artisans, the disabled, and those from the SCs/STs not having house sites, distribution of farmers' registers, administering the *Aam Admi Bima Yojana* and personal accident insurance scheme for the farmers, in addition to being the administrative department of the State Government for the Revenue Board, the Consolidation Commissionerate and the Directorate of Land Acquisition.

The Revenue Board

The Revenue Board, in the then united provinces, was established by the British in the year 1831 at Allahabad, for looking after the various aspects of land and revenue management. In 1932, the Board was entrusted with the responsibility of appointing, posting and transferring the *tehsildars* and the *naib tehsildars*, as well as control over the works of the district collectors and divisional commissioners. Certain changes were made in the administrative arrangements and scope of work of the Board since Independence, and currently the Board functions as the apex-level field office of the Revenue Department of the UP government. The following is a snapshot of its activities over the past few years.

Distribution of Land Pattas to the Landless

Under the UP Zamindari Abolition Act of 1950, preference is given to the landless agricultural labourers from the SC/ST categories, followed by the landless agricultural labourers from other castes, for the distribution of agricultural land *pattas*. The SC/ST who are landless with respect to agricultural land and who have been in possession of the *Gram Panchayat* land prior to 30 May 2007 have also been conferred rights over such lands. The following table indicates the distribution of agricultural land of *Gram Samaj* during the past few years:

Year	Target (ha.)	Achievement (ha.)
2006–2007	6,768	8,876
2007–2008	8,000	17,511
2008–2009	8,000	19,190
2009–2010	8,000	11,010[a]

Note: [a]Up to November 2009.

Distribution of Rural Homestead Land

Under the UP Zamindari Abolition Act, 1950, homestead land sites are allotted in rural areas to the SCs/STs, OBCs, general castes under the BPL, rural artisans and disabled persons living in rural areas who do not have adequate land for homestead purposes. In addition, the *Gram Samaj* lands on which houses had been built by the eligible persons prior to 30 May 2007 are also settled with those very families. The following table indicates the distribution of rural house sites during 2006–2010:

Year	Target (Number of families)	Achievement (Families)
2006–2007	53,337	59,310
2007–2008	60,000	98,244
2008–2009	60,000	1,32,649
2009–2010	60,000	73,096[a]

Note: [a]Up to November 2009.

Allotment of Ponds for Fishery

The State Government allots ponds to the fishermen community for helping them earn livelihood through fishery activities. The following was the performance in this regard during 2006–2010:

Year	Target (ha.)	Achievement (ha.)
2006–2007	25,349	8,543
2007–2008	3,000	12,347
2008–2009	3,000	8,088
2009–2010	3,000	4,001[a]

Note: [a]Up to November 2009.

Allotment of Land for Afforestation

Land *pattas* are allotted by the UP government to individuals for carrying out afforestation on the allotted lands, the rights being limited to the trees and their produce. The performance over 2006–2010 is indicated below:

Year	Target (ha.)	Achievement (ha.)
2006–2007	2,069	2,357
2007–2008	2,500	3,079
2008–2009	2,500	3,467
2009–2010	2,500	2,899[a]

Note: [a]Up to November 2009.

Commissionerate of Consolidation

Consolidation of landholdings has been an important priority for the UP government. The land consolidation operations were begun in UP way back in the year 1954; it has been going on since then. This is an important land reform measure with significant contributions towards rural economy, rural development and ushering in Green Revolution in the state. This also helps in the updation of the land records for the plots that come under consolidation.

Survey and Settlement Operations

The survey and settlement operations are carried out as per the provisions of the UP Land and Revenue Regulation of 1901 and the Survey and Land Record Rules of 1978. The survey and settlement operations are reportedly going on in 28 districts falling under the five survey units located at Faizabad, Ballia, Sonbhadra, Unnao and Gorakhpur. In addition, notifications have also been issued for taking up the survey and settlement operations in certain villages of the following districts, as per the UP Government's Annual Report of 2010–2011: Muzaffarnagar (16 villages), Saharanpur (28 villages), Bijnor (72 villages) and Gautam Buddha Nagar (14 villages).

Computerisation of Land Records

UP has made considerable progress in computerisation of land records over the past two decades. Of all the 313 *tehsils* under all the districts, the *khataunis* of the 99,949 villages which are not under the consolidation operations have been computerised, and the abstracts from the computerised land records are made available through the *tehsil*-level computer centres on payment of ₹15. Legal sanctity has been conferred on the computerised land records by a State Government notification of 14 July 2005. Manual issuance of RoRs has been completely stopped. A system has been put in place for the updation of land records through computers by the authorised officials in a timely manner. The computerised land records have also been placed at the official website of the UP Revenue Board (http://bor.up.nic.in), which is also of help to the banks, sugar mills, farmers, etc., in accessing the land records.

For the distribution of digitally signed *khataunis*, common service centres have been established, one for every six villages, and this facility has been made available across all the districts in UP from 1 August 2012 under the State Service Delivery Gateway.

District-level Land Record Data Centres

Under the centrally sponsored scheme of Computerization of Land Records (CLR), the setting up of district-level land records data centres is almost complete in 70 districts of UP. These centres will have vertical e-link connectivity with the field level as well as the state headquarter.

Establishment of Digital Revenue Record Rooms

Another important initiative of the UP Revenue Board under the CLR scheme is to scan and digitise all the records of the Revenue Record Rooms at the *janpad* (district) level. Work has been completed at the three pilot sites: Lucknow, Ghaziabad and Gautam Buddha Nagar districts, and work has been taken up in 18 other districts (Saharanpur, Meerut, Agra, Mathura, Aligarh, Bareilly, Moradabad, Jhansi, Banda, Kanpur *Nagar*, Sitapur, Mirjapur, Azamgarh, Varanasi, Gorakhpur, Gonda, Basti and Faizabad). Connectivity shall be established between the digital record rooms and the revenue courts. Apart from preservation of the records and facilitating their retrieval, this initiative will also help prevent unauthorised manipulation of the land records.

Computerisation of Certificates and Uniformity in Numbering

Various certificates based on the land records and allied data, such as the residence, income and caste certificates, are issued to citizens from the *tehsils*. For the sake of uniformity in their numbering, an 11-digit coding system has been introduced. These certificates are issued through computers and have a unique 11-digit number, which helps in verification of the authenticity of these certificates through the UP Revenue Board's website (http://bor.up.nic.in).

Computerisation of the Revenue Courts

The Revenue Courts at the UP Revenue Board, Lucknow and Allahabad have been computerised and the cause lists are issued through computers. For the benefit of the litigants, a touchscreen kiosk has been set up at the Revenue Board, through which the status of the cases can be found out with ease.

'Revenue Soft' Software

The UP government has deployed the web-based 'Revenue Soft' software, using which the information sought from the districts by the Revenue Board and the state government for the purposes of various plans and schemes are being obtained, and transfer and retrieval of information has become efficient.

While the above-mentioned initiatives of the UP government will certainly help in better land management in the state, there still is scope for establishing a modern and comprehensive land information system in the state, as may be appreciated from the following discussion.

Need for a Comprehensive Land Information System

Land is a critical resource for all human endeavours, and even the virtual world needs some real property for locating its technical and human resources. One can hardly emphasise the need for establishing a well-designed land information system with the appropriate mix of technology, process reengineering, institutional reforms and legal framework changes.

A sound land records' maintenance system is necessary for the security of property rights, which, in turn, is a *sine qua non* for an efficiently functioning market economy. In the constitutional and legal framework of many nations, the right to property finds its place next to the right to life and liberty. In India also, although no longer a fundamental right, it is a constitutional right. Quite often, land or property disputes rob much of life, liberty or pursuit of happiness—and faulty land records have their fair share behind the misery. Peaceful and legitimate enjoyment of land-based entitlements, such as tenancy rights, land rights of tribals and other traditional forest dwellers, rights conferred through various land reforms and distributive justice programmes—even the effective design and administration of such schemes—requires correct and up-to-date land data and records.

Land market operations lose efficiency on account of information asymmetry (which usually favours the holder of the information, leading to scope for rent seeking, fraud and abuse) and negative externalities arising out of faulty land and property information, which also make true price discovery and private acquisition of land via market mechanisms difficult. The case becomes complex when the area of land required is large, and a comprehensive land information system well equipped with accurate and current data and records in a suitably secure and accessible form with display facilities of a GIS is not in place. Under such circumstances, options for assessment of alternative sites may become cumbersome, or may not be feasible. Land acquisition, planning for rehabilitation and resettlement of the affected families, periphery development around project sites and corporate social responsibility activities based on land data may suffer in the absence of land records and other data being available in the form and manner best suited for the purpose.

In fact, in the absence of a modern land information system, carrying out developmental, regulatory or disaster management activity, or other land-use planning by public or private initiatives, may become inefficient, and effective delivery of citizen services based on land data may prove to be a tall order.

Finally, accurate and up-to-date property and ownership records and a mechanism that maintains the records updated on a continuous basis and makes them available to the user through a single-window are necessary for ushering in conclusive titling with title guarantee.

Although conclusive titling and title insurance have been possible even before the advent of modern technology, information technology applied to land data and records, plus modern survey technology, would make it possible to introduce the system much faster and help sustain it. Such a system will also facilitate title insurance operations, whether via private players, the state or both. Thus, a modern land information system would be an enabler for the Torrens system.

Attributes of a Comprehensive Land Information System

A well-designed land information system must comprehensively address the following aspects in a holistic and integrated systems approach in a digital (and, if possible, dematerialised, or demat) environment:

1. Updation and computerisation of all *textual RoRs* and titles (variously known as *khata, khatian,* etc.) and other attributes of data (such as land use and soil types), preferably using standard data codes applicable across the jurisdictions, while Unicode could be used for the Indian language computing and interface.

2. *Updation and digitisation of all spatial records and the maps-to-scale for each RoR or title*: Since the survey and settlement records are out-of-date, and the task needs to be completed within a defined timeframe, adoption of modern survey technology would be imperative. Such technology includes total station (TS), global positioning system (GPS), aerial photography, high-resolution satellite imagery (HRSI), laser-based distance measurement (e.g., airborne laser terrain modelling, or ALTM), etc. These could be used in combinations best suited to the local situation. Rastorisation of map data with physical details, geo-referencing using GPS and differential GPS (DGPS), vectorisation of data,

ground truthing and mosaicing of parcel boundaries would be required to be carried out.

3. *Integration of the corresponding textual and spatial records,* so that giving RoRs with maps-to-scale could be possible, and changes in one could be reflected in the other simultaneously.

4. *Computerisation of the registration process,* including online availability of the applicable deed or document formats, circle rates or valuation details, encumbrance information, etc., and facility for electronically receiving the stamp duty and registration fees (so that stamp papers could be abolished).

5. *Updation and computerisation of all mutations,* transaction records and records of charges for each RoR or title, including all backlogs of the registration, mutation and legacy encumbrance data, and scanning and archiving of the relevant records.

6. *A system for automatic and automated mutation* following each change in title, so that the records are continuously updated. Horizontal and vertical connectivity should be provided within the land records' maintenance system and between this and the registration system. The state should build a system for keeping all textual, spatial and transaction records in a continuously updated state, and arrange for their integration using information technology for *single-window service delivery* and conclusive titling.

7. *A comprehensive GIS,* built by seamlessly integrating and harmonising the spatial data from satellite imagery or aerial photography, the Survey of India and Forest Survey of India map data, and adding the cadastral layer from digitised revenue records data and other layers, e.g., administrative boundaries, watersheds, road and rail networks and so on.

8. *Data architecture, data codes and Indian language computing:* Common data codes with Indian language interfaces should be developed and the Unicode adopted as encoding standard with recognised fonts for the sake of inter-operability and collaboration on data interchange. Open source and open standard architecture may be applied for operationalisation, delivery and storage of data and services, so that the system is not fettered by proprietary data standards and architecture.

9. *Delivery organisation:* 'Anytime-anywhere' access to the data could be provided via web-based solutions with proper

authentication and access control. Access to the system could also be provided to the banks, treasuries and other financial institutions such as cooperative banks, etc., for ease of credit operations and financial transactions.

In addition, key delivery points could be set up to facilitate service delivery for the lay public at the following levels: *tehsils*, blocks, service centres or kiosks dovetailed to the common service centres of the Department of Information Technology, which can also be used for information, education and communication (IEC) purposes.

10. *Data security, backup/disaster recovery and business continuity plans*: The entire system should be robust. For maintaining confidentiality, integrity and authentication aspects of the secure system, an appropriate security policy should be formulated and applied at various layers, such as operation, delivery and storage. In order to build such a secure system, various security technologies such as digital signatures, smart cards, biometrics, firewalls and centralised data repositories and archives with backup/disaster recovery mechanisms and business continuity plans will have to be given due priority.

   For non-repudiation and maintaining uniqueness in terms of ownership and access in the privilege system, proper relationship management amongst the various entities based upon a well-defined identity management system would need to be created with unique transaction IDs.

   Backup and disaster recovery systems for critical resources may be located in a geographically distributed manner, keeping in mind geological features, earthquake zoning, etc., and other security considerations.

Collaboration with Technical Agencies

Collaboration with the technical agencies such as the Survey of India (SoI), National Remote Sensing Agency (NRSA), Indian Space Research Organization (ISRO), National Informatics Centre (NIC), Centre for Development of Advanced Computing (C-DAC), Forest Survey of India, Soil & Land Use Survey of India, etc., and the private players in the field may be the need of the hour.

The system could also work with the National Natural Resources Management System (NNRMS) in a collaborative framework. The NNRMS is a key initiative with the Department of Space as the nodal department to create, *inter alia*, spatial thematic maps of various scales for natural resource layers for the entire country.

Similarly, collaboration could be established with the work being done under various other organisations, e.g., the National Spatial Data Infrastructure (NSDI), National e-Governance Programme (NeGP), electoral photo-ID card system, UID/Aadhar, etc. International experiences could be taken as learning models for adopting best practices.

Role of the Private Sector

The solutions of NIC, NRSA, SoI, etc., may not always be adequate, and these may be supplemented by critical resources from other sources. Outsourced delivery models could be used to the extent necessary and feasible including the public–private partnership (PPP) models in non-sensitive areas.

Time-bound Deliverables and Milestones

Time-bound action will have to be a hallmark of the programme for establishing a comprehensive land information system, and massive efforts will have to be mobilised to meet the challenge.

Capacity Building

Inadequacy of human resources shall have to be mitigated through a carefully thought-out plan for training and capacity building of revenue, IT and other staff and officials from the grassroots levels and upwards across the system. From the *tehsil* level upwards, fully trained and adequate staff would need to be provided for managing the programme.

Interconnectivity

Interconnectivity will have to be established, both vertically and horizontally, among all the land record offices, from the state level to the district, sub-division and *tehsil* levels and all the registration offices, via local area network (LAN) and wide area network (WAN), dovetailing with the state wide area network (SWAN) and the NICNET networks, in an appropriate configuration based on the technical and functional requirements, and using leased lines, broadband with virtual private network (VPN), VSAT satellite link, microwave, radio or any appropriate medium depending on the local conditions for last-mile connectivity.

Institutional Changes and Process Reengineering

Creating a unified command, or at least a single-window delivery mechanism for citizen interface, for all related systems such as land revenue, survey and settlement, consolidation, map organisation, stamps, registration, mutation and titling, shall be the most important change required in the institutional set-up. Structural integration, although desirable, may not be immediately forthcoming, because of the legacy systems with different cadres for functionaries, different ministries, etc. However, technology-mediated functional integration of all these coupled with system reforms and process reengineering may suffice, along with the necessary legal changes.

Process reengineering may not remain confined to the land revenue and registration systems. It may involve other allied functions as well, e.g., the process for issue of succession certificate may need to be simplified.

Legal Changes

Legal framework changes will include the appropriate amendments to the Registration Act, 1908, and a number of other Acts including the Transfer of Property Act, Code of Civil Procedure, Indian Evidence Act, Succession Act, Power of Attorney Act, Limitation Act, Stamp Act, etc., as well as the revenue regulations and revenue manuals. A law on conclusive titling may also have to be developed. As land is a state subject under the Constitution, the state government could take the initiative and work with the related agencies in the central government as required.

Important Land Management Policy Responses

Major initiatives of the Government of India (GoI) in response to the above-mentioned challenges in land management include:

1. Launching of a nation-wide programme for comprehensive modernisation of the land records management system — the National Land Records Modernization Programme (NLRMP)
2. Decision to support ushering in of the conclusive property titling system with title guarantee (on the pattern of the 'Torrens' system prevalent in many other countries) to replace the current presumptive title system, and drafting of the model Real Property Titling Bill
3. A renewed focus on the unfinished task in land reforms, including the issues related to agrarian relations, ownership reform, tenure security, land use and common property resources

The State Government of UP also has taken a number of initiatives to meet the challenges in land management referred to earlier, and the important among them are consolidation of landholdings, agrarian reforms to favour the traditionally disadvantaged sections of the rural society, computerisation of land records and property registration and joining hands with the Union Government on implementation of the National Land Records Modernization Programme.

Major policy initiatives in land records management (of GoI and UP) are discussed further.

Land Records' Management Initiatives of Government of India

Initiatives for modernisation of the land records management system and computerisation of land data in India began in the late 1980s, soon after the use of computers was introduced in the public sector. The two centrally sponsored schemes of Strengthening of Revenue Administration & Updating of Land Records (SRA&ULR) and CLR, under implementation since 1987–1988 and 1988–1989, respectively, have been main initiatives of the central government in this direction. In fact, the scheme of CLR has been one of the first e-governance programmes in the country.

Moreover, around the same time, steps were initiated for studying the Torrens system. A One-man Committee on Records-of-rights in Land was constituted by the Planning Commission in 1987, which studied and reported on the system in a number of countries and recommended switchover to the conclusive titling system. However, the country had to wait for over two decades, until the Union Cabinet made a positive decision along those lines in August 2008.

SRA and ULR

The scheme of SRA&ULR was introduced for helping the states and UTs in updating the land records, strengthening their survey and settlement organisations and setting up and strengthening the training infrastructure for revenue and survey staff. Financial assistance was also provided for purchase of equipment of various kinds including modern survey equipment such as differential global positioning systems (DGPS), GPS, electronic total stations (ETS), for carrying out aerial surveys, etc.

CLR

The CLR scheme was launched with the aim of bringing efficiency, transparency and easy accessibility to the system of land records.

Pilot projects were initiated in eight districts, and the scheme was subsequently extended to cover 582 districts. Financial assistance was provided to states and UTs for setting up computer centres at the *tehsil* (or *taluk* or block or circle) level, sub-divisional level, district level and a monitoring cell at the state level; data entry of the RoR and other land attributes' data; and training on computer applications to revenue officials. Digitisation of maps was also allowed under the CLR scheme.

Achievements and Shortcomings of the Schemes of SRA&ULR and CLR

Although significant progress has been made under these initiatives, the desirable outcomes are yet to be achieved. Under the scheme of SRA&ULR, the states made progress towards adopting modern technology for survey and resurvey of land. However, the existing survey and settlement organisations have not completed their job of periodic resurveys for updation of land records. Records are outdated or not in good shape in most states. In some northeastern states, even the original survey has not taken place in many districts. A similar situation prevails in some UTs and also in some parts of other states. The earlier technology of tape and chains for survey is cumbersome, painfully time-taking and costly.

Under CLR good progress has been made, but not consistently across the country. Many states have digitised basic land records data and have started the process of effecting mutations and distribution of RoRs through computers. A number of states have stopped manual distribution of RoRs by totally relying on computerised systems for more than a year now. Many other states are making good progress in shifting to the computerised system. Some states have also placed land records' data on the Internet.

However, the emphasis of CLR so far had been more on computerisation and digitisation of records, and less on having a system that maintains accurate and up-to-date RoRs and securely generates such records on demand. Also lacking were the integration of textual and spatial data on RoRs, linkage of registration with mutation and updating of RoRs, backend reconciliation of village records and a comprehensive and standard database of land records across the country that is necessary for understanding land and immovable property markets and for efficient administration and policy-making in a modern economy.

Computerisation of registration is another area where some progress has been made in a number of states, although this component was not covered by CLR or SRA&ULR. The main focus of these initiatives had been on automation of the deed registration procedures, and there was hardly any linkage with the land records' management system.

Moreover, the systems for computerisation of land records, digitisation of maps, updation of land records and computerisation of registration had been functioning in a stand-alone manner. They had been without a comprehensive framework to collate and integrate the data into a seamless system of land information management, which could run on a GIS platform and provide land data, other land records-based information as well as any location-specific information for decision support to various stakeholders in the public and private sectors.

The probable reasons for such sporadic, intermittent and uneven progress include the absence of a national framework for comprehensive land information management, limitations of the available technology, limited technical knowledge base, inadequate training and capacity building of human resources deployment and the lack of local language interface for IT applications. Also, until the late 1990s, due to non-availability of network connectivity, it was difficult to achieve the necessary degree of data exchange and information collaboration amongst the key players. The e-governance structure was in its initial stages, and there had been much prevarication and indecision in respect of digitisation of land data and records. The situation has changed now. Today, there is a vast difference in the scenario vis-à-vis the challenge. Significantly superior technology is available and willingness of the key players for technology adoption has greatly improved. The national e-governance initiative is taking shape, and digital connectivity across the country is being established through extensive wide area networks. Finally, the decision makers are receptive to putting in place the necessary institutional and legal framework, in the absence of which merely technological interventions could not give the desired results.

With this backdrop, the scheme of Comprehensive Modernization of Land Records (CMLR) was conceptualised as a major e-governance and system reforms' initiative that could be concerned not merely with the computerisation, updation and maintenance of land records or the validation of titles, but as a programme that would add value and provide a comprehensive database for planning and decision-making for development planning as well as regulatory activities where there is need for location-specific information. The disconnects and redundancies in the system would be reduced and a better reform model would be re-engineered, so that the spatial and non-spatial land-related data for the entire country could be available as a national enterprise knowledge base for both public and private stakeholders. The proposed CMLR scheme was later renamed as the National Land Records Modernization Programme (NLRMP).

The National Land Records Modernisation Programme (NLRMP)

In August 2008, the Union Cabinet approved merger of the two schemes of CLR and SRA&ULR and their replacement with a centrally sponsored scheme in the shape of the NLRMP with the long-term goal of bringing in the system of conclusive titles with title guarantee in India. The following is an outline of the components and activities of this programme:

1. Computerisation of land records
   i. Data entry/re-entry/data conversion of all textual records including mutation records and other land attributes data
   ii. Digitisation of cadastral maps
   iii. Integration of textual and spatial data
   iv. *Tehsil*, sub-division/district data centres
   v. State-level data centres
   vi. Interconnectivity among revenue offices

2. Survey/resurvey and updating of the survey and settlement records (including ground control network and

ground truthing) using the following modern technology options:

i. Pure ground method using electronic total station (ETS) and global positioning system (GPS)
ii. Hybrid methodology using aerial photography and ground truthing by ETS and GPS
iii. High-Resolution Satellite Imagery (HRSI) and ground truthing by ETS and GPS

3. Computerisation of registration

   i.   Computerisation of the sub-registrar's offices (SROs)
   ii. Data entry of valuation details
   iii. Data entry of legacy encumbrance data
   iv. Scanning and preservation of old documents
   v.   Connectivity to SROs with revenue offices

4. Modern record rooms/land records management centres at *tehsil* (or taluk, circle or block) level
5. Training and capacity building

   i. Training, workshops, etc.
   ii. Strengthening of the survey and revenue training institutes

6. Core GIS

   i. Village index base maps from satellite imagery, for creating the core GIS
   ii. Integration of the three layers of data:
       (a) spatial data from aerial photograph or high-resolution satellite imagery;
       (b) Survey of India and Forest Survey of India maps; and
       (c) cadastral maps from revenue records

7. Legal changes

   i.   Amendments to the Registration Act, 1908
   ii. Amendments to the State Stamp Acts
   iii. Other legal changes
   iv. Model law for conclusive titling

8. Programme management

   i. Programme Sanctioning & Monitoring Committee in the GoI

  ii. Core Technical Advisory Group in the centre and the states/UTs

 iii. Programme Management Unit (PMU) in the centre and the states/UTs

 iv. Information, education and communication (IEC) activities

  v. Evaluation

NLRMP Implementation Strategy

The strategy is to proceed with all the activities in a systematic, ladder-like manner with a primary ladder for reaching the conclusive titling stage, and a secondary ladder for archival purposes and strengthening of revenue administration. All primary activities will converge in the district, and the district will be the unit of implementation. Each state/UT was supposed to take up at least one or two district(s) in the first year (2008–2009), while those willing to take up more districts can do so, and could go for PPP models in non-sensitive areas. The plan is to cover all the districts in the country by the end of the Twelfth Five Year Plan period.

The states/UTs shall have to carry out the process re-engineering involved, which will be a condition of the memorandum of understanding (MoU) to be entered into with them.

Key Deliverables of NLRMP

The deliverables of NLRMP fall under three domains: 'government-to-citizen', or G2C domain; 'government-to-government', or G2G domain; and 'government-to-business', or G2B domain.

Citizen Services (G2C Domain)

Citizen services (mediated through technology) would be the primary deliverables of the programme. Such 'government-to-citizen' (G2C) services would bring, *inter alia*, the following benefits:

1. Real-time records of land titles with maps to scale will be available to the citizen.
2. Since the records will be placed on the websites with proper security IDs, property owners will have free access to their records while maintaining confidentiality.
3. Free accessibility to the records will reduce interface between the citizen and the government functionaries, thereby reducing scope of rent-seeking and harassment.
4. PPP mode of service delivery will further reduce citizen interface with the government machinery, while adding to the convenience.
5. Abolition of stamp papers and payment of stamp duty and registration fees through banks, etc., will also reduce interface with the registration machinery.
6. With the use of IT inter-linkages, the time for obtaining RoRs, etc., will be drastically reduced.
7. The single-window service will save the citizen time and effort in obtaining RoRs, etc.
8. Automatic and automated mutations will significantly reduce the scope of fraudulent property deals.
9. Conclusive titling will also significantly reduce litigation.
10. These records will be tamper proof.
11. This method will permit e-linkages to credit facilities.
12. Market value information will be available to the citizen.
13. Certificates based on land data (e.g., domicile, caste, income, etc.) will be available to the citizen through computers.
14. Information on eligibility for government programmes will be available, based on the data.
15. Issuance of land passbooks with relevant information will be facilitated.

Government-to-Government (G2G)

The ultimate goal is to link the conclusive titles to the development process, such as credit institutions, disaster management, land acquisition and R&R, land-use planning, agricultural census, irrigation census, cropping pattern, food security, civic amenities planning, wasteland management and other secondary data such as issue of various certificates, etc.

Moreover, the system will make available layers of GIS data such as: cadastral maps with plot numbers and unique ID for each land parcel; forest, water bodies and other physical attributes of land; land-use details; administrative unit boundaries from village level upwards including panchayat, block, *tehsil*, circle, sub-division, district, division, state and national boundaries, etc., for any purpose where location-specific information is required.

Government-to-Business (G2B)

The knowledge base created through the programme will be available to private enterprises for various location-specific purposes, e.g., determining location of new projects, planning and managing transport and tourism circuits, laying pipelines, fibre-optic channels, mobile phone towers, etc.; construction industry including housing, roads, bridges, etc.; marketing; banking and credit institutions (e.g., location of branches, field offices), etc.

Once the stage of conclusive titling is reached and the necessary legal changes are in place, title indemnity funds and title guarantee arrangements shall have to be put in place, for which several alternatives are possible, in various combinations of public and private delivery mechanisms. Title assurance funds could be created by charging a small levy, ad valorem or per transaction, on property registrations, or the governments could provide budgetary support, maybe at least initially. The experiences of Australia, the United Kingdom, etc., indicate that these funds do not run into solvency problems, because efficient administration of the land records maintenance and titling system helps avoid too many cases of indemnification.

Title assurance or guarantee corporations could be created statutorily, or the private sector could be allowed to establish and operate such entities under statutory regulation, or both sectors could exist, in partnership models or independently, expanding the options for the public. Business success of the American title insurance companies could be taken as a learning model here.

Strata title system could be adopted for apartment ownership or other multi-unit properties, where the individual lot is recorded against the title holder along with his/her interest in the common property such as the driveways, stairwells and gardens. The legislations and administrative mechanisms applied in other countries, e.g., Australia, Singapore, South Africa, Canada, etc., could be studied in this regard.

With the implementation of the initiatives along the lines described earlier, it is hoped that the maintenance of error-free RoRs in real property and conclusive titling will be possible, a major cause of market failure in this area shall be mitigated and a new era will dawn in land sector governance in all the states in the country including UP.

Progress Made by the State of UP under the NLRMP Scheme of GoI

UP has been participating in the NLRMP, as it had been under the predecessor schemes of SRA&ULR and CLR, albeit not very enthusiastically. The RoR data have been computerised and placed on the website. The state government has stopped the manual issue of RoRs and has accorded legal sanctity to the computerised copies of the RoRs. However, the state has yet to start effecting mutations using computers. Also, it is not confirmed as to whether the RoR data are updated in real time and whether the digitisation of cadastral maps has been completed.

Since 2008–2009, the state has received ₹18.52 crore of the NLRMP funds, of which only ₹0.26 crore has been reportedly utilised (as of May 2012); moreover, the state had unspent balances of ₹19.70 crore under SRA&ULR and ₹14.23 crore under CLR.

NLRMP is being implemented only in a few, out of the 75, districts in UP (Allahabad, Ghaziabad, Mathura, Barabanki, Jaunpur and Khiri). The *khasra* records are being computerised in these districts.

The digitisation of spatial records has been accomplished in Ghaziabad and Mathura districts, and the work is going on in Barabanki and Jaunpur districts.

For the capacity building of the revenue staff, NLRMP cells are being established at the Survey Training Institute at Hardoi and the Lekhpal Training School at Allahabad.

The survey/resurvey works using modern technology are being taken up in Allahabad, Ghaziabad, Mathura, Barabanki and Jaunpur districts.

Modern record rooms are going to be established in the *tehsils* of Ghaziabad, Mathura, Barabanki and Jaunpur during the year 2012–2013 under NLRMP. Funds have also reportedly been made available for establishing interconnectivity and for data entry/re-entry of *khasra* records for the *tehsils* under Allahabad, Ghaziabad, Mathura, Barabanki and Jaunpur districts.

The state-level data centre under NLRMP is being set up at the Revenue Board headquarter, which will have data from all the districts in UP. However, the state's NLRMP programme management unit (PMU) was not yet operational (as of May 2012).

The Way Forward: Some Thoughts

The importance of putting in place a comprehensive land records management system based on modern technology and backed up by the necessary process reengineering and statutory changes can be hardly emphasised, considering the importance of land in the economic development of a state like UP. At the same time, given the vast size of the state and its local land-holding pattern, which involves a large number of small plot holders, at least some of who may not have clear land titles, or at times there are many claimants for the same plots, claiming a plethora of land rights, which are not always well defined, the task of modernisation of land records management system is a significant challenge. This gets compounded by the fact that the extant real property laws allow for only presumptive titling and not conclusive and guaranteed titles. Since a modern land records system is yet to be firmly in place, the RoRs and maps of the plots are frequently out-of-date and may not be easily accessible, leading to wastage of time and resources, exposure to rent seeking and increase in transaction costs. Lack of a comprehensive GIS with cadastral details precludes optimal planning and options assessment of potentially alternative sites for locating the projects and making market-based purchase decisions.

Given their inherent limitations, highly efficient land markets don't always prevail. The factors mentioned earlier contribute to significant information asymmetry and market failure in land, particularly for private enterprises.

Hopefully, the state government will accelerate its efforts in modernisation of the land records management system and rapidly cover all the districts in the state as per a well-defined timeline and work plan, and again show the way to others, as Raja Todarmal's work had accomplished in the same area during the reign of Akbar the Great.

16

Land Management: Land Acquisition and Rehabilitation and Resettlement*

Ajay Kumar Singh

Introduction

Uttar Pradesh is among the largest of the 35 states and union territories of India, with an area of 294,411 sq. km, or 8.9 per cent of the total area of the country, which makes it almost half the size of France, thrice that of Portugal and four times of Ireland in terms of land area. The challenge of land management is accentuated by the fact that, being the most populous state in the country, UP supports almost 17 per cent of the population of India, and is beset with a large number of small landholdings: over 75 per cent of the holdings are less than 1 ha. in size, the average size of 90 per cent of small and marginal farmers' holdings being only 0.55 ha. In terms of livelihoods, dependence on land is still paramount, as two-third of the working population of UP is in the primary sector (as opposed to 53 per cent in India), and about 77 per cent of the rural households (spread over more than 97,000 villages in 75 districts) are in farming. Despite covering only 8.9 per cent of the country's land area, the state's land under agriculture and allied activities produces 19 per cent of the food grains, 22 per cent of vegetables and 38 per cent of potatoes, as well as the highest quantities of milk, sugarcane and sugar in the country, and it is reported that two or more crops are grown even on ceiling-surplus lands distributed to the beneficiaries, in most cases, with the help of private irrigation facilities (despite the possibility that such lands could be of somewhat inferior quality and subject to

---

*Disclaimer: The views expressed are that of the author only and do not reflect the stand of the government on the subject.

sub-optimal utilisation for various reasons). This little snapshot of the land economy of UP should form the necessary backdrop for understanding the complexities of land acquisition (LA) and the rehabilitation and resettlement (R&R) of the involuntarily displaced in the state. The discussion proceeds in the following manner: an outline of the legal framework for land management and problems inherent therein (section titled 'Legal Framework for Land Management and Problems Therein'); structural issues in land markets contributing to market failure (section titled 'Structural Aspects of Land Markets and Market Failure'); public policy responses to the challenges in LA and R&R (section titled 'Some Important Land Management Policy Responses'); and some observations on the way forward (section 'New R&R Policy and Associated Legislative Measures of GoI').

Legal Framework for Land Management and Problems Therein

As per the scheme of the Indian Constitution, 'land' is a state subject, included in the State List, which brings matters related to land management under the exclusive jurisdiction of the states, and the centre has only an advisory and coordinating role in such matters. However, 'land acquisition' has been placed in the Concurrent List, thereby giving both the centre and the states the powers to make laws on the subject. Therefore, LA takes place under a number of central and state acts. The Land Acquisition Act, 1894 (LA Act), is the main act governing LA in the country, to which the states (including UP) have made amendments to suit their needs and circumstances. The National Highways Act, the Railways Act, the Ancient Monuments Act, the Requisitioning & Acquisition of Immovable Properties Act, etc., are examples of other central acts under which acquisition of real property takes place.

The LA Act has been in force since 1 March 1894. It provides for the procedure for compulsory acquisition of land, determination of the compensation (including the market value, an additional amount as solatium in consideration of the involuntary nature of the acquisition and interest on delayed payments) and apportionment of the amount among the persons interested. It also provides for acquisition of land by the state for private companies and the Land Acquisition (Companies) Rules, 1963, framed under the principal Act apply to such acquisitions. The act has been amended several times, e.g., in 1914, 1919, 1921, 1923, 1933, 1937, 1948, 1950, 1962, 1967 and 1984, and is proposed to be replaced with a new act to provide for land acquisition and rehabilitation and resettlement (LA&RR) comprehensively, because the LA Act has come under severe criticism on many counts.

A major criticism of the LA Act is that it does not fare well on the equity front (high on efficiency, low on equity), which goes against the grain of the welfare state concept and the widely accepted doctrine that the exercise of the *eminent domain* powers by the state should be subject to careful consideration of (1) public purpose, (2) just compensation and (3) due process of law. The LA Act has been found lacking in all these aspects.

'Public purpose' has been defined liberally, giving extensive scope for the exercise of *eminent domain* powers. Use of state power to help private interests, at times even where market mechanisms could work and probably could do a better job, has come under extensive popular criticism. There is no provision for options' assessment in terms of site and/or technology so as to go for acquisition of an optimum area of land and its full utilisation, avoiding unnecessary acquisition of land and large areas of the acquired land remaining unutilised, at times for several years.

Except for some provisions under the LA rules for acquisition for companies, the law has no reference to the land-use policies of the state, nor places any restriction on acquisition of farmland, particularly irrigated and/or multi-cropped land, giving rise to implications for food security, and more importantly, the adverse impact on the livelihoods of those dependent on such land.

The LA Act (1894 or its amendments since) makes no reference to the social and environmental impact assessments of the project, nor does it create any legal obligation on the requiring body for mitigating any adverse impact of the acquisition, thus allowing scope for negative externalities without imposing costs on the creators of such externalities. In the absence of any legally guaranteed rights for rehabilitation and resettlement (R&R), those adversely affected by the acquisition, whose lives and livelihoods may be disrupted, often permanently, are left to fend for themselves or to appeal to the discretion of the requiring bodies.

On fairness aspect of the transaction, the landowners are often forced to subsidise the acquirers, as the price discovery device built into the law (the market value-determination mechanism) is seriously flawed, leading to under-valuation of the property being acquired, at times significantly, and the recourse left is to approach the courts and wait. Even then, an equitable resolution may be elusive. In fact, some of the longest running court cases in the country relate to land matters (including the LA Act, 1894).

There is no mechanism built into the law to capture (for the landowner) the increase in the market value of the property in the wake of coming of the project for which land is acquired, while (with few exceptions) there is manifold increase in the property values in such cases, often immediately, and also over time.

Once a piece of land is notified for intent of acquisition, its safety net and asset value for the owner are blocked immediately by law, but completing the transaction may get delayed, at times inordinately. Timeline beyond the stage of collector's award is not well defined in the current law, allowing the acquisition pro-ceedings to drag on. There is no linkage between the government taking over the possession of the acquired land and the payment of the compensation amount to the landowner. Nor is there any mechanism for fast-track adjudication of the disputes arising out of the action under the Act.

Practically unfettered powers for the exercise of the urgency clause for land acquisition, which are used quite commonly under the current law, even for circumstances that could not probably be categorised as true public emergencies, often lead to heartburn among those adversely affected.

These are the major challenges built into the structure of the legal framework for land acquisition, and apply to the country in general, but get highlighted in the context of states like UP, for the very reasons mentioned in the beginning of this discussion.

Beyond these, there are structural aspects of the local land markets that contribute significantly to market failure and efficient operation of the market mechanism for obtaining land for projects requiring significant land areas, thereby forcing taking recourse to statutory land acquisition.

Structural Aspects of Land Markets and Market Failure

Despite serious flaws, the attractiveness of the LA Act lies in its ability to overcome the structural issues in land markets and to mitigate the market failure in land. The LA Act has stood the test of time and proved effective in affecting compulsory acquisitions of private lands, vesting them absolutely in the government free of all encumbrances, which are then transferred to the new owners clear of any infirmity in the title. This facet is particularly desirable when a rather big area of land is required, which, given the local landholding pattern, involves a large number of small plot holders, at least some of whom do not have clear land titles, since the real property laws allow for only presumptive titling and not conclusive and guaranteed titles. Also, at times there are many claimants for the same plots, claiming a plethora of land rights, which are not always well defined.

Since a modern land records' system is yet to be firm in place, the records of rights (RoRs) and maps of the plots are frequently out-of-date and may not be easily accessible, leading to wastage of time and resources, exposure to rent seeking and increase in transaction costs. Lack of a comprehensive geographic information system (GIS) with cadastral details precludes optimal planning and options' assessment of potentially alternative sites for locating the projects and making market-based purchase decisions.

Moreover, statutory acquisition by the exercise of the *eminent domain* powers helps taking care of the hold-out issues (another important source of market failure in land) and facilitates 'specific land-taking' to ensure continuity, contiguity and connectivity issues (which the requiring bodies often face in arranging land through private efforts through open market). In such situations, statutory acquisitions may actually turn out to be efficient (lower transaction costs) and effective (goal attainment/public interest).

Given its inherent limitations, highly efficient land markets don't always prevail in practice. The factors mentioned here contribute to significant information asymmetry and market failure in land, adding to the appeal of the LA Act, particularly for private enterprises, because under the current law, the states can exercise their eminent domain powers and come to the aid of such projects as long as they do bring some public benefit.

Although these are some of the 'generic' aspects of land markets in India, the story in UP is not any different with respect to land markets.

Some Important Land Management Policy Responses

From the foregoing discussion, it is obvious that the public policy responses need to focus both on fixing the problems in the legal and regulatory framework for LA and R&R and on ushering in a modern land records management system with conclusive property titling so as to minimise the market failure in land. The following discussion covers such responses made so far with respect to LA and R&R, outlining some crucial interventions of the Central Government (to the extent they form the general backdrop for local action by the states) and some major initiatives of the state government of UP. Chapter 15 covers the policy responses related to land records management, property titling and minimising the market failure in land.

Major initiatives of the Government of India (GoI) in response to the above-mentioned challenges in LA and R&R include the proposed amendments to the Land Acquisition Act, 1894, and its replacement with a comprehensive LARR Act covering the legislative proposals for the R&R of the affected families as well; and the notification of the National Rehabilitation and Resettlement Policy, 2007 (NRRP-2007), to replace the NPRR-2003.

The state government of UP also has taken a number of initiatives to meet the challenges in land management referred to earlier, and these include: the UP state amendments to the LA Act, 1894; the UP state policies on LA and R&R of the affected families; and the UP government's initiatives on consolidation of landholdings, agrarian reforms to favour the traditionally disadvantaged sections of the rural society, progress made in computerisation of land records and property registration and joining hands with the union government on implementation of the National Land Records Modernization Programme. Major policy initiatives in LA and R&R (of GoI and

UP) are discussedin the next section, while the other initiatives are covered in Chapter 15.

New R&R Policy and Associated Legislative Measures of GoI

On 31 October 2007, GoI notified the National Rehabilitation and Resettlement Policy, 2007 (NRRP-2007), formulated by the Department of Land Resources in the Ministry of Rural Development, to replace the earlier National Policy on Resettlement and Rehabilitation for Project Affected Families, 2003. Shortly after that, on 6 December 2007, the Union Government had introduced two Bills in the *Lok Sabha*: (1) the Rehabilitation and Resettlement Bill, 2007, formulated on the lines of NRRP-2007 for giving a statutory basis to the policy, and (2) the Land Acquisition (Amendment) Bill, 2007, formulated to amend the Land Acquisition Act, 1894, so as to align the provisions of the principal Act with the goals and objectives of NRRP-2007.

The Parliamentary Standing Committee on Rural Development had examined both the Bills, held hearings on them with a wide range of stakeholders including the concerned government departments, states and union territories (UTs), eminent academics, experts, activists, etc., and presented their reports to *Lok Sabha* and laid them in *Rajya Sabha* (i.e., both houses of the Parliament) on 21 October 2008. They have placed on record their appreciation for these legislative efforts, describing them as historic, path-breaking and landmarks in this field. However, with the dissolution of *Lok Sabha* in 2009, these two bills lapsed. A new Land Acquisition and Rehabilitation and Resettlement (LARR) Bill to replace the Land Acquisition Act, 1894, and to provide for R&R alongside the LA provisions had been introduced in *Lok Sabha* in 2011, on which the Parliamentary Standing Committee on Rural Development gave its report in May 2012 for further consideration of the union government. After incorporating the official responses, it is now proposed to bring in the Right to Fair Compensation, Resettlement, Rehabilitation and Transparency in Land Acquisition Bill, 2012, before *Lok Sabha* during the Monsoon Session of 2012.

Salient Features of the National Rehabilitation and Resettlement Policy, 2007

Objectives: The objectives of the policy have been expanded to: (a) promote, as far as possible, non-displacing or least-displacing alternatives; (b) ensure adequate rehabilitation package and expeditious implementation of the rehabilitation process with active participation of affected persons; (c) ensure that special care is taken for protecting the rights of, and ensuring affirmative state action for the weaker segments of the society, especially members of SCs and STs and to create obligations on the state for their treatment with concern and sensitivity; (d) provide a better standard of living than before and a sustainable income above the poverty line to affected families; and (e)integrate rehabilitation concerns into the development planning and implementation process.

Applicability: NPRR-2003 was applicable only to the projects displacing 500 or more families *en masse* in plain areas or 250 or more families *en masse* in tribal or hilly areas, Desert Development Programme (DDP) blocks or areas mentioned in Schedule V or Schedule VI to the Constitution. The NRRP-2007 applies to all cases of involuntary displacement irrespective of the cause and the number of persons affected, although certain provisions of the policy, such as social impact assessment (SIA), tribal development plan, provision of comprehensive infrastructural facilities and amenities in the resettlement zone, and procedural requirements like appointment of the administrator for R&R (of the rank not below collector) and notification of the affected zone, are mandatory to cases involving displacement beyond defined thresholds.

Coverage has also been extended to not only those whose land is acquired, but also to others who are adversely affected, including the tenants and lessees who are involuntarily displaced, agricultural or non-agricultural labourers who have been residing in the affected area for a defined length of time immediately preceding the acquisition. Illegal encroachers *per se* have not been recognised as such, and the only occupiers who have been covered are the STs in possession of forestlands prior to 13 December 2005, which is in line with the recently enacted Forest Rights Act.

Social impact assessment of projects: A new chapter on Social Impact Assessment (SIA) has been introduced in NRRP 2003 for options assessment purposes for projects involving physical displacement of 400 or more families *en masse* in plain areas, or 200 or more families *en masse* in tribal or hilly areas, Desert Development Programme (DDP) blocks or areas mentioned in Schedule V or Schedule VI to the Constitution. The SIA report will be prepared considering various alternatives, and using agencies accredited for the purpose. Where both SIA and environmental impact assessment (EIA) are required, both SIA and EIA will be carried out simultaneously. Public hearings in the affected area will be mandatory. The report will be examined by experts including social science and rehabilitation experts. SIA clearance from the designated governmental authorities and following the conditions of the clearance by all concerned will be mandatory.

The only exemption from the SIA has been allowed in cases of emergency acquisitions for defence or national security purposes, that too, only for the minimum area to be acquired, and subject to such institutional safeguards as may be prescribed for protecting the interests of the affected families.

Concern for the vulnerable population: Special concern for the vulnerable population has been reflected across the policy.

The R&R benefits have been extended to the eligible landless families, and housing entitlement offered to those without homestead land.

Annuity policies for lifetime monthly pension for the affected persons above 50 years of age, disabled, orphans, unmarried girls, abandoned women, widows and destitute (who are not provided or cannot immediately be provided with alternative livelihood and are not otherwise covered as part of a family) have been introduced.

Special provisions for the STs include a tribal development plan for projects displacing 200 or more families, preference in allotment of land-for-land, restoration of rights in alienated lands, financial assistance for loss of usage of forest produce or customary rights, consultation with tribes advisory councils and mandatory consultation with the *Gram Sabhas* as per the PESA Act in Schedule V areas and as per the relevant laws in Schedule VI areas, resettlement preferably in the same schedule area and in a compact block, 25 per cent extra monetary R&R benefits if resettled outside the district. Also, it is provided that one-third of the compensation amount for land for the tribal affected families will be paid at the outset.

Special provisions for the SCs are new features of the policy, which include preference in allotment of land-for-land (after STs) and fishing rights.

Continuation of the reservation benefits at resettlement sites has been provided for both SCs and STs.

People's participation: Scope for extensive public participation has been built into the policy at all stages of the R&R process, right from mandatory public hearings at the SIA stage to wide publicity for the survey results and R&R plan, consultation with *Gram Sabhas* and public hearings on draft R&R plan in urban and rural areas not having *Gram Sabhas*, representation of the affected persons including women, SCs, STs, NGOs, *panchayats*, MPs, MLAs, etc., on the R&R committees and accessibility for all to the grievance redressal mechanism — all designed to provide a voice to the people and to enhance transparency in the entire process.

Rehabilitation package: The rehabilitation package applies to assistance to be provided over and above the monetary compensation awarded under the Land Acquisition Act. The main elements can be broadly outlined as under:

Land-for-land: This benefit is subject to availability of government land in the resettlement area. While allotting land-for-land, preference will be given to scheduled tribes, followed by scheduled castes. In land development projects, in lieu of land-for-land or employment, affected families would be given a site or apartment within the project.

House sites: In addition to those losing houses, the housing benefits will also be available to the below poverty line (BPL) affected families without homestead land, as per the scales defined. This benefit is to be provided free of cost to the affected families.

Employment: A new feature in NRRP-2007 is to ensure at least one job for each affected family, subject to availability of vacancies and suitability of the affected persons for the employment; job training, scholarships and other skill development opportunities where required; preference to groups and cooperatives of affected persons in outsourced contracts and other economic opportunities; and preference to willing landless labourers and unemployed affected persons in wage employment. This is an important intervention for the sake of livelihood security of the affected families.

Fishing rights: Fishing rights enjoyed by the affected families have been protected in irrigation or hydel projects. In other cases also, unless there are special reasons, fishing rights will be given to the displaced families preferentially.

Rehabilitation grant: One-time rehabilitation grant equivalent to 750 days minimum agricultural wages has been offered to the affected families who do not receive land-for-land or employment.

Shares in companies: The eligible affected families have been given the option to take a part of their rehabilitation grant amount in the form of shares or debentures of the requiring body, if the requiring body is a company authorised to issue shares and debentures, as per the guidelines to be prescribed by the central government.

Moreover, the affected families entitled to get compensation for the land or other property acquired have been given the option of taking a part of the compensation amount due in the form of shares or debentures, if the requiring body is a company authorised to issue shares and debentures.

Shifting and transit assistance: Transit and temporary accommodation shall be provided to the displaced families. They will also get one-time financial assistance for shifting to the resettlement areas.

Subsistence allowance: This will be paid to the affected families for 1 year from the date of displacement.

Other financial assistance: One-time financial assistance shall also be provided to the eligible affected families for agricultural production, development of allotted culturable wasteland or degraded land, cattle shed, working shed or shop.

Infrastructural facilities: In projects displacing 400 families or more *en masse* in plain areas, or 200 families or more *en masse* in tribal or hilly areas, DDP blocks or areas mentioned in Schedule V or Schedule VI to the Constitution, comprehensive infrastructural facilities and amenities shall be provided. Basic infrastructural facilities and amenities such as health, education, drinking water, power, roads, etc., will be provided in other projects also.

Periphery development: The appropriate government may require the respective bodies to undertake developmental activities in a defined geographical area along the periphery of the project sites.

Indexation of monetary benefits: The rehabilitation grant and other monetary R&R benefits offered under the policy have been linked to the Consumer Price Index, and will also be revised appropriately at suitable intervals.

Linear projects: The ex-gratia grant to be paid to the affected persons will be in addition to the compensation/benefits due for loss of land, house or other property. Those becoming reduced to the status of a small or marginal farmer due to such LA shall be eligible for all R&R benefits under the policy.

Institutional mechanism for monitoring and grievance redressal: A multi-level monitoring and grievance redressal institutional set-up has been provided. This includes R&R committees at the project level and standing R&R committees at district level. Provision has been made for appointment of ombudsman by the appropriate government for time-bound disposal of grievances. A national monitoring committee has been provided for monitoring the imple-mentation, and it has been made mandatory for the states and UTs to share relevant information with this committee. The National Monitoring Committee is to be serviced by a national monitor-ing cell in the Department of Land Resources, GoI. Also, internal oversight committees are to be set up in the concerned ministries/departments of the appropriate government.

Further, a provision has been made for setting up of a national rehabilitation commission for the purpose of exercising external oversight over the R&R of the affected persons covered by this policy.

The NRRP-2007 provides for the minimum requirements, and the requiring bodies in the union government's various depart-ments and PSUs are free to offer better R&R packages, and the state governments are supposed to adopt or improve upon the basic framework for the R&R of the involuntarily displaced provided for in the national policy.

Policy Responses of the State Government of UP on LA and R&R

As the subject of 'land acquisition' falls under the Concurrent List in the Constitution, enabling the states and their legislatures to have an important say in the matters connected with LA and consequential involuntary displacement necessitating R&R of the affected families, UP has made a number of state-specific amend-ments to the central law, as well as taken important policy steps aimed at striking a balance between the imperatives of meeting the requirement of land for various public purposes and for development on the one hand, and protecting the interests of the landowners and others connected with the land involved in acquisition, on the other.

UP State Amendments to the LA Act, 1894

Taking into consideration the amendments to the LA Act made since Independence, it is seen that way back in 1954, UP had found a role for the Act in effecting redistributive land reforms by acquiring land for settlement for agriculture with the weaker sections and had amended the Act accordingly. At the same time, UP had recognised the value of the LA Act in arranging land for planned area development and townships, and had made the necessary amendments. In 1959, UP had amended the LA Act to cover the improvement schemes under the *UP Nagar Mahapalika Adhiniyam,* 1959, and in 1974, to cover the planned development of lands in regulated areas under the UP (Regulation of Building Operations) Act, 1958. Some more state amendments had been made.

Surprising as it may seem, the fact remains that these provisions do not effectively address the issues behind popular protests against LA and involuntary displacement in the state. It is also generally true that the state amendments to the LA Act, 1894, have largely remained procedural in nature, and have not attempted to substantively address the issues raised commonly against statutory acquisition. However, instead of taking the legislative route, a number of states, UP included, have come up with policies designed to address such issues.

UP Government Adopted NPRR-2003

Prior to coming up with the UP Policy of 2011 on land acquisition, the state government had adopted the National Policy on Resettlement and Rehabilitation for Project Affected Families, 2003 (NPRR-2003) of GoI. This policy (which had been approved by the central government on 15 January 2004, and had come into force on 17 February 2004) was the precursor to NPRR-2007 discussed earlier. NPRR-2003 had laid down minimum provisions for resettlement and rehabilitation of the project's affected families, while the states, public sector undertakings or other requiring bodies were free to offer better benefit levels.

While NPRR-2003 had addressed many problems of development-induced displacement, several issues were still thought to be inadequately addressed. Mainly, these related to having a holistic approach to the entire gamut of issues, appraising the desirability and justifiability of projects, minimising displacement and options assessment for non-displacing or least-displacing alternatives, avoiding the use of agricultural land for non-agricultural purposes, assessing the social, economic, cultural and demographic impacts of projects, ensuring a better standard of living for the affected families, having sensitivity to the concerns of the vulnerable sections such as the SCs, STs, women, destitute, etc., and putting into place a more participatory and transparent process for the entire R&R exercise.

That policy did not prescribe a complete timeframe for R&R, nor did that lay down a timeframe for utilising acquired lands and disposal of excess land acquired. Also lacking were an external oversight mechanism for independent monitoring, and mechanisms for speedy redressal of grievances and disputes.

Moreover, NPRR-2003 did not have provisions for livelihood security, its applicability was limited to projects displacing families beyond a defined (and rather high) threshold, and cases of involuntary displacement of a permanent nature arising out of causes other than LA were not covered. Most significantly, NPRR-2003 did not have a statutory basis.

As the UP government had adopted NPRR-2003, its R&R regime became subject to these shortcomings, although the state government was always free to offer a better policy package. In view of the issues mentioned above, GoI had decided to formulate the new R&R policy, NRRP-2007, which replaced NPRR-2003. It also decided to give a statutory basis to the new policy and to suitably amend the legal framework for land acquisition, for which the LARR Bills were introduced in *Lok Sabha* between 2007 and 2012. The state government of UP, in the meantime, responded to the challenges emerging in the realm of LA via administrative action and, later, with its LA policy of June 2011.

UP Government's Land Acquisition Policy of June 2011

It is to the credit of the UP Government that large-scale infrastructure development initiatives have been taken up in the state over the years since Independence as well as in the recent years in various sectors, e.g., urban development, integrated townships, industrial and institutional areas, health and educational facilities, power generation, flood protection, canals, roads and expressway projects, etc., where application of the LA Act has played an important role. However, in the past few years, particularly since 2007, there have been significant controversies and incidents of public protest, even violence, in LA for certain expressway and other infrastructure projects in UP.

The Yamuna Expressway case could be taken as a recent example. Important components of the project include the 165-km-long Yamuna Expressway connecting the National Capital Region (Delhi NCR) and Agra, and dedicated land areas for industrial and urban development along the way. The expressway project involves about 1,182 notified villages in Gautam Buddha Nagar, Bulandshahr, Aligarh, Mahamaya Nagar (Hathras), Mathura and Agra districts in UP.

LA for the project was largely completed by July 2010, but in mid-2010, Tappal in Aligarh district (the location of one of the townships proposed under the project) emerged as the epicentre of farmers' agitation over land acquisition. The primary demands of the farmers included compensation at the rates applicable for the New Delhi suburb of Noida (in UP), negotiations between the farmers and the project developers (instead of forced acquisitions from unwilling farmers) and a package of benefits no less than that offered in the neighbouring state of Haryana under the latter's LA policy (which offered a rather generous compensation package, including annuity payments for 33 years with annual hikes, developed plots to the erstwhile landowners, livelihood skill development, social infrastructure in the affected villages for public benefit, etc.).

By the beginning of September 2010, this agitation had forced the state government to offer a number of measures, which included keeping in abeyance any forcible acquisition of land, no construction of townships along the expressway without consent of the farmers, an annuity payment of ₹20,000 per acre of land for 33 years and annual hikes of ₹600 per acre (or a lump-sum payment of ₹2.40 lakh per acre), an additional ₹1.85 lakh (equivalent of 5 years' agricultural wages) to the farmers' families rendered landless by land acquisition, company shares to the extent of 25 per cent of land value in projects of private companies, reserving for housing purpose 7 per cent of the total area acquired and distributing 17.5 per cent of this reserved area among the erstwhile landowners, who were offered a minimum of 120 sq. m of developed land for house construction.

However, in May 2011, violent protests flared up at another location: Bhatta Parsaul village in Bulandshahr district, near Greater Noida in UP. Beginning on 6 May 2011, the violence and related incidents continued until 19 May 2011. The circumstances around the events are shrouded in much controversy and political bickering, but it is believed that farmers' discontent over LA for the expressway project was one source of trigger for them.

On 2 June 2011, the UP government formally announced the new state policy on LA and rehabilitation, the salient features of which include:

1. Payment of a lump-sum amount equivalent to 5 years' daily agricultural wages (₹1.85 lakh at the time), to each family of farmers rendered landless due to the acquisition
2. An annuity payment of ₹20,000 per acre for 33 years in addition to the compensation amount
3. Annual hike of ₹6,00 per acre in the annuity payments, payable every July
4. A lump-sum rehabilitation grant of ₹2,40,000 per acre to the farmers unwilling to opt for the annuity payments
5. Option to take company shares equivalent to 25 per cent of the lump-sum rehabilitation grant, if the acquisition is for a company
6. In acquisitions for the 'Land for Development scheme', 7 per cent of the acquired land to be allotted to the affected farmers for residential purposes, with a minimum plot area of 120 sq. m
7. In acquisitions for the 'Land for Development' projects, employment in the concessionaire company to one member of the family rendered completely landless, consistent with the person's qualifications

8. Provision of 17.5 per cent reservation for the affected families in the allotment of plots on the acquired land for housing schemes
9. LA to be done under the *Karar Niyamavali*, or a mutual agreement process, under the UP LA — Determination of Compensation Rules
10. Recourse to compensation, damages and remedial measures for the farmers whose lands have been fraudulently transacted
11. Developers of private projects to obtain prior consent of 70 per cent of the affected farmers and to give back to them 16 per cent of the developed land

Many of these provisions are similar to the offers made by the UP Government in September 2010 in the wake of the Tappal agitation. In addition, they compare well with the Haryana policy on land acquisition, which had become a reference point for the agitating farmers.

However, whether these policy provisions will actually help the state government in acquiring land for developmental purposes without widespread public resentment will depend upon many more things, e.g., (a) creating a perception among the landowners that they are getting a fair deal and (b) minimising the sense of deprivation and heightened disparity among the erstwhile landowners, post acquisition. These perception issues are really important from the point of view of managing LA for any project, because what the landowners perceive they believe to be the 'reality' and then respond accordingly. In the context of LA by states for private companies, or where the acquired land is handed over to private parties (e.g., PPP projects, etc.), it is well recorded that the landowners believe that the private operators have made 'unimaginable' amounts of profit. Such situations may call for proactive action on the part of the state authorities, not only offering fair and transparent deals (whether through *karar*s or otherwise) but also quelling rumours in time and managing perceptions of the landowners and their opinion-makers.

The aspects mentioned earlier are also borne out of the recent experience of another problematic LA situation in UP, which had flared up in early 2011: the LA cases of Noida Extension, a part of Greater Noida adjoining Noida across the river Hindon. There, the lands acquired earlier had been transferred by the Greater Noida Authority to a number of builders for taking up housing projects, mostly multi-storied apartment complexes. Following protests and litigation by a section of the erstwhile landowners, many of these projects had to be suspended, modified or (a few) even abandoned, causing much resentment and concern among the buyers in these projects (who had flocked to them in droves, attracted by the location and reasonable prices).

In these cases, even the Supreme Court was forced (in July 2011) to raise two issues: (a) adequacy of the compensation offered and (b) development for whom? Looking at the situation from the point of view of the erstwhile landowners, their perception of not getting a fair deal in these LA cases got heightened once the builders began marketing their projects aggressively and the prevailing market prices became widely known. Such situations raise question marks on the adequacy of compensation offered, and bring to focus the inability of the compensation mechanism to capture the rise in market value of the acquired land in the wake of the project. Also, when residential and commercial complexes, malls, multiplexes and other developments start coming up on the acquired lands, but the erstwhile landowners have not been given any stake in the projects, a sense of deprivation and disparity crops up among them, contributing to resentment and protests.

While the policy-makers have to remain sanguine to these aspects, those interested in this field of enquiry need to study the behavioural economics of land acquisition, a field of inquiry where not much empirical and research work has been done.

Changes Proposed in the LA Policy of UP (April 2012)

Although the LA and rehabilitation policy of UP has been in force for only a few months (since June 2011), the state government is reportedly considering revisions to the policy. Although the revised provisions have not been finalised, reports have come out (in April 2012) that the state government has sought input from some major departments involved in land acquisitions in the state for a new policy. Reportedly, two important changes are under consideration:

1. Payment of compensation at rates six times higher than the prevalent circle rates
2. A ban on acquisition of two-cropped land

More details of the revised policy are yet to emerge, yet the proposals mentioned earlier can be examined.

In addition, some other relevant issues may be discussed in the context of revising the State LARR policy.

Fixed-multiples formula for the compensation amount: The working of the provision for payment of compensation at rates six times higher than the prevailing circle rates, if actually made, will depend on the relationship between the circle rate and actual market rate at the given location and time (before and after project announcement).

If the circle rate is much lower than the market rate, or if the circle rate is not adequately revised to capture the rise in market value of the land in the wake of the project, this provision will help the landowner get adequate compensation.

However, if the circle rate is close to the market rate, offering compensation at a high multiple of the circle rate may not only have a bearing on the project cost, but also distort open market transactions in land at the potential project location and open up scope for speculative land deals in anticipation of the statutory acquisition. Excluding the compensations paid through the LA process from the circle rate determination and revision process may not help. The potential sellers may opt out from open market sales in favour of the acquisition, and the speculative buyers may offer high prices to the (willing, or coerced) sellers to make purchases in anticipation of even higher gains when those lands do get acquired.

A somewhat similar formula has been discussed in the context of the LARR Bill pending before the Parliament: compensation at two to four times the market rate (not circle rate) in rural areas (the sliding scale depending on the distance of the project site from the urban area) and twice the market rate in urban areas (including solatium), the market rate figures being based on the past land sale deeds. This provision has come under criticism for (a) the multiples used in the formula not having any scientific basis; and

(b) the market values derived from the sale deeds not being a true reflection of the going market rates.

In this regard, a better policy solution would be to make the circle rates realistic by making the circle rate revision a dynamic process, which takes into account the rise in local market rates of land following the project announcement. Also, to some extent, the future increase in the market value of land could be captured by basing the compensation amounts on the intended category of use of the land being acquired, instead of the land's pre-project category (i.e., based on the rates for the new category — industrial, commercial or housing, etc., rather than the earlier category — agricultural, barren, etc.). Moreover, the reference date could be the date when the collector's award is made, rather than the date of the original notification. In any case, a 'one-size-fits-all' solution may not be universally helpful, and a careful assessment of the situation, state-wide, may probably be in order.

Acquisition of multi-cropped land: Regarding ban on acquisition of two-cropped lands, a blanket ban provision may have its own consequences. From a 'micro' perspective, this may impact certain projects adversely, particularly when the continuity, contiguity or connectivity issues are involved, or there is a 'specific land taking' situation where land at only a certain location is required. From a 'macro' perspective, such a provision may even impact the economic development of the state, by edging industries out and hampering urbanisation, infrastructure creation and such other effects.

The UP policy proposal apart, the LARR Bill under consideration of the Parliament proposes a 5 per cent limit on the acquisition of multi-cropped land in a district, while the Parliamentary Standing Committee has recommended a complete ban on such acquisitions. However, it is emerging that, since land is a state subject under the Constitution, and since different states may have different imperatives on land acquisition, the decisions in this regard may be left with the state governments, who may be in a better position to balance the issues of economic development and agricultural production in their respective jurisdictions. If that actually happens, under the umbrella of the enabling provision of the principal legislation, different states will have different formulations, which may even change with time and situation, depending upon how the legal provisions are constructed in the principal law and the state laws that may come out in due course. This may accentuate the inter-jurisdictional competition for attracting industries, both inter-state and intra-state (i.e., inter-district). A fine balancing act may be required on the part of the public policy-makers, between satisfying popular votes and risking that the industries may vote with their feet.

In this context, the following statistic about the composition of land area in UP is worth keeping in mind:

Geographical area ('000 ha.)	Agricultural land ('000 ha.)	Agricultural land (%)	Forest land ('000 ha.)	Forest land (%)	Agricultural and forest land (%)
24,093	19,179	79.60	1,658	6.9	86.5

This data indicates that after taking into account the agricultural and forestlands in the state, and lands under other uses already or lands not fit for use, very small percentage of the state's land area would be available for acquisition. Of course, not all the agricultural land is double- or multi-cropped, yet, given the fertility pattern of agricultural land in UP, dependence of a high proportion of the state population on agriculture and allied activities, and increasing density of people per unit area of land, such a provision does have its appeal, in terms of food security, as well as in protecting the livelihoods of those dependent on agriculture, which is an important consideration in UP.

'Well-off' vs. 'less well-off' landowners: Restrictions on acquisition of multi-cropped lands may have one more dimension—a social one, since the owners of multi-cropped lands are more likely to be relatively well-off farmers, while those having single-cropped lands are more likely to be less well-off or belonging to the socially disadvantaged groups. Thus, limiting the acquisition of multi-cropped lands may probably direct the acquisition efforts towards single-cropped lands, with likely (although unintended) consequences for the socially vulnerable.

A careful GIS mapping of the state's farmlands (which may be based on the Soil and Land Use Survey of India [SLUSI] data) may be of help in working out the details so that a truly feasible proposal is worked out. One more policy solution is to have a well-defined land-use policy, announced *a priori*, and making all land acquisitions subject to that policy.

Need vs. greed: Not having a policy provision for options' assessment for the land requirements of the project may lead to situations where greed for land on the part of the requiring body may take the upper hand over any rational assessment of the need of land for the project. The options' assessment could be in terms of sites, or technology, or a combination of the relevant factors so as to minimise the requirement of land for the project, and also for finding the least displacing alternative. For example, in quite a few cases of LA for setting up industries, it has been well known that for a plant of similar capacity the organisation had managed with much lesser area than what was sought to be acquired, or a larger area was sought than was required. Making the relevant provisions in the LA policy for options assessment in a transparent and objective manner would go a long way in optimising land requirements for projects.

Current vs. future generations: Land is a finite resource, and excessive acquisition of land for projects of today (than the areas truly required) may create limitations on the availability of land for future projects. For example, in many projects taken up in the past, it is seen that large tracts of land were acquired, and often big areas of land remain unutilised even after several years. In the absence of policy provisions for minimising the areas of land to be acquired and the provisions for resuming the unutilised lands after a certain period, say 5–10 years, future generations may find it difficult to find land for desirable projects. A good LA policy should care about such inter-generational aspects of land acquisition.

Dispossession vs. displacement: LA with least effect on the *abadi* or inhabited areas would also be least likely to cause actual displacement of people and will help avoid the consequences of physical displacement of human settlements (the owners, their families, cattle and other possessions). Although rehabilitation may still be needed for the sake of livelihood security of affected families, need for the resettlement part of the R&R package would probably be reduced if the LA policy solutions are sanguine to these aspects. In this context, one can look at examples of LA cases in Delhi post Independence, where the Delhi Development Authority (DDA) has generally avoided acquiring the *abadi* areas and uprooting of the settled villages (in contrast to the land acquisitions by the British for creating New Delhi, which led to disappearance of entire villages like Malcha and some others). Of course, such a solution may have its own consequences (e.g., creation of over 200 'urban villages' in Delhi — a massive challenge for the civic planners), or solutions like this may not always be feasible, but having such a policy provision may at times help.

Public use vs. public purpose: While much debate has been there on defining and re-defining 'public purpose' in the context of legal framework for land acquisition, the fine distinction between 'public use' and 'public purpose' seems to have received scant attention. A project of public purpose may meet the legal criteria as such, but may not be for something of public use (which entails the twin elements of continued access and continuation of use by the public) or beneficial to the larger public cause. Examples are elite golf courses created on lands acquired for defence department, high-end malls and multiplexes (or other purely commercial projects) created on lands acquired from common people and so on. Although it may not be feasible to restrict LA on such grounds, the credibility of statutory action is much higher in public perception in cases where land is acquired for projects of public use. The state LA policy may be sensitive to such nuances.

Public vs. private projects: The LA Act, 1894, Chapter VII, provides for acquisition of land by the state for private companies. Use of these provisions by the states (including UP) has been quite common, and such use of the eminent domain powers by the states has also been a cause for public outcry against land acquisition. Opinions have been divided on this aspect, with some (including the Parliamentary Standing Committee) calling for no role for government in LA for private projects, while others have sought to allow for the state to come to the aid of the private party if that party has already arranged land to the extent of 70 per cent of the required area (the LAA Bill, 2007), or for public–private partnership (PPP) projects where 80 per cent of the project's affected families (likely to be changed to 80 per cent of the landowners concerned) have consented to part with their lands (the LARR Bill, 2011). While it is true that the entry of state-backed private players does distort the already less-than-efficient land markets, it is also true that some support from the state may be required for the private parties in successfully arranging large areas of land, given the state of land records and land markets in the country (including UP). Although the last word on this aspect can come only from the Parliament, pending such an event, the state policy could probably lay down the parameters for state involvement in private projects (e.g., provision of public goods and services under certain conditions). Doing so would not only give clear signals to the industry, but also help contain public resentment against LA in the state.

Urgency clause – to use or not to use: The use of the urgency clause in the LA Act, 1894, has been so commonplace that it has become more the norm than the exception that it was supposed to be. Many states, UP included, have fallen into this habit and have often been chastised by the courts of law for their undue invoking of the law in this regard. Now, the legal changes under consideration of the Parliament are likely to restrict the use of such provisions to true emergencies. Pending the changes in the law, the state policy could proactively adopt self-imposed limitations along those lines, and reap the benefits of less public resentment and litigation.

R&R benefits in private projects – to impose or not to impose: This has been an area of debate in the wake of proposals contained in the LARR Bill, 2011, which have sought to bring private projects above a certain threshold in terms of the land area involved, under the requirements of the R&R provisions. Those for the idea claim that such a provision helps eliminate the duality between public and private acquisitions of lands for projects with respect to the R&R benefits to the affected families, since those who are affected by statutory acquisitions (for public or private projects) would be entitled to get R&R benefits, but those who part with their lands for private projects through private negotiations would not get any such benefits. Those at the opposite end of the spectrum aver that bringing even private land sale cases under the R&R provisions would not only distort land markets but also amount to undue enrichment of those who have voluntarily accepted the sale prices for their lands, in addition to adding to the project costs. This is a difficult area of public decision making, and the final word will come from the Parliament (and later from the courts of law). However, it is likely that the Parliament may only legislate on the enabling provision in the law and leave the implementation decisions (including the threshold for triggering the provision) to the states. Some forward thinking along these lines on the part of the state policy-makers may probably be considered.

Borrow ideas: Moreover, in revising the state's LA policy, the UP Government could also benefit from many other ideas that have been proposed in this space: in the LARR Bill before Parliament,

is a very concise and well-written story of institutional reform and agricultural growth and change in Vietnam since the 1990s. There are sub-stories of achievements in institutional change, both in land relations and in incentive, support and disincentive systems for the sector, structural change, diversification and globalisation and consequent impacts on the rural and agricultural economies and its regional and distributional aspects. It is largely an uplifting story of high achievements. The authors are careful and there are underlying currents of concerns, of falling profitability, declining sources of growth and nutritional and poverty impacts for some classes of the population and some regions.

The authors state the problems squarely as follows:

> While poor households need loans to meet daily necessities or occasional large expenditures, richer households need bigger, longer-term loans for investment purposes. Bank loans, on the other hand, have usually been short-term and only available to the better off. The government has adjusted credit policy for households several times by, for example, increasing the non-collateral credit limit from 10 million to 30 million VND per household. However, banks are reluctant to take risks and access to formal credit remains limited for many households.

Apparently, globalisation does not help:

> Price volatility, particularly downward pressure on prices and a proliferation of intermediaries in supply and marketing chains have disadvantaged more vulnerable farmers. In addition, an underdeveloped rural infrastructure limits rural inhabitants' access to information about markets and technology, education and health services, putting those in more remote areas at a disadvantage.

The sweet and sour nature of the paradigm of Asian agriculture comes out in the following quote:

> Development of the household economy in agriculture has, therefore, played an extremely important role in Vietnam's emerging market economy, sustaining growth and employment during the crucial transition years. Only in the last five years have we been able to see any significant tendency for agricultural employment to diminish and this has largely been achieved without increasing unemployment in urban areas. While poverty among these farming households has diminished rapidly over the past decade, agriculture

has also fallen behind relative to the urban sector. In 2003, while urban poverty had fallen to a quarter of its 1993 level, rural poverty was still over half its previous level. Among ethnic minority households in remote and mountainous areas, the level of poverty remained at 80 per cent of its 1993 level. The proportion of the country's poor living in rural areas has risen. Renewed efforts to develop the rural economy are therefore important if Vietnam's positive experience to date is to continue.

If this was the story in the fastest growing Asian economy of the period, the marginalisation of small holder agriculture and the plight of landless labour in Asiatic peasant agriculture may be surmised. As the Vietnamese experience suggests, vulnerability is seen more in less-fertile or less-populated areas, the forest, the 'remote and mountainous areas' and the 'ethnic minorities'. The Indian experience is not different. The policy reform mode gets into tough problems in this case.

Forest Rights

Land rights and a market for land transactions, which protects the rights of tenants, are some such tough issues. It is tougher when we get to forest dwellers. *Adivasi* is a translation to the category aboriginal from colonial times. This definition is wrong, because tribe refers to the political organisation of the community while aboriginal means one present from the beginning (origin) or of the sunrise (literal meaning). This genetic sub-text may have some limited validity in the New World but none in our country. Hinduism as a religion of the people was propagated by the saints of India. The poets of the Bhakti movement, the Sufis or the Sikhs were the saints of the people of India who in a big part were Dalits, *adivasis* or the OBCs. Gandhi ji started the Bhil Seva Mandal when the then government hanged a nationalist Bhil leader. The Gandhians in fact called them *ranipaja, vanyajati* or *girijan.*

Forest land has always been an issue to the Indian State from the time of the Mauryas. Recent history begins with the Forest Act of 1864 and the Indian Forest Act of 1927. There is also The Forest Policy of 1952, the Wild Life Protection Act of 1972 and the Forest Conservation Act of 1980. Finally, we have the Scheduled Tribes and Other Traditional Forest Dwellers Recognition of Forest Rights Act of 2006, notified in January 2008. N.C. Saxena has pointed out that the rights of 'other forest dwellers' are inadequately recognised and so 'many claims are being erroneously rejected'. Eleven states are to implement the law. Saxena says that the number of claims processed is very low in Gujarat, Jharkhand and Tamil nadu. The then minister Jairam Ramesh said that the Indian Forests Act of 1927 will be suitably amended and could be introduced in the 'next' session of Parliament, another important reform lying with our sovereign elected masters. He also feels that measures to recognise communal rights need to be taken up urgently.

Recognition of land rights is central to reform in rural India because land can then be collateral for investment. This can be observed in states such as Gujarat, Karnataka and Andhra Pradesh, where progress has been made and this is also very important for forest areas. The fact is that forests are a source of wealth—not just green wealth but GDP. Demand for forest products is rising very fast in India and it is becoming a major importer of forest products. This could be a leading sector with growth rates of around 7 per cent annually. India wisely does not allow trees to be cut but forests produce a lot of wealth apart from wood. We used to call this somewhat contemptuously 'minor forest produce'. We do not have organisations like producer companies or financing mechanisms, including special financial products for forest economies since trees need long-term funding. Today, a forest dweller with rights can grow a tree for 5 years but for the 6th year, funding can be a problem if the dweller runs out of cash, because there is no collateral. Community collateral is also not accepted. The minister is quite right in saying that we cannot go on with a government-owned forest model. In the Bhopal Declaration on community-based organisations, we lamented the bureaucratisation of Joint Forestry Management. The Eleventh Plan accepted this but progress in creating market-savvy institutions is slow.

Apart from producer organisations linked with trading and processing companies and financing mechanisms, the question of trade policy is also never raised. Take a product like vanilla, which did gain acceptance as a profitable crop in the *ghats* a few years ago. Although in great demand, it has been overtaken by synthetics and subsidised imports. There are no standardisation rules or tariff policies in place. This is applicable to a large number of forest products demanded by a fast-growing economy. There is an urgency to all this since in the REDD+ process at Cancun we have agreed to a system in which rewards will be there for improving on deforestation rates as also safeguards for fair treatment to indigenous people (forest dwellers?).

The Institute of Rural Management, Anand (IRMA), which I chaired, has a vested interest in all this. When Rahul Gandhi came to IRMA I asked him what we will do if the young scholars who had worked on PESA were jailed. He said he would go with them. Now Sonia Gandhi has, following Indira Gandhi, asked for the land the Jarawas need to survive in the Andamans to be protected. One of Prime Minister Indira Gandhi's last orders was a study of the Andamans to provide living space to the *adivasis* from the advancing timber-using industries, which I was asked to do. More generally, with policy and institutional support, forests and their dwellers can be the next growth sector.

Working Models for Reversing Trends

Working models with stakeholder groups need much greater attention. Land scarcity is going to be perhaps the single greatest constraint to Indian development. Local bodies are the repositories of what are called common resources. This problem is particularly severe in tribal areas, conventionally a concern of land reform law. Those who work or live off a resource are obviously the first to be affected and need to be consulted. We need to build models of co-operation rather than clash. These are not simple matters and while best practice cases exist, we do not as yet have working systems. The idea that land is not an economic good in the market, which lies behind tenancy legislation, is irrelevant in practice because the greatest change that has taken place in rural India is land, which is also being transferred voluntarily from very small peasants to middle-class peasants.

Our advocacy on land question is that the powers of Land Acquisition Act are gone; with the reestablishment of land rights, the market would take over and if we are clever we would also wrap the *kisan* as a stakeholder in partnerships. Thus, the lone rangers who would not sell at any cost would be isolated and easy to manage. Functioning examples of change are there (Alagh, 2011). The flip side is business as usual, the might of the state and the brutality that runs when contractors run and fund the roost. Farmers should be stakeholders in the change that is India when their land is used for development. But contractors were not too happy at the Sardar Sarovar rehabilitation plan and also the one that C.H. Hanumantha Rao designed for Tehri. I know because I have been there before.

Land Use and Land Acquisition

There are worthies who argue, quoting Ricardo, that the land price has not risen on account of the farmers' own efforts and so they do not have unlimited rights. This is the argument for acquiring *jantri* rates for the land. Of course, the fact that no one ever buys or sells land at *jantri* rates, normally a quarter of the market rates, is another matter, since the rest changes hands without paying stamp duties or other taxes. It is true that land prices are rising on account of economy-level factors. The point is that we are mismanaging soils and water and the demand for food and commodities is rising in a booming economy. If land under crops and cropping intensity does not rise because irrigated area is constant, while agricultural demand goes up by 4–5 per cent annually, you do not have to be David Ricardo to say that land rents and prices will rise. Notice that while the farmer did not exactly earn it, it is not quite his fault either and it is not fair to paint him as the villain of the piece.

When everybody is making money with rising prices with money incomes rising at twice the rate of the supply of goods, there is little logic in denying the farmer his share when he owns and claims it for the first time in history. Instead of making the farmer a sullen outsider, make him a stakeholder. That way he will enhance, and not be a bottleneck to, the change you want. We had argued for producer companies of farmers. Would they get a large chunk of equity. Not so, although a share could be considered instead of cash compensation, for then they would have a direct incentive not to obstruct, but to expedite. However, they could be encouraged to set up businesses around the developments to take place and be trained or financed for that. Also there would be outsourcing of services, which are a substantial part of additional employment. The use of locals enhances loyalties for the business.

All these would add up to costs. But it is a real cost emerging from real scarcities and has to be paid. We are so used to a subsidy culture that even hardnosed business men expect the state to give them freebies and then lecture to others on the virtues of free market. If you cannot afford the land, your project is unviable and do not ask for a subsidy. Nobody dares to give that message. At best, the message is not given because the other chief minister does not give it and there is a genuine beggar thy neighbour policy. The more uncharitable interpretation is that the *Sethji* pays the piper. The faster urbanisation spreads, the worse the problem will be.

There are other ways of solving the problem. But they involve planning, which is no longer fashionable. If you ask policymakers to do land-use planning, they look at you blankly. They are from the land ceiling days so used to monkeying around with plots of land that the idea that there is a larger solution is not seen. You could build urban spaces on barren land and make the barren land central by transport planning. Transport is the other side of distance as villages become large villages and large villages become towns, which need markets, infrastructure and land for economic activities.

It is not wise to alienate the farmer. Civilisations like India, Egypt and China have existed because of their peasantry. Invaders came and went. Sometimes they looted villages but left them alone in the main. The ones who stayed back learnt to deal with the farmer without shaking his world. The great transition has begun in India as the small village becomes the large village or the small town. The spread of markets is dense as earth satellite pictures show. The rural urban continuum has to be managed in harmony and not in conflict. The stakes are too high for us to fail.

Private organisations are expanding in groundwater exploitation, as seen in places like Kaira District in Gujarat, where there are small water storage tanks in private plots (Antisar). The economic interest in land and water has to be at the heart of any reform process. Groups of stakeholders, including the smallest peasants, can cooperate for well-defined and limited purposes for land development and water projects. Farmer-level irrigation management systems, watershed development projects and groundwater cooperatives are all thriving, and many more and very promising possibilities are there.

Newer Models

There are at present different agricultural diversification models. Amul is the classical cooperative. But corporates work with different models. Some work with producer associations of farmers, e.g., the DCM Harayali model works with Producers Association and does not get into farming, so also the Tata Khetse. However, other corporates have a Farm to Fork model.

As a socialist, to me the central principle is whether the small farmer and/or the landless labourers will be stakeholders in the institutional processes of organising agriculture or not. I also believe that such stakeholder participation is efficient, but I am sufficiently well trained in economics to accept that this is a concept of dynamic and not short-run efficiency.

There is now a wider acceptance of these ideas. Alan de Jainvry, with whom we have worked earlier also, said that the Bank (WDR 08 on agriculture, and before them FAO, 07) wanted the Producers Association to bargain for farmers' rights. Tenancy records have to be straightened so that tenants who farm around two-fifth of the land can leverage their assets in bargains with the corporates. Some want to operate from the farm to the fork all by themselves if allowed to, which is rare, but others span the whole range, and do not enter the field or the last-line retailer. In fact, with large foreign tie-ups some have explicit strategies of strengthening producer companies as also the mom and pop stores.

However, life is not always a bed of roses. The CII has now lobbied that the Producers Association, part of the Companies Act, second amendment (2002) should be abolished. It has correctly argued that producers' association does now follow corporate profit-maximising principles since they are based on the 'one share one vote' principle. This argument is at present in flux and having created the text of the Company Law Amendment, we have lobbied with the prime minister to promote producers' associations to continue. However, now the Companies Affairs Ministry has, for all practical purposes, killed the Producer Company Legislation, which emerged from a Committee I chaired saying that the second amendment to The Companies Bill 2002 will only be an addendum until the government changes its mind, and the consultations proposed for local bodies and farmers groups are whitewashing the issues.

Some Future Trends

FAO/World Bank says that we have reached a stage of inflection and explosive agricultural demand growth and diversification.

> The contrast to South Asia is particularly striking for Sub-Saharan Africa where almost 65 percent of the rural population is found in areas with either low agricultural potential or poor market access, and 15 percent live in areas with both characteristics. The figures for South Asia are 25 and 3.5 percent respectively.

> Where the contrast between Indian agriculture and other countries looks particularly stark is in post-harvest aspects. One of the most striking is the low level of supermarket penetration and organisation of the supply chain from farm to retail outlet.

It is early hours yet and the mixture of public and private initiatives in strategic organisations is an issue with experimental possibilities. The question of the organisation of small farmers and their links with higher level organisations like input supplying or selling companies, or irrigation systems, is a complex one. Possibility of small farmers to form their own companies, without loss of control on their land, now exists under the law and needs to be strengthened. Later on, they may be allowed to have joint ventures with big companies, if they so decide. A problem visualised in contract farming is the organisation of farmer groups to interact with large companies. One answer is to encourage farmer groups in this context.

Urbanisation is gobbling up land. In Gujarat 'large villages' have become actually towns as per Census definitions, if we take into account the doubling of urban growth from 2.87 per cent annually to 5.06 per cent, which is close to double the earlier estimated change and makes a big difference to land use and forecast urban needs.

Barbara Harris' work has shown that an informal sector agro-processing and distribution in urban areas is now under great stress with the privatisation of land earlier under the use of 'commons'.

Even if distribution of agricultural produce is corporatised, there will be the need of the kinds of strategic policies that China followed of integrating informal sector distribution and artisan-based urban activities with super markets. There is a clear-cut case for pre-empting urban land for informal sector distribution and artisan-based processing and industry in the brave new world of the mall culture. The FAO is correct in saying that penetration of supermarkets in India is the lowest in the world and so is the Commission on Unorganised Sector correct in saying that the employment consequences of substitution of the distribution trade by the organised sector can be very large. At the least a strategic policy is required to integrate both.

There is a possibility that the state is now not receptive at the operational level to such ideas. In that case, there is a need for broad-based civil society initiatives to keep the issue alive.

Post Script

When I was editing my chapter for the proposed volume on land reforms for the Giri Institute, the Parliamentary Standing Committee had submitted its report and union ministers have contested it. This section visits the controversy in the light of this chapter.

The land question keeps on returning and every time there is no learning. During the last two decades at least four issues were I thought resolved by studies, reports, experience and so on, as argued earlier. The first was that tenancy had increased in a big way but in many areas the middle farmer was leasing in land, in what was called reverse tenancy. Most of this was unrecorded since tenancy is officially frowned upon and the state keeps up the mirage that it provides land to the tiller, so he cannot be a tenant. Two corollaries were known. Some states had done a great job in issuing *patta*s and some in fact had set up ICT-based systems for instantaneous service. In tribal areas largely land rights were historical and not recorded and so the poor *adivasi* was at the mercy of rapacious exploitation. Yugandhar, B.K. Sinha and others following them had left a lot of evidence in revenue studies, chief minister's conferences and so on.

The second was that we were merrily chugging along but in the 1990s we see real pressure on agricultural land. In earlier decades 2 per cent or less land would get out of agriculture in a decade. Now it was happening in some states in a year. I am a declared lefty but have to admit that the Urban Land ceiling was the worst legislation we had and very little came out of it for the poor although *babus* and

land racketeers made fortunes in implementing this part of 'socialism'. With the 1990s' 'reform', we actually gave up the concept of
land-use planning. The Land Use Boards and High Level Committees
never met. Now all that is official. As Kirit Parikh wrote in his excellent history of plan modelling, the government and planners do not
believe in perspective planning any more. He paid himself and some
of us great compliments, quite the boy on the burning deck for the
past work, but made it quite clear it was the past. Arun Maira was to
give us a new vision but his work never saw the light of the day. The
last three documents from Yojana Ayog scrupulously stayed away
from a perspective chapter. Now both the Planning Commission
and the Union Budget, while suggesting plan schemes, also want
the concept examined that plan schemes and resources for them be
scrapped. Not quite the background for the state to play a dominant
role in the land market, a genuinely long-term issue.

Third, this meant that earlier concepts of unearned incomes or
rentier surpluses were given up. In the global bazaar the border
price was mantra and so be it. Fourth, the policy makers were ignoring the big population movements taking place. People like me kept
on saying: the farmer is going to the bazaar in small and big towns
and many times the farmer is a lady, and let's do something for
small towns. At least call them towns when the Census says so but
the government in its wisdom ignores it. In 2011 the Census boys
said the *charawak*s like Alagh are OK (Alagh, 2011). Forty million
people have moved to small towns called census towns but these
are not even called towns by the government. So much for land
use and the state-led 'Dominant Domain' principle.

The Parliamentary Standing Committee on Rural Development's
Thirty First Report on Land Acquisition (released in May 2012)
does not want the dominant domain principle extended to PPPs,
and the faith of private sector projects in eminent domain, land-
use and district planning is touching. With all this we wanted the
market to play a role. That is what the land record business was all
about. There are two problems in all this. The market is alright, but
you can have the old person who will not let h(er)is land go when
everybody else has agreed and that may stall a school, a road or
a great manufacturing project. So you may need a state role after
all, in a classic public policy expenditure sense.

The second is what is the market when the land price will go
up in the future as development takes place. This is where the

suggestion was to consult local groups or better still form cooperatives or producer companies of small landholders, who in fact become a part of the negotiation and sharing of future benefits and opportunities' process. The Standing Committee is strangely silent on the '80 per cent affected' clause in the Bill. Also to give to the states all the powers it wants is inconsistent with its main thrust. There is again an implied rebuff to the concept of sharing of the sellers of land in equity or possible future benefits. A senior bureaucrat took this very seriously for land for industrial estates. The farmers were to get a first price but their producer company could get contract work later and also maybe equity in future price increases of the estates' assets. His work was so good that he was transferred. The Standing Committee would make him irrelevant.

The land acquisition bill states that if a company got 80 per cent of its land needs from the bazaar the state may intervene for the balance. The Parliamentary Committee seems to have sidestepped that and we are now in the realm of the dialogue of the deaf. But that is not an argument for draconian powers for the state as some ministers, I hope, have been wrongly quoted as demanding. That state did not help in the growth or the poor or *adivasi* and forests for the last century and a half, and it is too late to resurrect it now. The market can be relied upon and those who would misuse it can be punished by law. In the special cases of eminent domain as defined earlier the state must have the powers. I wish we also will have laws to use land well, but that is a revolutionary hope today.

References

Alagh, Y.K. (2011), 'The Rural Urban Continuum', *Indian Journal of Agricultural Economics*, March, pp. 1–18.

FAO (2007), *Accelerating Agricultural Growth in India*, GOI, Rome, Delhi.

Planning Commission, Government of India (1989), *Proceedings and Papers of the Seminar on Land Reforms-A Retrospect and Prospect*, Manager of Publications, Government Press, Faridabad.

Son, D.K., N.N. Que, P.Q. Dieu, T.T. Trang and D. Beresford (2006), *Agricultural Transformation in Vietnam*, FAO, Bangkok; also see Y.K. Alagh's chair comments at expert meeting at Seoul.

World Bank (2008), *World Development Report*, World Bank, Washington, D.C.

18

Land Policies for Agricultural Growth with Equity: An Agenda for Uttar Pradesh

Santosh Mehrotra and Ajit Kumar Singh

This chapter pulls together for the benefit of policy-makers the policy implications emerging from this book. The book's chapters have documented the chronic and acute stress that the farmers of UP (as in many states of India) are in. The 200 million citizens of UP deserve better. Despite many state 'schemes', agriculture and rural citizens are in a state of crisis.

Farm sizes have been shrinking inexorably with a rise in population, and UP still has, along with Bihar, the dubious distinction of having the highest total fertility rate in India (3.7 children on average for every woman of reproductive age between 15 and 49). The well-known demographer, Ashish Bose, was responsible for the evocative acronym BIMARU states (or sick states) — referring in the 1990s to the undivided Bihar, Madhya Pradesh and UP, along with Rajasthan. Today, only UP and Jharkhand (and to a much lesser extent Bihar, on account of its very significant turnaround since 2005) would qualify for that dubious distinction. UP's successive governments in recent decades have failed its poor, especially its rural citizens, so signally in regard to investments in health, nutrition, education, water and sanitation, that human development outcome indicators, despite improvement, remain among the worst in the country (see the *India Human Development Report 2011* [IAMR, 2011]). It is these poor basic social services that account for the low health status, high infant mortality and consequent high fertility. Poor, illiterate parents see boys as a personal insurance against old age, and in search of boy children tend to overcompensate — which raises their fertility. The low levels of schooling of married women of reproductive age have further contributed to this high fertility rate (on UP's health system, see Mehrotra, 2008).

In any case, the rural distress has resulted in large-scale migration away from rural UP to urban UP as well as to rural and urban areas of the rest of India (especially to Delhi and Maharashtra, especially Mumbai). In fact, NSS data show that UP and Bihar together account for half those in India who left agriculture for non-agricultural employment in just five years, between 2004–2005 and 2009–2010 (Mehrotra et al., 2013). Over 3 million persons abandoned farming in UP in these 5 years.

This large-scale male migration out of rural UP (and Bihar) has meant that an equally widespread feminisation of agriculture is taking place in UP—more widespread in UP (and Bihar) than in other parts of rural India, although all states are so affected. What this means is that the state governments should have been responding to this rural crisis, but seems to have remained almost oblivious to it—as chapter after chapter in this book has demonstrated. The politicians of the state have responded by mobilising the lower castes (one party focusing on the scheduled castes [SCs]) and other backward classes (OBCs, or more particularly Yadavs, being mobilised by another UP political party). This mobilisation, however, has not resulted in a focus on agricultural output yields, or a special emphasis on the SC farmers who are mostly landless or small/marginal farmers.

The historic failures of land reform in UP have been well documented in this book. The only reform that has ever been implemented was the Zamindari Abolition Act of 1950, but all that it managed to do was to eliminate absentee landlords, but without doing away with landlordism. The land ceiling legislation of 1960 became quickly mired in litigation. In any case, the proposal to introduce a bill to impose rural land ceiling was announced well in advance by the then state government, almost to enable the large landowners to get their land in excess of the proposed ceiling transferred in fictitious (*benami*) transactions to family members to prevent the land from being declared surplus (i.e., in excess of the bill's ceiling). Whatever land was declared as surplus, only a small proportion of it was actually transferred to beneficiaries, which was ensured by means of a landowner–bureaucrat–politician nexus. Such land as was transferred often had litigation initiated in their case. Often the transferred land was of the worst quality, so the poor beneficiary, with little or no credit or other input support coming from the state, was unable to utilise it. Often the land was only transferred in the records, but in actual fact possession remained with the original owner. In other words, every trick in the book was used to prevent the noble intent of the land ceiling law from being realised.

As though this history of injustice was not enough, the caste dimension of the gross injustice has been highlighted by our authors. UP is unusual among the Indian states since it has a much higher than the national average share of SCs in its total population (around 20 per cent as opposed to 15 per cent for India). They are the ones with the smallest size plots, and constitute a significant share of the landless labourers and marginal farmers (Saha and Mehrotra, Chapter 2). Caste and class thus overlap in rural UP. However, despite this overlap and despite the SC social and political mobilisation carried out by one political party in particular, their situation improved only in terms of intangibles (i.e., their sense of self-esteem and their ability to assert themselves socially, on which see Kapur et al. [2010]), but in terms of their access to land or even in terms of their human development outcomes, there was no significant turnaround (on the latter, see Mehrotra, 2006).

However, as we will argue in this final chapter, there are a series of policy measures that are within the realm of the 'doable' and feasible, provided a committed government in UP was willing to put its mind to the task. As a first step, we would recommend that since land is a state subject, the UP government creates a land commission, required to recommend specific actions by different individual land-related departments of the government of UP, within a specific timeframe. The Commission's term should be restricted to 5 years.

Its agenda for action is suggested below, based on the research presented in this book.

1. Legalise tenancy to enable use of fallow land, reassure landlords/tenants and counter farm size shrinkage.
2. Intensify land consolidation to counter adverse effects of farm size shrinkage and reduce in efficiency.
3. Implement land ceiling, at least to ensure homestead rights to homeless.
4. Develop a public land bank to enable tenancy.
5. Encourage group farming to enable small and marginal farmers to get access to inputs and enter the contract farming market.
6. Develop a land-use policy for the state to restrict inefficient conversion of agricultural land to non-agricultural use.

7. Adopt the new land acquisition bill, and especially the rehabilitation and resettlement measures for old and future displaced.
8. Implement the central government's land records modernisation programme.
9. Stop the diversion of forestland for non-forest use to protect tribal people.
10. Ensure women's rights in land through legal changes.

We will discuss each of these issues in turn.

Legalise Tenancy

There are four categories of Indian states depending on the nature of restrictions in tenancy laws:

1. Where leasing out agricultural land is legally prohibited without exception (Kerala and Jammu & Kashmir)
2. Where leasing out of agricultural land is allowed only by certain landowners, i.e., disabled, minors, widows, defence personnel (UP, Bihar, Jharkhand, MP, Chhatisgarh, Uttarakhand, Orissa, Telengana area of Andhra Pradesh, Karnataka)
3. Where leasing out of agricultural land is permitted, but the tenant acquires right to purchase the tenanted land after a specific period of creation of tenancy (Punjab, Haryana, Gujarat, Maharashtra, Assam)
4. Where there are no restrictions on leasing out land (Andhra area of Andhra Pradesh, Rajasthan, Tamil Nadu, West Bengal) (Report of the Committee on State Agrarian Relations, 2008)

In colonial times, agricultural tenancy was part of the feudal, exploitative agrarian structure. Tenancy was not legally protected by any form of security of tenure or regulation of rent. After 1947 some state governments gave ownership/occupancy rights to the existing tenants, but also put legal restrictions on future leasing. Several states that permitted leasing out by certain categories of landowners also prescribed the levels of fair rent. UP, however, practically does not permit tenancy.

Nevertheless, NSSO (2003) reports that the share of rural households leasing in land is 12.8 per cent in UP. Unfortunately, the most exploitative form of tenancy is the most prevalent in UP. Of all tenants, 52 per cent are paying a share of produce; 15 per cent of tenants pay fixed money; another 21 per cent pay a fixed produce; and 12 per cent have other terms. Even worse, most of those leasing-in land are either landless (7.8 per cent) or own less than 0.5 ha. (70 per cent) or own between 0.5 and 1 ha. of land (13.2 per cent) — together accounting for 90 per cent of those leasing-in land; in other words, only 10 per cent of those leasing-in land are medium or large farmers.

Tenancy contracts by such landless or marginal/small farmers with their landlords are oral since they are in violation of law; the tenants' position is precarious and he may have little incentive to cultivate land efficiently. On the other hand, the ban on tenancy encourages both larger and smaller landowners to keep land fallow.

Legalising tenancy would have several benefits. First, if tenancy is permitted for a long enough period (while protecting the rights of the landlord) it would encourage investment in the leased-in land, encouraging greater agricultural productivity. Second, legalising tenancy would reduce the land lying fallow, since that land would be leased out — thus again raising output and incomes for both. Third, we have seen earlier that 10 per cent of tenants are those who are middle/large farmers, who are leasing-in land from the small-marginal farmers, thus giving rise to 'reverse tenancy'. Legalising tenancy could have the effect of encouraging this phenomenon, thus enabling marginal/small farmers to lease-out their land and seek better employment opportunities in non-agricultural activities. The transition to non-agricultural employment has been happening in India (as in UP) as we noted earlier, and the share of the workforce in agriculture in India declined from 60 per cent in 1999–2000 to 57 per cent in 2004–2005, and further to 53 per cent in 2009–2010 and 49 per cent in 2011–2012. But this transition is not happening fast enough, despite an increase in non-agricultural output.

Even if tenancy were legalised in UP, there is a possibility that marginal/small farmers might still find it too risky to lease out their land to bigger farmers out of fear of losing their title. To offset this risk, the UP government should create a public land bank. As proposed by a Working Group on Disadvantaged farmers for the Twelfth Plan, this bank would accept 'deposits' of land parcels from landowners wishing to lease out their land, with the deposit being for one season, one year or three years and more at a time. On deposit the farmer would get first a small payment as incentive, even for fallow land; second, a rent for land that gets leased out; third, development of the leased-out land in terms of soil conservation under MGNREGA works; and finally, a government guarantee that owners can withdraw the land from the bank after giving notice.

There would be many advantages. First, it would activate a lot of the fallow land, which, as Chapter 14 notes, is very significant in the case of UP—hardly surprising given the large numbers of people leaving agriculture. Second, it would enable small farmers to lease-in land, which often they are unable to compete for in the open market. Third, it could encourage leasing-in of land by groups of small farmers, thus enabling them to engage in contract farming (as we discuss later). Finally, land banks would be banned from leasing out land to corporates and large farmers, which would prevent further concentration of land operated.[1]

Intensify Consolidation of Fragmented Holdings

Binswanger et al. (1995) identify the disadvantages associated with farm size shrinkage combined with fragmentation of holdings: physical problems (increased labour time, land loss, need for fencing, transportation costs and limitations to access); operational difficulties (unsuitability of certain equipment, greater difficulty with pest control and management and supervision, foregone improvements such as irrigation); and social externalities (need for extensive road and irrigation networks). With 83 per cent of all farms being either small or marginal (i.e., less than 2 ha.), fragmentation multiplies the disadvantage of farm size shrinkage.

The problem of consolidation efforts of the UP government is that they have in the past been beset with corruption. Consolidation of fragmented holdings will only work well if it becomes part of another measure discussed later—modernisation of land records, based on surveys, proper mutation of names of owners and titling.

---

[1] Thus, the Working Group report (2012) (Planning Commission.nic.in) notes that there has been an amendment of tenancy laws in Punjab to permit leasing-in of agricultural land by corporates—which is a retrograde step.

Redistributive Land Reform, Especially to Give Homestead Rights to Landless

A land ceiling law was introduced in UP (as in most states) 10 years after *zamindari* abolition in 1950, as a redistributive measure to promote equity. If it had been implemented effectively, it could also have improved efficiency, by transferring land from less-productive large units to more-productive, small family-based units (as discussed by Saha and Mehrotra in Chapter 2). But as we have noted above, this intention was sabotaged by the landlords, with the implicit and explicit support of politicians (often themselves landlords) and petty local bureaucrats.

Redistributive land reform has similarly failed in other countries as well. Many ambitious land reforms simply fail because full compensation of old owners at market prices imposes fiscal costs that governments are unwilling to meet, which was what happened to land reforms in Brazil, the Philippines and Venezuela. Some reforms have tried to overcome this problem by compensating landowners with bonds whose real value erodes over time. Of course landowners vehemently oppose this action, and such reforms have proved possible only in conditions of political turmoil (Cuba, Japan, Korea after the Second World War, Taiwan or Vietnam). The only state in India where redistributive land reforms were successfully implemented was in Kerala in the early 1950s during the rule of the Communist Party government, and the same is true for West Bengal in the early 1980s (though the latter was confined to securing the insecure rights of share-cropping tenants).

Had the land ceiling surplus been seriously redistributed in UP (and other states) soon after the land ceiling legislation was passed in 1960, it would have had both the efficiency and equity-enhancing effect that the theoretical literature discusses. In 1960–1961 the large farmers (tilling farms larger than 10 ha.) accounted for 4.5 per cent of all operational holdings, but they also farmed 29 per cent of the total operated area in India. The medium farmer (cultivating 4–10 ha. size holdings, which were 14 per cent) controlled 31.2 per cent of the operated area. So together they controlled 60 per cent of the operated area. In 2002–2003 they controlled only 34.8 per cent of the operated area. Even if the ceiling limit is reduced and re-fixed now, with new limits of 5–10 acres of irrigated land, as has been suggested in the Report of the Committee on State Agrarian Relation (Government of India, 2008), it remains unclear how this would significantly alter agrarian relations, even if it was politically feasible. Hence, as an alternative we are suggesting that at least three measures are still feasible, though even the first two of these are likely to face major political hurdles. First, in cases where the land has been distributed but the beneficiary has been dispossessed or does not have a title to the land such cases should be surveyed and the land restored. Second, religious trusts hold much land — both used and unused — which has been allotted by the state to them under exemptions from the Land Ceiling Act. A huge number of exemptions were granted to them, making ceiling legislation ineffective.[2] Religious establishments of all denominations (e.g., temples, masjids, gurudwaras, churches) existing since the 1950s should be allowed one unit of 15 acres, and even if temples have numerous deities on different pieces of land they will have only ceiling (*Report of the Committee on State Agrarian Relations,* Government of India, 2008).

Third, redistributive land reform should include distribution of wasteland to totally landless households. An estimated 13–18 million families in rural India are landless (i.e., without any agricultural land), of which about 8 million lack land even for a home of their own. The total area of wasteland in India is estimated to be 63.85 million ha., or 20.2 per cent of the geographic area.[3] These wastelands cannot be cultivated but they support a substantial part of the rural and forest people. Till March 2002, 6 million ha. of wastelands had been distributed to the landless. UP has distributed 1 million ha. of wasteland, but more could be done.

Fourth, redistributive land reform in its new phase must provide for homestead for the 8 million of the landless rural households who do not even have land to build their own homes. At least one-sixth of this number are living in UP. They live on a house constructed on the land of others or provided by landowners in

---

[2] The BJP-ruled Chhattisgarh government in recent years decided to allot thousands of acres of land to religious trusts exempted from the ceiling limit. This case shows that there will be political difficulties to reversing such decisions.

[3] Of this total wasteland 30 per cent is 'land with or without scrub', another 22 per cent is 'under utilised/degraded notified forest land, sands/coastal land 7.8 per cent, degraded pastures/grazing land 4 per cent, and water-logged and marshy land 2.5 per cent (Government of India, 2008).

return for forced labour. The Eleventh Plan had proposed that all such families should be allotted 10–15 per cent land to build a home, which would enable them to grow some vegetables on the plot. This agenda remains incomplete.

Finally, redistributive land reform should include a government programme to facilitate the landless and land poor to themselves purchase land, preferably by groups of small/marginal farmers. There are several advantages to group farming by small/marginal farmers (as has been demonstrated already in several states, e.g., Andhra Pradesh, Kerala, Gujarat), facilitated by the state government. As individual farmers, small and marginal farmers are disempowered. But as a group they can pool land, engage in joint crop planning, invest in lumpy inputs like irrigation, buy recurrent inputs jointly at better prices and engage with corporate to undertake contract farming, which is currently occurring only with medium/large farmers. Besides, their lands could be developed through joint activity using MGNREGAs' funds.

While the state government should facilitate groups of small farmers purchasing land, the government should not purchase the land for them (the Working Group cautions), with a view to leasing out the land to them (as the AP government has done). Government purchases will raise the market price of land, thus making the programme exclusionary, rather than inclusive.

Encourage Group Farming by Small and Marginal Farmers

The marginalisation of small holder farming remains a problem in agriculture in India and other fast-growing Asian economies. Globalisation-induced price volatility introduced in these economies downward pressure on prices and a proliferation of intermediaries in supply and marketing chains, which have disadvantaged vulnerable farmers. Vulnerability is more in less-fertile or less-populated areas, the forest, the remote and mountainous areas and the ethnic minorities.

To address the problem, group farming by small farmers has to be encouraged to improve their access to input and output markets. Several organisational options are possible and are in fact being practised in parts of the country. As Alagh points out in his chapter

(Chapter 17) producer companies of farmers should be promoted to overcome the problems of small farmers and improve their bargaining strength. Tenancy records have to be straightened so that tenants who farm around two-fifth of the land can leverage their assets in bargains with the corporates. The question of the organisation of small farmers and their links with higher-level organisations like input supplying or selling companies, or irrigation systems, is a complex one. Possibility of small farmers to form their own companies, without loss of control on their land, now exists under the law and needs to be strengthened. Later on, they may be allowed to have joint ventures with big companies, if they so decide. Groups of stakeholders, including the smallest peasants, can cooperate for well-defined and limited purposes for land development and water projects. He points out that farmer-level irrigation management systems, watershed development projects, groundwater cooperatives are all thriving and with very promising possibilities.

Developing a Land-use Policy for UP

The chapter on land-use policy in UP (Chapter 14) points out that in the absence of a land use policy and a perspective plan for land use for UP there are several issues that are crying out for attention. A land-use policy is required for several reasons. First, the land put to non-agricultural use was 24.4 lakh ha. in 2000–2001, when Uttarakhand was separated from UP. This area has grown to 28 lakh ha. in the year 2009–2010, showing a growth in the 2000s much faster than before. The rate of conversion from agricultural to non-agricultural use has gone up to 40,000 ha. per year during the 2000s. It is critical that a land-use policy specifies in descending order of priority the categories of land that should be considered for conversion to non-agricultural use. Urbanisation, infrastructure development and industrialisation are certainly required in a predominantly agrarian state like UP but there must be a rational policy for the conversion of land use. The first category of land that should be converted is barren and uncultivable land. The area under such land was 6.5 lakh ha. in 2000–2001, which came down to 4.49 ha. in 2009–2010, on account of the establishment of industrial estates and urban habitations in these areas. This is precisely the kind of land that should be used for such purposes in the future as well. Recent history of conversion of multi-cropped land in UP and elsewhere (Battaparsaul in 2011 in UP, Singur 2008 in West Bengal) shows that there is likelihood of serious farmers' resistance to conversion to non-agricultural use of irrigated and multi-cropped land (an issue we discuss again later under land acquisition–related recommendations).

Second, culturable wastelands are a category of land that could be used for distribution to the landless and marginal farmers. By using MGNREGA and the central government funds for watershed development, such culturable wastelands can be regenerated by means of actions to promote soil and water conservation, thus enabling group farming to take place by the landless or marginal farmers on such lands.

Third, permanent pasture and other grazing lands are a common property resource that needs to be preserved for the benefit of the community. It is inappropriate to allocate such lands to landless persons (as has been done in UP), rather than the other kinds of land that could be used (e.g., ceiling surplus land, culturable wastelands). The cattle population in the state of UP should rise and animal husbandry should be supported by the state as the means of livelihood diversification by poor farmers, but they can maintain their cattle only if there is permanent pasture and other grazing land available in the village. Hence, the policy of allocating government or *Gram Sabha* land to landless persons should be discontinued, when the land in question is common grazing land.

Fourth, current fallows constituted 10.9 lakh ha. in 2000–2001 in UP and that category of land increased in size by 20 per cent to 12.3 lakh ha. in 2009–2010. As we suggested in Chapter 1, this is a process that can be reversed. A number of actions are necessary, which we have discussed in this book (and in this last chapter as well). First, marginal/small farmers are risk averse when it comes to leasing their small plots of land out to other farmers, even when they themselves are unable to cultivate their own land. Often the male adult members in such marginal/small farming households have migrated in search of other means of livelihood, leaving the spouse and children behind. The spouse and children often are unable to cultivate the land and yet the land lies fallow and unutilised. This is an unsustainable situation in a state where the number of those living below the poverty line has gone on increasing (even though the headcount ratio of the proportion of the population below the poverty line is falling). Net sown area also cannot increase on account of the non-availability of cultivable land. With adult and child malnutrition levels high, a situation where large areas of cultivable land lies fallow must be reversed, whereby current fallows come down and total agricultural output increases. Therefore, two actions are urgent and necessary, which must be taken by the UP state government. First, tenancy, which remains illegal, must be legalised. Second, even when tenancy is legalised marginal/small farmers may still consider the leasing out of their fallow land as too risky to bigger farmers, who in UP often belong to upper castes while the marginal/small farmers belong to lower castes including SCs. Hence, we have suggested earlier that the UP state government should create a public land bank, in which such current fallow land could be deposited, with the objective of leasing out by the land bank to other farmers, thus ensuring that the risk to the lessor is minimised.

Finally, between 2000 and 2010 there has been no significant change in the area under fallow under UP. Although we will discuss what actions are necessary in regard to forest land in the following section, there has been a degradation of forests, and therefore we suggest that as part of land-use policy the state government should undertake a rejuvenation of degraded forest land and plant trees outside of forests under MGNREGA works to increase the forest cover and protect agricultural land from ecological degradation in the face of future climate change. It must be noted that small and marginal farmers do not have the capacity to make investments on their own to counteract the increasing effects of weather change resulting from global climate change forces. Hence, the responsibility for such collective action must lie with the state and central governments together.

Adopt and Implement the Central Land Acquisition and Rehabilitation and Resettlement Measures

The Parliament passed in late 2013 an Act that combines a new land acquisition bill with new resettlement and rehabilitation measures included within the bill. This is a huge advance upon the erstwhile Land Acquisition Act (LAA) of 1894, as well as the rehabilitation and resettlement policy of the Union Government of 2007. The new bill, once it becomes an act, will replace not only the Land Acquisition Act of 1896 but also the R&R policy of 2007.

It would be in the interest of the UP government to move rapidly to implement the new Act. In this section, we will deal with some of the criticisms of the main principles underlying the new Act. First, a suggestion has been made that the LAA 1896 and the new Act are similar in that they retained the notion of 'eminent domains', thus allowing the state to acquire land compulsorily, and hence the critics make the case that the principle of eminent domain must be eliminated. However, this is an untenable position. Critics argue that since capital and labour cannot be acquired forcibly then neither should land. However, this argument ignores the fact that unlike capital and labour, land is not fungible, land is limited in quantity and is also immoveable. The state is the ultimate judge of public good and it should be vested with the power of eminent domain. The new law significantly moderates the scope of eminent domain in the 1894 law. The state should have a role in acquisition since land markets are highly imperfect in India, and also because there are huge power and information asymmetries between buyers and sellers.

Critics also suggest that there should be no acquisition of agricultural land, regardless of whether it is single- or multi-cropped land. However, this suggestion of the critics, if adopted, would pose serious hurdles for development in rural areas. The new bill leaves the exact limits of acquisition by the government/purchase by private companies of single-/multi-cropped land to be decided by each state in line with its own development priorities, and the UP Government will be able to take decisions in regard to single or multi-cropped land, as local needs demand, as the state governments sees fit. The Act also states that acquisition of multi-cropped land is to be undertaken only as a last resort and in 'exceptional circumstances'. Moreover, it states that if such land is acquired then an equal plot of alternative land is to be identified for agricultural purposes. Finally, the Act even provides for state governments to impose ceilings on such acquisitions taking place within a district as a unit.

Third, critics argued that the definition of 'public purpose' for which land can be acquired in the new bill is poor, and Medha Patekar had even argued that it is defined 'in a manner worse than in the British Act' (the *Hindu*, 29 August 2012). However, this criticism does not recognise that the new Act defines public purpose such that it qualifies it by establishing processes whereby such public purpose needs to be clearly and properly validated. The Social Impact Assessment Process, identified in the new Act, is such that all those affected, including those whose livelihood is disturbed, including representatives of Panchayati Raj institutions, must be invited to deliberate as to where public purpose is in fact served by such acquisition. Moreover, this assessment is then vetted by an independent expert group and finally a decision is taken by a high-level committee headed by the chief secretary of a state. These safeguards are further reinforced by the high level of consent required (80 per cent). It may be noted that none of these processes were provided for in the British Act.

Finally, critics have argued that the bill is weak on rehabilitation. However, this criticism too is seriously unfounded. More than five chapters and two schedules in the bill have been dedicated to describing elaborate processes for R&R. The second schedule outlines the benefits such as land for land, housing, employment and annuities that will accrue in addition to the one-off cash payment. Moreover, drawing upon the lesson learnt from past displacement, the new Act provided a guarantee that none of those individuals whose land has been acquired shall be dispossessed unless alternatives, as enumerated in the bill, are provided for (Section 37). There has not been any such protection enshrined in a national statute ever before.

Land Record Management, Registration and Titling

Land titles and registration reduce the problems of asymmetric information, and hence proper land record management provides the institutional framework to facilitate both legal tenancy and land sales. Such transfers can enhance efficiency by transferring land from those farmers unable to cultivate to other farmers and by facilitating the use of land as collateral in the credit market. To reduce these informational efficiency and the related welfare losses, societies develop institutional arrangements to reduce risk, such as the requirement in the *Arthashastra* (4th century BC) that land transactions be conducted in public with witnesses or the establishment of a centralised public register that tracks those who have rights over plots of land (Binswanger et al., 1995).

Land record management in India and in UP has suffered from a number of infirmities. First, the land revenue administration in all states is included within non-plan expenditure, and it has been generally starved of funds. It is also a subject very low in the order of state government's priorities. It is for this reason that the Report of the Committee on State Agrarian Relations (2008) recommends that land revenue administration must be placed under the plan head. The second problem with land record management historically is that land is a state subject and, as just noted, has been neglected, while the major initiatives in land record management and surveying have come from the central government. Ministry of Rural Development (Land Resources Department) has taken the initiative to strengthen revenue administration, updating our land records and their computerisation in 1988–1999 and the digitisation of maps with 100 per cent financial assistance. However, it has been the experience that even in such centrally sponsored schemes on sharing basis with the states, the states have failed to commit resources to take advantage of the inflow of central funds.

Historically land records are based upon survey and settlement operations, which should be conducted periodically after a gap of almost 15 years as both land ownership and the practical conditions undergo change, but in fact they have been taken up only after 30 years. Survey and settlement operations have two objectives: updating land records including changes that may have taken place in the features of the land and updating the revenue to be paid by the tenants on the basis of these changes. These operations have since Independence suffered from serious problems. They have taken not less than 30 years because of the six stages involved and have also encouraged rent-seeking behaviour. Most surveyors (Amins) are employed on a work charge basis and hence they have a high propensity to indulge in rent seeking.

Recognition of Rights in Forest Land and the Protection of Forests

One issue in regard to forests has already been discussed above briefly, i.e., the need for the protection of forests. Data on the state-wise diversion of forest area for development projects in India for the period 1980–2003 suggests that nearly 76,000 ha. in UP was so diverted, which is clearly a cause for concern since it accounts for around 9 per cent of all such land diverted in the country. In fact, only in two other states (Madhya Pradesh and Maharashtra) the area diverted from forest land to development projects exceeds the forest land diverted in UP in this period.

However, an equally if not more important issue is the recognition of the rights of forest dwellers in UP. Chapter 14 notes that the revenue land that was not acquired under Zamindari Abolition Act was vested with the Forest Department. In UP, Bihar and Bengal the forest was vested under UP Private Forest Act enacted in 1948 just before our Constitution came into existence and before the enactment of Zamindari Abolition Act in 1950. Moreover, the notification of the Zamindari Abolition Act was delayed for many years in areas like Bihar and Sonbhadra district of UP. The revenue lands were appropriated by the landlords and the forest land was appropriated by the forest department. The forest department extinguished all rights enjoyed by the people in such forestland after Independence. Choudhary and Roma (Chapter 14) argue that both forest and revenue departments claim the same land in their records, and have been showing separate actions in their respective land records relating to the same land for the last 50 years. Examples of such disputes are common in the UP districts of Chitrakoot, Sonbhadra, Mirzapur, Chandauli, Lakhimpur Kheri and Bahraich. In other words, they argue that in most forest areas disputes arose after Independence, which were between the forest department and the village, revenue department and the village and the forest department and the revenue department.

They also note that after Independence no serious work was done to prepare land records in such disputed areas. They also point out that land in the forest regions was appropriated in the Tarai region of UP where residents of Punjab and some so-called environmentalists (such as Billy Arjan Singh) managed to grab thousands of hectares of land. The authors note the serious disputes that occurred in the entire Kaimur region of UP, consisting of Sonbhadra, Mirzapur and Chandauli districts. These areas also became the centres for armed groups later, on account of the injustice caused by these disputes.

There is clearly a strong case for the preparation of a village register, which becomes the basis for the resolution of the disputes related to forestland. There is thus a case for serious investigation of the status of land and its redistribution among forest dwellers in this region, as per the provisions of the new Forest Rights Act 2006, which can be the basis for the resolution of these disputes. This is a matter that the UP government needs to pursue urgently, if it does not want these southeastern districts of UP becoming part of those contiguous districts of Madhya Pradesh, Bihar and Jharkhand that are Maoist infested.

Ensuring Women's Land Rights and Encouraging Women's Farming SHGs

Several chapters in this book have noted that employment in agriculture in UP has been declining. Saha and Mehrotra (Chapter 2) found 3.5 million workers left agriculture between 2004–2005 and 2009–2010 in UP, which accounts for 25 per cent of all those workers who shifted from agriculture to non-agricultural occupations during the second half of the 2000s. The migration of males out of agriculture is a nation-wide phenomenon, but the extent of rural poverty in UP is so great, and the degree of rural distress is so high, that male migration out of rural UP (in Bihar) is more visible in UP than in other states of the country. The implication of this male migration and the decline of male workers in agriculture are a growing feminisation of agricultural activities, especially but not only in UP and Bihar. There are major policy implications of this phenomenon.

First, there are historic gender inequities in land relations, but only some states have taken action to enable land rights for women to be realised. States like Karnataka, Tamil Nadu and Andhra Pradesh have amended the Hindu Succession Act to facilitate succession by women. The Hindu Succession Amendment Act 2005 gives equal right to daughters to succession and the Act should be implemented in UP as well.

In addition, the report of the Committee on State Agrarian Relations and the unfinished Tasks in Land Reforms (of the Department of Land Resources, Ministry of Rural Development, Government of India), 2008, recommends that there should be mandatory joint entitlement (for both women and men) and ownership rights through central initiatives. The Committee has also recommended that the new Land Acquisition Act should require that all females above the age of 18 should be recipient of the government notice to acquire land, and unmarried daughters/sisters, physically challenged women, female orphans, widows and women divorcees should be treated as separate families in the rehabilitation and resettlement section of the Act.

Finally, there are other ways of empowering women farmers in this age of growing feminisation of agriculture. There is evidence from Kerala and Andhra Pradesh which have shown how this can be done. The Kudumbashree collective farming initiative in Kerala facilitated land leasing by small groups of women, typically women's self-help groups (SHGs). SHGs undertaking group farming can be registered as Joint Labour Groups—a NABARD scheme—and given financial and technical support. The state government provides support for land preparation and reclamation (linking it with MGNREGS in some districts), and subsidised seeds, manure, electricity for farming machines. Similarly, Andhra Pradesh has demonstrated that group farming by women can be a successful enterprise. The AP Mahila Samatha Society is working with about 175 women's groups across five districts of Andhra Pradesh, involving over 4,000 women farmers, mostly small and marginal farmers and landless labourers. The UP Government should supplement the legal changes to the Hindu Succession Act suggested earlier, with similar support to groups of women farmers, especially in cases where male migration out of the village has left them with fewer choices, and has forced the household to leave land they own as fallow land instead of cultivating it.

The 10-point land reforms agenda we have outlined earlier to promote agricultural growth and equity in the context of UP is relevant to other states as well. This book is based on independent research; yet it is notable that there is an echo of these 10 points in the agreement on land issues signed between movement of poor, SC and ST farmers and the Government of India in 2012 (see Annexures to this chapter). The agenda takes into account the present-day political and economic realities in mind, which are quite different from the situation that prevailed soon after Independence. In our opinion, the agenda could be politically acceptable and administratively implementable. It will encourage agricultural growth and address the issues of agrarian distress and marginalisation of holdings. Postponing action on the agenda will further aggravate the situation of agrarian distress and discontent and give rise to violent protests, which are occurring in other parts of the country and are knocking at UP's door. The alarm bells are ringing. We only hope that the political masters and policy-makers are listening to them.

Appendix

AGREEMENT ON LAND REFORMS BETWEEN THE MINISTRY OF RURAL DEVELOPMENT (GOI) AND JAN SATYAGRAHA

1. **National Land Reforms Policy**: While land reforms is clearly a state subject under the constitution, the MoRD acknowledges that a National Land Reforms Policy announced by the Central Government could have its own importance. The MoRD will initiate a dialogue with States immediately and put out a draft of this policy for public debate and discussion in the next 4-6 months and to be finalized soon thereafter. The draft Land Reforms Policy prepared by the Jan Satyagraha organized by Ekta Parishad will be an important input into the preparation of this draft. Civil Society Organisations will also be actively involved in this exercise.
2. **Statutory Backing to the Provision of Agricultural Land and Homestead Land**: MoRD will proactively initiate the dialogue process with States to take up steps on the issue of giving statutory backing (like MGNREGA and FRA) to (a) provision of agricultural land to the landless poor in the backward districts; and (b) provision of Homestead Rights to the landless and shelter less poor of rural areas, all over the country, so as to guarantee 10 cents of homestead to every landless and shelter less rural poor household.
3. **Homestead Land**: MoRd will propose doubling the unit cost to enable provision of 10 cents of land as homestead for every landless and shelter less poor family as a component of the Indira Awas Yojana (IAY).
4. **Enhanced Land Access and Land Rights for the Poor, Marginalised and Deprived Landless**: The MoRD agrees to

issue detailed advisories in the next two months exhorting the States to focus on the effective implementation of various laws enacted by legislatures aimed at protecting the land right to dalits, adivasis and all other weaker and marginalized sections of society. Details of these advisories will be worked out in consultation with civil society organizations active on this issue. MoRD will also, through a set of advisories exhort and support the State Governments to take up a time-bound programme, for securing access to land to specific categories of marginalized and deprived landless families.

5. **Fast Track Land Tribunals**: The MoRD agrees to initiate a dialogue with States to establish Fast Track Land Tribunals/ Courts for speedy disposal of the cases pending in revenue and judicial courts. In addition to the Central Scheme for legal aid, States too will be exhorted to extend legal aid to all the persons belonging to socially deprived sections, whose lands are involved in litigation, particularly dalits and tribal communities.

6. **Effective Implementation of Panchayats (Extension to Scheduled Areas) Act, 1996 (PESA)**: MoRD will work with the Ministries of Tribal Affairs and Panchayati Raj to complete stakeholder consultations over the next four months so that detailed circulars to States could be issued for ensuring effective implementation of PESA by empowering the Gram Sabhas to exercise the powers given to them under the Act.

7. **Effective Implementation of Forest Rights Act**: Ministry of Tribal Affairs has issued a comprehensive set of revised rules on 13th September, 2012 under the Scheduled Tribes and Other Traditional Forest Dwellers (Recognition of Forest Rights) Act, 2006. States will be actively exhorted and supported for effective implementation of the Forest Rights Act in the light of the revised rules and directives issued by the Ministry of Tribal Affairs and in light of suggestions received from civil society organisations.

8. **Forest and Revenue Boundary Disputes**: MORD agrees to issue an advisory to States to set up joint teams of Forest and Revenue Departments to undertake a thorough survey of the forest and revenue boundaries to resolve disputes. The Gram Panchayats and Gram Sabhas will be fully involved in the survey and settlement process.

9. **Survey, Updating of Records and Governing Common Property Resources**: The MoRD will exhort and support the States to carry out survey of Common Property Resources (CPRs) with the direct involvement of the Gram Sabha and the Gram Panchayats concerned. The States will also be advised to ensure full implementation of recent Supreme Courts' directions on this matter.

10. **Task Force on Land Reforms**: The MoRD will immediately set up a Task Force on Land Reforms headed by the Union Minister for Rural Development to implement the above agenda Members of the Task Force will include representatives of MoRD, state governments, civil society organizations working on land reform issues and all stakeholders concerned.

In light of this Agreement Jan Satyagraha agrees to discontinue its present march and work with the MoRD to carry forward this agenda.

Sd/-   Sd/-
Jairam Ramesh,   PV Rajagopal
Minister for Rural Development,   Jan Satyagraha
Drinking Water and Sanitation,
Government of India

Dated: October 11th 2012,
Agra

Annexure 1: Suggested Agenda for Action to Secure Access of Land to the Poor

1. **Protection and development of lands belonging to Dalits and Adivasis**: Measures to prevent alienation Government lands assigned to Dalits; Identification of Govt./assigned lands encroached by ineligible persons for restoring back to the original assignees; Identification of tribal lands alienated to the non-tribals in contravention to the existing land transfer regulations for restoring the land back to the tribals and thorough inventory of land belonging to SCs/STs for

taking up development of the lands and provision of irrigation facilities under MGNREGS and other programmes;

2. **Assignment of land to the landless poor**: Regularization of unobjectionable occupations on the government lands in favour of landless poor and issuance of title deeds (in scheduled areas, in favour of tribals only); Resumption of land acquired, purchased and/or leased out to industries etc. or acquired for development projects but remaining unutilized, for distribution to the landless poor and State Governments to identify all categories of lands available for assignment to the poor and taken up assignment of the land to the poor, giving priority to the poorest of the poor; To secure access to land to the specific categories of marginalized and deprived landless people such as, Nomads, Particularly vulnerable Tribal Groups, single Women, HIV Affected People, Siddhis (Gujarat & Karnataka), Fisherfolks, slum inhabitants, Hawkers, Leprosy affected people, Physically & Mentally Challenged People, Tea Tribes, Salt Workers, Pastoral communities, Bonded Labourers, Mine Workers, Bidi Workers, Internally Displaced People; Re-survey and physical verification of Bhoodaan lands to recover the Bhoodaan lands from encroachers, for allotment to the poor and to revisit the ceiling limit and implement ceiling laws, undertake reclassification of the lands and assign the surplus lands to the poor.

3. **Land related issues of the poor**: Identify land related problems being faced by the poor and take up a programme for their resolution in a time bound manner; recording of tenancy to enable the tenants secure loans from the Banks; Protect/provide burial grounds and pathway to burial grounds, especially to the most vulnerable communities in the villages; and management of land records at the village in a transparent manner.

4. **Land to the Nomad**: To issue appropriate directives to the State governments to take up a campaign to settle the nomadic communities, by providing minimum homestead and agricultural land for sustaining their livelihoods.

5. **Women Land Rights**: To ensure that land owned by a family is recorded either in the name of a woman or jointly in the name of the man and the woman.

Annexure 2: Suggested Agenda for Action for Ensuring Effective Implementation of the PESA, 1996 and FRA, 2006

1. **PESA**

   Align all State revenue laws and land related relevant laws with PESA 1996 to recognise powers of Gram Sabha over land matters; provide mandatory intimation to Gram Sabha in writing through the Gram Panchayat of any proposed sale of transfer including mortgage of any land/transaction in the village; authorize Gram Sabha to call for relevant revenue records, conduct a hearing and direct SDM for restoration of alienated land in necessary cases; inform any changes in the land record including mutations to the Gram Sabhas; expand the list of Schedule V villages by including all the eligible but left out habitations; enforce in letter and spirit, the 'Samata Judgment' in all acquisition of tribal land for private companies and implementation of PESA to be strengthened by notification of appropriate rules and directives under it; given overriding effect in the State, over all other laws, with appropriate amendments being carried out in all the State laws that are in conflict with PESA within a period of one year.

2. **Forest Rights Act**

   Securing to the Tribals, Bank credit facilities in respect of the land granted under Forest Rights Act and other land laws; ensuring vesting of all forest rights as defined under the Act, to the tribal communities, who were earlier displaced because of notification of National Parks and Wild Life Sanctuaries, and are rehabilitated under the provisions of Forest Rights Act; settlement of Forest Rights, both individual and community rights, in respect of lands proposed for acquisition, before land acquisition proceedings are commenced.

   All forest land where the Forest Rights Act applies and where the process of settlement of rights under the India Forest Act, 1927 has not been completed, it will be made clear that the process of recognition of forest rights under the Forest Rights Act will be completed first and then the Settlement process will be taken to its logical end facilitating absolute rights to the tribals. All particularly vulnerable/primitive tribal groups without their date of occupancy on a particular piece of land will be exempted from furnishing of evidence of residence as required under Forest Rights Act. This will be done through appropriate amendment to the Forest Rights Act.

'Orange Areas' in Madhya Pradesh and Chhattisgarh, where large extent of land is under dispute between Revenue Department and the Forest Department shall be settled expeditiously.

References

Binswanger, H., K. Deininger and G. Feder (1995), 'Power, Distortions, Reform and Revolution in Agricultural Land Relations', in J. Behrman and T.N. Srinivasan (eds.), *Handbook of Development Economics*, vol. 3B, North Holland, Amsterdam.

Government of India (2008), *Report of the Committee on State Agrarian Relations and the Unfinished Tasks in Land Reforms*, Department of Land Resources, Ministry of Rural Development, New Delhi.

Institute of Applied Manpower Research (2011), *India Human Development Report 2011*, Oxford University Press, Delhi.

Kapur, D., C.B. Bhan, L. Pritchett and S. Babu (2010), 'Rethinking Inequality: Dalits in Uttar Pradesh in the Market Reform Era', *Economic & Political Weekly*, 28 August, xlv (35), pp. 39–49.

Medha, P. (2012), 'Debate: Medha Patkar Responds', *the Hindu*, 29 August.

Mehrotra, S. (2006), 'Well-being and Caste in Uttar Pradesh: Why UP Is not Like Tamil Nadu', *Economic and Political Weekly*, 41 (40), pp. 4261–4271.

Mehrotra, S. (2008), 'The Public Health System in Uttar Pradesh: What Can Be Done?', *Economic and Political Weekly*, 6–12 December, 43 (49).

Mehrotra, S., A. Gandhi, B. Sahoo and P. Saha (2013), 'Turnaround in India's Employment Story: Joblessness and Informalisation Reversed', *Economic and Political Weekly*, 48 (35).

Planning Commission (2012), *Working Group Report on Marginalized Farmers*, report to the Planning Commission in preparation of the 12th Five Year Plan. Available at www.planningcommission.nic.in (last accessed 30 January 2014).

About the Editors and Contributors

Editors

Ajit Kumar Singh is retired director, Giri Institute of Development Studies, Lucknow. He holds degrees of MA and PhD in economics and PG Diploma in national and international development from the Institute of Social Studies, The Hague. He has been the faculty of economics at University of Lucknow and RML Avadh University, Faizabad. He was member of Second State Finance Commission, UP, Committee on Unfinished Agenda on Land Reforms in India appointed by the Ministry of Rural Development Government of India, 2008.

Santosh Mehrotra is the Director General, Institute of Applied Manpower Research (IAMR), New Delhi. He has an MA in economics from the New School for Social Research, New School University, New York, and Phd in economics from Cambridge University. He was associate professor in Jawaharlal Nehru University (1988–1991). He spent 15 years in the international public system from 1991 to 2006. He was chief economist of UNDP's Global Human Development Report (2002–2005), New York. He also led the research programme on developing countries at UNICEF's Global Research Institute, the Innocenti Research Centre, Florence (1999–2002). He has worked as head, Rural Development Division, and adviser, Social Sectors, and Head, Development Policy Division, Planning Commission. He led the team that prepared the *Second National Human Development Report*. He has authored nearly a dozen books on various aspects of development published by reputed publishers.

Contributors

Yoginder K. Alagh is an internationally reputed eminent economist. He is presently chancellor of the newly created Central

University at Ahmedabad. He holds a doctorate in economics from the University of Pennsylvania. He has taught at the University of Rajasthan, Indian Institute of Management Calcutta, University of Jodhpur, Swarthmore College and the University of Pennsylvania. A former member of Rajya Sabha, he was a minister of state for planning and programme implementation, science and technology and power, Government of India. He was also the member of Planning Commission, Government of India, and vice chancellor of Jawaharlal Nehru University, New Delhi. He was appointed as chancellor of Nagaland University. He has been chairman of several academic institutions including Institute of Human Development, New Delhi, Giri Institute of Development Studies, Lucknow, and IRMA, Anand. He has headed various institutions and commissions and acted as expert with a number of UN organisations. He has written extensively on issues related to agriculture and macro-economic policy.

Vasant W. Ambekar has a graduate degree in agricultural engineering. He worked in various capacities in the Department of Agriculture, UP, and retired as director of agriculture. He has worked in the area of soil conservation and watershed development and land reclamation activities. He was consultant in several World Bank–aided projects on agricultural development. He has also worked as national-level monitor with the Ministry of Rural Development, Government of India. He was associated with the study on 'Long Term Perspective Plan for Land Use in Uttar Pradesh', sponsored by Planning commission, UP. He has presented many papers related to agriculture and watershed development in national-level seminars and conferences.

Ashok Choudhary is associated with Vikalp, a social organisation working on issues of land rights of forest dwellers. He initiated the forest workers' cooperative along the Shivalik forest ranges in Sahranpur, UP, in the 1980s. He played a key role in the formation of the National Centre for Labour in the 1990s. He has been closely associated with the UP land rights network since 1997. He is the general secretary of National Forum of Forest People and Forest Workers and vice president of the New Trade Union Initiative (NTUI) since its inception in 2001. He is associated with Sangarsh, a common platform for campaigns working against the land acquisition and asserting rights over community rights and common resources.

Hiranmay Dhar is retired professor, the Giri Institute of Development Studies, Lucknow. He holds a PhD degree in economics. He started his career from AN Sinha Institute of Social Sciences, Patna, and later joined the Giri Institute of Development Studies, Lucknow. He was a visiting fellow at the Institute of Developing Economies, Tokyo, and senior fellow of ICSSR, New Delhi. He acted as a consultant with IAMR, New Delhi, and the Institute of Gandhian Studies, Varanasi. His areas of interest include land relations in UP and Bihar.

Siddharth Dube is a senior fellow at the World Policy Institute, New York. He is the author of *Words Like Freedom: The Memoirs of an Impoverished Indian Family, 1947–1997*. He works and writes on issues of poverty and social justice. His forthcoming books include a chronicle of 'outlawed love', tracing developments on prostitution and homosexuality against the backdrop of the AIDS pandemic, as well as an exhaustive sequel to *Words Like Freedom* based on research conducted through 2012.

Fahimuddin has worked in various capacities at the Giri Institute of Development Studies, Lucknow, and is presently professor at the Institute. He holds the degree of MA in economics from University of Lucknow and PhD from Chhatrapati Shahu Ji Maharaj University, Kanpur. His areas of specialisation are agricultural development, land-use planning, educational planning and condition of minorities. He has directed more than forty research projects sponsored by various state and national-level organisations including ICSSR and NABARD.

Pratap Singh Garia has worked in various capacities with the Giri Institute of Development Studies, Lucknow, and recently retired as fellow of the Institute. He obtained his PhD in economics from Chhatrapati Shahu Ji Maharaj University, Kanpur, on the role of hill women in agriculture. He is associated with a large number of research projects sponsored by various state and national-level organisations. He has a number of books and articles to his credit. His areas of interest have been women empowerment, agricultural development and educational planning.

Roma Malik has been working as a social activist on the issue of forest, land, wages and gender with Dalit, tribal and minority sections for the last 20 years. She is associated with the Uttar Pradesh Land Reform and Labour Rights Campaign Committee and New Trade Union Initiative, New Delhi. She is founder member and organising secretary of National Forum of Forest People and Forest Workers. She was nominated as people's organisation representative in the State Level Monitoring Committee constituted under Forest Rights Act, Uttar Pradesh. She was member of Joint Review Committee, constituted by Ministry of Environment and Forest and Ministry of Tribal, Government of India on Forest Rights Act to review the implementation of the Forest Rights Act in the country in 2010.

Partha Saha is an assistant professor and research coordinator of India Public Policy Report at the School of Public Policy of Jindal Global University. He has worked earlier at the Institute of Applied Manpower Research, New Delhi. He is a PhD from Jawaharlal Nehru University, New Delhi. He was the co-author of *India Human Development Report* brought out by the Institute of Applied Manpower Research, New Delhi. He has published in edited books and journals on issues related to agrarian relations, socio-economic development and employment creation.

Kripa Shankar is presently an honorary fellow of Govind Ballabh Pant Social Science Institute, Allahabad, and was a faculty member at the Institute. He was a senior fellow of the Indian Council of Social Science Research, New Delhi. DPhil from the University of Allahabad, he has been working on the problems of poverty, land issues and economic development in Uttar Pradesh. His publications include *Economic Development of Uttar Pradesh, Land Transfers in UP* and *Irrigation Dynamics*. He has been contributing research articles in books and journals including *Economic and Political Weekly*.

Ajay Kumar Singh, IAS, holds the degrees of MBBS, MBA and PhD. He held an internship at Johns Hopkins Bayview Medical Center, Baltimore. He has wide-ranging experience and expertise in the various aspects of land management and land policy. As director, Land Reforms Division, Department of Land Resources, Government of India, he played a key role in launching the National Land Records Modernization Programme. He has contributed significantly to formulating the Property Titling Bill, amendments to the Land Acquisition Act, 1894, and the Rehabilitation and Resettlement Bill for consideration of Parliament, and notification of India's National Rehabilitation and Resettlement Policy for the involuntarily displaced.

Richa Singh is UGC senior research fellow at Centre for Study in Regional Development, Jawaharlal Nehru University, New Delhi. She holds the degree of MA in economics from University of Lucknow and MPhil and PhD in economics from CSRD, Jawaharlal Nehru University, New Delhi. She was awarded Junior Research Fellowship of UGC. She also obtained the degree of Master of Public health from the School of Public Health and Information Sciences, University of Louisville. She has worked as consultant to World Bank on a project under the South Asia Poverty Reduction and Economic Management and to National Commission for Enterprises in the Unorganised Sector. Her articles have been published in various national-level journals.

R.K. Singh is a retired banker. He has an MTech degree in agri-cultural engineering from IIT Kharagpur. After serving Govind Ballabh Pant University of Agriculture & Technology, Pantnagar, Uttarakhand, as assistant professor for 4 years, he joined Bank of India in 1974 and served in various capacities including as Chairman of Regional Rural Bank. After retirement, he worked as consultant under several World Bank projects relating to rural and agricultural development and handled various national and inter-national assignments. He was associated with the study on 'Long Term Perspective Plan for Land Use in Uttar Pradesh', sponsored by Planning Commission, UP.

Prashant Kumar Trivedi is fellow, Giri Institute of Development Studies, Lucknow and associate fellow, Council for Social Development, New Delhi. He is PhD in sociology from University of Lucknow. Before joining the Giri Institute, he had been faculty at the Council for Social Development, New Delhi, since 2006. His research interests include political economy of land reforms, rural studies and Dalit issues with a special focus on Uttar Pradesh. He was co-author of *The Globalisation Turbulence: Emerging Tensions in India Society* and *Weapon of the Oppressed: An Inventory of People's Rights in India.*